Canceling Lawyers

Canceling Lawyers

Case Studies of Accountability, Toleration, and Regret

"Daddy doesn't slay dragons, dear—he represents them."

W. BRADLEY WENDEL, CORNELL LAW SCHOOL

Oxford University Press is a department of the University of Oxford. It furthers the University's objective of excellence in research, scholarship, and education by publishing worldwide. Oxford is a registered trade mark of Oxford University Press in the UK and certain other countries.

Published in the United States of America by Oxford University Press
198 Madison Avenue, New York, NY 10016, United States of America.

© Oxford University Press 2024

All rights reserved. No part of this publication may be reproduced, stored in a retrieval system, or transmitted, in any form or by any means, without the prior permission in writing of Oxford University Press, or as expressly permitted by law, by license, or under terms agreed with the appropriate reproduction rights organization. Inquiries concerning reproduction outside the scope of the above should be sent to the Rights Department, Oxford University Press, at the address above.

You must not circulate this work in any other form
and you must impose this same condition on any acquirer.

Library of Congress Cataloging-in-Publication Data
Names: Wendel, W. Bradley, 1969– author.
Title: Canceling lawyers : case studies of accountability, toleration, and regret /
W. Bradley Wendel, Cornell Law School.
Description: New York : Oxford University Press, 2024. |
Includes bibliographical references and index. |
Identifiers: LCCN 2023050060 | ISBN 9780197673423 (hardback) |
ISBN 9780197673447 (epub) | ISBN 9780197673430 (updf) | ISBN 9780197673454 (online)
Subjects: LCSH: Attorney and client. | Practice of law. |
Lawyers—Corrupt practices. | Rule of law. | Toleration.
Classification: LCC K126 .W46 2024 | DDC 174/.3—dc23/eng/20231025
LC record available at https://lccn.loc.gov/2023050060

DOI: 10.1093/oso/9780197673423.001.0001

Printed by Sheridan Books, Inc., United States of America

Note to Readers
This publication is designed to provide accurate and authoritative information in regard to the subject matter covered. It is based upon sources believed to be accurate and reliable and is intended to be current as of the time it was written. It is sold with the understanding that the publisher is not engaged in rendering legal, accounting, or other professional services. If legal advice or other expert assistance is required, the services of a competent professional person should be sought. Also, to confirm that the information has not been affected or changed by recent developments, traditional legal research techniques should be used, including checking primary sources where appropriate.

(Based on the Declaration of Principles jointly adopted by a Committee of the American Bar Association and a Committee of Publishers and Associations.)

You may order this or any other Oxford University Press publication
by visiting the Oxford University Press website at www.oup.com.

Contents

Preface ... vii

1. Case Study: Swiss Banks and Nazi Gold ... 1
   Crisis at Cravath ... 1
   Against nonaccountability ... 4
   The justification of John Adams ... 7
   The Freedman-Tigar debate ... 10
   "Ethics rules" and client choice for American lawyers ... 14
   Contested meanings ... 17

2. Philosophical Perspective: Accountability, Reactive Attitudes, and the Meaning of Actions ... 38
   Morality beyond duties and rights ... 38
   Reactive attitudes ... 40
   Reactive attitudes and reasonable expectations ... 45
   Reactive attitudes and the scope of the moral community ... 50

3. Case Study: Harvey Weinstein, Ronald Sullivan, and Harvard University ... 66
   Joining Weinstein's dream team ... 66
   Answering "The Question" ... 69
   Making clients radioactive ... 74

4. Philosophical Perspectives: Blame, the Meaning of Actions, and the Ethics of Blame ... 101
   Blameworthiness vs. wrongness ... 101
   What do you mean by that? ... 105
   The ethics of blaming ... 108
      1. How wide is the circle of blame? ... 109
      2. What standards apply to determine blameworthiness and appropriate blaming responses? ... 113
      3. Toleration ... 116
      4. Don't feed the trolls ... 119

5. Case Studies: Boycotts of Law Firms and the Ethics
   of Informal Social Sanctions 132
   The "obsequious servants of business"? 134
   Down with Big Oil 135
   Reasonable disagreement and the role of the legal system 141
   Formal and informal power 145

6. Philosophical Perspective: The Challenge of Role Morality . . . 163
   The persistence of the personal 164
   Three mistakes about professional roles 167
       Mistake #1: Too much weight on the duties of the role 167
       Mistake #2: Too little appreciation for the significance of the role 169
       Mistake #3: Excluding personal identity altogether 171
   Roles and professional ethics 175
   Are roles exclusionary or just very weighty? 181

7. Case Studies: McCarthyism or Legitimate Criticism? Canceling
   Government Lawyers 199
   From the Trump administration back to polite society? 199
   Blame and the Big Lie 205
   Whose side are you on? The "Department of Jihad" 211
   Fidelity to law vs. abusive legal advice 216

8. Philosophical Perspective: Regret and Moral Costs 233
   Excruciating cases 233
   How moral remainders arise (and what to do with them) 237

9. Some Concluding Thoughts 262

Acknowledgments 271
Index 275

Preface

People have been criticizing lawyers since . . . well, probably since there were lawyers.[1] Lawyers have been mocked, mistrusted, ridiculed, or loathed in Ancient Greece and Rome,[2] the Bible,[3] the England of Shakespeare's time,[4] and in the American colonies.[5] Negative public perception of lawyers has been based on a number of consistent themes, such as greed, duplicitousness, self-interest, taking the side of the rich and powerful over the rest of us, stirring up dissension and disputes, bringing frivolous lawsuits, needlessly prolonging litigation, manipulating the law at the expense of justice, and being social parasites instead of contributing to economic prosperity.[6] This book considers a persistent type of criticism of lawyers—the claim that they should be held up to scorn, shunned, or made to suffer some social sanction for representing unpopular, controversial, or repugnant clients.[7]

There is a fairly standard pattern, enacted in tweets, blog posts, and editorials in the *Wall Street Journal* or *Washington Post*, in which critics express outrage that a lawyer is representing some client the critic believes to be a terrible person or corporation and lawyers patiently (or not so patiently) respond that representing nasty clients is what lawyers do, and so all this criticism is completely misguided. This happens every. single. time. I don't know about you, but my hunch when there is a recurring set piece of points and counterpoints like this is that there is something deep and interesting going on.

The idea to be explored in this book is that the intractability of the debate has something to do with the complexity of our practices of critically evaluating the conduct of others. I'll be developing this idea in two ways that I hope are related and mutually reinforcing. The first is through case studies of public criticism of lawyers for the clients they represent. Recently there's been a lot of noisy public controversy about lawyers representing Hollywood mogul and convicted rapist Harvey Weinstein, alleged terrorists, big multinational corporations, or the Trump campaign in its challenges to the 2020 presidential election. But this debate goes way back, literally to the early days of the American Revolution when a lawyer, civic leader, and future president named John Adams decided it would be a shrewd political move to serve as defense counsel for the British soldiers involved in the Boston Massacre.

The second approach makes reference to moral philosophy, which is just the academic discipline of getting clear about what's going on when we critically evaluate others' actions, reasons, attitudes, and character. My aim is to use some of the tools developed by moral philosophers to sort out the public criticism of lawyers. The arguments put forward by both sides—lawyers and their critics—turn out to be a lot more complicated (and interesting) than their opponents sometimes appreciate.

I realize there's a risk here. A television comedy series called *The Good Place* ran on NBC from 2016 through 2020. The premise of the show is that four people find themselves in the afterlife, thinking they are good people and made it to the "good place." The brilliant plot twist is that the protagonists have actually ended up in the bad place, designed by demons to torture them for all eternity.[8] The four set about trying to become better people and earn passage to the good place. A recurring joke is that one of the four, Chidi Anagonye, was a professor of moral philosophy on earth, but is completely hopeless at figuring out what to do in any practical situation, because he is so caught up in abstract theory and all its contradictions. His companions, particularly his enthusiastic student and eventual girlfriend, Eleanor Shellstrop, constantly remind Chidi that everyone hates moral philosophers.

I loved *The Good Place*. While I have no illusions that this book will be similarly entertaining, I do hope to use the tools of philosophy to make some progress in seemingly never-ending debates about the responsibility of lawyers representing nasty clients. My aim is not to involve readers in dense, technical discussions, although there may be a couple of places where the arguments here will aim to intervene in ongoing academic debates. Like Chidi, however, I do think there is a point to reading moral philosophy.* We may be able to better understand an important and long-running controversy in professional ethics by considering insights of philosophers about the nature of interpersonal morality, including the often-neglected topics of blame, blameworthiness, and the ethics of blame; and how blame relates, or does not relate, to permissibility and wrongfulness.[9] A different strand of the literature in political ethics proposes that some social roles, including that of a lawyer or a judge, may sometimes require one to do something only with

---

* By the way, I use the words morality and ethics interchangeably, as is common in philosophy. We will take up in various places the idea of "legal ethics" used by lawyers, incorrectly, to describe the legal rules of professional conduct.

a sense of regret or reluctance. My hope is that these contributions to moral theory can provide resources to help public discussion of lawyer accountability escape the frustrating, seemingly endless "lather, rinse, repeat" cycle of the same critiques and responses that appear to be talking past each other when lawyers are criticized for representing unpopular clients.[10]

I think criticism of lawyers for representing unpopular clients is an excellent case of something that isn't particularly well developed in academic professional ethics. Recent work in moral philosophy shows that there are multiple dimensions on which we can evaluate actions. In particular we can distinguish between whether something is morally permitted and what the action shows about the attitudes a person has toward others. This sounds very abstract, I know, but in working on this book I found that it becomes quite a bit clearer in the context of these case studies of public criticism of lawyers. In writing the book I tried to develop the philosophical themes organically. The principal theoretical ideas of accountability, permissibility, meaning, blameworthiness, toleration, the rule of law, regret, and reluctance should emerge from reflection on the case studies. I do think theory matters, however, and the most ambitious claim *about* this book (as opposed to claims made within it) is that borrowing some insights from contemporary moral philosophy can help make progress in this fascinating but seemingly interminable debate.

As the title of this book suggests, some may regard public criticism of lawyers as part of the much-lamented phenomenon of "cancel culture."[11] This term has been overused to the point of meaninglessness. Consider, for example, that in the wake of Russia's invasion of Ukraine, Vladimir Putin said that Western protests were an instance of cancel culture, comparable to online criticism of *Harry Potter* author J.K. Rowling for her comments about transgender people.[12] And in an amusing hall-of-mirrors episode, a federal court of appeals judge sought to cancel Yale Law School by discouraging conservative judges from hiring Yale graduates as law clerks. Yale's offense? Canceling conservative speakers and student groups.[13] Cancelation may also be used loosely to refer to the collateral consequences of having been found guilty, or at least credibly accused, of some act that is clearly a crime or a grave moral wrong. Harvey Weinstein and Bill Cosby, for example, will never have the power and influence they once enjoyed, as a result of their criminal sexual abuse of women.[14] But this is not cancel culture in any meaningful sense. The most heated debate over cancel culture pertains not to people found to be serious wrongdoers, but to those accused of what might be called thought crimes.[15] Stand-up comedian Dave Chappelle, for example, has faced criticism and the occasional literal cancelation of his performances in response to his jokes about transgender people.[16] Cancelation in this case refers to penalties for challenging a prevailing orthodoxy, something which stand-up comedians believe is literally their job.[17] Lawyers may be able to help themselves to a similar defense—representing clients effectively sometimes involves upsetting people. As one of my early mentors in academia liked to say, it is the duty of lawyers to comfort the afflicted and afflict the comfortable.[18]

The position I will defend, which will require some theoretical development (and patience on the part of the reader), is that the intractability of the debate over lawyers representing unpopular clients is the result of a structural tension inherent in the law itself. The law supports toleration in a liberal society characterized by deep and persistent disagreement. It does so, however, by imposing an official, formal resolution of disagreement on everyone, even those who object sincerely and on moral grounds. Law stands in opposition to anarchy and mob rule, but it also may stand in opposition to justice and the values that should be affirmed by the community.[19] Lawyers, for their part, act within a professional role that emphasizes service as faithful agents of clients, who have their own point of view about justice and the public interest. This role may prompt indignation or anger from observers who disagree with the beliefs or actions of the lawyer's client.

The complexity created by the coexistence of professional roles and background, "regular folks" morality is illustrated by a question addressed to the *New York Times Magazine*'s "Ethicist" column. The writer was a law student who entered law school with the aspiration of practicing law in the public interest but now, as a result of substantial student debt, found themselves considering a job offer from a law firm whose practice includes "defending large corporations that I'm ethically opposed to, including many polluters and companies that I feel are making the apocalyptic climate situation even worse."[20] In response, philosopher Kwame Anthony Appiah defended the importance of skilled legal advice and representation for all clients, even big corporations, and not just in defense against accusations of criminal wrongdoing but in ordinary civil litigation, transactions, and legal compliance matters.

So far so good, but the writer was asking about his or her own moral agency, not the ethical ideals to which the legal profession is committed. In response to this question, Appiah said something quite interesting:

Again, for an adversarial legal system to function justly, there have to be lawyers who are willing to serve clients they disapprove of. If that's a demerit, it has to appear on somebody's moral scorecard. *But surely it can't be both good that somebody does it and a demerit for the person who has done it.* (You can regret having to do something as part of your job, even if that something isn't itself wrong.)[21]

The sentence emphasized in this passage takes a position that is very common among moral philosophers. Appiah contends, in effect, that if there is a good argument that can be made in justification of some action, such as representing big fossil fuel companies in transactions (say, to obtain permits for a new oil refinery) or defending them in environmental litigation, then the justification has to carry through to anyone who occupies the role of lawyer for one of these clients. There is no room, on this view, to consider whether this particular lawyer has ethical commitments, values, or relationships that are in tension with the ends to which a social institution, like the legal profession, is committed.[22] Those ends might be good ends, and Appiah may be correct that the world would be worse off if big corporations could not find lawyers who will work diligently for them regardless of any disapproval they may feel toward their client's activities. On this view, however, the goods of the institutional role outweigh or exclude altogether the lawyer's own moral commitments.

I agree very much with Appiah that the role of lawyer requires diligent work notwithstanding a lawyer's own moral qualms. Lawyers cannot agree to represent a client and then undermine their client's legal interests by doing a halfhearted job, or even engaging in some kind of covert sabotage. I do not believe, however, that the lawyer's moral qualms simply disappear or are obliterated by the goods of the role. Using Appiah's language, it may be that the indifference of big fossil fuel companies to the impact they are having on the earth's climate is a demerit for the lawyer who accepts a job at a law firm representing these clients.[23] That demerit may be experienced as a sense of regret or reluctance, even if the lawyer concludes that, on the whole, she is justified in taking the job. What should be done with the qualms that accompany some of the characteristic, and permissible, actions of professionals is, in my view, a vital but relatively unexplored issue in legal ethics. A richly textured moral analysis should attend not only to whether a representation or an action taken on behalf of a client is permissible (although that is important), but should also consider the first-personal experience of those who participate in it, including a sense of regret or guilt.[24]

One of the main theoretical ideas to be developed in this book is that it *can* be good for someone to do something *and* can be a demerit for the person who has done it. That is a paradoxical idea, I know, but I believe it follows necessarily from the paradox of law itself, as something that responds to both the world as it is and the world is we wish it would be. Professional ethics too often denies this deep contradiction, usually by emphasizing the justification for what lawyers do when they represent unpopular clients. I agree with much of the traditional defense of the lawyer's role, but I believe it is important to attend to the qualms and regret that sometimes accompany even a permissible representation.

When I began thinking about this book, the first draft featured an opening chapter with a series of case studies of lawyers who had been criticized for the clients they represented, followed by subsequent chapters setting out and applying ideas from modern moral and political philosophy. The downside of this approach soon became apparent. The series of stories felt like the caricature of history sometimes misattributed to Arnold J. Toynbee: "just one damned thing after another." The subsequent philosophy chapters seemed remote and unconnected from the stories and, frankly, kind of felt like homework. To address these concerns, the book alternates between "Case Study" chapters containing of stories about lawyers who have been criticized for the clients they represent, with a bit of theory mixed in, and "Philosophical Perspectives" chapters that are more theoretical, with some real-world stuff mixed in. Therein lies the danger. Nonspecialist readers may be tempted to read only the even-numbered chapters and skip over the odd-numbers philosophical chapters. It's a high burden, but I hope to convince you that without engaging both the practical and theoretical parts of this analysis, we'll never get past the endless assertion of the same old arguments back and forth about the accountability of lawyers for the clients they represent.

References, digressions, and down-the-rabbit-hole theoretical refinements are in endnotes, not the footnotes more familiar to readers of legal scholarship. The publisher's reference guide asks authors whether we expect readers to engage with the note material. I really don't, although there may be many places where specialist readers will want to consult the notes for additional information. I tried—perhaps unsuccessfully—to minimize the name-dropping and shorthand references to positions (like "Scanlonian blame") that characterize scholarly writing, while providing enough connection to academic debates to invite engagement and criticism. Nerds (I include myself in that group) are welcome to read the endnotes first.

Notes

1. Robert C. Post, "On the Popular Image of the Lawyer: Reflections in a Dark Glass," 75 *Cal. L. Rev.* 379 (1987); A.W.B. Simpson, "Legal Iconoclasts and Legal Ideals," 58 *U. Cin. L. Rev.* 819 (1990). For an interesting exploration of 16th-century English cases in which lawyers brought defamation lawsuits after being accused of disloyalty, see Jonathan Rose, "Of Ambidexters and Daffidowndillies: Defamation of Lawyers, Legal Ethics, and Professional Reputation," 8 *U. Chicago L. Sch. Roundtable* 423 (2001). Although the charge of being an "ambidexter" is analogous to the modern claim that a lawyer has a conflict of interest, Rose's study shows that it was much more associated with public opprobrium and threats to reputation than today's highly technical conflict-of-interest doctrine. Importantly, the defendants in these defamation actions were not clients who accused their lawyers of disloyalty, but members of the community, that is, third-party observers, criticizing lawyers—very much the subject of this book. Someday I hope to work the word "daffadowndilly," meaning a lawyer with divided loyalties, into an expert affidavit in a conflicts proceeding.
2. Max Radin, "The Ancient Grudge: A Study in the Public Relations of the Legal Profession," 32 *Va. L. Rev.* 734 (1946); James Boyd White, "Plato's *Gorgias* and the Modern Lawyer: A Dialogue on the Ethics of Argument," in *Heracles' Bow: Essays on the Rhetoric and Poetics of Law* (Madison: University of Wisconsin Press 1985), pp. 215–37.
3. Luke 11:46, reporting Jesus's admonition: "Woe to you lawyers also! for you load men with burdens hard to bear, and you yourselves do not touch the burdens with one of your fingers." Martin Luther went one better and proclaimed, "I shit on the law of the pope and of the emperor, and on the law of the jurists as well." John Witte, Jr., "Luther the Lawyer: The Lutheran Reformation of Law, Politics, and Society," 178 *Law & Justice—Christian L. Rev.* 6, 8 (2017).
4. The frequently quoted line, "The first thing we do, let's kill all the lawyers," is just as frequently misunderstood. It is from *Henry VI, Part II*, Act IV, scene II, and is spoken by Dick the Butcher, intended to be seen by the audience as a buffoonish peasant. Dick is an associate of Jack Cade, who had been hired by the Duke of York to cause disorder so that it would be easier to overthrow the king. As a lawyer and literary scholar has argued, Shakespeare's point is really that "[t]o have a successful revolution, you must get rid of the lawyers." Daniel J. Kornstein, *Kill All the Lawyers? Shakespeare's Legal Appeal* (Princeton: Princeton University Press 1994). Similar to the theme running through John Adams's defense of the British soldiers following the Boston Massacre, which will be considered in Chapter 1, lawyers are held up as the alternative to chaos and mob rule. Be that as it may, there were many lawyer jokes circulating in Elizabethan times with themes that are familiar to modern readers—for

example, that lawyers are unethical, given to overcharging their clients, and uninterested in helping poor people. Thomas W. Overton, "Lawyers, Light Bulbs, and Dead Snakes: The Lawyer Joke as Societal Text," 42 *UCLA L. Rev.* 1069, 1094–96 (1995).

5. Post, pp. 379–80; Marc Galanter, *Lowering the Bar: Lawyer Jokes and Legal Culture* (Madison: University of Wisconsin Press 2005), pp. 4–5.

6. Galanter, pp. 3–9, 16–19.

7. Right out of the gate there a problem with terminology. A long-standing literature exists on criticism of lawyers but scholars and commentators equivocate among the labels to be used to identify clients for whom lawyers come in for criticism for representing. Are they "unpopular"? Perhaps, but this may show that they are members of a persecuted or widely disliked minority, as was the case with suspected Communists in the 1940s and 1950s. Some clients may be unpopular with a currently powerful majority, and good on them for that. Civil rights protesters in the South were about as unpopular as a client could be, but their objectives were in line with ideals of justice and equality, to which lawyers should be dedicated. On the other hand, a client like Harvey Weinstein, who is the subject of the principal case study in Chapter 3, is *deservedly* unpopular, owing to what he has done. Weinstein was proven beyond a reasonable doubt to have committed numerous criminal sexual acts and was sentenced to 23 years in prison. Colin Dwyer, "Harvey Weinstein Sentenced to 23 Years in Prison for Rape and Sexual Abuse," *NPR* (Mar. 11, 2020). He may indeed be an unpopular client, but that is because he was credibly accused, and ultimately convicted, of doing terrible things, seemingly without remorse. Compare the observation that the use of the words "unsavory" or "troublesome" to refer to allegations ranging from exploitation to physical violence, by the author David Foster Wallace, are standing in the way of moral clarity about the subject. See Mary K. Holland, "The Last Essay I Need to Write about David Foster Wallace," in Mary K. Holland & Heather Hewitt, *#MeToo and Literary Studies: Reading, Writing, and Teaching about Sexual Violence and Rape Culture* (London: Bloomsbury 2021). Weinstein should be seen clearly as someone who has done terrible things, not merely as someone who is crosswise with the powers that be. Are the clients, instead, merely "controversial"? Maybe, but like "unsavory," this word has the feel of a euphemism when applied to clients credibly accused of horrific wrongdoing, such as Dylann Roof, who killed numerous members of a historic Black church in Charleston, South Carolina, during a Bible study. Surely Roof is more than "controversial." It may be controversial to *represent* Roof, but he himself is noncontroversially a wrongdoer (although one might disagree whether anyone deserves to be killed by the state, no matter how evil their actions). The rules of professional conduct for American lawyers use the term "repugnant," which in my view is meant to signify that a lawyer must have more than a mere disagreement with a client before refusing a representation. The client's disagreeableness must rise to the level of repugnance in order to permit withdrawal from representing a client (Rule 1.16(b)(4)) or refusal to accept a court appointment (Rule 6.2(c)). I avoid the word "repugnant" precisely because it has been incorporated into the rules of professional conduct, and I want to avoid resolving the moral issues here with reference to the rules. For an interesting look at the use of the term "repugnant" in the Model Rules,

see Vanessa A. Kubota, "Subjective Feeling or Objective Standard? The Misuse of the Word Repugnant in the Model Rules of Professional Conduct," 35 *Geo. J. Legal Ethics* 259 (2022). I sometimes use terms like "nasty" or "obnoxious" clients when referring to social attitudes, not to signify my own disapproval. Finally, the term "antisocial" is sometimes used by critics who believe lawyers in some instances should refuse to act on behalf of clients with interests that are contrary to the common good. The social-trustee conception of professionalism is discussed in Chapter 5 in connection with the student-led boycotts of law firms representing fossil fuel companies. On that subject, see Michael Ariens, "The Rise and Fall of Social Trustee Professionalism," 2016 *J. Prof. Law.* 49 (2016). In keeping with one of the principal themes of this book, the trouble with the term "antisocial" is that there is considerable disagreement about what is in the public interest and, in my view at least, one of the functions of the law, the legal system, and the legal profession is to facilitate cooperation and common projects among people who disagree about rights, justice, and the common good.
8. The structure is an excellent riff on Sartre's play *No Exit*, in which the characters are imprisoned together and learn that "hell is other people."
9. R. Jay Wallace, *The Moral Nexus* (Princeton: Princeton University Press 2019); Susan Wolf, *The Variety of Values: Essays on Morality, Meaning, and Love* (Oxford: Oxford University Press 2015); T.M. Scanlon, *Moral Dimensions: Permissibility, Meaning, Blame* (Cambridge, Mass.: Belknap Press 2008); Stephen Darwall, *The Second-Person Standpoint: Morality, Respect, and Accountability* (Cambridge, Mass.: Harvard University Press 2006).
10. The debate is often described as both "endless" and "confused"—see, e.g., G.S. Hans, "Being a Lawyer Doesn't Make You Immune from Criticism," *Balls and Strikes* (Apr. 25, 2022), available at https://ballsandstrikes.org/legal-culture/is-lawyer-criticism-ok-a-very-important-debate/
11. The term, now used indiscriminately in public discourse, has its origins in Black culture and originally gained currency on so-called Black Twitter. The word traces back to a Nile Rodgers song called "Your Love is Cancelled," which was referenced by Wesley Snipes's character in the movie *New Jack City*. See Clyde McGrady, "The Strange Journey of 'Cancel,' from a Black-Culture Punchline to a White-Grievance Watchword," *Wash. Post* (Apr. 2, 2021). Cancelation, and the related phenomenon of calling out, originated as a protest by marginalized people against discrete, individualized episodes of wrongdoing, such as workplace bigotry, but the term has since transformed into a signifier of moral panic by powerful, usually white, speakers claiming that they have been victimized by an online mob. For an insightful overview of this history, see Meredith D. Clark, "DRAG THEM: A Brief Etymology of So-Called 'Cancel Culture,'" *Communication and the Public* 5(3–4): 88–92 (2020). As used in both Clark's paper and the *Washington Post* article referenced above, cancel culture is a defensive term used by people with power or privilege as an attempt to "quash any attempts to critique their social position." Brown, p. 90; see also Aja Romano, "The Second Wave of 'Cancel Culture,'" *Vox* (May 5, 2021). It has tended to take on a particular political valence in contemporary usage, mostly deployed by the right to claim that artists, writers, academics, or other public figures risk career

or social penalties for espousing conservative positions. This is ironic given that one of the first high-profile examples of career penalties imposed on an artist as a result of concerted social pressure is the criticism, death threats, and country music radio blacklist directed at the bestselling band formerly known as the Dixie Chicks (now just the Chicks) in response to their criticism of President George W. Bush and the Iraq war. See, e.g., Alan Light, "The Dixie Chicks, Long Past Making Nice," *N.Y. Times* (June 10, 2016). In any event, I will use the term more neutrally, to cover criticism aimed at influencing others to shun or ostracize a wrongdoer (which is to say an aspect of informal or non-legal social ordering), leaving the power dynamics in each situation as an open question for analysis. Chapter 5 on boycotts of law firms by law students seeking to influence climate policy will have more to say about the ethics of boycotting, shunning, shaming, and other efforts to use informal (that is, nongovernmental) power for social change.

12. Pjotr Sauer, "Putin Says West Treating Russian Culture Like 'Cancelled' JK Rowling," *Guardian* (Mar. 25, 2022).

13. Nate Raymond, "Trump-Appointed Judge Boycotts Yale for Law Clerks Over 'Cancel Culture,'" *Reuters* (Sept. 30, 2022); Avalon Zoppo, Brad Kutner, & Christine Charnosky, "In Slamming 'Cancel Culture,' Judge James Ho Boycotts Yale Law Clerks," *Nat'l L.J.* (Sept. 29, 2022). His comments and appeal to other judges to join him in boycotting Yale graduates were criticized by Judge Jerry Smith, a conservative member of the same court. Nate Raymond, "Judge's Yale Clerk-Hiring Boycott 'Regrettable,' Conservative Colleague Says," *Reuters* (Oct. 5, 2022). See also Scott Altman, "Using Cancel Culture's Tools to Dismantle Cancel Culture?," *The Hill* (Oct. 7, 2022). Judge Ho's boycott appeared to have worked, however, because he and another federal judge who had joined the effort were invited by Dean Heather Gerken to attend a program at Yale on freedom of speech and intellectual diversity. David Lat, "Is Yale Law School Turning Over a New Leaf?, *Substack* (Oct. 20, 2022); Steven Lubet, "Yale's Perplexing Invitation to Judicial Bullies," *The Hill* (Nov. 2, 2022).

14. Cosby's conviction was reversed by the Pennsylvania Supreme Court based on an immunity agreement negotiated between Cosby and a prosecutor who had offered a deal promising not to prosecute Cosby if he gave up his Fifth Amendment privilege against self-incrimination and testified in a civil action brought by Andrea Constand, the Temple University employee he was accused of drugging and sexually assaulting. *Commonwealth v. Cosby*, 252 A. 3d 1092 (Pa. 2021). See also Graham Bowley & Julia Jabobs, "Bill Cosby Freed as Court Overturns His Sex Assault Conviction," *N.Y. Times* (June 30, 2021); Maryclaire Dale & Alanna Durkin Richter, "Explainer: Why Bill Cosby's Conviction Was Overturned," *Associated Press* (June 30, 2021). The decision was based on the then-prosecutor's judgment that obtaining a conviction in a criminal case would be difficult, so the best thing to do would be to force Cosby to testify in the civil case brought by his accuser. Many commentators saw the Pennsylvania court's decision as a setback for the policy objective, exemplified by the online #MeToo movement, of holding powerful men accountable for sexual misconduct and abuse of power. See, e.g., Merrit Kennedy, "Bill Cosby Is Released from Prison After Court Overturns Sexual Assault Conviction," *NPR* (June 30, 2021). However, as

a factual matter one would be justified in believing that the allegations proven beyond a reasonable doubt against Cosby in his criminal trial are true.

15. A retired partner at the law firm Hogan Lovells alleged, in an op-ed in the *Wall Street Journal*, that she was fired by the firm for speaking up in defense, on a firm-wide call, of the Supreme Court's *Dobbs* decision, overruling the constitutional right to abortion recognized in 1973 in *Roe v. Wade*. Robin Keller, "No Dissent on Abortion Allowed at Hogan Lovells," *Wall St. J.* (Nov. 29, 2022). The headline may be misleading, however, because Keller's firing offense seems to be not failing to share others' "anger and outrage" about *Dobbs* but making a comment about "disproportionately high rates of abortion in the black community, which some have called a form of genocide." Nevertheless, Keller saw the firm's action as "kowtowing to the woke faction," which is to say, imposing a serious career penalty for stating a view that many within the firm found to be offensive. This is the sense in which the term "cancel culture" is frequently invoked. For this usage in connection with this case, see David Lat, "Biglaw's Latest Cancel-Culture Controversy," *Original Jurisdiction—Substack* (Dec. 1, 2022).

"Woke" is another word, like "cancel," that originated in Black culture but subsequently got picked up as a term of abuse by conservative commentators and politicians, such as Florida Governor Ron DeSantis. See, e.g., Aja Romano, "A History of 'Wokeness,'" *Vox* (Oct. 9, 2020); Bijan C. Bayne, "How 'Woke' Became the Least Woke Word in U.S. English," *Wash. Post* (Feb. 2, 2022); Ashley Parker & Liz Goodwin, "Republicans Use 'Wokeism' to Attack Left—But Struggle to Define It," *Wash. Post* (Feb. 21, 2023). As Benjamin Eidelson notes, the word "is now used almost exclusively by critics of the attitudes it names, so it is difficult to use the word without channeling the critics' skeptical tone." Benjamin Eidelson, "The Etiquette of Equality," 51 *Phil. & Pub. Aff.* 97, 110 n. 44 (2023).

Among other interesting details of the history of the word, Romano's *Vox* article reports that it may have been popularized by a Lead Belly (a/k/a the blues musician Huddie Ledbetter) song about the Scottsboro Boys. In his usage, to stay woke means a caution to Black Americans to be alert to racially motivated threats of violence. Similarly, Bayne's article argues that to be woke means to be aware of racial subjugation by whites, making the usage of DeSantis and others, to describe white progressives, incoherent. In late 2022 a federal district judge issued a blistering opinion holding the "Stop W.O.K.E. Act" championed by DeSantis unconstitutional. The opinion opened with an allusion to Orwell's *1984*, never a good sign for a government defendant in a First Amendment case:

> It was a bright cold day in April, and the clocks were striking thirteen," and the powers in charge of Florida's public university system have declared the State has unfettered authority to muzzle its professors in the name of "freedom." To confront certain viewpoints that offend the powers that be, the State of Florida passed the so-called "Stop W.O.K.E." Act in 2022 – redubbed (in line with the State's doublespeak) the "Individual Freedom Act." The law officially bans professors from expressing disfavored viewpoints in university classrooms while permitting unfettered expression of the opposite viewpoints. Defendants argue that, under this Act, professors enjoy "academic freedom" so long as they

express only those viewpoints of which the State approves. This is positively dystopian. It should go without saying that "[i]f liberty means anything at all it means the right to tell people what they do not want to hear." *Pernell v. Florida Board of Governors of State University System*, 641 F. Supp. 3d 1218, 1229–30 (N.D. Fla. 2022). As the court reports in a footnote, DeSantis's proposal was originally entitled the "Stop Wrongs to Our Kids and Employees (W.O.K.E.) Act." Nothing better illustrates the trajectory of "woke" from a term of racial liberation to a right-wing talking point than its appropriation as the title of a piece of performative legislation introduced by a politician notorious for picking fights in the ongoing culture war.

16. See, e.g., Timothy Bella, "Dave Chappelle's Show in Minneapolis Canceled by Venue After Backlash," *Wash. Post* (July 21, 2022).

17. Comedy historian Kliph Nesteroff points out that many comedians have seen their role in society as speaking uncomfortable truths. In the pre-social media era, criticism by ordinary people might be represented by the 1 of 100 letters to the editor of the local newspaper that was actually printed, whereas today a deluge of tweets or YouTube comments may make the criticism appear more intense or widely shared. Sonaiya Kelley, "The Rise and Fall of Cancel Culture in Comedy," *L.A. Times* (Dec. 12, 2022). Nesteroff also points out that instead of informal social sanctions like calling out and shaming, comedians in previous generations like Lenny Bruce, Richard Pryor, and George Carlin were subject to harassment, arrest, and prosecution by police officers who were not terribly concerned that the obscenity laws they were attempting to enforce had been held unconstitutional.

18. Thanks to Washington and Lee law professor Uncas McThenia for this, which I've returned to many times over the years. I believe the original source of the line is the fictional Irish bartender Mr. Dooley, created by humorist Finley Peter Dunne. See Sam Roberts, "He Skewered Politics and New York, Without Actually Existing," *N.Y. Times* (Aug. 29, 2012). Whatever its origin, I got the line from Uncas and very much appreciated his insistence that the highest calling of a lawyer is sometimes to be a pain in the ass.

19. Post, p. 383.

20. Kwame Anthony Appiah, "Ethicist: Is It OK to Take a Law-Firm Job Defending Climate Villains?," *N.Y. Times Magazine* (Sept. 6, 2022).

21. Appiah, above.

22. Smith, above, considers the age-old ethical issue of cross-examining a truthful witness in order to discredit her testimony, only not from the impartial point of view but from the first-personal perspective of a self-identified feminist struggling to reconcile those commitments with the ethical justifications for criminal defense representation.

23. See also Arthur Isak Applbaum, "Professional Detachment: The Executioner of Paris," 109 *Harv. L. Rev.* 458 (1995), one of my favorite contributions to the theoretical legal ethics literature and one I will have occasion to cite frequently. The paper takes the form of an imagined dialogue between a writer and the executioner of Paris and is notable for some pretty good arguments on both sides. On the subject of something

being a social good and nevertheless a demerit for the person doing it, the executioner, Sanson, contends that "[i]t is incoherent to desire that capital punishment be executed and condemn the executioner." The writer, Mercier, responds that "citizens may with consistency applaud your performance on the scaffold, but damn *you* for what you have done with your hands, and abhor *you* for building a career out of the bones of your victims." See Applbaum, p. 479. While my sympathies incline toward Sanson throughout most of the dialogue, I'm with Mercier on this point.

24. In this respect, the claim defended here is a tweak to the theoretical position I have supported for quite some time. A strong (but fair) critic of that position has written: "Unhindered by situational or local moral dilemmas, Wendelian lawyers can and should go about their robust advocacy on behalf of any and all clients 'without any moral qualms.'" Allan C. Hutchinson, *Fighting Fair; Legal Ethics for an Adversarial Age* (Cambridge: Cambridge University Press 2015), p. 25. I continue to maintain many of the views that Hutchinson objected to, including locating substantial ethical value in the rule of law, and I have always been sympathetic to the idea of recognizing qualms and moral remainders. This book puts much more weight on these qualms, as well as moral sentiments and the post-Strawson tradition more generally.

1
Case Study: Swiss Banks and Nazi Gold

Crisis at Cravath

Founded in 1819 in New York City, Cravath, Swaine & Moore is the paradigm of an elite, "white shoe" law firm, with a long history of representing financial institutions, industrialists, publishers, and wealthy individuals. It hires only the highest-ranking graduates of the very top of the American law school hierarchy and then runs them through the rigorous "Cravath system" of professional development and evaluation, inviting only a tiny fraction into the partnership ranks. The hardy few Cravath associates who survive the long hours of work and internal tournament for promotion can look forward to profits per partner on the order of $4.5 million.[1] More of a bastion of power, prestige, and privilege within the American legal profession is difficult to imagine.

In 1997, Cravath was asked by its long-standing client Credit Suisse, a Swiss bank, to provide "strategic advice" related to the bank's role in laundering gold that had been looted by Nazi Germany from countries it occupied during World War II. Some of the gold had been stolen from Jewish victims of the Holocaust. According to reports by U.S. and British intelligence based on wartime intercepts, Credit Suisse accepted deposits of gold bars by Nazi officials and then provided loans in Swiss francs to Hitler's government. Other deposits had been made into Swiss banks by Jewish citizens of European countries who were concerned about increasing persecution. After the war the banks steadfastly denied that they had collaborated in Nazi atrocities and stonewalled efforts to trace the ownership of assets. Criticism by the international community grew to the point that, in the mid-1990s, Swiss bankers and government officials began to cooperate with investigations conducted by historians and international lawyers. Then the chairman of Credit Suisse proposed the creation of a $70 million fund to pay reparations to Holocaust victims, financed by itself and two other banks. This is the matter on which Credit Suisse sought the advice of lawyers at Cravath.[2]

The prospect of the firm advising a Swiss bank on its interests, given the evidence of its culpability in one of the worst moral horrors of the 20th century, was not met with universal approval. Twelve associates wrote a memo to the partnership of the firm, asking whether a concern for justice for the victims of the Holocaust could be squared with a defense of Credit Suisse:

> It is our conviction that one cannot represent Credit Suisse in its role as bankers to those who committed genocide and do the justice we are all obliged to do to the victims and survivors of the slaughter. The two are simply incompatible. It seems implausible that Cravath could both serve Credit Suisse and bring about a fair and honorable resolution for those who suffered at the hands of the Nazis and their collaborators. We suspect, even with the best intentions, Credit Suisse's interest may be too closely connected with containing the financial consequences of scandal for justice to be served by our representation of them.[3]

The associates' concern turned out to be prescient. The Swiss banks were indeed interested in minimizing their culpability for laundering Nazi gold. After a historic settlement of the claims of Holocaust victims and the establishment of a fund to pay reparations, according to a federal judge in the United States the banks "filed a series of frivolous and offensive objections to the distribution process" that were "based on an egregious mischaracterization of historical accounts."[4] Although Cravath was not representing any of the banks at this stage in the process, at the outset, when Credit Suisse first sought Cravath's representation, the associates might well have believed that the client would seek the firm's assistance in minimizing the financial cost of restitution to the families of victims and, in the process, to deny or minimize its complicity in Nazi atrocities. They were concerned that doing so would be in conflict with something deeper and more fundamental—doing the right thing, "the justice we are all obliged to do."[5]

The controversy over Cravath's representation of Credit Suisse would have been strictly internal to the firm if the associates' memo had not been leaked and reported in the press. Even so, the case did not lead to a big public outcry. There was no attempt to organize a boycott or embarrass the firm with other clients. This episode therefore differs from some of the others we will consider, such as the law student-led effort to stigmatize law firms representing fossil fuel companies and the campaign waged on social media to embarrass law firms representing the Trump campaign in challenges to the 2020 presidential election. If one sees criticism of lawyers as something akin to a moral panic or mob rule, the Swiss bank case is not an instance of that.

It is also important to see that the associates did not suggest that the representation of Credit Suisse would involve any violation of *professional* norms, such as the prohibition on bringing unfounded claims. While the district judge supervising the class-action litigation subsequently did criticize the banks for raising frivolous objections,[6] this was not the basis for the associates' objection to the firm taking on the matter for Credit Suisse. Rather, they were concerned that the bank's objectives would be to minimize the financial consequences of the revelations of its role in laundering gold looted by the Nazis. It would be wrong, they contended, for the firm to lend its assistance to that objective, not as a matter of professional ethics but as a matter of "real ethics," that is, moral standards that exist apart from laws and legal procedures. That is the significance of the reference to "the justice we are all obliged to do to the victims and survivors of the slaughter."

Finally, the associates' contention was not that the firm would be assisting Credit Suisse in violating the law. Large law firms have many flaws, but they very seldom assist clients in out-and-out lawbreaking. The memo, and the subsequent debate within the firm, were instead motivated by the assertion of accountability to moral standards that apply to decent, conscientious people in their dealings with other individuals and the moral community as a whole. Helping powerful institutions evade responsibility for assisting Nazi Germany in financing its war machine with assets stolen from victims of genocide is not something that ordinarily decent people should do. It is an obligation of background morality to avoid participating in such an injustice. The associates admitted that there is tension here between this obligation, as human beings, and what they take to be the obligations lawyers have to a client they have agreed to represent, that is, "containing the financial consequences of scandal." This tension between the duties that follow from occupying an institutional role, like that of lawyer, and the importance of remaining connected with universal moral principles even when acting in a professional capacity, is the source of much of the divergence between the permissibility and meaning of lawyers' actions.

Journalistic accounts of the firm's decision-making process described a great deal of "soul searching" and a sometimes-angry internal dispute. This is consistent with thoughtful people wrestling over a difficult moral issue, but inconsistent with a position that is believed to be part of the furniture of legal ethics. In response to criticism for the clients they represent, lawyers often reach for some kind of shield or force field—something that will rule out such criticism across the board, as out of bounds or incoherent, and therefore not deserving of a substantive response.[7] This has been referred to as the Principle of Nonaccountability.[8] One of the main arguments in this book is that the Principle of Nonaccountability is wrong and should be discarded from our thinking about lawyers' ethics. Lawyers, in short, are accountable to others for the clients they represent.

Against nonaccountability

The blanket assertion of the Principle of Nonaccountability to block all criticism of lawyers has never sat quite right with me, even though for my entire career I have been a staunch defender of the centrality of the ideal of the rule of law in thinking about legal ethics.[9] There has always seemed to be a whiff of elitism in many lawyers' response to public criticism—you unschooled, unsophisticated people simply do not understand the esoteric mysteries of the practice of law. While is true that some of what lawyers do is not easy for a non-lawyer to understand fully, lawyers are accountable not only to their clients but potentially also to the wider moral community. The organized legal profession tends to proclaim loudly that the practice of law is not a "mere" business (not that there's anything wrong with business), but that lawyers practice their profession in the public interest. If that is the stance taken by the profession, then lawyers cannot wish away public criticism for the clients they represent.

It is certainly true, and a position I will defend in this book, that lawyers have distinctive obligations to their clients, the courts before which they practice, and the legal system as a whole. However, the standards belonging to a professional role are not a force field protecting lawyers from moral criticism. Instead, the "role-differentiated" morality of the legal profession *itself* requires a defense. Public criticism of lawyers rightly raises this demand for a justification, in terms that are acceptable to the community as a whole, of the representation of all sorts of clients—the good, the bad, and the ugly— and the things that lawyers do in the course of representing those clients. That justification will turn out not to yield an across-the-board Principle of Nonaccountability for lawyers, but a much more nuanced assessment of the permissibility and meaning of representing unpopular clients. It will also vary to some extent by the context of the representation. Not all lawyers are advocates for clients in litigated disputes, let alone criminal defense lawyers. Lawyers may also be subject to public criticism for representing clients in transactional matters, or for the legal advice they have given to clients.

As you might have guessed, the word "nuanced" means it will not always be as clear and simple as lawyers would like it to be. We in the legal profession do a job that sits at the intersection of competing interests and values about which people feel very strongly. Any compromise worked out by a political and legal system is bound to be imperfect and unsatisfying. Yet I do not believe being a lawyer is equivalent to doing other necessary but unglamorous jobs, like being a garbage collector.[10] Lawyers rightly feel proud to work in an admittedly flawed system but one that aims at fairness, equality, and protecting human dignity. At the same time, however, critics of the system or of particular types of clients (fossil fuel companies, gun manufacturers, private prison corporations, suspected terrorists—insert your own prototypical "bad guy" here) understandably experience resentment or indignation as a result of, among other things, the ability of powerful individuals and corporations to employ legal procedures for their own benefit. These reactions by others, which are an essential part of living together in a society, are not so easily waved off by lawyers' invocations of legal values such as due process of law and loyal client service. A justification premised on the social value of the legal system—which I believe is the one lawyers should offer—is bound to be incomplete and unsatisfying. Any decent society will recognize some extralegal avenues, such as civil disobedience, conscientious objection, protests, boycotts, and public shaming campaigns, as a way of acknowledging moral objections to unjust laws. Public criticism of lawyers functions in this way, as a way of recognizing the gap between a legal system that necessarily reflects compromise and values that citizens do not believe should be compromised.

In a society in which people seem to disagree about everything, morally based criticism of lawyers is likely to come from all sides. As I see it, one of the most important justifications for the legal system is rooted in the capacity of law to enable us to get along with each other despite all the things we disagree about. This means, by the way, that the justification for representing unpopular clients applies not only to criminal defendants, or to parties in litigated disputes, but also to clients who seek legal advice or the assistance of lawyers in transactions, such as entering into contracts or issuing securities. In a liberal society—and by "liberal" I mean one that regards individual liberty as central—the law provides a means by which people can deal with others having beliefs or engaging in actions they believe to be wrong. Law embodies the value of toleration, which is necessary only against a background of suspicion and the desire to repress the beliefs and practices with which one disagrees.[11] Toleration coexists uneasily with the moral sentiments of resentment and indignation that are essential to the community's practices of holding others accountable. Not surprisingly, the tension between toleration and accountability often surfaces in the intense debates over lawyers who represent unpopular clients.

I want to be as clear as possible up front because this is a point that may be lost or misconstrued in the context of the discussion of some of the cases. To say that lawyers are *accountable* to others for the clients they represent and what they do in the course of that representation is not to say they are wrongdoers. It is, instead, to observe that lawyers must give an account for themselves, that is, offer a justification in terms that others can accept. It is possible to overlook the necessity of giving a justification because it is already well understood that there are good reasons for representing a particular client. When it comes to advocating on behalf of accused persons in criminal matters—even those defendants accused of doing terrible things—lawyers have a powerful moral justification for their actions. There are also many compelling reasons why criminal defense lawyers believe a full-on, zealous defense is warranted for clients accused of even the worst crimes. These include resisting the carcereal state, with its overcriminalization and excessively punitive sentences;[12] the brutal conditions behind bars awaiting anyone sentenced for a serious crime, including shocking indifference to basic human rights of prisoners;[13] understanding and sympathy for the poverty, racism, lack of educational and employment opportunities, and other social factors underlying many crimes;[14] commitment to the ideals of due process and fairness in the treatment of persons accused of crimes and the importance of checking the power of the state;[15] preventing a rush to judgment, particularly in highly emotion-laden cases;[16] ensuring that the government plays fair and complies with obligations of truthfulness in pleading and representations to the court, and disclosure of evidence favorable to the defense;[17] and an appreciation for the inherent dignity of all human beings.[18]

These are general values and commitments; lawyers are prohibited by rules of confidentiality from divulging information about their specific clients' cases. By giving an account, I do not mean here that lawyers should throw their clients under the bus or reveal confidential information.[19] Lawyers also need not *actually* provide a justification in any given case but should think through what that justification would be and be prepared to offer it. The cases discussed in this book can serve as what law professors refer to as "hypos"—hypothetical examples illustrating difficult cases for the application of competing principles. Observers and commentators on these cases are not restricted by duties of confidentiality, even though the actual lawyers involved may not have been able to actually provide the justification we attribute to them. I mention this point about the professional duty of confidentiality because it is important to understand the idea of accountability in terms of reasons that *could be* offered in justification, not as an obligation that lawyers actively representing a client give those reasons in violation of confidentiality obligations.

The case made by lawyers is often persuasive. For example, I have found, in spending more time on Twitter than is probably good for one's sanity, that people tend to get why criminal defense lawyers represent accused murderers.[20] The ideals of fairness and treating the accused with dignity make sense to people outside the legal profession, even if they do not always act consistently on those values. Lawyers seem to come in for the most severe and sustained criticism where there is some larger injustice that a powerful individual or corporation appears to be exploiting, with the assistance of high-priced legal counsel. Robust criticism for this kind of representation is healthy in a democracy. It helps remind lawyers that the legal system may be deserving of respect, but it is not the only source of guidance that matters to people. Background moral considerations such as equality, fairness, human dignity, and respect for differences are often more important than the requirements of formal law in how people think about what they owe to each other. The persistence of these ordinary moral considerations may lead to a sense of regret or reluctance, which may have the effect of mitigating or avoiding unnecessary harms to others. That theme will be explored in considerably more depth in the last chapter of the book.

The justification of John Adams

In refusing to take seriously any public criticism for the clients they represent, lawyers may have learned the wrong lesson from a lawyer often invoked as a hero for standing up to this type of public criticism. This lawyer is future signer of the Declaration of Independence and second President John Adams, then a practicing lawyer and political leader in Boston, who supposedly braved the scorn of his fellow Bostonians to represent the defendants in the Boston Massacre trial.[21] In reality, however, Adams understood himself from the very outset to owe an explanation to fellow Patriots for his representation. The explanation for his decision touches on one of the themes to be developed in this book—respect for the rule of law and the legal system as important public values in a society in which people disagree about justice.

Adams accepted the representation of eight British soldiers and Captain Thomas Preston, their commanding officer, charged with murder after firing into a boisterous crowd that had gathered near the Customs House.[22] The standard narrative, a "splendid image and a splendid myth,"[23] is that Adams bravely put aside the risk to his law practice and even his personal safety posed by a mob of townspeople braying for the soldiers' blood because he believed that justice would best be served by a vigorous defense of the accused. Many years later he remembered that he had to withstand public criticism for his role in the legal proceedings: "The Part I took in Defense of Captain Preston and the Soldiers, procured me Anxiety, and Obloquy enough. It was, however, one of the most gallant, generous, manly and disinterested Actions of my whole Life, and one of the best Pieces of Service I ever rendered my Country." Historical accounts show, however, that contrary to Adams's self-congratulatory perception in hindsight, he made the decision to represent the defendants after careful consideration of how to use the legal proceedings to advance what he believed to be the political interests of British North Americans in his beloved home city of Boston.

In the wake of the shootings, the competing Patriot (Whig) and Loyalist (Tory) presses offered starkly different versions of events: Did things just spiral out of control on the evening of March 5, 1770, leading the soldiers to fire in self-defense, or was this a premeditated act—a "horrid massacre"—by the British authorities? Pamphlets and other appeals, including Paul Revere's famous engraving showing the troops taking aim and firing at the unarmed crowd, with an officer in the background giving the command to fire,[24] sought to influence the court of public opinion. Adams privately entertained doubts that the firing had been intentional and considered the possibility that the townspeople, the rioters, should themselves be prosecuted.[25] He also had a deep-seated suspicion of disorder and lawlessness and worried that if Boston was perceived as too radical, it would hamper its struggle for rights within the British empire.[26] The imperial authorities feared that Adams would let his politics get in the way of providing a vigorous defense of the British troops.[27] On the other side, Patriot leaders seem to have assumed that the fix was in and there was no way that local jurors would acquit the soldiers and Captain Preston, so the perception of a just result would be enhanced by having high-quality representation provided to the defendants.[28] Having a defense lawyer like Adams, who considered himself a British subject and was not identified with the radical Sons of Liberty, could therefore be politically useful to the Patriot cause.

In fact, Adams's politics may have complicated his performance as a defense lawyer, but not in the way the British authorities feared. He was no radical like his second cousin Samuel Adams but was nevertheless a severe critic of abuses of power by the colonial authorities. Importantly, he was particularly keen to protect the reputation of Boston and its inhabitants, even if that potentially led him to pull his punches in his defense of his clients.[29] There was a risk apparent to sharp observers like Adams that Parliament would take steps to tighten the Crown's control over its restive colony if Boston was perceived to be sliding into anarchy.[30] Thus, Adams resisted the urgings of his co-counsel Josiah Quincy to introduce evidence that the townspeople had been looking for trouble before the events of March 5, roaming the streets in a chaotic mob armed with sticks.[31]

On the other hand, Adams showed little compunction about sullying the reputation of the crowd into which the soldiers had fired. He referred to them as "a motley rabble of saucy boys, Negroes and mulattoes, Irish teagues and outlandish jack tars" (with a reference to Crispus Attucks, now regarded as America's first Black hero).[32] Adams later claimed his representation of the troops exposed him to public criticism. That criticism, however, was likely from contemporaries who thought he had put the town of Boston on trial, not from Patriots who objected to his representation of the soldiers.[33] In his later reflections on his role in the trial, Adams emphasized his opposition to "Riots, Routs, and unlawful assemblies." "Mobs will never do," he said, "to govern States or command armies."[34] Given that political commitment, Adams's closing argument separated the unruly crowd on the street from the town itself, allowing the jurors to find the soldiers not guilty while also avoiding blame for the disorder that had led to the shooting. In his telling, Adams managed to indict the presence of a standing British army in Boston while distancing the respectable population of Boston from the rabble that had formed on the night of March 5.[35]

The Adams case is often wrongly understood today as standing for the position that it is illegitimate to criticize lawyers for the clients they represent. In fact, however, Adams expected criticism but believed he had a good response to it. In other cases, lawyers or law firms may conclude that they do not have a good reason for representing a particular client. Consider the case of a large multinational law firm, Mayer Brown, that withdrew from the representation of the University of Hong Kong after being asked for advice on what it initially referred to as a "real estate matter."[36] The matter turned out to involve the removal of a statue from the university campus commemorating the 1989 Tiananmen Square massacre, which had become a focal point for pro-democracy demonstrators. Members of Congress and numerous nonprofit organizations had called upon the firm to defend the right of free expression against yet another crackdown by the Chinese-influenced government of Hong Kong.

Although the firm said nothing publicly about its reasons for withdrawal, it would be a fair inference that firm lawyers were uncomfortable with the meaning and significance of representing a client that was seeking to do the bidding of the Chinese government. One might see this as simply caving into political pressure, cancel culture, and a public-relations crisis fueled, once again, by misunderstanding about the importance of zealous client representation in maintaining the rule of law. Certainly John Adams's justification of supporting the rule of law would ring hollow in a legal system that fails to safeguard that ideal. (Of course, it would be harder to make this argument when the representation occurs within a political system that does not itself respect the rule of law.) On the other hand, one person's public-relations crisis is another's demand for accountability, and the firm may not have believed it had an adequate response. Reliance on the Principle of Nonaccountability in this case might have led the firm to dig in against public criticism without providing a response that addressed the ethical concerns related to supporting the government's crackdown on pro-democracy protests in Hong Kong.

The Freedman-Tigar debate

A famous debate about the accountability of lawyers involved a law professor, Monroe Freedman, and a prominent civil rights lawyer, Michael Tigar. It arose out of Tigar's representation of John Demjanjuk, accused of being the notorious guard known as "Ivan the Terrible" at the Treblinka extermination camp.[37] Tigar was no stranger to controversial clients and would later represent one of the defendants in the Oklahoma City bombing case. He represented Demjanjuk in proceedings seeking to prevent his deportation to

Israel for trial, leading Freedman to write an impassioned demand that Tigar give an account for his decision:

> Is John Demjanjuk the kind of client to whom you want to dedicate your training, your knowledge, your extraordinary skills? Did you go to law school to help a client who has committed mass murder of other human beings with poisonous gases? Of course, someone should, and will, represent him. But why you, old friend?[38]

The language of Freedman's accusation was an intentional echo of a question Tigar had asked him two decades previously. Freedman had defended the representation by a large law firm of General Motors, after Ralph Nader led a group of law students in protests against GM for its air pollution.[39] In that earlier debate, Tigar had said the students should ask themselves two questions: Is this the kind of client to which I want to dedicate my training, my knowledge, my skills? and, Did I go to law school to help a client that harms other human beings by polluting the atmosphere with poisonous gases? Freedman came away from the earlier debate convinced by Tigar that lawyers have a "burden of public justification" for the clients they represent and what they do for them.

Tigar's response was fascinating. It seeks both to give an account for his decision to represent Demjanjuk and to resist being held accountable. Tigar first bristles at Freedman's conclusion from the first debate, contending that he could not possibly have meant to say that lawyers must account for the clients they represent:

> To put lawyers under such a burden of public justification undermines the right to representation of unpopular defendants. It invites the kind of demagoguery that we are now seeing in the attacks on lawyers for defendants in capital cases. It even invites the kinds of unwarranted attacks on zealous advocacy that have often been directed – and quite unjustly – at Professor Freedman.[40]

This is, of course, the Principle of Nonaccountability, which Tigar believes is necessary to ensure that controversial clients can find lawyers willing to represent them and represent them zealously.[41]

But Tigar does not stop there. He goes on to provide a powerful response to the demand for accountability, one which not only establishes that it was morally permissible to represent Demjanjuk but that a lawyer should be seen as admirable for doing so:

> When the most powerful country on earth gangs up on an individual citizen, falsely accuses him of being the most heinous mass murderer of the Holocaust, and systematically withholds evidence that would prove him guiltless of that charge, there is something dramatically wrong. When that man is held in the most degrading conditions in a death cell based on those false accusations, the wrong is intensified. When the government that did wrong denies all accountability, the judicial branch should provide a remedy. I have spent a good many years of my professional life litigating such issues. I am proud to be doing so again.[42]

If Tigar really believed in the Principle of Nonaccountability, he would not have given that inspiring defense of his professional commitments to defending the dignity of every person, even accused mass murderers, and insisting that powerful governments respect the rights of individuals.[43] Instead, Tigar accepted accountability and justified his representation of Demjanjuk as a way of resisting the abuse of government power. The "denaturalization" proceeding to revoke his U.S. citizenship on the basis of having lied on his immigration application was tainted by allegations that the Department of Justice withheld evidence that would have shown that Demjanjuk had been misidentified as "Ivan the Terrible."[44] Perhaps more importantly the representation was justified in this case because the crimes of which Demjanjuk was accused were in part enabled by the abuse of government power:

> We must remember the Holocaust, and we should pursue and punish its perpetrators. We dishonor that memory and besmirch the pursuit if we fail to accord those accused of Holocaust crimes the same measure of legality and due process that we would give to anyone accused of wrongdoing.[45]

Rather than simply relying on the remote possibility that unpopular clients would have a hard time finding counsel—after all, Tigar took the case despite the criticism leveled at him—Tigar's acceptance of accountability opened the door to a substantive defense based on the moral value of individual dignity and the political ideal of legality.

If he had relied solely on the Principle of Nonaccountability, Tigar also would have been unable to stand by his earlier criticism of lawyers who chose to dedicate their knowledge, training, and skills to defending General Motors. Tigar clearly wanted to see himself, and to justify himself publicly, as the kind of lawyer who sticks up for the little guy against powerful forces, whether governments or big corporations, even if his clients are accused of having done terrible things. If you find Tigar's commitments admirable, as I do, you have to let go of the Principle of Nonaccountability.[46] It would be incoherent to hold that lawyers can never be *criticized* for representing a particular client or a category of clients, while at the same time holding out some lawyers as admirable, even heroic, based on the clients they represent. You can see this in one of Tigar's other responses to Freedman. He says if he can be criticized for representing his client, then we'd better "hurry to the library, and re-write *To Kill a Mockingbird*" because Atticus Finch is not a hero.[47] The better response would be to accept that the fictional Atticus Finch was accountable for his decision to represent Tom Robinson, a Black man wrongfully accused of raping a white woman, despite considerable social pressure in the small town of Maycomb, Alabama, in the 1930s. Having conceded Atticus's accountability, it is not difficult to establish that defending Tom was an admirable thing to do, given the risk to Atticus's social position and physical safety, even if some readers have some hesitation about the tactics he employed at trial.[48] Ironically, insisting on the Principle of Nonaccountability would also mean not being able to regard Atticus as a hero. If lawyers are simply fungible robot-like devices that are no more accountable than any other tool, then praise and admiration, as well as criticism, are preempted by the lack of accountability placed upon intentionless objects.[49]

Upon reflection on this famous debate, I think it is clear that Freedman is right about the burden of public justification. Accountability is an inescapable feature of morality that carries through when someone is acting in a professional capacity. This does not mean, however, that you have to be persuaded by Tigar's criticism of the law firm representing General Motors. Yes, those lawyers are accountable, but accountability is not the same thing as a conclusion that someone is a wrongdoer. Accountability means that someone stands in a relationship with another person or group having the authority to address a demand.[50] The demand for accountability seeks a justification, and a justification must be based on reasons that others can accept.

However, people can disagree in good faith over the soundness of the justification offered as well as the meaning of the action that called forth the demand for justification. People may sometimes be mistaken or wrongheaded in their criticism of lawyers. The representation of the accused Nazi may satisfy a reasonable demand for accountability, just as Atticus Finch did the right thing in representing Tom Robinson. However, the lawyers in both cases may have to endure vitriolic criticism. Non-lawyers (which is what lawyers call regular folks) may fail to appreciate the way in which providing legal representation to everyone, even someone accused of having been a guard at a Nazi death camp, is justified by the ideal that criminal punishment or other adverse consequences should be imposed only after a fair process that respects the rights of even disreputable people. Someone may find Tigar's representation of Demjanjuk abhorrent even in the facts of Tigar's justification, perhaps because they believe that the value of legality is outweighed by the importance of punishing the perpetrators of genocide. The standard lawyerly appeals to human dignity, due process, and the rule of law tend to sound like weak tea in comparison with the things the defendant is accused of having done. Outside the context of criminal defense, lawyers may also have a hard time communicating the idea that loyal and effective representation of unpopular clients is an aspect of the rule of law, which supports at least some degree of social solidarity and stability despite intense disagreement about values and deep polarization. The only thing for lawyers to do in these cases is to be resolute, shrug off the public criticism, and stand up for their clients. Others might concede reluctantly that a lawyer's representation was permissible but nevertheless feel some disquiet or qualms about the lawyer's motivations or character. That is a subtle, almost paradoxical position that will be developed in the last chapter of this book.

"Ethics rules" and client choice for American lawyers

The decision to represent a client like Credit Suisse or John Demjanjuk is entirely discretionary for American lawyers. There is no legal requirement to accept the representation of any given client and a lawyer can refuse for good or bad reasons, or no reason at all, to represent a prospective client.

What lawyers have an unfortunate tendency to refer to as "ethics rules" are law, plain and simple. The regulation of the legal profession is a bit complicated, but the short version is that lawyers have traditionally been regarded not only as representatives (agents, in legal terms) of clients but also as "officers of the court," whose authority derives from that of the judiciary. In the United States, with its federal system of government, lawyers are subject to regulation by the highest court in any state in which they seek admission to practice.[51] Courts adopt rules of conduct for lawyers and enforce them through an elaborate structure of investigation and grievance committees, which can recommend sanctions such as public and private reprimands, suspension, and disbarment. The rules for lawyer discipline are based, in all U.S. jurisdictions, on models prepared by committees of lawyers, judges, and law professors organized by the American Bar Association (ABA). The ABA is a purely voluntary organization with no regulatory authority, but it has a long history of opining on professional conduct and proposing rules to govern the activities of lawyers. Its most recent effort at establishing standards of conduct for all lawyers is known as the Model Rules of Professional Conduct. Some version of the Model Rules is in effect in every U.S. state, forming the basis for legally binding rules adopted by state courts, the violation of which could subject a lawyer to discipline. "Discipline" here refers to some sort of penalty related to a lawyer's license to practice law, such as being disbarred or suspended from practice. Lawyers potentially face other sorts of legal problems beyond license-related sanctions, such as civil liability to clients for malpractice, but they typically do not refer to these legal doctrines as part of the "ethics" of the profession.[52]

The professional ethics rules, such as they are, have remarkably little to say about the representation of unpopular clients. One provision of the Model Rules says that lawyers are permitted to decline an appointment by a judge to represent a client only for good cause, including a conflict of interest, an unreasonable financial burden, or that "the client or the cause is so repugnant to the lawyer as to be likely to impair the client-lawyer relationship or the lawyer's ability to represent the client."[53] It is interesting that the rule does not just say "repugnant," let alone a weaker adjective such as "unpopular." Plenty of clients may be regarded as repugnant, but this rule contemplates declining a court appointment only if the client or the client's cause is *so* repugnant that it is likely to interfere with the lawyer's ability to provide competent representation. The rule has a kind of negative implication, which is that most lawyers, most of the time, should be able to hold their noses and represent even repugnant clients. In any event, this rule only applies to lawyers who have agreed to accept appointments by courts to represent clients, usually clients who are indigent. Most lawyers do not put themselves on the roster of lawyers willing to accept appointments and so are not subject to this rule.[54] However, there is some recognition in professional custom, although not formal law, that if one were the proverbial "last lawyer in town," it would not matter if a court did not order the representation—the lawyer would be obligated to represent the client.[55]

The word "repugnant" turns up in another provision of the Model Rules, this one governing withdrawal from representation. Once a lawyer-client relationship has been established, lawyers cannot drop the client without a good reason. (Clients, on the other hand, are free to fire lawyers at any time.) In addition to a couple of contexts in which a lawyer must withdraw from the representation, there are several permissive grounds for terminating the lawyer-client relationship, including situations in which "the client insists upon taking action that the lawyer considers repugnant or with which the lawyer has a fundamental disagreement."[56] When I teach this rule to my law students, I point out the second clause, talking about a "fundamental disagreement" between lawyer and client. As a matter of rule interpretation, including reading the rule in parallel to the rule on declining judicial appointments, I think the word "repugnant" ought to be understood as a type of moral conflict that goes beyond mere disagreement and crosses over into something so serious that it impairs the professional relationship.[57] The idea is that the lawyer would be unable to work as diligently as possible because of repugnance felt toward the client. Whenever the word "repugnant" appears in the rules it tends to be in the neighborhood of language denoting a fundamental breakdown in the lawyer-client relationship. The upshot is that the rules expect that lawyers will overcome ordinary moral disagreement and represent even disagreeable clients with competence and diligence.[58]

Supporting this interpretation is a provision of the conflict-of-interest rules having to do with personal interests of the lawyer. The rule states that "a lawyer shall not represent a client if . . . there is a *significant* risk that the representation of one or more clients will be *materially* limited by . . . a personal interest of the lawyer."[59] The italicized language, "significant" risk and "material" limitation indicates that lawyers should not lightly assume that a moral objection to the client or the client's objectives creates a conflict of interest. Most of the disciplinary and malpractice cases involving personal-interest conflicts arise out of family ties to opposing counsel, sexual relationships with clients, or service on the board of directors of a corporate client.[60] In extraordinary cases, a lawyer's racial or religious bias may interfere with the duty of loyalty and the ability to provide competent representation to a client. The Massachusetts Supreme Judicial Court is currently considering an appeal from an indigent criminal defendant, who is a Black Muslim, who claimed his lawyer was laboring under a conflict of interest because later-discovered Facebook posts showed that the lawyer had racist and anti-Islamic beliefs.[61] The level of bigotry displayed by the lawyer in that case certainly appears to rise to the level of a material limitation on his representation of his client. In most cases, however, moral disagreement with one's client's position is not disqualifying, because moral disagreement is only to be expected in a society in which people reasonably disagree about a wide range of matters. The legal system has, as one of its most important goals, establishing a basis for people to interact peacefully and resolve disagreements despite a lack of consensus on foundational questions about justice and rights. Lawyers play a role in that system by representing clients notwithstanding disagreements they might have about the morality of their client's objectives, at least as long as the disagreements are within the range of reasonable. The lawyer in the Massachusetts case, however, is not merely disagreeing with his client, but exhibiting the level of contempt and hatred that makes a normal representation impossible.

Considered as a whole, the rules of professional conduct can be read as seeking to disassociate the representation of a client from the moral qualms that one might feel toward that client or their objectives. This stance is embodied in an odd provision of the Model Rules—odd because it does not expressly state any duties on the part of lawyers. The rule states that "[a] lawyer's representation of a client, including representation by appointment, does not constitute an endorsement of the client's political, economic, social or moral views or activities."[62] The rule does not tell a lawyer to represent clients regardless of disagreement with their political, economic, social, or moral views or activities. In fact, it seems addressed to non-lawyers who might incorrectly assume that lawyers do endorse the views or activities of their clients. The rule appears to be an official statement by the organized legal profession of the Principle of Nonaccountability but aimed at critics of lawyers. Overlooking the strangeness of addressing a rule regarding the professional conduct of lawyers to the general public, the point appears to be to urge the Principle of Nonaccountability upon lawyers as an ideal to which they should aspire.[63]

Contested meanings

The Swiss bank case and Michael Tigar's defense of John Demjanjuk also show something important about morality that is often unappreciated: there is a difference between the permissibility of an action and its meaning—that is, its significance for others in evaluating the actor.[64] Many deep puzzles in moral philosophy touch upon this distinction, and contemporary treatments of problems like that of free will and responsibility consider the intentions and attitudes of the actor. What makes something wrong is that some consideration counts decisively against it; what makes an actor blameworthy is not having taken the right considerations into account in the right way.[65] To turn this point around, the process of soul-searching promoted by the associates' memo within the Cravath firm is important, because it ensured that the firm lawyers did more than merely conclude that there were no decisive moral reasons against accepting Credit Suisse as a client. As part of its deliberations about whether to take the case, partners consulted lawyers who were leaders in New York's Jewish community to consider, in effect, whether the client deserved the efforts and talents of Cravath lawyers.[66] The firm's decision was based in part on its assessment that Credit Suisse had behaved honorably in breaking an impasse that had developed between the Jewish community and Swiss banks concerning the responsibility of banks to make reparations. The firm's managing partner stated that the firm had agreed to represent the bank because the firm's involvement would make a terrible situation better.[67]

This is a subtle point to which we will return over the course of the book. The distinction between permissibility and the significance or meaning attributed by others has the potential to affect the way lawyers conduct themselves even where, as a baseline matter, there is no question that the representation would be permissible. Hypothetically, suppose that there are two courses of action available to the bank, both of which would be permitted by American substantive and procedural law: First, the bank could acknowledge that monetary compensation is owed to victims and their families. It could agree to participate in a process that would seek to make a just measure of restitution to claimants. This might mean establishing procedures to ensure that claims were not duplicative or fraudulent, but the bank would not contest the basic entitlement of victims and family members to recover, nor would it deny the historical record of its wrongdoing. I do not mean to suggest that making restitution for financial crimes is the only response consistent with the moral obligation to remember and respond to victims of genocide. For example, Abraham Foxman, director of the Anti-Defamation League and a Holocaust survivor, argued that making financial restitution would be a desecration of victims and a trivialization of the Holocaust, because most victims did not have Swiss bank accounts and were killed not for their money but because they were Jews.[68] Nevertheless, one available response could be for the bank to acknowledge its financial responsibility at the outset, while ensuring that the restitution process is orderly and fair.

The second option would be to do what large law firms like Cravath sometimes do for their clients, which is to provide all-out, no-holds-barred zealous advocacy.[69] This might include filing numerous motions to slow down the resolution of the claims, conducting extensive discovery on the factual basis for the plaintiffs' claims, and seeking every possible legal angle to deny the claims—for example, that the bank had not knowingly received deposits of looted assets or that jurisdiction in U.S. courts over this action was inappropriate. This approach would be permitted by the American law of lawyering, provided that there was a sufficient legal and factual basis for the positions taken by the firm on behalf of its client and the firm's actions were not taken for no purpose other than to "embarrass, delay, or burden" the opposing parties.[70] The predominant attitude of lawyers is that aggressive or "hardball" litigation, to the extent it does not violate any of the rules of professional conduct, is permissible full-stop—both legally and morally.[71]

To be clear, this is a hypothetical; I am not contending that the bank considered the latter approach. But notice how these two options affect the terms of the professional engagement between Cravath and Credit Suisse. The law firm might have simply agreed to do whatever the client instructed it to do, provided of course that the client's objectives and the means used to accomplish them did not violate the law. Alternatively, the law firm could have sought to negotiate an agreement that the bank would not use the firm's services to resist the victims' entitlement to restitution nor to seek to revise the historical record. The rules of professional conduct also permit this type of limitation on the scope of the representation.[72] If firm lawyers really were engaged in a process of soul-searching, however, they should consider representing the bank only if it were willing to pursue the first approach of participating in good faith in an orderly process to ensure a just measure of restitution for victims. According to the *Washington Post*, this is exactly what happened. A sense of reluctance regarding the representation of a Swiss bank in this reparation proceeding motivated the lawyers to consider all available options, including the firm negotiating a limitation on the scope of representation with its client.

In my view, it would have been morally permissible for the firm to represent even a bank that denied responsibility and wanted to fight hard (but fairly, and within the law) against the reparations claims. This is a controversial position that I have defended in the past and continue to stand by.[73] What I understand better now, after a great deal of reflection on public criticism of lawyers, is the same *permissible* act can have multiple meanings, the significance of which depends on the intentions, attitudes, and character of the lawyers involved. Tigar, for example, responded to Freedman's demand for accountability by appealing to his history of defending the liberty of individuals against the power of the state and to the importance of legality in a free society. Significantly, senior lawyers at Cravath pointed to the acceptance of responsibility Credit Suisse as one of the reasons they agreed to represent the bank. They were very much aware that standing on the legal and moral permissibility of the representation was not enough. They recognized that they had to address the demand for accountability expressed powerfully in the associates' memo but undoubtedly shared by other observers of the firm. The response they provided did not merely rehash platitudes about everyone deserving a lawyer. Instead, they addressed the meaning imputed to their action by observers, connecting the representation of Credit Suisse with the bank's efforts to work with the families of Holocaust victims toward a just resolution of their claims.

Cravath did not have to do this. Management could have told the associates to pound sand. By engaging with the criticism, however, the firm helped shape the meaning of its representation of the bank. This is the kind of dialogue that is made possible when lawyers do not reflexively deploy the Principle of Nonaccountability in an attempt to shut down criticism but instead recognize that the reactions of observers should be taken seriously as part of professional ethics. The meaning placed on actions by other members of the moral community may also lead a lawyer to engage in the representation of a client with a sense of trepidation or regret. Defending a client accused of profiting from genocide should not be a straightforward matter, morally speaking. The representation should prompt a conscientious person to slow down the decision-making process and think hard about whether all options have been exhausted. This includes considering whether there is a way to carry out one's duty as a lawyer, which includes providing an effective, even "zealous" defense of the client, consistently with the assessment felt by any decent person that this is a difficult matter calling for ethically informed judgment.

One problem with the Principle of Nonaccountability is that it risks shutting down the exercise of judgment at an early stage in the process, by encouraging lawyers to think that they do not owe a response to a demand for accountability such as that expressed by the Cravath associates. The firm deserves considerable credit for accepting responsibility and seeking to modify its representation of Credit Suisse in a way that appropriately reflects the acknowledgment of its client's complicity in a horrific injustice. This was an appropriate recognition of the moral costs of the representation.[74] The firm did not see itself as walled off from the rest of society or otherwise exempt from the demand for moral accountability that any member of the society would have to address. By accepting the obligation of providing a justification for its actions, the firm engaged with the broader set of moral resources available to reflective members of the political community exercising judgment in a difficult ethical dilemma.

One final point about the Cravath and Credit Suisse case: it did not arise out of the representation of a criminal defendant. Much of the conversation about legal ethics refers, expressly or by implication, to the situation of the lonely, powerless individual facing the massed power of the state. Much of the rhetoric around representing unpopular clients similarly assumes a criminal defense case. The claim that "everyone deserves a lawyer," including the constitutional right to counsel, the concern that no one be deprived of a lawyer because they are controversial or unpopular, and the overarching concern to check the abuse of government power are firmly rooted in the tradition of criminal defense. The John Adams story, which recurs in lawyers' justifications for representing unpopular clients, is a criminal defense story. In a way so is Michael Tigar's representation of John Demjanjuk. Although the client did not technically face criminal charges, the prospect of deportation to Israel was a serious threat to his liberty, tantamount to a criminal penalty. The Cravath/Credit Suisse case flips the usual balance of power. Now the lawyers facing criticism for their choice of client cannot claim to be riding herd on the government to ensure against abuse of its power. Nor can the firm say it is standing up for the little guy in civil litigation. The Swiss bank client was clearly the 800-pound gorilla in the scenario.

Chapter summary

To say someone is accountable to others means they owe an explanation for their actions. Lawyers like to assert the Principle of Nonaccountability to avoid providing an explanation for representing unpopular clients. The Cravath associates' memo and the firm's response show that lawyers are accountable for the clients they represent. The representation by John Adams of the British soldiers shows that lawyers frequently have a good explanation for their client-selection decision. Legally speaking, American lawyers have almost unlimited discretion to decide which clients to represent. Morally speaking, however, lawyers are accountable for those choices.

Notes

1. The $4.5 million number represents profits per equity partner (PEP) in 2021, as reported by the *National Law Journal*. The Cravath system is described in a privately printed book, *The Cravath Firm and Its Predecessors, 1819–1948*, an excerpt of which is included as Appendix 2 in James B. Stewart, *The Partners: Inside America's Most Powerful Law Firms* (New York: Simon & Schuster 1983). This approach proved to be extremely influential, and most large American law firms adopted some version of it. See Thomas D. Morgan, *The Vanishing American Lawyer* 100–102 (Oxford: Oxford University Press 2010); Milton C. Regan, Jr., *Eat What You Kill: The Fall of a Wall Street Lawyer* (Ann Arbor: University of Michigan Press 2004).
2. The internal controversy at Cravath was reported in a number of newspaper articles. See John J. Goldman, "Venerable Firm in Spotlight for Holocaust Assets Case Role," *L.A. Times* (Apr. 3, 1997); Blaine Harden & Saundra Torry, "N.Y. Law Firm to Advise Swiss Bank Accused of Laundering Nazi Loot," *Wash. Post* (Feb. 28, 1997). For a summary of the background on the conduct of Swiss banks during World War II, see Alan Cowell, "Swiss Acknowledge Profiting from Nazi Gold," *N.Y. Times* (Dec. 14, 1996). For book-length accounts, see, for example, Jean Ziegler, *The Swiss, the Gold, and the Dead: How Swiss Bankers Helped Finance the Nazi War Machine* (New York: Harcourt 1998); Tom Bower, *Nazi Gold: The Full Story of the Fifty-Year Swiss-Nazi Conspiracy to Steal Billions from Europe's Jews and Holocaust Survivors* (New York: HarperCollins 1997).
3. Quoted in Blaine Harden, *When Client, Justice, Are "Incompatible,"* *Wash. Post* (Mar. 13, 1997). A similar associates' protest led the Washington, D.C., law firm of Covington & Burling to reconsider its representation of South African Airways during the apartheid era. See William H. Simon, "Ethical Discretion in Lawyering," 101 *Harv. L. Rev.* 1083, 1094–96 (1988).
4. See the opinion of U.S. District Judge Edward Korman, in *In re Holocaust Victims Assets Litigation*, 319 F. Supp. 2d 301, 303 (E.D.N.Y. 2004).
5. I don't know if it was intentional, but I hear in the associates' memo the invocation of the declaration from the Torah, also central to the Christian tradition of public ethics: "Justice, justice thou shalt pursue." Deuteronomy 16:20. Notably the Hebrew word *tzedek*, translated as "justice," also means righteousness, or doing the right thing. It is not limited to legal justice.
6. *In re Holocaust Victims Assets Litigation*, 319 F. Supp. 2d 301, 303 (E.D.N.Y. 2004).
7. Journalist Matthew Yglesias, writing about the representation of Harvey Weinstein by Harvard Law School Professor Ronald Sullivan, which will be the principal case study

in Chapter 3, says "[t]he legal profession itself has a strong belief that there is an important principle by which it is wrong to subject lawyers to social sanction or strong moral criticism for working on behalf of bad people." Matthew Yglesias, "The Raging Controversy Over Ronald Sullivan, Harvey Weinstein, and Harvard, Explained," *Vox* (May 17, 2019). Similarly, a progressive critic of elite litigator Neal Katyal objects to the Principle of Nonaccountability "as a kind of force field preventing lawyers from facing any social or professional repercussions for their actions on behalf of their clients." Alex Pareen, "Neal Katyal and the Depravity of Big Law," *New Republic* (Dec. 8, 2020). This is what I mean by the magic shield or force field claim or, more formally, the Principle of Nonaccountability.

8. The prominence of the Principle of Nonaccountability in theoretical legal ethics scholarship can be traced back to an important early article. See Murray L. Schwartz, "The Professionalism and Accountability of Lawyers," 66 *Cal. L. Rev.* 669 (1978). Schwartz's Principle of Nonaccountability became one of three principles that comprised what came to be known as the Standard Conception of legal ethics—partisanship, neutrality, and nonaccountability. An alternative term for the Standard Conception is Neutral Partisanship. See W. Bradley Wendel, "Legal Ethics as Political Moralism or the Morality of Politics," 93 *Cornell L. Rev.* 1413 (2008), citing David Luban's use of both terms. Bill Simon uses the term "Dominant View," although ironically that label is the least frequently used. See William H. Simon, *The Practice of Justice* (Cambridge, Mass: Harvard University Press 1998). All three of these terms are defined in the same way, with substantially identical sub-principles of partisanship, neutrality, and nonaccountability.

In a nutshell the Standard Conception maintains that lawyers should be (1) partisan, in zealously pursuing their client's objectives regardless of costs to third parties, whether in litigation, transactional, counseling, compliance, or any other type of legal representation; (2) neutral, in not refraining from pursuing their client's objectives out of concern for the impact on others or as a result of moral qualms about the justice of the objectives; and (3) nonaccountable, which is to say not subject to criticism in moral terms for having complied with the first two principles. The name of this position and its three component parts coalesced in two highly influential articles published around the same time as Schwartz's. Gerald J. Postema, "Moral Responsibility in Professional Ethics," 55 *NYU L. Rev.* 63 (1980); William H. Simon, "The Ideology of Advocacy: Procedural Justice and Professional Ethics," 1978 *Wis. L. Rev.* 29. Other foundational articles in theoretical legal ethics emphasizing the Principle of Nonaccountability include Charles Fried, "The Lawyer as Friend: The Moral Foundations of the Lawyer-Client Relation," 85 *Yale L.J.* 1060 (1976); and Stephen L. Pepper, "The Lawyer's Amoral Ethical Role: A Defense, a Problem, and Some Possibilities," 1986 *Am. B. Found. Res. J.* 613. For this history of the field, see David Luban & W. Bradley Wendel, "Philosophical Legal Ethics: An Affectionate History," 30 *Geo. J. Legal Ethics* 337, 343 (2017). A couple of articles by scholars who were primarily lawyers, but also trained in other disciplines, questioned whether philosophers had the lawyer's model of ethics right. See Ted Schneyer, "Moral Philosophy's Standard Misconception of Legal Ethics," 1984 *Wis. L. Rev.* 1529; M.B.E.

Smith, "Should Lawyers Listen to Philosophers About Legal Ethics," 9 *Law & Phil.* 67 (1990). More recently Kate Kruse has argued that philosophers tend to overemphasize or artificially sharpen the conflict between role obligations and ordinary morality by imputing to clients the nastiest objectives, regardless of whether a flesh-and-blood client would actually want to do the antisocial thing. Katherine R. Kruse, "Beyond Cardboard Clients in Legal Ethics," 23 *Geo. J. Legal Ethics* 103 (2010).

My take on all of this is that the Standard Conception is alive and well; it accurately describes the approach taken by lawyers to morally troubling cases (many of which will be considered in this book). Tim Dare and I have both defended a moderate version of the Standard Conception, in which the legal rights and duties of clients, not mere client interests, inform the Principle of Partisanship. W. Bradley Wendel, *Lawyers and Fidelity to Law* (Princeton: Princeton University Press 2010); Tim Dare, *The Counsel of Rogues? A Defence of the Standard Conception of the Lawyer's Role* (London: Ashgate 2009); see also Alice Woolley, "The Lawyer as Advisor and the Practice of the Rule of Law," 47 *U.B.C. L. Rev.* 743 (2014); Christine Parker & Adrian Evans, *Inside Lawyers' Ethics* (Cambridge: Cambridge University Press, 3d ed. 2018); Donald Nicolson & Julian Webb, *Professional Legal Ethics: Critical Interrogations* (Oxford: Oxford University Press 1999)(using the term Neutral Partisanship). The latter two books are critical of the Standard Conception. However, the point of the citations to Dare, Woolley, Parker and Evans, Nicolson and Webb is to indicate that the Standard Conception is accepted broadly by lawyers in other common law jurisdictions (New Zealand, Canada, Australia, and the United Kingdom, respectively) as the theoretical foundation of their role, even if it comes in for academic criticism.

9. W. Bradley Wendel, *Lawyers and Fidelity to Law* (Princeton: Princeton University Press 2010); W. Bradley Wendel, "Legal Ethics Is About the Law, Not Morality or Justice: A Reply to Critics," 90 *Tex. L. Rev.* 727 (2012); W. Bradley Wendel, "Legal Advising and the Rule of Law," in Kieran Tranter et al., eds., *Reaffirming Legal Ethics: Taking Stock and New Ideas* (Abingdon: Routledge 2010); W. Bradley Wendel, "Legal Ethics and the Separation of Law and Morals," 91 *Cornell L. Rev.* 67 (2005); W. Bradley Wendel, "Civil Obedience," 104 *Colum. L. Rev.* 363 (2004).

10. In a justly famous article, law professor Barbara Babcock reviewed the reasons that could be given by criminal defense lawyers for representing clients they know, or at least strongly suspect, are guilty of the charged offense. One of the reasons she calls the "Garbage Collector's Reason"—that is, "yes, it's a dirty job, but someone must to do it." Barbara Allen Babcock, "Defending the Guilty," 32 *Clev. St. L. Rev.* 175, 177 (1983–84). We will return to Babcock's article in Chapter 3 on the defense of Harvey Weinstein.

11. The concept of toleration applies to beliefs, actions, or practices that one regards as wrong; a state tolerates a minority religion, or a citizen of a liberal democracy tolerates hateful expression or a practice one believes to be immoral. Rainer Forst, "Toleration," *Stanford Encyclopedia of Philosophy* (rev'd 2017); Rainer Forst, *Toleration in Conflict: Past and Present* (Cambridge: Cambridge University Press: Ciaran Cronin, trans., 2013); David Heyd, ed., *Toleration: An Elusive Virtue* (Princeton: Princeton University Press 1996).

12. Abbe Smith, "Representing Rapists: The Cruelty of Cross Examination and Other Challenges for a Feminist Criminal Defense Lawyer," 53 *Am. Crim. L. Rev.* 255, 257–59 (2016).
13. See, e.g., Ken White, "Thirty-Two Short Stories About Death in Prison," *Atlantic* (Aug. 13, 2019).
14. Barbara Allen Babcock, "Defending the Guilty," 32 *Clev. St. L. Rev.* 175, 178 (1983–84); Abbe Smith, "Defending Defending: The Case for Unmitigated Zeal on Behalf of People Who Do Terrible Things," 28 *Hofstra L. Rev.* 925, 951–52 (2000).
15. Charles J. Ogletree, Jr., "Beyond Justification: Seeking Motivations to Sustain Public Defenders," 106 *Harv. L. Rev.* 1239, 1246–58 (1993); David Luban, *Lawyer and Justice* (Princeton: Princeton University Press 1988), pp. 58–66.
16. Smith, "Representing Rapists," p. 289.
17. Smith, "Representing Rapists," pp. 289–90. As Smith rightly observes: "The Government's constitutional and ethical obligations are the same, whether or not my client is guilty."
18. David Luban, "Lawyers as Upholders of Human Dignity (When They Aren't Busy Assaulting It)," in *Legal Ethics and Human Dignity* (Cambridge: Cambridge University Press 2007), p. 65; Smith, pp. 295–97.
19. I am grateful to Lonnie Brown for pressing me on this point.
20. For a counterpoint, see Barry Sullivan, "Private Practice, Public Profession: Convictions, Commitments, and the Availability of Counsel," 108 *W. Va. L. Rev.* 1, 3–4 (2005), recounting a story of a lunch with a former president of the American Bar Association at which the author, then in practice at Jenner & Block, discussed handling, on behalf of the defendant, an appeal of a death sentence imposed for killing two police officers. The facts and constitutional issues involved were compelling, but all the former ABA president could say was "Well, I suppose someone has to represent people like that."
21. Adams's representation of the British soldiers remains the go-to trope in the long-running debate over lawyer accountability for representing unpopular clients. See, e.g., Eugene Scalia, "John Adams, Legal Representation, and the 'Cancel Culture,'" 44 *Harv. J. L. & Pub. Policy* 333 (2021); Paul Clement & Erin Murphy, "The Law Firm That Got Tired of Winning," *Wall St. J.* (June 23, 2022); Andrew C. McCarthy, "Not Everybody Is Entitled to a Lawyer," *National Review* (Mar. 22, 2022); Eric H. Holder, Jr. "'Lawyers Know Better': Criticizing Lawyers for Defending Unpopular Clients Is Risky, 'Disturbing,'" *Nat'l L.J.* (Dec. 29, 2020) (lawyers "have been steeped in a tradition that goes back to John Adams's defense of British soldiers in the Boston Massacre"); and innumerable bar journal articles. An Atlanta lawyer retained to represent Donald Trump in the ongoing criminal investigation of attempting to interfere in the Georgia election was formerly a fierce critic of Trump, for example having referred in 2017 to "the racist architect of fraudulent Trump University." Predictably enough, however, in an interview with the *New York Times*, "Mr. Findling explained his decision to take on Mr. Trump by referring to John Adams, who took the unpopular position of representing British troops after the Boston Massacre." Danny Hakim & Richard Fausset, "Trump Hires #BillionDollarLawyer," *N.Y. Times* (Aug. 12, 2022).

22. Eric Hinderaker, *Boston's Massacre* (Cambridge, Mass.: Belknap Press 2017); Neil L. York, *The Boston Massacre: A History with* Documents (Abingdon: Taylor & Francis 2010); Hiller B. Zobel, *The Boston Massacre* (New York: W.W. Norton 1970); Farah Peterson, "Black Lives and the Boston Massacre," *American Scholar* (Winter 2019): 34–43; John Philip Reid, *A Lawyer Acquitted: John Adams and the Boston Massacre Trials*, 18 *Am. J. Leg. Hist.* (July 1974): 189–207. For readers who are lawyers, yes, the concurrent representation of Capt. Preston and the soldiers under his command would today be regarded as a conflict of interest, probably not waivable. The soldiers' best defense was almost certainly that they were following the orders of Capt. Preston, the disobedience of which would have resulted in their punishment and perhaps even execution. Capt. Preston's best defense would have been that the soldiers panicked and fired without authorization. Effective defense of all these clients simultaneously would have been impossible given the conflicting defense theories unless defense counsel sought to harmonize the position of the soldiers and their commanding officer by arguing that they fired in self-defense, which would have required characterizing Boston residents as an unruly and dangerous rabble, which Adams was reluctant to do.
23. Reid, p. 189.
24. York, pp. 30–32; Zobel, p. 221.
25. Reid, p. 190.
26. York, p. 45; Hinderaker, pp. 133, 165–67, 261–63, 273.
27. Reid, p. 195.
28. Zobel, pp. 220–21.
29. Hinderaker, p. 188 ("Boston itself was on trial...").
30. Hinderaker, pp. 192–93.
31. Reid, p. 200–201. In a recent political history of the Boston Massacre, Eric Hinderaker observes that Adams's desire to protect the reputation of Boston "threatened to compromise his effectiveness as a lawyer for the defense." Hinderaker, pp. 202–203.
32. Reid, p. 202; Hinderaker, p. 206; Zobel, p. 214. Legal historian Farah Peterson focuses on Adams's reference to "Attucks with his myrmidons" coming onto the scene, and his argument to the jury that the soldiers seeing "reinforcement coming down under the command of a stout Molatto fellow, whose very looks, was enough to terrify any person" to show how Adams sought to support the theory of self-defense while avoiding characterizing the respectable (which is to say, white) citizens of Boston as a mob. Peterson, above.
33. Reid, pp. 204-05.
34. Reid, p. 205 (quoting Letter From John Adams to Benjamin Hichborn, 27 January 1787.)
35. Hinderaker, p. 204. As Farah Peterson puts it, Adams found a solution to a seemingly intractable political problem by narrowing the scope of the community that matters—in this case, by discounting the value of Black lives. Peterson, above.
36. Adam Taylor & Shibani Mahtani, "U.S. Law Firm Mayer Brown to Cease Work for University of Hong Kong in Dispute over Tiananmen Memorial's Removal," *Wash. Post* (Oct. 15, 2021). Mayer Brown is indeed based in the United States, but it has

offices all over the world, including Asia (China, Hong Kong, Japan, Vietnam, and Singapore). The legal regulation of the conduct of lawyers, which as noted in the text is sometimes misleadingly referred to by lawyers as "legal ethics," can involve complex choice-of-law analysis when a representation crosses national borders. Interestingly, though, in this case the firm seemed motivated to respond to morally grounded outrage in its home jurisdiction.

37. See Monroe H. Freedman, "Must You Be the Devil's Advocate?", *Legal Times* (Aug. 23, 1993): 19; Michael E. Tigar, "Setting the Record Straight on the Defense of John Demjanjuk," *Legal Times* (Sept. 6, 1993): 22. These columns are reprinted in Monroe H. Freedman & Abbe Smith, *Understanding Lawyers' Ethics* (2d ed. New York: LexisNexis 2002), pp. 397–402, and can be found in Tigar's papers at the University of Texas School of Law. The debate is recounted in a *New York Times* article, which gives some sense of its prominence in legal culture. David Margolick, "At the Bar; The Demjanjuk Episode, Two Old Friends and a Debate from Long Ago," *N.Y. Times* (Oct. 15, 1993). See also W. William Hodes, "Accepting and Rejecting Clients – The Moral Autonomy of the Second-to-the-Last Lawyer in Town," 48 *U. Kan. L. Rev.* 977, 985–88 (2000). The firm involved in the GM controversy was Wilmer, Cutler & Pickering, which later merged into the firm now known as WilmerHale.
38. Quoted in Margolick, above.
39. Monroe H. Freedman, "Are There Public Interest Limits on Lawyers' Advocacy," 2 *J. Legal Prof.* 47 (1977).
40. Tigar, "Setting the Record Straight."
41. American lawyers love the phrase "zealous advocacy." Bob Gordon refers to it as the central ethical norm followed by litigators. Robert W. Gordon, "The Ethical Worlds of Large-Firm Litigators: Preliminary Observations." *Fordham Law Review* 67 (1998): 709–38, p. 733. An important early article on the standard conception of legal ethics referred to the zeal of advocates. Murray L. Schwartz, "The Zeal of the Civil Advocate," in David Luban, ed., *The Good Lawyer* (Totowa, N.J.: Rowman & Allanheld 1983). "Zealous advocacy" appeared prominently in the American Bar Association's Model Code of Professional Responsibility, promulgated in 1969. The Model Code grouped both duties and aspirational ideals under nine "Canons," reflecting the 1908 ABA Canons of Professional Ethics. Canon 7 of the Model Code, which was the grouping of duties and aspirations pertaining to representing clients in litigation, stated that "A lawyer should represent a client zealously within the bounds of the law." The first statement of aspirational ideals under this Canon, EC 7-1, repeated that "The duty of a lawyer, both to his client1 and to the legal system, is to represent his client within the bounds of the law," and the first enforceable rule of professional conduct, DR 7-101, was headed "Representing a Client Zealously," although the content of the duties stated under this heading was more specific, having to do with duties under agency, fiduciary, and tort law to pursue the lawful objectives of the client. In the current ABA Model Rules of Professional Conduct, the idea of zeal is relegated to a comment on the rule requiring lawyers to act diligently: "A lawyer must also act with commitment and dedication to the interests of the client and with zeal in advocacy upon the client's behalf." ABA Model Rule 1.3, cmt. [1].

Beyond the rules of conduct proposed by the ABA and adopted by state courts, lawyers are very fond of quoting, of all people, an English barrister's justification of his threat to reveal King George IV's secret marriage to a Catholic, as part of a strategy to defend the king's estranged wife from charges of adultery. The barrister, Lord Henry Brougham, justified this aggressive strategy by claiming that an advocate must zealously represent a client, even if doing so causes harm to others:

> An advocate, in the discharge of his duty . . . knows but one person in all the world, and that person is his client. To save that client by all means and expedients, and at all hazards and costs to other persons, and among them, to himself, is his first and only duty; and in performing this duty he must not regard the alarm, the torments, the destruction which he may bring others.

Quoted in, among innumerable sources on the ethics of lawyers, Monroe H. Freedman, "Henry Lord Brougham, Written by Himself," 19 *Geo. J. Legal Ethics* 1213, 1215 (2006) (quoting 2 *The Trial of Queen Caroline* (1821), p. 3); see also Eberhard P. Deutsch, "The Trial of Queen Caroline," *ABA J.* 57: 1201–1208 (Dec. 1971). For a lively and funny recounting of the story, see Tim Dare, *The Counsel of Rogues? A Defence of the Standard Conception of the Lawyer's Role* (London: Ashgate 2009), p. 6. Dare's account of the trial of Queen Caroline contains several amusing details and is worth referring to as the best source for this famous quote. As frequently as this speech is quoted by American lawyers, it gives us little reason to believe that observers today would look with approval upon a lawyer who proclaimed indifference toward "the alarm, the torments, the destruction" brought upon others, particularly in a case less extraordinary than the trial of the Queen.

Many lawyers lament the removal of the word "zeal" from enforceable rules of professional conduct, believing it central to the ethical justification of the lawyer's role. Fittingly, given the opening story in this chapter, one of those lawyers is a former partner at Cravath. He writes:

> "Zealous advocacy" is the time-honored response to the question lawyers often receive: "How can you represent someone who is guilty?" It permits the Army JAG lawyer who is representing a young Private who is frightened about what might happen to him and who has never spoken to an officer before to say to his client: "I am on your side and only on your side." "Zealous advocacy" is what clients expect, and it is what they deserve.

Paul Saunders, "Whatever Happened to Zealous Advocacy?", *N.Y. L.J.* (Mar. 11, 2011).

I have long found the devotion to the term "zealous" somewhat tiresome and have argued that it is better understood in legal terms as a shorthand for the competence, diligence, and loyalty that lawyers owe clients in the context of a highly fiduciary relationship. W. Bradley Wendel, *Lawyers and Fidelity to Law* (Princeton: Princeton University Press 2010), § 2.2.3, p. 77; W. Bradley Wendel, "Understanding the Complex Loyalty of Lawyers: Dual-Commission, Governance Mandate, and Intrinsic-Limit Analyses," in Paul B. Miller & John Oberdiek, eds., *Oxford Studies in Private Law Theory: Volume II* (Oxford: Oxford University Press 2023); W. Bradley Wendel, "Constructing a Legal Field: The Restatement of the Law Governing Lawyers," in Andrew S. Gold & Robert W. Gordon eds., *The American Law Institute—A Centennial*

History (Oxford: Oxford University Press 2023). This is how the term was used in a recent letter submitted by a group of prominent lawyers seeking the disbarment of former Trump administration ethics counsel Stefan Passantino for trying to persuade a witness, Cassidy Hutchinson, to lie at the January 6 Commission hearing. The opening paragraph of the section detailing Passantino's misconduct states:

> Well established is the expectation that, when a person engages a lawyer to represent his or her interests, the lawyer's subsequent advice will not be affected by differing interests others may have in the same matter. That well-established expectation is the result of decades, if not centuries, of activity by lawyers who zealously pursued the interests of their clients in a manner that was unaffected by competing interests of others. Sometimes they did so at great personal cost. But, in the end, they produced a rule regarding fidelity to client interests that now lies at the heart of the lawyer-client relationship. That fidelity also is at the center of ethical rules regarding client relationships and at the core of the public's understanding of what clients should expect when they hire an attorney.

Lawyers Defending Democracy, letter submitted March 6, 2023, to the Office of Disciplinary Counsel of the District of Columbia Court of Appeals.

"Zeal" here is a shorthand for fiduciary loyalty, in this case the obligation to provide independent advice to the client unaffected by the interests of anyone who was paying the lawyer's fees. Hutchinson realized she needed a lawyer not beholden to what she referred to as "Trump World." And Passantino's advice in the course of preparing her for the hearing was consistently slanted toward protecting the legal and political interests of the former president. This is exactly the concern underlying Rule 1.8(e) of the District of Columbia Rules of Professional Conduct, which prohibits lawyers from accepting compensation from anyone other than the client unless the lawyer obtains the client's "informed consent after consultation" (a redundant formulation underscoring the importance of full disclosure) and ensures that there will be no interference with the lawyer's independent judgment. If zeal is used as a summary term to mean fiduciary loyalty free from conflicts of interest, that's fine, and perhaps that is all that is intended in the Cravath partner's reference to it as an ideal. But I still find the invocation of it as a talismanic word a bit perplexing.

In working on this book, which takes reactive attitudes seriously, I have come to appreciate the attachment lawyers have to the emotional punch of the word "zealous." Nevertheless, I believe it is misleading to summarize the duties of lawyers, even those serving as advocates, as requiring "zealous" advocacy, in part because the idea of fiduciary loyalty should be sufficient, also because it tends to make lawyers forget the second half of the phrase, that is, "... within the bounds of the law," and perhaps most importantly because references to zealous *advocacy* subtly encourage lawyers to import norms that make sense in the context of adversarial litigation into other contexts, such as counseling clients or transactional representation.

As my Italian-American in-laws would say, *basta cosi!*—enough with this. Clearly the term "zealous advocacy" gets me worked up.

42. Tigar, "Setting the Record Straight."

43. Tim Dare suggested in conversation that I am misinterpreting the Principle of Nonaccountability (PNA) and that none of its defenders would ever have thought that it should block a lawyer like Tigar from offering a defense like this one. Rather, the PNA only blocks an inference from specific client conduct (or objectives) to a conclusion that the lawyer is a moral wrongdoer. Nothing prevents lawyers from giving a general institutional account for what they do, or observers from regarding lawyers well or poorly based on the clients they represent. That is the suggestion in a marvelous paper by political philosopher Arthur Applbaum, written in the form of an imagined dialogue between the executioner of Paris, Charles-Henri Sanson, who seamlessly transitioned from serving the corrupt justice system of the *ancien régime* to guillotining the victims of the Reign of Terror, and the essayist Louis-Sébastien Mercier. Arthur Isak Applbaum, "Professional Detachment: The Executioner of Paris," 109 *Harv. L. Rev.* 458 (1995). Mercier questions whether anyone should take on the role of executioner, since it requires one to commit bad acts: "One should be *morally* good, a good man, Charles-Henri. If a good professional must be a bad man, then it is immoral to be a good professional." To this, Sanson responds with the PNA:

> I do not deny the possibility of a bad professional role that is not worthy of anyone's commitment. But that is a judgment made about the role itself, not a particular action the role requires. I have already explained to you why I believe the role of executioner is worthy of a person's commitment, and you half-believe it yourself. Having made such a commitment to the role, I cannot then reject the reasons for action the role provides. Only if the overall justification fails is any particular performance no longer an "execution," but a murder. As I said, I am not an instrument. I must judge my role. But the judgment is of a life in a role, not the particular acts the role requires me to perform.

Applbaum, pp. 484–85. Sanson's argument is that the moral permissibility of roles is evaluated at the wholesale, rather than the retail level. Once a role is justified, if an act is required (or maybe even merely permitted) by the role, there is nothing more to say about it. There is certainly no room for criticism from a perspective external to the role, in ordinary moral terms, of actions that are undertaken pursuant to the role. This is consistent with Dare's reliance on the Rawlsian two-level approach to justifying practices and acts within them. See Dare, *Counsel of Rogues*, pp. 43–51. Once a practice is on-the-whole justified, the only critical stances available, from which to say that a practitioner acted wrongly, are internal to the practice (e.g., a lawyer violated the duty of confidentiality, or knowingly introduced false evidence), or an external critique meant to disprove that the practice is on-the-whole justified. But particular moves in the game, so to speak, cannot be criticized except in terms of the rules of the game. This is, in effect, the PNA, although Dare does not refer to it as such in his discussion of Rawls and Applbaum's objection to this strategy.

My understanding of the PNA is that it preempts evaluation at a retail level of acts performed within a role, on the assumption that the role is justified at a wholesale level, as a socially useful one. Mercier's response in the dialogue is that the social value of the role does not remove the stigma of serving as an executioner because "the death penalty turns men into killers, and killers are abhorrent." Applbaum, p. 479. Sanson and Dare do understand the PNA as blocking that inference. But I believe it is a fair interpretation of the PNA that it blocks all retail-level evaluations of acts performed in a professional role, whether choosing to represent a given client or the tactics used in the course of the representation. Rather than attacking a straw version of the PNA, I think the argument in the book is faithful to the fictional Mercier's insistence that "killing is odious *from the inside*" (Applbaum, p. 480)—that is, that human moral agency remains when one acts within a role and establishes an evaluative standpoint from which role-occupants (executioners, lawyers, etc.) may be coherently criticized, even on the assumption that the role itself is justified. The magic shield or force field interpretation of the PNA, which is the way I interpret many of the responses of lawyers to being criticized for representing obnoxious clients, is consistent with Sanson's wholesale-level justification of the role and refusal to engage with criticism of particular acts within the role. One of the recurring issues in the book will be the extent to which a wholesale or system-level justification is an adequate response to criticism of an action taken by a lawyer that is unambiguously permitted by the practice rules that constitute the lawyer's professional role. Proponents of the PNA would say it is always an adequate response and if people persist in criticizing the lawyer they must be mistaken. That is what I aim to challenge here.

44. *Demjanjuk v. Petrovsky*, 10 F.3d 338 (6th Cir. 1993). The government subsequently instituted a second round of denaturalization proceedings contending that while Demjanjuk may not have been "Ivan the Terrible" at Treblinka, he nevertheless did serve as a guard at the Majdanek, Sobibor, and Flossenburg death camps. *U.S. v. Demjanjuk*, 838 F. Supp. 2d 616 (N.D. Ohio 2011).

45. Tigar, "Setting the Record Straight."

46. Jerold Auerbach relates the story of a successful New York corporate lawyer who retired from law practice to become a college professor, but returned to practice in 1951, at the age of 70, in response to pervasive anti-Communist hysteria. The lawyer, Royal W. France, explained his decision this way: "I could not be at peace with myself until I had genuinely and without reserve offered myself, at a crucial moment in history, to defend the principles which lay at the basis of my philosophy of life. To do so required defending Communists." Jerold S. Auerbach, *Unequal Justice: Lawyers and Social Change in America* (Oxford: Oxford University Press 1976), p. 257. In the civil rights era, lawyers like William Kunstler similarly explained their decision to lend their professional energies to the representation of Black clients in civil rights cases in similar terms, as a realization that neutrality about client selection is actually a personal and political stance and one they did not want to adopt. See Auerbach, pp. 267–68. The public-interest lawyering movement, which is well established in American law schools and the wider profession, seeks to prepare lawyers to represent subordinated clients and communities to challenge structural racism, economic inequality, and other social injustices. See, e.g., Catherine Albiston, Scott L. Cummings, & Richard L. Abel, "Making Public Interest Lawyers in a Time of Crisis: An Evidence-Based Approach," 34 *Geo. J. Legal Ethics* 223 (2021).

47. Michael E. Tigar, "Setting the Record Straight on the Defense of John Demjanjuk," *Legal Times* (Sept. 6, 1993), p. 22. The rhetorical punch of Tigar's response to

Freedman comes from the standing of the character of Atticus Finch, in the novel and as portrayed by Gregory Peck in the film version of *To Kill a Mockingbird*, as an icon of virtue, both as a lawyer and as a human being. In a 2003 American Film Institute list of top 100 movie heroes, Atticus Finch came in at #1, ahead of Indiana Jones, Han Solo, James Bond, and Rocky Balboa. See Galanter, p. 7. The list is available at https://www.afi.com/afis-100-years-100-heroes-villians/ Atticus was mentioned along with the old warhorse John Adams in a letter from Senate Majority Leader Mitch McConnell to the chief judges of the federal circuit courts of appeal. McConnell was pretending to be upset by the decision of Kirkland & Ellis to stop representing gun manufacturers in constitutional litigation after the Uvalde massacre, reportedly after pressure from the firm's corporate clients. McConnell's letter said: "As Americans we used to be taught to revere John Adams and Atticus Finch; it's a good thing they didn't have institutional clients." *See* James Arkin, "GOP Sens. Quiz Circuit Chiefs Over Kirkland Gun Cases Shift," *Law360* (Aug. 18, 2022).

48. "Finch could not have had a more righteous cause in Tom Robinson, a poor black man falsely accused of rape by a troubled white woman in the Jim Crow South." Smith, "Representing Rapists," p. 265. There is a lively literature arguing over whether Atticus Finch is a morally admirable character, to which many leading legal ethics scholars have contributed. Teresa Godwin Phelps, "Atticus, Thomas, and the Meaning of Justice," 77 *Notre Dame L. Rev.* 925 (2002); Tim Dare, "Lawyers, Ethics, and To Kill a Mockingbird," 25 *Phil. & Lit.* 127 (2001); Steven Lubet, Reconstructing Atticus Finch, 97 *Mich. L. Rev.* 1339 (1999); Randolph N. Stone, "Atticus Finch, In Context," 97 *Mich. L. Rev.* 1378 (1999); Rob Atkinson, "Liberating Lawyers: Divergent Parallels in Intruder in the Dust and to Kill a Mockingbird," 49 *Duke L.J.* 601 (1999); Michael Asimow, "When Lawyers Were Heroes," 30 *U.S.F. L. Rev.* 1131 (1996); Monroe H. Freedman, "Atticus Finch – Right and Wrong," 45 *Ala. L. Rev.* 473 (1994); Thomas L. Shaffer, "The Moral Theology of Atticus Finch," 42 *U. Pitt. L. Rev.* 181 (1981). This is in addition to the countless articles and president's columns, many platitudinous, in bar journals celebrating the virtues of Atticus. The existence of all of this writing stands as a kind of ostensive refutation of the Principle of Nonaccountability. If lawyers really believed in the Principle of Nonaccountability there would be nothing interesting to say about Atticus Finch. Ironically, as this book was in the editing process, several progressive teachers in a high school in Washington State proposed removing the book from the list of mandatory readings for high school English students. "To Kill A Mockingbird centers on whiteness," the teachers wrote in their challenge, adding that "it presents a barrier to understanding and celebrating an authentic Black point of view in Civil Rights era literature and should be removed." Hannah Natanson, "Students Hated 'To Kill a Mockingbird.' Their Teachers Tried to Dump It," *Wash. Post* (Nov. 3, 2023). As the article notes, the political right, which is behind most efforts to remove books from public school curriculums, saw this as an attempt to "censor a classic in service of a woke agenda."

As noted previously, Tim Dare thinks the Principle of Nonaccountability, properly interpreted, never meant to exclude this sort of debate about whether it is good that Atticus defended Tom Robinson, or whether anything he did in connection with that representation was good or bad. Again, I'm not so sure about that. At least in the way lawyers tend to deploy the Principle of Nonaccountability in response to public criticism, it stands for a kind of absolute prohibition on acting based on anger, resentment, etc., when lawyers represent obnoxious clients. The mirror image of the PNA for nasty clients would be not lionizing a real or fictional lawyer like Atticus Finch.

49. In his "Executioner of Paris" dialogue, Applbaum has the character of Sanson avoid reliance on the mindless "just following orders" defense. "Sanson, like Eichmann, aspires to respectability," Applbaum writes; but for Sanson "the thoughtless banality of the bureaucrat is never a possibility. *Something* goes on in that head of his, because Sanson is forced to explain himself." Applbaum, p. 473. When Mercier points out that the public prosecutor, Fouquier-Tinville, had argued, "Je suis la hache! On ne punit pas la hacle!", Sanson disclaims the defense that he is a mere instrument. Applbaum, p. 481.

50. Stephen Darwall, *The Second-Person Standpoint: Morality, Respect, and Accountability* (Cambridge, Mass.: Harvard University Press 2006).

51. Charles W. Wolfram, *Modern Legal Ethics* (St. Paul, Minn.: West Publishing Co. 1986)§ 2.2. New York is an oddball exception, with lawyers admitted not by the state's highest court, the Court of Appeals, but in four different appellate divisions of the Supreme Court, which is actually the trial court of general jurisdiction in the state.

52. In conversation Gautam Hans raised the interesting possibility that public criticism of lawyers, or the public's reluctance to accept the system-level justifications offered by lawyers for the clients they represent, may be due at least in part to the profession's failure to regulate itself in the public interest. There is a long-standing critique of the ABA's rulemaking process, and the organized bar's self-regulation more generally, as being self-protective, self-interested, and aimed at excluding competition from the market for legal services. See, e.g., Richard L. Abel, "Why Does the ABA Promulgate Ethical Rules?", 59 *Tex. L. Rev.* 639 (1981); Deborah L. Rhode, "Why the ABA Bothers: A Functional Perspective on Professional Codes," 59 *Tex. L. Rev.* 689 (1981); Daniel R. Fischel, "Lawyers and Confidentiality," 65 *U. Chi. L. Rev.* 1 (1998). I am sympathetic to this critique, but the self-regulation train has long since left the station in the United States. Far more important than the ABA Model Rules and the enforceable versions adopted by state courts, at least for most lawyers most of the time, is the possibility of civil liability to clients for negligence or breach of fiduciary duty, occasional claims by third parties against lawyers (e.g., for aiding and abetting client fraud), litigation sanctions, loss of the evidentiary attorney-client privilege, and similar penalties not administered by the state-court grievance process. The usual concern of emerging industries is that if we don't regulate in the public interest we'll be regulated far more rigorously by the government. That happened with the legal profession and it was clear 50 years ago that it was happening. Hans may have a point that criticism of the legal profession may reflect the public's sense that lawyers are allowed to get away with assisting clients in a lot of anti-social conduct. If that's true, then the law regulating the activities of clients should also come in for criticism if it permits the clients' activities.

53. ABA Model Rules of Professional Conduct, Rule 6.2.

54. After the law firm of Kirkland & Ellis announced that it would no longer represent firearms manufacturers in constitutional litigation, Senate Majority Leader Mitch McConnell wrote to the chief judges of each federal circuit, urging them to ensure that the firm would "see through all existing or future appointments in the absence of any *traditional* attorney-client conflicts," to ensure that firm lawyers appearing before the courts make all reasonable constitutional arguments, and to inquire of all firms with more than 500 attorneys whether they have placed any restrictions on their litigation advocacy positions due to the political position of firm management of firm clients. James Arkin, "GOP Sens. Quiz Circuit Chiefs Over Kirkland Gun Cases Shift," *Law360* (Aug. 18, 2022). This request is a *legally* meaningless act of political grandstanding, even if it reflects the sort of demand for ethical accountability that I generally support. Appellate judges make very few appointments of counsel and seldom encounter requests by lawyers to withdraw from pending cases. U.S. Courts of Appeal have no authority to inquire into internal client-selection decisions by law firms except in the unusual circumstances of a refusal of a court appointment or a request to withdraw from a specific representation. The Kirkland/Clement rupture over gun litigation is also discussed in Chapter 3.

55. See, e.g., W. William Hodes, "Accepting and Rejecting Clients—The Moral Autonomy of the Second-to-the-Last Lawyer in Town," 48 *U. Kan. L. Rev.* 977, 984 (2000); Teresa Stanton Collett, "Common Good and the Duty to Represent: Must the Last Lawyer in Town Take Any Case," 40 *S. Tex. L. Rev.* 137 (1999); Charles Fried, "The Lawyer as Friend: The Moral Foundations of the Lawyer-Client Relation," 85 *Yale L.J.* 1060, 1078–79 (1976).

56. Model Rules, Rule 1.16(b)(4).

57. This principle of interpretation is known as *noscitur a sociis*, a delightful Latin expression which basically means "you know someone (here to include words) by who they hang around with." 2A Norman Singer & Shambie Singer, *Sutherland Statutory Construction* § 47:16 (7th ed. & Supp. 2021). The "fundamental disagreement" language usefully highlights that the client's repugnance is a subjective matter, that is, it depends on the lawyer regarding the client as repugnant to the lawyer's own values, beliefs, or commitments. For example, a Roman Catholic lawyer might regard Planned Parenthood as repugnant, while a progressive secular lawyer would see it as morally praiseworthy. See Teresa Stanton Collett, "Speak No Evil, Seek No Evil, Do No Evil: Client Selection and Cooperation with Evil," 66 *Fordham L. Rev.* 1339 (1998).

58. Competence and diligence are basic obligations owed to every client, as stated in Rules 1.1 and 1.3 of the Model Rules.

59. Model Rules, Rule 1.7(a)(2).

60. See American Bar Association Center for Professional Responsibility, *Annotated Model Rules of Professional Conduct* (9th ed. 2019), pp. 155–57; Geoffrey C. Hazard, Jr., W. William Hodes, & Peter R. Jarvis, *The Law of Lawyering* (New York: Wolters Kluwer Law & Business, 3d ed., 2014), § 11.17.

61. Allie Reed, "Lawyer's Racism Sparks Court Debate Over Fair Representation," *Bloomberg Law* (Feb. 8, 2023); Allie Reed, Lawyer's Racist Posts Test Conflict of Interest Standards," *Bloomberg Law* (Feb. 7, 2023). I am grateful to Lonnie Brown for pointing this case out to me. The hard question in this case is whether this type

of conflict—and I believe there is a conflict here under Rule 1.7(a)(2)—is one that relieves the defendant/petitioner of the requirement of showing constitutional prejudice under the second prong of *Strickland v. Washington*, 466 U.S. 668 (1984). The Supreme Court has held that prejudice is presumed when the lawyer had a conflict of interest. *Cuyler v. Sullivan*, 446 U.S. 335 (1980). *Cuyler* involved the concurrent representation of co-defendants, which is a uniquely pernicious type of conflict for criminal defense lawyers. Whether other types of conflicts, including those arising from the successive representation of clients whose interests are materially adverse in the same or substantially related matters, or the personal-interest conflict at issue in the Massachusetts case, also relieve the petitioner of showing prejudice is a murky issue after the subsequent case of *Mickens v. Taylor*, 535 U.S. 162 (2002).
62. Model Rules, Rule 1.2(b).
63. See Charles W. Wolfram, *Modern Legal Ethics* (St. Paul, Minn.: West Publishing Co. 1986), § 10.2.2, at 571 ("[A]nciently and now one hears it said that lawyers are obliged to represent every person who wishes to become a client."). Gautam Hans suggests that the rule is most useful for supervisors of reluctant junior lawyers needed to staff a matter for an unpopular client. When I graduated from law school, the paradigmatic unpopular client that required a ton of associates on its matters was a cigarette company involved in products liability litigation brought by the families of dead smokers. I recall students looking at the client lists of law firms to see if Philip Morris, R.J. Reynolds, etc., were on there. Since then it seems that cultural and political polarization has increased to the extent that a category of client regarded as undesirable by one group of junior associates, or law students considering competing job offers, would be attractive to others. For example, Chapter 3 will consider the decision of the law firm Kirkland & Ellis to discontinue representing firearms manufacturers in constitutional litigation, a decision that led to the departure of former U.S. Solicitor General Paul Clement as the firm's head of appellate litigation. Paul Clement & Erin Murphy, "The Law Firm That Got Tired of Winning," *Wall St. J.* (June 23, 2022). Rather than being seen as a generally disfavored type of client, however, gun manufacturers are on one side of a profound cultural divide. See, e.g., Todd C. Frankel, Shawn Boburg, Josh Dawsey, Ashley Parker, & Alex Horton, "The Gun That Divides a Nation," *Wash. Post* (Mar. 27, 2023). Lawyers representing unpopular clients now inevitably get drawn into broader culture-war issues, which contributes to the intensity of the debate.
64. An important theme of Scanlon's recent work. T.M. Scanlon, *Moral Dimensions: Permissibility, Meaning, Blame* (Cambridge, Mass.: Belknap Press 2008).
65. T.M. Scanlon, "The Illusory Appeal of Double Effect," in *Moral Dimensions: Permissibility, Meaning, Blame* (Cambridge, Mass.: Belknap Press 2008), pp. 22–23.
66. A *Washington Post* article about the controversy reported that the firm's managing partner consulted with Arthur Liman, among other lawyers outside the firm, as part of its consideration. Blaine Harden & Saundra Torry, "N.Y. Law Firm to Advise Swiss Bank Accused of Laundering Nazi Loot," *Wash. Post* (Feb. 28, 1997).
67. Blaine Harden & Saundra Torry, "N.Y. Law Firm to Advise Swiss Bank Accused of Laundering Nazi Loot," *Wash. Post* (Feb. 28, 1997)(quoting presiding partner Samuel C. Butler).

68. Michael J. Bazyler, "Suing Hitler's Willing Business Partners: American Justice and Holocaust Morality," 16 *Jewish Pol. Stud. Rev.* 171, 174 (2014). This is a powerful objection, but for the purposes of the ethics of representing Credit Suisse, the law firm had only the options available to the bank, and the bank's most plausible response to the demand for accountability would be to offer financial restitution. In addition, the families of the victims whose assets had been looted were ultimately morally responsible for determining what action would best honor their families' memory.
69. Well documented in a sociological study conducted by the ABA Section on Litigation and reported in several articles including Robert W. Gordon, "The Ethical World of Large-Firm Litigators: Preliminary Observations," 67 *Fordham L. Rev.* 709 (1998); Robert L. Nelson, "The Discovery Process as a Circle of Blame: Institutional, Professional, and Socio-Economic Factors That Contribute to Unreasonable, Inefficient, and Amoral Behavior in Corporate Litigation," 67 *Fordham L. Rev.* 773 (1998).
70. ABA Model Rules of Prof'l Conduct, Rule 4.4(a). Rule 3.1 requires that the firm ensure that there is a non-frivolous basis for every issue within the proceeding that it "assert[s] or controvert[s]" on behalf of the client, where non-frivolous is defined as an objectively reasonable basis in law and fact for doing so.
71. Two key findings of the ABA Litigation Section study were:

    1. "Ethically inappropriate behavior (in the standard take) is defined narrowly as a violation of the rules. Any eyebrow-raising behavior that is not a rule violation is classified as a matter of questionable 'morality' or 'bad manners' or 'hardball' or 'asshole' behavior, a defect or mannerism of individual character or personality."
    2. Given the basic norm of the adversary system, which is the duty of zealous representation of client interests within the rules, much of what is characterized as aggressive or 'hardball' behavior is legitimate and functional in view of valid litigation objectives and the conventional norms of the adversary game. 'You stay within the rules; to the extent it's within the rules, you have a duty to do everything you can for the client's interest.'"

    Gordon, p. 710. The first finding does refer to questionable morality, but it is clear from the rest of the sentence—and the article more generally—that morality as used here is equivalent to manners or personal character and that big-firm lawyers do not take seriously the possibility that they may not be morally permitted to engage in hardball litigation.
72. Model Rule 1.2(c).
73. W. Bradley Wendel, *Lawyers and Fidelity to Law* (Princeton: Princeton University Press 2010); W. Bradley Wendel, "The Limits of Positivist Legal Ethics: A Brief History, a Critique, and a Return to Foundations," 30 *Can. J. L. & Jurisprudence* 443 (2017); W. Bradley Wendel, "Legal Ethics Is About the Law, Not Morality or Justice: A Reply to Critics," 90 *Tex. L. Rev.* 727 (2012). I hope this book does more than furnish an occasion to clean up a few nagging problems in my overall theoretical position. The phenomenon of public criticism of lawyers seems interesting in its own right.

74. Gerald J. Postema, "Moral Responsibility in Professional Ethics," 55 *NYU L. Rev.* 63, 80 (1980). Postema's early, influential article sounds many of the themes that I will address throughout the book, including the centrality of the appropriate attitudes and reactions to a moral situation—not just "getting our moral sums right" (pp. 68, 70), the idea that even justified actions may carry "moral costs" with them (p. 69), and personal and social costs of adopting an extreme attitude of detachment toward any considerations that would interfere with the lawyer's "zealous and scrupulously loyal pursuit of the client's objectives" (p. 78).

2
Philosophical Perspective: Accountability, Reactive Attitudes, and the Meaning of Actions

Morality beyond duties and rights

It is fairly common to think that the subject of morality has to do with what we are obligated to do or, negatively, what we must *not* do. Morality did not have to become equated with this stringent language of duty, however. For ancient philosophers, the subject of ethics had to do with pursuing ends that are truly valuable, having a good character, or enjoying a life characterized as happy, in Aristotle's rich sense of flourishing.[1] Along the way, however, probably through the influence of Christianity, ethics acquired the characteristics of law, including a preoccupation with notions of duties, permission, excuse, guilt, penalties, and so on.[2] Even if we have given up the idea of a divine lawgiver, we have hung on to ideas of being bound by law-like requirements. And even if we don't talk in legalistic terms, the subject of ethics still deals largely in absolutes, or else complex structures of duties and excusing conditions, with the ultimate goal being to settle on some course of action that is permissible. As the modern moral philosopher T.M. Scanlon has famously argued, we owe it to others to act only in ways we can justify to them, based on principles they cannot reasonably reject.[3] The focus is on the act itself and whether it is justified.

The approach to ethics taken by this book emphasizes the interpersonal or relational dimension of morality without limiting the questions to those regarding duties, prohibitions on actions, and whether an action is justified. Morality is richer than that, and while academic philosophers know this, they are inclined to work on the theoretical problems that tend to be discussed in the scholarly literature. As a philosophically inclined lawyer, however, I am more drawn to challenging problems that arise in the real world. From that perspective, the memo written by the associates at Cravath in response to the firm's representation of Credit Suisse raises a number of interesting questions. The questions, however, do not really have to do with whether a lawyer in general or this law firm in particular is morally prohibited from representing the bank. Clearly the representation is legally permitted. As for why the firm is *morally* permitted to work on behalf of a corporation that admitted to having assisted the government of Germany in laundering assets stolen from victims of a genocide, that is a complex argument that will develop over the course of the book; the short version is that in a society in which we disagree constantly about right and wrong, having political rights and a legal system to determine their content answers to a deep human need—that is, it is morally valuable. If that is true, then the firm's representation of the bank is morally as well as legally permissible.

I believe it to be important to look not only at permissibility but also at the *meaning* of actions. Meaning is the significance attributed to actions by those directly affected by them and to other members of the community who are sizing up the action, trying to figure out what sense to make of it, and how that affects their relationship with the actor. Meaning has to do with the intentions, motivating reasons, or attitudes toward others that one expresses in actions. These attitudes can be positive, such as respect or caring, or negative, such as contempt or indifference. Intentions and attitudes have a great deal to do with how we understand the significance of others' actions.[4] We care not only about what people choose to do but about the attitudes underlying those choices. "Our evaluations of ourselves and our actions depend not only on getting our moral sums right but on having the appropriate attitudes and reactions to the moral situation in which we act."[5] An impartial, system-level justification of an action may not fully describe the moral situation of someone who performs the action in the context of a professional role.[6] The moral analysis may also have a great deal to do with the actor's attitudes and intentions and how those things affect the relationship between the actor and those affected by the action.[7]

Before delving into the significance of attitudes and intentions for the practice of blaming others, which is the subject of Chapter 4, we need to start chipping away at the Principle of Nonaccountability. That begins with understanding morality as the maintenance of relationships of mutual accountability. The account of morality I am developing here is indebted to many historic and modern thinkers, including one of the major figures of the Scottish Enlightenment, David Hume.[8] Hume was interested in the nature of human beings and their psychology. Morality for Hume was not matter of highly abstract reasons but the way people actually interact with one another. One of Hume's primary concerns was to connect morality with the emotions or sentiments, not rationality alone. The feelings that an observer would have, upon witnessing some act, gives rise to reactions of praise or blame. These reactions arise as a result of the sympathy we as sensitive beings naturally have toward those we perceive as similar to ourselves in relevant ways.

Hume gave a simple illustration of this process at work.[9] Suppose David has a swollen, painful toe. Another person comes along and steps on David's toe, causing David to cry out in pain. Now what? The exclamation of pain functions as an urgent request that the other person do something—certainly remove his foot, and probably also offer some explanation to David for why this unfortunate foot-treading incident happened (jostling on a crowded subway car, for example, or killing a poisonous spider that is about to crawl up David's pant leg). In addition, David's reaction also creates a reason for the other person to move his foot. The cry of pain operates as an authoritative demand, establishing David's claim that the other person must do something. The relationship between David and the foot-treader is one of equality and, as such, grounds a structure of accountability in which one person may reasonably demand something of another.[10] To fail to remove one's foot from David's swollen toe therefore manifests a failure to respect David's dignity or standing as a person who may not be treated in this way.[11]

Reactive attitudes

David, of course, would have a perfectly natural response to his toe being stepped on. He would experience what the British philosopher Peter Strawson referred to as "reactive attitudes," including indignation, blame, hurt feelings, contempt, or resentment.[12] These attitudes hold others to account for violating a justified expectation—for example, that one not gratuitously cause pain to others.[13] David's attitude of resentment holds accountable the person who stepped on his toe, *to David*, not to some kind of impartial tribunal of reason.[14] The violation of a justified expectation is a wrong to another, not an abstract or impersonal wrong (if there is such a thing), or a conclusion about what is best in some general sense.[15] Rather, it is part of normal interpersonal relationships that we tend to feel and express sentiments like indignation toward people who disregard the interests of others without sufficient justification.[16] The term "attitude" suggests something in a cool emotional register, like reappraisal or reevaluation. However, Strawson himself is drawn to more highly charged affective states, like indignation or anger.[17] Most of the cases we will be talking about in this book involve people getting mad at, or about, lawyers.

Conversely, people express positive reactive attitudes, including approval, gratitude, and forgiveness toward actions that manifest respect for the interests of others. Reactive attitudes are expressed from the standpoint of being a participant in normal human relationships, as opposed to a detached, impartial observer.[18] This participant stance involves treating others as we regard ourselves—as fully competent beings capable of being moved by reasons.[19] In the lingo of moral philosophy, this is the point of view of seeing others and ourselves as *moral agents*. One reason the Principle of Nonaccountability is such a contentious part of legal ethics is that it appears to deny the agency and responsibility of lawyers for acting in ways that are harmful to the interests of others. Lawyers seem to be foisting responsibility off onto an institution like the legal system, without accepting any personal responsibility for harms caused in the course of their representation of antisocial clients.[20] The existence of reactive attitudes in the community is compelling evidence that lawyers are not walled off by a magic shield or force field from other members of the community, somehow immune to moral criticism. Nor should they be, for there must be some connection between the interests and concerns of the broader community and the evaluative standards followed by professions that have any plausible claim to legitimacy within the community (as opposed to a malevolent organization like the Sicilian Mafia or Mexican drug cartels).[21]

Reactive attitudes are adopted in response to the actions of others and the reasons and attitudes that underlie those actions. In this way they form a part of a social practice of holding people responsible. Many philosophical discussions of responsibility are concerned with big issues such as whether it is appropriate to blame someone for something that is beyond their control due to their factors such as their DNA or life history.[22] There is a worry that we do not originate our actions but are merely a confluence of causal processes that long predate our existence.[23] It would not be appropriate to hold someone responsible if their actions were causally determined by some prior state of the universe and the laws of nature. People suffering from severe addictions or mental illness, for example, do not deserve blame for the actions caused by an organic process over which they have no control.[24]

Metaphysical worries about the causal determination of actions have long been at the center of philosophical debate about moral responsibility.[25]

One of Strawson's innovations was to reverse the usual order of explanation. Reactive attitudes do not follow from a conclusion that someone is responsible for their actions, and they are not merely emotional side effects of or social sanctions for wrongdoing.[26] On Strawson's account, there is nothing more basic than the social practices of feeling resentment, ascribing blame, expressing indignation, arousing contempt for others, feeling guilty or remorseful for one's own offenses, and so on. Rather, these practices are *constitutive of* moral responsibility. To be responsible oneself, and to regard others as responsible, simply *is* to be subject to these reactive attitudes. Interactions among members of a moral community take the form, among other things, of demands and expectations that are addressed to others, and responses to wrongdoing "in the general key of blame."[27] Reactive attitudes in this same key reflect a concern, internalized by members of the community, for the interests of individuals, their entitlement to be treated with dignity and respect, and the expectation that others will justify actions that infringe on the rights of others. Moreover, as Strawson argues, we cannot help doing this because we are human. "What I have called the participant reactive attitudes are essentially natural human reactions to the good or ill will or indifference of others towards us, as displayed in *their* attitudes and actions."[28] In this way Strawson follows in the tradition of Hume, by grounding morality in observations about the kinds of creatures we are. The concerns and demands expressed through reactive attitudes are part and parcel of our fundamental nature.

On this way of looking at the subject, morality is at its roots *relational*, having to do with the claims others have against us by virtue of the fact that we live alongside other people and have the power to affect them by our actions.[29] We presuppose that others are free, rational, and equal, just as we are, when we engage in ordinary interpersonal interactions, which are characterized by practices of feeling indignation, assigning blame, expressing attitudes of approval or disapproval, and all the other perfectly ordinary ways we deal with one another.[30] Making a conscientious effort to take account of the interests of others satisfies the demand that we act responsibly. However, actions revealing disrespect for others' concerns or the standards of appropriate behavior prevalent in the moral community may prompt the resentment or indignation of others.[31] Reactive attitudes and the practices they support are ways a moral community maintains standards for treating others with respect and dignity.

Resentment and indignation are expressed in daily life through characteristic forms of social behavior such as direct criticism, attempts at persuasion, gossip, shaming, shunning, ostracism, protests, and boycotts.[32] John Stuart Mill, who was strongly opposed to coercive social control over individuals, nevertheless observed in *On Liberty* that it is natural for people to wish to avoid those we regard as wrongdoers:

> We have a right, also, in various ways, to act upon our unfavourable opinion of any one, not to the oppression of his individuality, but in the exercise of ours. We are not bound, for example, to seek his society; we have a right to avoid it (though not to parade the avoidance), for we have a right to choose the society most acceptable to us.[33]

Many cultures and subcultures throughout history have developed elaborate public rituals to target social disapproval at those individuals perceived to have transgressed community norms.[34] These include tarring and feathering, riding offenders out of town on a rail, and charivari rituals involving noisy public parades and aimed at adulterers and other violators of community sexual norms.[35] Social media has created additional avenues for the expression of reactive attitudes, through practices such as calling out wrongdoers.[36] Sometimes negative reactive attitudes can motivate calls for formal actions, such as employers suspending or firing perceived wrongdoers, "de-platforming" unpopular speakers by rescinding invitations to speak at universities or in other public forums, or refusing to go through with a proposed transaction.[37]

These concrete manifestations of reactive attitudes are central to the moral life of communities, even while they are also susceptible to characteristic dysfunctions. Spreading false rumors may unfair harm another's reputation, social media pile-ons can lead to disproportionate punishment for relatively minor offenses,[38] and social sanctions may be directed toward relatively powerless members of the community. As a method of persuasion, getting in someone else's face and telling them they are a wrongdoer is pretty much the worst possible approach. People tend not to take very well to being called out or shamed and often respond by doubling down on the action or position for which they are being criticized.

Another problem with informal social expressions of reactive attitudes can be explored by analogy with denial of due process of law. Cancelation may be associated with the imposition of tangible and greatly disproportionate penalties, such as losing a job or an entire career, unconstrained by anything like a formal procedure in which the "cancellee" would have an opportunity to present evidence of innocence or in mitigation of punishment.[39] Someone who is fired by an employer after an inartfully worded social media post may object along these lines to having been canceled. So far nothing like this has happened to many of the performers or public figures who seem to relish taking controversial positions. These claims of cancelation thus appear insincere or performative. But lurking in the background of many invocations of cancel culture is the very real fear that unruly social processes, unconstrained by the requirements of formal lawmaking and law application, will have serious economic repercussions on people who express ideas that are unacceptable to the unappointed mandarins of political correctness. Relatedly, another pathology of cancel culture is that it involves evaluations of the character of a person that are very difficult to rehabilitate.[40] Critics do not assert merely that Dave Chapelle did something wrong by doing bits about transgender rights but that he is a hateful person. That is the sort of stigma that is hard to come back from, and if cancelation does involve a potentially erroneous judgment about one's character, it becomes even more terrifying to those who take unpopular positions on behalf of others.

Some of what gets labeled as cancel culture should be seen as an effort by relatively powerless people to leverage the limited tools that are available, including social media, to focus attention and outrage on wrongdoers who otherwise would escape responsibility. The trouble with informal mechanisms like calling out, shaming, and shunning is precisely that they are informal. They are not governed by standards that are clear, public, predictable, and apply in the same way to similarly situated people. In other words, they are not responsive to the ideal of the rule of law; nor are they democratically legitimate. A sophisticated version of the cancel culture critique would therefore seek to restrict certain decisions about what constitutes a wrong, who is a wrongdoer, and what punishment is appropriate for wrongdoers, to an official public process like voting, passing legislation, or rendering judicial decisions.[41] We should decide important questions such as who deserves to lose their job or be treated as an outcast, how severe the punishment should be, or how long someone should be regarded as a social pariah only through formal procedures designed to ensure the fairness and legitimacy of the punishment. This version of the argument from cancel culture is a serious one and may be a powerful response to public criticism of lawyers, but it requires a sophisticated engagement with the question of the proper boundaries between the public and private spheres.

Although informal avenues of accountability can be unruly, formal law and legal procedures are no panacea. One problem with formal law is that it may be used or abused to protect powerful people.[42] The rights and privileges available under formal law may also have been established by a superficially open, inclusive, and democratic process that nevertheless excluded or undervalued certain groups or political viewpoints. Those with diminished access to official power may feel drawn to informal techniques such as shunning, shaming, or boycotts. Informal mechanisms of accountability, such as criticism, shunning, shaming, and boycotts, are therefore an important feature of public life in a lively, disputatious liberal society. It's true that no one likes to be publicly shamed,[43] and intense, personal public criticism is generally not a particularly good way of persuading others.[44] Lawyers, however, who are very comfortable with ethical norms centered on the rule of law, tend to believe that there is something *conceptually* wrong with basing criticism on nonprofessional ethical standards. This is precisely what makes public criticism of lawyers such an interesting phenomenon from the point of view of legal ethics. It reveals the divergency between the background morality and the moral universe of lawyers and, in turn, requires lawyers to understand, explain, and justify what they do in terms that are responsive to the demand for accountability that underlies public criticism for representing unpopular clients.

Reactive attitudes and reasonable expectations

Strawson reframes the debate within moral philosophy from one concerning the power to control one's actions to a focus on whether it would be appropriate to hold people responsible, through reactive attitudes and practices such as blaming, criticizing, calling out, or even "canceling." Reactive attitudes are a pervasive feature of ordinary morality and reveal that people are not paralyzed by doubts about whether moral responsibility is compatible with a scientific account of the causes of behavior.

However, facts about the world, including social practices, folk morality, and reactive attitudes, may not, by themselves, be enough to underwrite an evaluative judgment—that is, one labeling an action or a person as good or bad, right or wrong, praiseworthy or blameworthy, and so on.[45] Philosophers who have been influenced by Strawson have therefore sought to establish a connection between reactive attitudes and the rational evaluative standards that arise when people stand with others in relationships of mutual respect and concern. One approach would be to emphasize the expectations and attitudes that constitute relationships, not sentiments like resentment and indignation.[46] Alternatively it could be that to experience a reactive attitude involves believing that another has violated an expectation to which one holds that person.[47] Reactive attitudes might therefore be related to standards that structure social relationships in terms of expectations that people owe to each other.[48] In either case I believe we can speak of reactive attitudes as appropriate, fitting, or justified given the conduct of the other.

References to a reasonable belief that one has violated a justified expectation are meant to differentiate appropriate from mistaken reactive attitudes. The observers of an event may be interpreting it in light of what they assume, possibly incorrectly, to be the reasons for the action. Going back to the gouty toe example, maybe David and a friend were just horsing around and the friend had no reason to know about David's swollen toe. A stranger witnessing the act, having no way of knowing this, might think the person who stepped on David's toe was a jerk. The reasons underlying an action and the motivation for it are often opaque to outside observers, although in some cases they may be inferred based on the actor's words, prior actions, or the surrounding circumstances. Reasons and motivations can also be ambiguous or inconsistent. The phenomenon of acting out of mixed motives is familiar enough, but people also act impulsively, contrary to their considered intentions, or out of weakness of will. The upshot is that it is possible for others' reactive attitudes to be mistaken, and for this reason it is important to hold onto the evaluative terms that have been pervasive in this discussion—*appropriate* reactions to violations of *justified* expectations. There is an important step between simply experiencing a reactive emotion such as indignation and doing something to hold another person responsible. Slowing down, gathering information, considering all the evidence, withholding judgment until all the facts are in, and making an effort to view the matter sympathetically, from the point of view of the actor, and attempting to draw fair inferences are all part of the ethics of blame, a subject that will be considered further in Chapter 4.

As we will see in many of the cases in this book, including the Swiss bank representation from the previous chapter, much of the interesting debate in professional ethics relates to whether it is appropriate to criticize lawyers based on a negative reaction to learning that they are working on behalf of a client accused of having done, or intending to do, something unjust. People who engage in criticism, shaming, calling out, or advocating for social sanctions against lawyers ought to make sure they understand the facts of the matter and have taken into account the lawyer's reasons for representing that particular client. Of course, a great deal of public criticism is far from this paradigm of careful consideration of the appropriateness of blame, and lawyers are accustomed to ignoring unwarranted attacks. But this does not mean that all negative reactive attitudes are unjustified or can simply be ignored. One of the features of the Swiss bank case that makes it an excellent introduction to the problem of criticizing lawyers is that the moral questions were raised by associates at the law firm. The critics in this case were not only legally sophisticated but probably very well informed about the underlying facts. Lawyers take the protection of client confidences very seriously, so there are often facts not known to the general public that bear on the appropriateness of criticizing lawyers in a particular case.[49] Lawyers are authorized by the rules of professional conduct to share confidential client information within a law firm, however,[50] so the Cravath associates were not working with rumors and innuendo, but with as much of the relevant facts as the firm partners were willing to discuss internally. The associates' memo cannot be written off easily as factually mistaken. In some of the other cases we will be discussing, some initial public criticism may have been based on an incomplete factual record, and the lawyer's conduct may appear less objectionable once additional information is learned. Apart from factual uncertainty, many of these cases involve interesting questions regarding the interpretation of the factual record to support inferences regarding the reasoning and motivation of the lawyers involved. As a matter of the ethics of blame, which can be seen as an aspect of the virtue of toleration in a pluralistic society, people ought to make reasonable efforts to understand the relevant facts and draw fair inferences from them.

Another disanalogy between David with his swollen toe and the representation of Credit Suisse has probably already occurred to you. Even without the philosophical apparatus of reactive attitudes, most people would have no difficulty judging that it would be wrong to step on someone's painful toe without a good reason. The law firm's representation of the bank, however, is not wrongful—certainly not in legal terms, but I would contend, not in moral terms either. The moral case for the permissibility of representing clients who appear to be acting unjustly is something that will be developed over the course of the book, but the basic idea is simple enough to state: even in connection with something as clearly immoral as helping the Nazi government hide assets stolen from the victims of genocide, questions may arise about which reasonable people may disagree. There are substantive questions, such as the extent of the bank's obligation to make restitution and how closely related a claimant must be to the original victims of the theft. There are also procedural questions, such as the jurisdiction of U.S. courts to consider the matter and the extent of discovery that will be permitted into the underlying facts and documentary evidence. Laws, a process of adjudication, and lawyers representing all sides to a dispute help a political community resolve these issues in an orderly and fair manner. This is a good thing from the point of view of a society characterized by deep and often intractable disagreement. There is, or at least so I believe, a resulting moral permission for lawyers to represent even fairly nasty clients because legal procedures contribute to the good governance of the community.

Nevertheless, another important theme to be developed throughout this book is that some morally permissible actions carry with them a sense of loss and should be performed only with some reluctance or regret. I have long thought that one of the things that makes legal ethics such a fascinating area of applied moral philosophy is the occurrence of cases in which it is not simply, straightforwardly the case that a lawyer's conduct is either permissible or wrongful. This is not just a matter of it often being complicated, or a matter of judgment, to determine the right thing to do. More than that, there are a great many situations in which some sentiment or evaluation of wrongdoing accompanies an action that the lawyer reasonably judges to be the right thing to do. There is a much-discussed case in the legal ethics literature in which a man confessed to his lawyers that he had committed a murder for which another man, Alton Logan, was currently serving a prison sentence.[51] The lawyers were obligated by a stringent rule of professional conduct not to disclose any client information without the client's consent, there was no exception to the rule permitting disclosure to prevent the wrongful conviction of an innocent person, and the client strictly instructed them not to reveal his confession during his lifetime. What should the lawyers do?

My view has always been not only that this is a hard case, but that whatever the lawyers do, some harm, loss, or even wrong will remain. If the lawyers disclose, they will be in violation of one of the core duties of the legal profession, the near-absolute protection of client confidences, and subject themselves to potential disbarment. If they do not reveal their client's confidential communication, however, an innocent person remains in prison for a crime he did not commit.* Many non-lawyers (including many law students) see this as an easy case—the lawyers should disclose. Just about every lawyer I've ever talked with about this case sees it as easy on the other side.[52] In their view, the lawyers must keep the man's secret even if it means someone rots in jail unjustly. The legal system, not the man's lawyers, bears the responsibility for the injustice. Either way, however, the usual analysis of that case seeks to characterize the lawyers' actions as either right or wrong, and then that's the end of it. There is no consideration of the possibility that the lawyers may have been right but should nevertheless feel considerable discomfort or regret about what they chose to do.

One way the moral costs of representation can be brought home to lawyers is the expression of reactive attitudes, like indignation and anger, in response to representing certain clients. As we will discuss in Chapter 4, lawyers may be blamed even in cases like this one, where they had good reasons for doing what they did, if their actions reveal attitudes that were impaired in some way. (I do not believe that was the case with the lawyers in the wrongful conviction case.) Returning to the Swiss bank example, the indignation expressed by critics inside and outside of the firm—many, but not all Jewish, some of them including Holocaust survivors—motivated firm management to negotiate with its client and obtain the client's consent to a style of representation that was not the full extent of legally permissible zealous advocacy but was instead an approach that took into account the moral costs imposed on victims' families and a community-wide sense of obligation to honor the memory of victims of the Holocaust. Seeing the firm's representation of the bank as straightforwardly permissible, as opposed to permissible with regrets, might have caused the firm to think it had no obligation to reconsider its approach to the litigation to take into account these extralegal moral interests. The concern with getting their motivating reasons and attitudes

---

* In the real case, the lawyers disclosed their client's confession after he died in prison because they had the foresight to obtain their client's consent to the posthumous disclosure of his written affidavit admitting to the crime. Cook County, Illinois, prosecutors then dropped all charges and the wrongfully convicted man was released from prison, having lost 26 years of his life to a gross failure of justice.

right may have nudged the lawyers in that case toward a better style of representation of the bank.

Reactive attitudes and the scope of the moral community

Reactive attitudes may be criticized because they are based on mistakes about the facts. It is also possible to evaluate them as disproportionate to the offense. The observation that someone is "freaking out" or overreacting is an assessment of the proportionality of a reactive attitude. Similarly, one can say that a critic is engaged in moral grandstanding or virtue signaling, rather than pressing a sincere objection to the conduct.[53] There is a further issue with reactive attitudes that I want to consider here in connection with public criticism of lawyers. That is, who is a member of the relevant community that establishes and enforces expectations regarding appropriate standards of interpersonal behavior?

Returning to our gouty toe example from Hume, it is important to see that the wrongfulness of the action is not only of concern to David.[54] People other than the immediate victim of a wrong might also express reactive attitudes such as indignation, contempt, or anger at the person who acted without sufficient regard for David's interests.[55] Those who witnessed the event also might adjust their attitudes in response. "Watch out for that guy," someone might mentally note. Reactions by people other than the immediate victim of the wrong indicate that it is not a matter of indifference whether others comply with community expectations of appropriate behavior and attitudes. In this way, moral standards and the reactions of others provide a basis for a shared social life. Given the role of morality in securing the conditions of common existence among a community of people, it is reasonable for members of that community to hold each other accountable for violations of standards of appropriate conduct.[56] Someone may even be criticized by others for *not* calling out or shunning a wrongdoer.

At the same time, we are all familiar with the objection that the conduct of another is none of your business. One of the objections to cancel culture is that people spend a lot of time on social media becoming exercised, and riling up others, about someone's offenses that do not affect them in any tangible way. What business do most members of the public have criticizing lawyers for the clients they represent? Maybe other lawyers have standing to be involved in these debates because they share an interest in the integrity of the legal profession. Lawyers in the United States, for example, are required to inform professional disciplinary authorities when they know of conduct by a lawyer that "raises a substantial question as to that lawyer's honesty, trustworthiness or fitness as a lawyer in other respects," with the scope of reportable offenses further defined as "those offenses that a self-regulating profession must vigorously endeavor to prevent."[57] The ideal of a self-regulating profession and the interest in not having the public think any worse of lawyers than it already does probably give other lawyers a sufficient interest to warrant criticism of perceived misbehavior. It is also, arguably, open to members of the public to criticize lawyers because the monopoly that the legal profession enjoys over the provision of legal services is traditionally thought to be granted in exchange for a commitment to practice law in the public interest. Who better than members of the public to raise objections when lawyers do not act in the public interest?

Many cases involve what can be seen as concentric circles of accountability. In the Swiss bank case, there is one constituency with quite legitimate grounds to object to the firm's representation of the bank, and that is the Jewish community. A *Washington Post* article about the controversy reported that the firm's managing partner consulted with Arthur Liman, among other lawyers outside the firm, as part of its consideration.[58] Liman was not just any lawyer, but a prominent Jewish lawyer in New York City. The actions of the firm had the potential to interfere with a hard-fought struggle to hold accountable those institutions that profited from their collaboration with the Nazi government. Jewish leaders had the moral authority as well as the factual knowledge to comment on the impact the firm's representation would have on the campaign for reparations and acknowledgment of responsibility by the Swiss. For example, Elan Steinberg, the executive director of the World Jewish Congress, said, "We believe Credit Suisse has helped create a sea change between the Jewish community and the Swiss authorities," but that the bank must do further in "returning to victims or their heirs those assets that were stolen from them."[59] Understandably, Jewish lawyers in the firm saw themselves as accountable to their own community and sensitive to their attitudes in response to the firm's representation of Credit Suisse. A different way of putting the point, to be developed below, is that the relationship with members of their religious and national community is of particular importance to Jewish lawyers in the firm. This relationship is more real, tangible, and "thick" as philosophers sometimes say than the relationship with a pure stranger on social media who posts nasty things about the firm.

The predicament of Jewish lawyers at Cravath is reminiscent of a well-known case in legal ethics, which arose in East Texas in the mid-1990s.[60] The main character in the drama, Anthony Griffin, was the general counsel for the Port Arthur branch of the NAACP and a cooperating attorney with the Texas chapter of the ACLU. As these affiliations suggest, Griffin was a Black civil rights attorney, which led to alarm and anger (classic reactive attitudes) in the community when Griffin accepted the representation of a leader of the local Ku Klux Klan. The Klan had been engaged in a campaign of terror directed against Black residents who had moved into a housing project under a federal desegregation order. The Texas Civil Rights Commission, seeking to prosecute Klan members who had threatened the Black residents, sought discovery of the Klan's membership list. Griffin, recalling the Supreme Court's protection of NAACP membership lists when they were sought by segregationist Southern government officials during the civil rights movement,[61] agreed to represent the Klan and its leader in the litigation.

Writing about this case, law professor David Wilkins notes that, for Black Americans, "race . . . literally colors the way that we are perceived by the world at the same time that it shapes our self-perception"; moreover "group membership is an important source of pride and strength and therefore an important part of human flourishing."[62] Therefore, Griffin stood in a distinctive relationship of accountability with other members of the Black community who were troubled, to say the least, by his decision to lend his efforts and talents to protect the interests of the KKK, given the Klan's objective of preventing Black residents from moving into segregated public housing. As the head of the NAACP office put it, you can't represent the NAACP and the Klan at the same time.[63]

Griffin recognized this and consistently sought to explain why representing the Klan leader would ultimately be beneficial to Black citizens in East Texas and nationwide. He understood the constitutional right of free association as providing special protection for Black civil rights organizations.[64] Restrictions on free expression, similarly, have frequently been applied in ways that disadvantage less powerful minorities. These may not ultimately be persuasive arguments. As Wilkins points out, constitutional rights have frequently been applied in ways that are harmful to Black Americans.[65] He also gently chides Griffin for being too quick to resort to a slippery-slope argument (if the rights of the Klan aren't protected in this case, then the right will not be protected in other cases) when a principled distinction is available.[66] Nevertheless, he believes Griffin to be correct in assuming that he owes a response to a demand for accountability that asks specifically, what is a *Black* lawyer doing representing the Klan? Even if it seems a bit of a stretch to hold lawyers accountable to the entire political community, one of the narrower concentric circles of accountability would be to a distinctive religious, racial, ethnic, or other community. The Jewish lawyers in the Swiss bank case and Black citizens in East Texas and elsewhere in the country have a special position from which to demand accountability from lawyers for their representation of clients that appear to be detrimental to their interests.

It is worth a brief digression here to reiterate that the arguments in this book rely on reasons and justifications that a lawyer *might* give in response to a demand for accountability. As for what lawyers can *actually* say, there is the serious problem of demanding duties of confidentiality and loyalty that arise within the lawyer-client relationship. As a matter of both the rules of professional conduct for lawyers and the generally applicable law of agency and fiduciary duties, lawyers are prohibited from disclosing any information relating to the representation of a client, unless they have obtained the client's informed consent to the disclosure, the disclosure is impliedly authorized to carry out the client's objectives, or the situation falls into one of several narrowly tailored exceptions.[67] One application of the rule of confidentiality, recognized by ethics committees of the American Bar Association and several states, prohibits lawyers from responding to online criticism by former clients or others.[68] In addition, the common law fiduciary duty of loyalty prohibits lawyers from acting against the best interests of their clients.

None of this prevents others from talking about what a lawyer in Griffin's position should do, or whether the reactive attitudes of observers are warranted. The cases discussed in this book are offered as hypotheticals for discussion and debate, and sometimes assumptions are made about the motives or attitudes of the lawyers involved. It may seem unfair that the lawyers involved in the actual representations are duty-bound not to weigh in on these debates. But sometimes professional duties are demanding, and lawyers may have to simply accept that in some cases they will take flak from the public and be unable to respond fully.[69] Because of the duties owed to their clients, lawyers are in a different position than, say, a restaurant owner dealing with a negative Yelp review. Being part of a profession with very strict duties owed to clients sometimes means having to take your lumps from public criticism. When Anthony Griffin sought to explain and justify his actions by bad-mouthing the Klan and its leader who was his client, he very likely violated these professional obligations. It is entirely understandable that Griffin would want to make it clear to his critics that he understands the Klan to be a violent terrorist organization whose message of hatred should be condemned by all decent people.[70] As a lawyer currently representing the Klan leader, or even as a former lawyer for that client, however, he is not permitted to disclose information related to the representation or to do anything that would undermine the client's legal objectives.

There is still a question of why Griffin owes an explanation to *anyone* about his decision to represent the client. As mentioned previously, in connection with Jewish lawyers and Credit Suisse, all of us have relationships that are of particular importance. They may be with family, friends, neighbors, members of a religious community; those with whom we share racial, ethnic, or national origin characteristics or particular interests.[71] Philosophically speaking, these relationships can be said to be *constitutive* in the sense that they make up a great deal of what we care about in life.[72] Because of the importance of these relationships, we may feel that we owe others an account if we do something that arouses their indignation. Because these relationships are partially constitutive of what matters to us in our lives, failing to acknowledge others in the right way—including explaining to them why we acted in a particular way—would be in effect to deny something that matters to us. We care about our lives having meaning and purpose, and one way we experience meaningful lives is through relationships of reciprocal respect and concern. Some demands for accountability therefore build on the preexisting importance of these relationships.

For example, Monroe Freedman criticized Michael Tigar specifically as a professional colleague and a friend for the latter's decision to represent the accused death camp guard John Demjanjuk. That is a fairly close, historically constituted, "thick" relationship of accountability. Moving out slightly in terms of closeness, the managing partner at Cravath was concerned with the reaction of firm associates, because they were not only employees but junior lawyers to whom senior lawyers traditionally owe responsibilities of guidance and mentorship. Firm management also understood that Cravath had a relationship of accountability with the Jewish community, arising out of existing ties between firm lawyers and their Jewish neighbors and professional associates. And certainly Jewish lawyers in the firm may have felt special ties of accountability, similar to Anthony Griffin's recognition of an explanation owed to fellow Black East Texans and possibly to Black Americans more generally.[73] (That is the significance of David Wilkins's observation that race is an important source of pride and strength and therefore an important part of human flourishing.[74]) Many critics, however, are not those with whom a lawyer is in a preexisting relationship, let alone one that is sufficient important to be constitutive of a meaningful life. Does a lawyer owe anything at all to the community at large?

Some readers may bristle at the word "owe," which may sound like any nosy person or social media troll can command one's time and attention to respond to criticism, however poorly thought out. I do not mean to suggest that lawyers fall short of some kind of personal or professional duty if they do not explain themselves to everyone who objects to their representation of a controversial client. Whether a particular individual has any business demanding an account from another is an aspect of the ethics of blame, a subject to be considered in Chapter 4. For now, what is important about the accountability of lawyers is the embeddedness of the legal profession within a wider moral community. Lawyers are not walled off from the rest of society. In fact, lawyers are generally held to be under a duty to practice their craft in service of society or the public interest,[75] albeit through the service of particular clients. Thus, what lawyers owe to others in the course of representing clients, including whether they are accountable for the clients they choose to represent, is a question having significance for the entire community.

I believe it is appropriate for people to weigh in on the actions of lawyers in cases that present issues of importance to the community, including the decision to represent a client and the specific steps they take in the course of the representation. Again, to emphasize, the standing to weigh in on something does not automatically confer force to the criticism. People can be wrong about the underlying facts, assume an implausible view of justice, ignore or undervalue countervailing considerations, and otherwise miss the mark in their reactions. Reactive attitudes are a natural part of life, but a thoughtful, responsible person will pause to ensure that a feeling of anger or disgust is warranted. The associates in the law firm representing Credit Suisse and Black residents of East Texas who asked what a Black civil rights lawyer was doing representing the Ku Klux Klan were not wrong to experience attitudes of resentment or indignation.

As it happens, I believe the lawyers in those cases had a sufficient justification for taking on the clients that they did. Even though the lawyers were able to satisfy the demand for accountability, the controversies created by these client representations remain valuable as repositories of thinking about appropriate conduct by members of the legal profession. The Swiss bank case shows that there may be limits to permissible zealous advocacy on behalf of a client and the KKK case shows that there may be principled reasons for defending the civil rights of odious individuals. Lawyers who are too quick to assert the Principle of Nonaccountability are closing off an important connection between professional ethics and the considerations that members of the political community care about. The debate that begins with the demand for accountability is valuable in itself. It may be too much to expect, in many cases, that members of the community will come to agree on the meaning of a representation, dependent as that conclusion is on assumptions about the attitudes, motivations, and character of the lawyers involved. It is nevertheless an important aspect of the relationship between the legal profession and society as a whole that lawyers be deemed accountable for the clients they represent.

Chapter summary

Morality and accountability are not mysterious, transcendental, or abstract ideas beyond the understanding of ordinary folks and remote from everyday life. They are part of ordinary experience in the form of reactive attitudes such as resentment and anger. Social practices like shaming, shunning, calling out, and even "cancel culture" are ways of expressing reactive attitudes. Reactive attitudes can be evaluated as appropriate or fitting, or criticized as unfounded or excessive, with reference to expectations about what we owe to each other. Because morality is fundamentally relational, we can ask about the scope of the community to whom something is owed. The case of Anthony Griffin shows the possibility of ever-widening circles of concern, from a lawyer's immediate community to those who are situated in a way that gives them an interest in the representation of a particular client, to the political community as a whole. In many cases lawyers have a sufficient response to the demand for accountability from those in the relevant community. Responding to well-grounded demands for accountability can focus lawyers on the moral considerations that are important to society generally.

Notes

1. Gary Watson, "Morality as Equal Accountability: Comments on Stephen Darwall's *The Second-Person Standpoint*," *Ethics* 118: 37–51 (Oct. 2007), pp. 46–47; Nicholas

McBride, "Are There Any Moral Duties?," in Haris Psarras & Sandy Steel, eds., *Private Law and Practical Reason: Essays on John Gardner's Private Law Theory* (Oxford: Oxford University Press 2022). Practical ethics disciplines, including medical and legal ethics, generally put aside consideration of what constitutes a well-lived life to pursue issues specific to the professional domain. Benjamin C. Zipursky, "Integrity and the Incongruities of Justice: A Review of Daniel Markovits, *A Modern Legal Ethics*," 119 *Yale L.J.* 1948, 1956 (2010). In medical ethics, for example, informed consent, end of life care, and respecting patient autonomy while making professionally appropriate decisions regarding treatment are regarded as central issues. Legal ethics takes up many questions pertaining to professional secret-keeping, truthfulness in advocacy, and conflicts of interest in addition to the matters considered here pertaining to the representation of nasty clients.

2. This is Elizabeth Anscombe's contention in one of her most influential papers. See G.E.M. Anscombe, "Modern Moral Philosophy," *Philosophy* 33: 1–19 (Jan. 1958). Jay Wallace explicitly acknowledges the influence on his relational account of morality of the legal concept of relational duty as elaborated in tort law. See R. Jay Wallace, *The Moral Nexus* (Princeton: Princeton University Press 2019), p. xo.

3. T.M. Scanlon, *What We Owe to Each Other* (Cambridge, Mass.: Belknap Press 1998), pp. 189, 219.

4. See, e.g., Angela Smith, Responsibility for Attitudes: Activity and Passivity in Mental Life," 115 *Ethics* 236 (2005).

5. Gerald J. Postema, "Moral Responsibility in Professional Ethics," 55 *NYU L. Rev.* 63, 68 (1980).

6. Law professor and criminal defense lawyer Abbe Smith begins a powerful article on the ethics of defending rape prosecutions with a fairly standard list of the reasons why vigorous criminal defense representation is justified—for example, resisting the harshly punitive criminal justice system in the United States, preventing a rush to judgment, and warding off the power of the state. Importantly, however, she understands the ethical problem as also including a first-personal dimension, that is, "how it actually feels to confront and cross-examine alleged victims of sexual assault, knowing (or strongly believing) that they are telling the truth, and how to come to terms with those feelings." Abbe Smith, "Representing Rapists: The Cruelty of Cross Examination and Other Challenges for a Feminist Criminal Defense Lawyer," 53 *Am. Crim. L. Rev.* 255, 256, 289 (2016). The attitudes, intentions, character of lawyers, and the impact of what they do on their personal integrity are additional moral dimensions that are often underdeveloped in legal ethics but play an important role in the accountability of lawyers for the clients they represent.

7. T.M. Scanlon, *Moral Dimensions: Permissibility, Meaning, Blame* (Cambridge, Mass.: Harvard University Press 2008).

8. Annette Baier, "Hume's Place in the History of Ethics," in Roger Crisp, ed., *The Oxford Handbook of the History of Ethics* (Oxford: Oxford University Press, 2013), pp. 399–420; James Baillie, "Hume's Moral Sentimentalism," in Angela M. Coventry & Alex Sager, eds., *The Humean Mind* (London: Routledge 2018), pp. 236–47.

9. David Hume, "An Enquiry Concerning the Principles of Morals," in L.A. Selby-Bigge, ed., *Enquiries Concerning Human Understanding and Concerning the Principles of Morals* (Oxford: Clarendon Press 1985), p. 225.

10. Stephen Darwall, *The Second-Person Standpoint: Morality, Respect, and Accountability* (Cambridge, Mass.: Harvard University Press 2006), pp. 7–9.
11. Darwall, p. 84.
12. P.F. Strawson, "Freedom and Resentment," 48 *Proc. Brit. Acad.* 187 (1962), reprinted in Gary Watson, ed., *Free Will*, 2d ed. (Oxford: Oxford University Press 2003); and John Martin Fischer & Mark Ravizza, eds., *Perspectives on Moral Responsibility* (Ithaca, N.Y.: Cornell University Press 1993). Citations to Strawson's paper will be to the version in the Watson *Free Will* volume. See also Maria Alvarez, "P.F. Strawson, Moral Theories, and 'the Problem of Blame': 'Freedom and Resentment' Revisited," *Aristotelian Soc. Supp. Volume* xcv: 183–203 (2021).
13. Darwall, p. 17.
14. Stephen Darwall, Allan Gibbard, & Peter Railton, "Toward Fin de siècle Ethics: Some Trends," *Phil. Rev.* 101: 115–89 (Jan. 1992)("Moral realists, constructivists, and quasi-realists alike look to the responses and reasons of persons, rather than some self-subsistent realm, to ground moral practice.").
15. Susan Wolf, "Morality and the View from Here," 3 *J. Ethics* 203, 211 (1999).
16. T.M. Scanlon, "Blame," in *Moral Dimensions: Permissibility, Meaning, Blame* (Cambridge, Mass.: Belknap Press 2008), p. 128.
17. See Susan Wolf, "Blame, Italian Style," in R. Jay Wallace, Rahul Kumar, & Samuel Freeman, eds., *Reasons and Recognition: Essays on the Philosophy of T.M. Scanlon* (Oxford University Press 2011), p. 332. The emotional quality of angry reactive attitude like resentment comes from having internalized these moral standards, but internalization is also compatible with "cooler" expressions of disapproval. More to the point of the discussion here, Wolf talks about episodes in her family life, including her daughter's eye-rolling and slamming of doors and her irritation at her husband's tendency to forget something and cause delay when they are on a schedule. Because she stresses that her family is quite loving and close, her point is that some irritation-causing conduct does not reveal deficient attitudes of interpersonal respect and concern—it is not "indicative of impaired relationships" (p. 336). Derk Pereboom seeks to turn down the temperature of reactive attitudes in *Wrongdoing and the Moral Emotions* (Oxford: Oxford University Press 2021), relying on a stance of moral protest rather than angry reactive attitudes. The former has forward-looking objectives, including changing the dispositions of the target of the protest.
18. Strawson, "Freedom and Resentment," pp. 80–83. The discussion here also draws from Darwall, pp. 65–79; Wallace, *Moral Nexus*, Ch. 3; and Bennett W. Helm, *Communities of Respect: Grounding Responsibility, Authority, and Dignity* (New York: Oxford University Press 2017), pp. 58–69.
19. David Shoemaker, "Moral Address, Moral Responsibility, and the Boundaries of the Moral Community," *Ethics* 118: 70–108 (Oct. 2007).
20. See Postema, above, discussing Charles P. Curtis, "The Ethics of Advocacy," 4 *Stan. L. Rev.* 3, 8–9 (1951), which refers to the displacement of responsibility onto an institution as "Montaigne's solution," after a position about the ethics of politicians put forward by the French essayist Michel de Montaigne:

> The mayor and Montaigne have always been two people, clearly separated. There's no reason why a lawyer or a banker should not recognize the knavery that is part of his vocation. An honest man is not responsible for the vices or the stupidity of his calling, and need not refuse to practise them.

> We will have much more to say about "Montaigne's solution" in Chapter 7 on role morality.

21. Bernard Williams puts this point not in terms of rules of professional conduct but psychological dispositions that are acquired through professional training and socialization. Bernard Williams, "Professional Morality and Its Dispositions," in *Making Sense of Humanity and Other Philosophical Papers 1982–1993* (Cambridge: Cambridge University Press 1995). This theme will return in Chapter 9 on the moral costs of actions taken within a professional role.
22. This is familiar from ordinary life and popular culture, as in *West Side Story* where Riff and other members of the Jets gang explain to Officer Krupke that it would not be appropriate to blame them for their delinquency:

> Dear kindly Sergeant Krupke
> Ya gotta understand
> It's just our bringin' upke
> That gets us outta hand
> Our mothers all are junkies
> Our fathers all are drunks
> Golly Moses natcherly we're punks
>
> Gee, Officer Krupke, we're very upset;
> We never had the love that every
> Child oughta get
> We ain't no delinquents
> We're misunderstood
> Deep down inside us there is good!

Lyrics by Stephen Sondheim, from the 1961 film version. See https://www.westsidestory.com/gee-officer-krupke. Although the musical number is performed for laughs, it captures a deeply serious position within moral philosophy, that someone is liable to be punished, or otherwise socially sanctioned (like the Jets' ostracism from polite society), or to feel a sense of guilt or shame, only if they are responsible for it.

23. Gary Watson, "Introduction," in Gary Watson, ed., *Free Will*, 2d ed. (Oxford: Oxford University Press 2003), pp. 2–3.
24. Gary Watson, "The Trouble with Psychopaths," in R. Jay Wallace, Rahul Kumar, & Samuel Freeman, eds., *Reasons and Recognition: Essays on the Philosophy of T.M. Scanlon* (Oxford: Oxford University Press 2011); David Shoemaker, "Moral Address, Moral Responsibility, and the Boundaries of the Moral Community," *Ethics* 118: 70–108 (Oct. 2007). The participant stance may be contrasted with the detached perspective of seeing others as a kind of problem to be solved, to be understood and controlled in a manner that is in our interests, or in the interests of society. Strawson, "Freedom and Resentment," pp. 81–82. Darwall identifies the impersonal stance with

the moral point of view. Darwall, p. 67. As Susan Wolf notes, much moral theorizing relies on the image of a disinterested stance, the impartial spectator's point of view, the standpoint of universal law, the point of view of the universe, and similar ideas. Susan Wolf, "Morality and the View from Here," 3 *J. Ethics* 203, 204 (1999) (quoting Peter Singer, *Practical Ethics*). Utilitarian versions of the moral point of view rely on an aggregation of individual points of view while those of a more Kantian flavor assume a perspective of universality. Either way, the upshot is supposed to be a point of view that is more objective or rational than the personal point of view and hence has a claim to authority. However, this abstraction and universalizing can make obscure the connection between reasons from the moral point of view and anything that might constitute a reason *for us*. Wolf's paper defends a perspective in which one deliberated based on reasons that are non-self-interested but not necessarily strictly moral. Wolf, pp. 217–19.

25. See, e.g., Derk Pereboom, *Free Will, Agency, and Meaning in Life* (Oxford: Oxford University Press 2014); Derk Pereboom, *Living Without Free Will* (Cambridge: Cambridge University Press 2001). Pereboom argues that Strawson's is not the last word in the debate over free will and moral responsibility. Granting the centrality of reactive attitudes to ordinary social practices of accountability, it could be the case that people are mistaken in responding with indignation, resentment, etc., to actions that were caused exclusively by events, not by agents. However, the discussion here will not have much, if anything, to say about the metaphysical problem of free will but, in line with much recent scholarship on blame, will emphasize moral psychology and the significance of blame in ordinary moral life. See D. Justin Coates & Neal A. Tognazzini, "The Contours of Blame," in D. Justin Coates & Neal A. Tognazzini, eds., *Blame: Its Nature and Norms* (Oxford: Oxford University Press 2013), p. 4. I will, however, have something to say about Pereboom's suggestion that worries about free will should motivate us to attend to our responsibility practices in particular ways.

26. Gary Watson, "Responsibility and the Limits of Evil: Variations on a Strawsonian Theme," in *Agency and Answerability* (Oxford: Clarendon Press 2004), p. 220.

27. Wallace, *Moral Nexus*, p. 70.

28. Strawson, "Freedom and Resentment," p. 80.

29. Wallace, *Moral Nexus*, pp. 1–3. To say that morality is relational does not mean it only piggybacks on existing relationships but can arise out of the full range of interactions among individuals, where what matters is the claims we have on one another because we are persons, where the standards derive from the effects that one individual's actions have on the interests of others. To illustrate with an example from law, there is a fairly well-known torts case called *Mussivand v. David*, 544 N.E.2d 265 (Ohio 1989), brought by a husband against his wife's paramour, alleging that the paramour infected the wife with a sexually transmitted disease and she in turn infected the husband. Tort duties are often understood in relational terms, so one of the issues in the case was whether there was a duty running from the paramour to the husband, sufficient to support a legal claim for negligence. In this case, there was enough of a relationship to support a duty of reasonable care because it was foreseeable that if the paramour did

not inform the wife of his infection, she might become infected and then spread it to the husband. "If one negligently exposes a married person to a sexually transmissible disease without informing that person of his exposure, it is reasonable to anticipate that the disease might be transmitted to the married person's spouse." 544 N.E.2d at 272. The idea here is that "relationship" can refer to an interaction in which one has the capacity to affect the interests or well-being of another, not that there must be some preexisting ties of affection or loyalty. In this case, the husband and the wife's lover could not have been in a more antagonistic situation, yet the latter owed a duty to the former.

30. Darwall, pp. 74–75.
31. Wallace, *Moral Nexus*, pp. 73–74.
32. See, e.g., Monroe Friedman, *Consumer Boycotts: Effecting Change Through the Marketplace and Media* (New York: Routledge 1999); M.P. Baumgartner, *The Moral Order of a Suburb* (Oxford: Oxford University Press, reprint ed. 1991); James West, *Plainville, U.S.A.* (New York: Columbia University Press 1945); Linda Radzik, "Boycotts and the Social Enforcement of Justice," 34(1) *Social Phil. & Policy* 102 (2017); Tim Bartley & Curtis Child, "Shaming the Corporation: The Social Production of Targets and the Anti-Sweatshop Movement, 79 *Am. Soc. Rev.* 653 (2014); Sally Engle Merry, "Rethinking Gossip and Scandal," in Donald Black, ed., *Toward a General Theory of Social Control* (Orlando, Fla.: Academic Press 1980), p. 271.
33. J.S. Mill, "On Liberty," in Stefan Collini, ed., *On Liberty and Other Writings* (Cambridge: Cambridge University Press 1989), IV.6.
34. See, e.g., Bertram Wyatt-Brown, *Southern Honor: Ethics and Behavior in the Old South* (Oxford: Oxford University Press, 25th Anniversary Edition 2007); Elijah Anderson, *Code of the Street: Decency, Violence, and the Moral Life of the Inner City* (New York: Norton 1999); J.G. Peristiany, ed., *Honour and Shame: The Values of Mediterranean Society* (Chicago: University of Chicago Press 1966).
35. One judicial decision described a charivari as follows: "[A] bride and groom were taken against their will by force and placed on a wagon and drawn up and down the streets, making proclamation of their nuptials, [the mob] introducing them to people in burlesque speeches, drawing large crowds, and causing disorder and some tumult." *Cherryvale v. Hawman*, 101 P. 994 (Kan. 1909). See also *Bruno v. State*, 162 N.W. 167 (Wis. 1917) (describing charivari party's activities as "firing a gun and exploding dynamite near the house, ringing bells, beating on tin pans, and making the other noises which usually characterize this highly refined and humorous proceeding"); *Combs v. Ezell*, 24 S.W.2d 301 (Ky. 1930) (couple charivaried for 2–3 weeks by rotating shifts of men).
36. See, e.g., Adrienne Matei, "Call-Out Culture: How to Get It Right (and Wrong)," *Guardian* (Nov. 1, 2019); Aja Romano, "The Second Wave of 'Cancel Culture,'" *Vox* (May 5, 2021). See also Thomas Schramme, "Properly a Subject of Contempt': The Role of Natural Penalties in Mill's Liberal Thought," *J. Social Phil.* 51(3): 391–409 (Fall 2020) and open access at https://doi.org/10.1111/josp.12344. Schramme gives an example of the intense online reaction to a photo posted online that appeared to be expressing disrespect for the dead buried at Arlington National Cemetery. Schramme

refers to the result as a "shitstorm" but even that description appears to understate the ferocity of the criticism of the woman who posted the photo, who in addition to being subject to vicious online abuse, was fired and essentially rendered unemployable. The story is described in more detail beginning in Chapter 11 of Jon Ronson, *So You've Been Publicly Shamed* (New York: Riverhead Books 2015).

37. Cancel culture is an issue that tends to inspire polemical commentary, but some contributors aspire to some measure of evenhandedness. See, e.g., Ernest Owns, *The Case for Cancel Culture: How This Democratic Tool Works to Liberate Us All* (New York: St. Martin's Press 2023); Eve Ng, *Cancel Culture: A Critical Analysis* (New York: Palgrave Macmillan 2022); Dan Kowalik, *Cancel This Book: The Progressive Case Against Cancel Culture* (New York: Hot Books/Simon & Schuster 2021) Alan Dershowiitz, *Cancel Culture: The Latest Attack on Free Speech and Due Process* (New York: Hot Books/Simon & Schuster 2020). One of the most insightful short contributions is Amna Khalid & Jeffrey Aaron Snyder, "Cancel Culture," *Substack—Banished* (July 24, 2022).

38. Jon Ronson, *So You've Been Publicly Shamed* (New York: Riverhead Books 2015).

39. Journalist and long-time commentator on free speech issues Jonathan Rauch has a useful distinction between cancel culture on the one hand and the exercise of expressive rights to hold others accountable on the other: "Criticism marshals evidence and arguments in a rational effort to persuade. Canceling, by contrast, seeks to organize and manipulate the social or media environment in order to isolate, deplatform or intimidate ideological opponents." Jonathan Rauch, "The Cancel Culture Checklist," *Substack—Persuasion* (Aug. 6, 2020).

40. I owe this insight to Marie-Amélie George.

41. This is essentially the argument in Waheed Hussain, "Is Ethical Consumerism an Impermissible Form of Vigilantism?," 40 *Phil. & Pub. Aff.* 111 (2012). Legal historian and criminal law scholar James Whitman argues that shaming sanctions are wrong because they involve a dangerous complicity between official state processes and mob rule. James Q. Whitman, "What Is Wrong with Inflicting Shame Sanctions," 107 *Yale L.J.* 1055 (1998).

42. Joseph Raz argues that the rule of law, as generally formulated, is morally neutral: "[T]he rule of law is just one of the virtues which a legal system may possess and by which it is to be judged. It is not to be confused with democracy, justice, equality (before the law or otherwise), human rights of any kind or respect for persons or for the dignity of man. A non-democratic legal system, based on the denial of human rights, on extensive poverty, on racial segregation, sexual inequalities, and religious persecution may, in principle, conform to the requirements of the rule of law better than any of the legal systems of the more enlightened Western democracies." Joseph Raz, "The Rule of Law and Its Virtue," in *The Authority of Law* (Oxford: Oxford University Press 1979). Other philosophers, most prominently Lon Fuller, have contended that a legal system that conforms to the ideal of the rule of law is considerably less likely (although the possibility is not inconceivable) to be committed to wicked ends. Lon L. Fuller, *The Morality of Law* (New Haven: Yale University Press, 2d ed. 1964).

43. Jon Ronson, *So You've Been Publicly Shamed* (New York: Riverhead Books 2015).
44. For a contrary view, see Jennifer Jacquet, *Is Shame Necessary?* (New York: Pantheon 2015).
45. Social-scientific research into moral decision-making has revealed that, at least in some emotionally charged situations, people often make rapid, unconscious, intuitive assessments of wrongdoing and only later backfill the principled reasons that they believe support their judgment. Jonathan Haidt is one of the leading scholars in the psychology of moral decision-making. See Jonathan Haidt et al., "The New Synthesis in Moral Psychology," 316 *Science* 998 (2007); Jonathan Haidt, "The Emotional Dog and iIs Rational Tail: A Social Intuitionist Approach to Moral Judgment," 108 *Psych. Rev.* 814 (2001); Jonathan Haidt et al., "Affect, Culture, and Morality, or Is It Wrong to Eat Your Dog?," 65 *J. Person. & Soc. Psych.* 613 (1993). Haidt is careful, however, to avoid the naturalistic fallacy of inferring from the fact of an emotional reaction—for example, that it is wrong to eat the family dog—to the normative conclusion that eating the dog is wrong.
46. T.M. Scanlon, "Blame," in *Moral Dimensions: Permissibility, Meaning, Blame* (Cambridge, Mass.: Belknap Press 2008), pp. 128–29.
47. Wallace, *Responsibility and the Moral Sentiments*, pp. 19–21.
48. Wallace, *Moral Nexus*, p. 71; see also Victoria McGeer, "Civilizing Blame," in Coates & Tognazzini, above, p. 163 (arguing that negative reactions toward people who display attitudes inconsistent with what is owed to others by way of respect and equal regard are one of the practices that sustains a community's sense of appropriateness). I also want to make reference to one of my favorite articles in professional ethics, Arthur Isak Applbaum, "Professional Detachment: The Executioner of Paris," 109 *Harv. L. Rev.* 458 (1995). Applbaum explores the morality of professional roles through the character of Charles-Henri Sanson, who served as executioner under Louis XVI and then under various revolutionary tribunals, including the one that sentenced Louis to death. In an imagined dialogue with the essayist Louis-Sébastian Mercier, Sanson accepted that professional roles cannot be justified solely based on tradition or craft norms internal to the practice that cannot be understood by those not steeped in the lore of the profession. Mercier contended that Sanson's justification must be offered "on grounds that we can share" and Sanson agreed, undertaking to "show why my role is a socially useful and necessary one" (p. 476).
49. While working on the book I came to think of this as the "Soeharno objection" after Dutch lawyer and law professor Jonathan Soeharno who, being a good advocate, would not let me wriggle out from the problem that lawyers are unable to defend themselves in response to a demand for accountability, due to the stringent duties of confidentiality imposed by rules of professional conduct. I have included responses to the Soeharno objection in several places, including a brief mention in the introduction and a lengthier explanation later in this chapter in the main text. But I wanted to express my gratitude separately for his insistence that I take this problem more seriously than I had in an earlier draft.
50. ABA Model Rules of Prof'l Conduct, Rule 1.6, cmt. [5] (2013) ("Lawyers in a firm may, in the course of the firm's practice, disclose to each other information relating

to a client of the firm, unless the client has instructed that particular information be confined to specified lawyers.").
51. The Alton Logan case, which I use as an introductory problem and discuss extensively in W. Bradley Wendel, *Ethics and the Law: An Introduction* (Cambridge: Cambridge University Press 2014), pp. 3–5, and *passim*. After that book came out, Logan published his own version of the story, co-written with journalist Berl Falbaum—see Alton Logan with Berl Falbaum, *Justice Failed: How "Legal Ethics" Kept Me in Prison for 26 Years* (Berkeley, Cal.: Counterpoint Press 2018).
52. Falbaum's introduction to *Justice Failed* makes the same point, which clearly exasperates her—lawyers almost uniformly believe the two lawyers representing Wilson, who had confessed to the crime for which Logan was serving time in prison, did the right thing.
53. Jonathan Rauch, "The Cancel Culture Checklist," *Substack—Persuasion* (Aug. 6, 2020). Rauch borrowed the term "moral grandstanding" from Justin Tosi & Brandon Warmke, *Grandstanding: The Use and Abuse of Moral Talk* (New York: Oxford University Press 2020).
54. Wallace, *Moral Nexus*, p. 69 ("it is an additional element in the modern understanding of morality that the obligations of moral right and wrong have normative significance for parties other than the agent immediately subject to them"); Marina Oshana, "Moral Accountability," 32 *Phil. Topics* 255 (2004).
55. If the person who stepped on David's toe believes he is somehow privileged not to have to offer a justification, the appropriate reactive attitude is to regard him as an asshole. Aaron James, *Assholes: A Theory* (New York: Anchor Books 2012). As James argues, a belief that one is immunized against the complaints of other people is one of the central characteristics of assholes.
56. Wallace, *Moral Nexus*, p. 72.
57. Model Rules of Prof'l Conduct, Rule 8.3(a) & cmt. [3].
58. Blaine Harden & Saundra Torry, "N.Y. Law Firm to Advise Swiss Bank Accused of Laundering Nazi Loot," *Wash. Post* (Feb. 28, 1997).
59. Quoted in Harden & Torry, above.
60. David B. Wilkins, "Race, Ethics, and the First Amendment: Should a Black Lawyer Represent the Ku Klux Klan?", 63 *Geo. Wash. L. Rev.* 1030 (1995).
61. *NAACP v. Alabama*, 357 U.S. 449 (1958).
62. Wilkins, p. 1041.
63. Wilkins, p. 1061.
64. Wilkins, pp. 1043–44.
65. Wilkins, p. 1045 (discussing *R.A.V. v. City of St. Paul*, 505 U.S. 377 (1992), which struck down a city ordinance prohibiting cross burning as an act of racial terror).
66. Wilkins, pp. 1047–49. It is also possible that Griffin went a bit overboard in publicly proclaiming the truth—but something a lawyer for the organization should not say out loud—that the Klan is a hateful terrorist organization. Wilkins, p. 1053.
67. ABA Model Rules of Professional Conduct, Rule 1.6.
68. ABA Standing Committee on Ethics and Professional Responsibility, Formal Opinion 21-496 (2021). Tons of state opinions reaching the same conclusion are cited in footnote 5 of the ABA opinion.

69. Bill Hodes has an interesting variation on this view. He agrees that it is perfectly proper for others to criticize lawyers, in moral terms, for their choice to represent, or not represent, particular clients. He also says, however, that it is a lawyer's prerogative to refuse to provide a justification in response to the demand for accountability—in effect, saying to critics, "none of your business." W. William Hodes, "Accepting and Rejecting Clients – The Moral Autonomy of the Second-to-the-Last Lawyer in Town," 48 *U. Kan. L. Rev.* 977, 982 (2000). He says of Michael Tigar, in the Freedman-Tigar debate discussed in Chapter 1, that Tigar could have asserted a kind of privacy interest in response to Freedman and refused to give any justification for his decision to represent John Demjanjuk. Hodes, p. 988. Interestingly, however, Hodes does not ground this right of refusal on the professional duty of confidentiality owed by lawyers, and indeed Tigar seemed quite willing to speak publicly about his representation of Demjanjuk. This leaves Hodes's "none of your business" principle squarely in the realm of the ethics of blame. I do think he is correct to assert that people do not owe an explanation to every busybody who might observe and criticize our actions, and that goes for lawyers too. Subject to the duties of confidentiality and loyalty, however, there are individuals and communities to whom a heightened duty of justification is owed. If a member of Anthony Griffin's church, for example, asked him why he was representing a leader of the Ku Klux Klan, it might seem highly inappropriate to respond "none of your business," again with the proviso that lawyer-client confidentiality may constrain what Griffin may say in response.
70. Wilkins, pp. 1053–54.
71. T.M. Scanlon, "Blame," in *Moral Dimensions: Permissibility, Meaning, Blame* (Cambridge, Mass.: Belknap Press 2008), p. 145 ("Blame has the most substantial content for people who interact with the agent in some way, as friends or family members, or as neighbors or coworkers or fellow citizens."). The discussion that follows is indebted to a workshop at the University of Denver philosophy department which was extremely helpful in clarifying the scope of accountability and the sense in which one can be said to owe an explanation to others.
72. Susan Wolf, "Meaning and Morality," in *The Variety of Values: Essays on Morality, Meaning, and Love* (Oxford: Oxford University Press 2015), pp. 127–40.
73. Eli Wald asked me the following: "I'm a non-practicing Jew—would I owe an explanation to someone who criticized the firm if I were working at Cravath?" To which I think the answer is, "I don't know—do you think you do?" In other words, how important is Jewishness, as a religious commitment or a national identity or simply as aspect of being Israeli? The answers to these questions cannot be prescribed from outside but are a matter of what constitutes one's own practical identity.
74. Wilkins, p. 1041.
75. "A manifest and demonstrable commitment to the public good is what legitimately creates a profession . . . ." Richard Moorhead, "Precarious Professionalism: Some Empirical and Behavioural Perspectives on Lawyers," 67 *Current Legal Probs.* 447, 450 (2014).

3
Case Study: Harvey Weinstein, Ronald Sullivan, and Harvard University

Joining Weinstein's dream team

In 2017, investigative reporters for the *New York Times* and the *New Yorker* magazine published articles detailing decades of sexual harassment, assault, and forcible rape by Hollywood studio executive Harvey Weinstein against at least 13 women.[1] Although the conduct had long been an open secret in the industry, no one would accuse Weinstein on the record, fearing his power and demonstrated willingness to retaliate against anyone who crossed him. After the publication of the reports, however, several women proved willing to give evidence against Weinstein, and he was charged with rape and other criminal sexual assaults.[2] The allegations against Weinstein touched off the #MeToo movement in which previously silenced women spoke out against accused other powerful men whose sexual harassment and assault had long been ignored. For his part, as an extraordinarily wealthy man, Weinstein was not in need of counsel provided for him by the state. He paid for a "dream team" of private counsel including Jose Baez, Benjamin Brafman, Arthur Aidala, and Harvard Law School professor Ronald S. Sullivan, Jr.[3] Some of these lawyers were fired by Weinstein and others quit for various reasons, but the issue of accountability for a lawyer's choice of client was raised sharply by a disciplinary action initiated by Harvard University against Sullivan after his representation of Weinstein became known.

Sullivan is well known as a civil rights lawyer, having represented the family of Michael Brown, who was killed by police in Ferguson, Missouri; he worked to reform the system that had resulted in the wrongful incarceration of thousands of people in New Orleans in the wake of Hurricane Katrina and designed a review process for wrongful convictions in Brooklyn.[4] However, this reputation did not protect him from a firestorm of criticism by Harvard students outraged by his representation of Weinstein. Significantly, in addition to his faculty position at Harvard Law School, Sullivan served as the faculty dean of an undergraduate residential house. In that capacity he had responsibilities for providing academic and personal support to students living in the house. Faculty deans at Harvard live in the same building as the students they advise, eat many meals with them, host events for students in their apartment, and are expected to be a voice for students within the university. They also set the tone and culture of residential life at the university.

Some students, particularly women, questioned Sullivan's suitability for the position, reasoning that his representation of Weinstein demonstrated "hostility to survivors of sexual assault." "Whose side are you on?," read graffiti sprayed on a Harvard building. An op-ed by two students published in the Harvard *Crimson* argued that Sullivan's defense of Weinstein would be inconsistent with the obligation to establish a residential environment in which all students feel safe and supported.[5] The student pressure led to a "climate review" by Harvard administrators of Sullivan's residential house, consisting of interviews with students and a questionnaire asking whether they found the environment in the house to be sexist or hostile; after the climate review, the dean of Harvard College decided not to renew Sullivan's appointment as house dean.

The response by lawyers to this series of events was predictable. Fifty-two members of the Harvard Law School faculty signed a letter invoking the long professional tradition of representing clients accused of crimes, even those who are socially reviled or who are accused of having done terrible things.[6] The faculty letter also referred to legal advocacy in service of constitutional principles as well as principles of academic values—"the university's commitment to the freedom to defend ideas, however unpopular." Writing separately, in the *New Yorker*, Sullivan's colleague Jeannie Suk Gersen connected the due process rights of criminal defendants with the First Amendment values of freedom of thought and inquiry.[7] Our intellectual life is chilled by reluctance to express socially unpopular positions, she argued, just as a trial in which the voice of the accused cannot be heard would be a sham. Another colleague, Randall Kennedy, wrote in the *New York Times* that, applying the standards advocated by the student protesters, a long list of civil rights lawyer-heroes, including Charles Hamilton Houston and Thurgood Marshall, would be deemed unsuitable to serve as a faculty dean.[8] Sullivan himself blasted Harvard University for caving into the demands of student protesters, which he characterized as driven by "unchecked emotion" instead of rigorous arguments, evidence, and thoughtful reasoning.[9]

I think Sullivan's critics understood perfectly well the reasoned arguments put forth by lawyers in defense of representing clients like Harvey Weinstein. Lawyers apparently believe the public does not sufficiently appreciate the value of due process of law and the contribution made by skillful, sometimes aggressive criminal defense to the rule of law and the protection of human dignity. They also see public critics as being unable to separate a position taken by a lawyer as the representative of a client and the lawyer's own views. It is certainly true that representing a criminal defendant does not involve the lawyer in avowing her own pro-crime stance. The lawyer is speaking for the client, on the client's behalf, not in the lawyer's personal capacity. But give the public some credit. For the most part the criticism of lawyers for representing nasty clients does not assume that the lawyer endorses the client's nefarious objectives. It is more subtle than that. The criticism, instead, is that given all the worthwhile projects to which a smart, highly educated person can devote herself, why do *this*? Why represent . . . fill in the blank of the type of client you believe is up to no good—those accused of crimes, including those alleged to be murders, rapists, or terrorists; big bad corporations including tobacco companies, banks, fossil fuel companies; "Big Pharma"; or defense contractors. In this case, why regard the representation of Harvey Weinstein as a worthwhile use of one's time and energy, when there clearly is no possibility that he will face the government's accusations without the benefit of skilled counsel?

This often-overlooked aspect of justification and blameworthiness in professional ethics was apparent in an interview Sullivan gave to Isaac Chotiner of the *New Yorker* magazine.[10] Sullivan began the interview by describing criminal defendants as people without power in the system, overwhelmed by the resources of law enforcement and prosecutors' offices and often members of socially marginalized communities. Chotiner immediately pushed back, noting that what may be true of criminal defendants in general is not true of Harvey Weinstein, a very wealthy white man. Sullivan then pivoted to two principles that are often invoked as justification by lawyers: the long-standing constitutional value of due process and the separateness of lawyers from their clients, that is, the fact that representation of a client does not constitute an endorsement of the client's values or objectives. The fact of representing Weinstein does not, by itself, establish that a lawyer is somehow in favor of sexual assault. However, Sullivan admitted that many Harvard students were nevertheless genuinely upset by his representation of Weinstein. Here is where the interview got particularly interesting.

Chotiner stated, possibly disingenuously, that it made him "wince a little bit" that someone who believed in the value of due process and fair trials thought he owed any explanation at all to the students who had been attacking him. Sullivan responded that it was strange to have to offer his bona fides, given his long history of social-justice work, but admitted that his role was to engage with the students, not just talk at them.

This was a missed opportunity for Sullivan in the interview. My sense of the student criticism and the administration's response, particularly the emphasis on Sullivan's role in counseling and supporting survivors of sexual assault, is that Sullivan needed to do more, not to explain why *a lawyer* would be justified in representing Harvey Weinstein, but why *he* sought the engagement. As philosophers sometimes say, he needed to give reasons of the right sort. Sullivan kept falling back on the constitutional principles underlying criminal defense and his own history of work for civil rights. What was missing was any explanation of what motivated him, in light of his commitments and personal history, to take on Harvey Weinstein as a client. This was particularly important in light of the role Sullivan had assumed as a house dean at Harvard. Perhaps he did not owe any account to a stranger who criticized him on Twitter, but the Harvard students were people with whom Sullivan was in a relationship of trust. They are not too remote to be entitled to demand that Sullivan answer what has come to be known as "the Question" for lawyers.

Answering "The Question"

In a famous article, law professor and criminal defense lawyer Barbara Babcock referred to The Question that every criminal defense lawyer has heard a thousand times: "How can you represent people you know to be guilty?"[11] (Progressives have pointed out that prosecutors should have to answer The Question too, given how much power they have and in light of the impact that decisions about the deployment of law enforcement resources have on communities of color and other marginalized groups.[12]) Importantly, Babcock faces up to The Question with its implied emphasis on the moral agency and accountability of individual lawyers. She hears it with emphasis on the personal dimension: "How can *you* represent . . .?" In terms of some of the concepts from moral philosophy introduced in the previous chapter, Babcock's recognition of The Question follows from the reactive attitudes, such as indignation, expressed by many people toward criminal defense lawyers. These reactive attitudes respond to what observers take to be objectionable reasons and motivations for representing people accused of doing terrible things. The appropriate response to The Question, for lawyers who are inclined to engage in these discussions, would therefore be to give reasons and motivations that are appropriate in light of the moral community's standards regulating interpersonal relationships.

Babcock reviews a variety of answers given by lawyers to The Question, including sympathy for underdogs and those on the margins of society, many of whom have been affected by poverty, racism, and other injustices; the desire to resist the exercise of power by the state and specifically abuses by law enforcement of that power; the importance of seeing those who have experienced disadvantage and shunted to the margins as real people in our society; and the desire to work on challenging and exciting cases. Throughout her article she assumes that lawyers have a choice. Even if they work as public defenders or court-appointed lawyers, and thus do not pick and choose individual clients, no one forced them to become criminal defense lawyers in the first place.

Babcock's article also presupposes that lawyers should be prepared to provide a justification in response to a demand for accountability—that is, The Question is not out of bounds but something a decent and conscientious person should be prepared to answer. Many defense lawyers accept the reasonableness of the demand for accountability. For example, capital defense lawyer David Bruck wrestled with the representation of Dylann Roof, a white supremacist who murdered nine Black church members who had gathered for a Bible study.[13] Bruck has written eloquently about the unequal imposition of the death penalty, which in states like South Carolina often seems reserved for Black defendants accused of killing white victims.[14] Now he intended to use his skill and experience to save the life of a white supremacist from a practice Bruck condemned as racist in its application. As Jelani Cobb wrote in the *New Yorker*, family members of the victims of the Emmanuel Church massacre "murmured uneasily" at points during the trial when Bruck's suggestion that the death penalty was inherently tainted by racism seemed difficult to square with his defense of Roof.[15] Importantly, however, Bruck never relied on the Principle of Nonaccountability. He always accepted that he had to answer The Question, even though it would be unlikely that everyone would accept his justification.

Given what experienced defense lawyers have said about their motivations, Ronald Sullivan could have given a number of different answers to The Question, in the form of explanations for why *he* decided to represent *this* client, Harvey Weinstein. To be clear, this list is entirely hypothetical—I am not suggesting that Sullivan was actually motivated by any of these considerations, and some of them would have only inflamed the students further—but they are all plausible explanations that a lawyer in his position could have offered:

- *Criminal defense work is difficult and rewarding*.[16] Many people are drawn to working as a lawyer by the intellectual excitement and challenge, and criminal defense work provides these rewards to a greater extent than, say, complex commercial litigation or transactional practice. As Barbara Babcock noted, winning is particularly sweet for criminal defense lawyers because the cards are stacked in favor of the prosecution.[17] High-profile cases are even more difficult, given the tenor of public opinion against the defendant. Representing Harvey Weinstein could be the ultimate demonstration of one's ability as a criminal defense lawyer—a kind of professional Mt. Everest. In the words of John F. Kennedy, we choose to go to the moon not because it is easy but because it is hard.[18]
- *Fight the power*. Public defenders often report being motivated by mistrust of law enforcement and government power as well as the desire to stick up for the little guy.[19] Sullivan could appeal to this explanation if he had been challenged for his representation of Michael Brown's family in response to his killing by Ferguson police. Harvey Weinstein is by no stretch of the imagination a powerless individual, and there are no allegations of police abuses in the investigation of the allegations against him. However, it is still possible to see his prosecution as a potential abuse of some kind of power, perhaps in response to (understandable) public outrage over his conduct. This would be different from the usual defense lawyer's motivation to resist the power of the state, but it would still tap into a lawyer's motivation to stand by a friendless individual.
- *Sympathy for the devil*. Some lawyers are drawn to flawed humanity. Law professor and defense lawyer Abbe Smith has written, provocatively, "I like guilty people."[20] She quotes Clarence Darrow reporting that he learned a great deal about humanity and about himself by visiting inmates of prisons. Seeking out the humanity in a deeply flawed, broken

person—trying to determine "how did he turn out this way?" may be a rewarding aspect of representing defendants in a criminal case.
- *This #MeToo thing is getting out of hand.* Weinstein's trial counsel, Donna Rotunno, came to the representation with a history of defending men in prosecutions for sexual assault.[21] She objects to a cultural environment in which men are presumed guilty until proven innocent. In response to the criticism by many advocates for women's rights, she contends that social attitudes have changed in a way that undermines the assumption that women are fully responsible agents. The potential injustice facing Harvey Weinstein is therefore not the same as that facing poor defendants or people of color but is nevertheless a type of injustice to be resisted. Alternatively, one might believe that we rely too much on a harsh, highly punitive criminal justice system to address social problems.[22]
- *It's a lucrative gig.* After a career of laboring in the vineyard for social justice, there is nothing wrong with getting paid well by a client who happens to be able to afford high-priced private counsel.[23] Government lawyers and judges sometimes move into private practice because they have children to put through college or other pressing financial needs and the salary disparity is too great to ignore. Alternatively, a lawyer may effectively subsidize pro bono or low-cost representation to poor clients by working for a few rich ones. A lawyer may also seek the nonmonetary reward of public recognition for having been selected to an elite defense team.

What these hypothetical explanations show is that the same action may be associated with a variety of meanings. Looking at client representation solely in terms of permissibility has the effect of flattening out the moral landscape for lawyers. We intuitively recognize a difference between representing an unpopular client out of a desire to make money and undertaking the same representation out of a belief (whether well founded or not) that larger issues are at stake. To emphasize, this is a question of the meaning of an action, not its permissibility. It is legally and morally permissible both to represent Harvey Weinstein and to earn a substantial return on one's professional skills and reputation. Whether one sees Sullivan's actions as something we should grudgingly tolerate or regard as admirable, however, depends to a great extent on Sullivan's attitudes and motivations.[24] The same *permissible* action—representing Weinstein—might be evaluated very differently depending on whether Sullivan's motivation was to take on an exceptionally challenging case, to slow down the public's rush to judgment, or to make a few bucks.*

At least as I read Sullivan's explanation, it failed to engage with what were *his* reasons in particular, as opposed to the reasons that any lawyer could offer, for deciding to represent Weinstein. Critics, including Harvard students in his residential house, wanted to know what it was about *Ronald Sullivan* that made defending Harvey Weinstein seem like a good idea. For all we know, Sullivan could have provided an answer that would have addressed this concern, at least in principle, although students may have continued to object and the Harvard administration may have decided that the headache of student protests was sufficient reason to dismiss Sullivan as house dean. Or the protests may have quieted down as many of the students came to understand better why Sullivan was interested in working on the case. In retrospect, however, Sullivan missed an opportunity to offer a sufficient justification in response to his critics' demand for accountability. The right sort of explanation would have to refer to the attitudes and expectations he had not only with respect to his client, Weinstein, but with respect to others with whom he was in a preexisting relationship of accountability. This likely includes Harvard University and the students in his residential house and, more controversially, may include his relationship with broader communities, such as #MeToo activists or anyone interested in accountability for powerful men.

Many Harvard students and university administrators believed Sullivan's representation of Harvey Weinstein was incompatible with the duties he owed as house dean. On the other side, I believe most lawyers would contend that it was a mistake to impose the sanction of removing him as house dean, reflecting ignorance or misunderstanding of the ethical obligations of lawyers. Sullivan did not do anything wrong *as a lawyer*, in the sense of violating a provision of the rules of professional conduct or some other professional duty. There is no question that Harvey Weinstein is entitled to the assistance of counsel for his defense and that a lawyer would be justified in representing him in connection with the charges against him. As far as I know, no one claimed that anything Sullivan did in the course of representing Weinstein was a violation of the rules of professional conduct

---

* To be clear, I don't think wanting to make money is a bad thing, but it is not necessarily, in itself, admirable. A lawyer who explained the acceptance of an engagement by a particularly nasty client by saying, "I've got kids to put through college" or "I've got some boat payments coming due" would be missing the force of criticism that is looking for a positive attitude or trait of character to explain the representation. At least in my view, however, a representation motivated solely by financially gain is morally neutral.

for lawyers, or even an aggressive, if legally permitted, tactic.[25] But an action justified in terms of political or professional values, such as the constitutional rights of litigants or the importance of the rule of law, may not have the same meaning to observers not steeped in the values and traditions of the legal profession.

It is tempting, as a lawyer and a legal scholar, to simply write public criticism off as the result of ignorance or unfamiliarity with what lawyers do. Much of the writing in defense of lawyers like Ronald Sullivan implicitly adopts the view that the lay public needs to be better educated about the importance of the Bill of Rights and the principle that criminal defendants have a right to counsel. It may be the case, however, that the public understands perfectly well what lawyers do, and in many instances even accepts the justification offered by lawyers like Sullivan on its own terms. People understand that everyone deserves a defense, even Harvey Weinstein. Ensuring that every criminal defendant receives the effective assistance of skilled legal counsel is an important principle of political morality in a society committed to the rule of law. But that justification is not necessarily the end of the matter when considered from the point of view of other social roles, such as university administrator. It also must be connected in the right way to the considerations that are part of ordinary morality, which a moral agent acting in a professional role would consider when thinking about the permissibility and meaning of his actions. We will return to the issues around the distinctiveness of professional duties later, in particular, Chapter 7.

Making clients radioactive

I expect many lawyers to be aghast at my openness to accepting any kind of criticism, let alone stronger informal social penalties, for representing an unpopular client. That goes even for clients like Harvey Weinstein who almost anyone would agree richly deserves his notoriety. Unless the legal profession and the legal academy fights back hard and consistently against the public criticism of lawyers who choose to represent these clients, the next controversial or unpopular would-be client may be unable to secure legal counsel.[26] Lawyers may not want to have anything to do with individuals or groups who are socially radioactive. If an individual or group is unfairly or unjustly marginalized, remaining silent while lawyers are subjected to criticism or more severe social sanctions like ostracism has the effect of perpetuating and amplifying the injustice. It is no answer to assert that some clients deserve to be shunned and stigmatized, because this depends on a social judgment that is not constrained by the requirements of due process of law, including a full investigation into the facts, an opportunity for both sides to present arguments, and the presence of a neutral decision maker.[27] Maybe Harvey Weinstein did not do the things he is accused of doing, and even if he did, there is a further question regarding the magnitude of the punishment he should suffer. The last thing lawyers should tolerate is the intrusion of unruly, unregulated "cancel culture" into a decision as important as choosing to represent a client. The effect of not standing firm against public criticism of lawyers could be the weakening of two of the bedrock political rights of American citizens, the right to the assistance of counsel and the right to due process of law.

Acknowledging the power of this defense in the abstract, the rhetoric of "mob rule" is overblown in most of the cases that actually lead to criticism of lawyers. A few harsh editorials in the Harvard *Crimson* and some graffiti do not equal a breakdown in social order. And a vanishingly small number of clients nowadays have difficulty finding competent counsel to represent them. Still, there is a serious concern here that needs to be explored. There is a difference between the legal rights of clients, unpopular or otherwise, and the judgment that they are moral wrongdoers. One of the social functions of the legal profession is to reconcile the value of the rule of law with the morality of responsibility and accountability. The rule of law is an important political value, but it can be realized only through social institutions and procedures that may distance professionals, such as lawyers and judges, from the practices that sustain relationships of moral responsibility and accountability. The Principle of Nonaccountability is intended to support the rule of law by barring criticism of lawyers for representing unpopular clients.

The lawyerly version of the Principle of Nonaccountability is often referred to in the United Kingdom as the "cab-rank rule." As the name suggests, the cab-rank rule imagines lawyers as being like taxicabs queued up at the airport, waiting to take passengers in turn, as opposed to choosing which passengers will get a ride. The fictional barrister Horace Rumpole explains that a barrister is "a black taxi, plying for hire; I'm bound to accept anyone, however repulsive, who waves me down and asks for a lift."[28] Technically it applies only to self-employed barristers, that is, in-court advocates, and not the solicitors who do the behind the scenes work of interviewing witnesses, preparing written filings with the court, and counseling clients.[29]

Specialization of practice also means that, for instance, family law barristers are never faced with the prospect of turning down a brief from a solicitor instructed by a defendant in a criminal prosecution.[30]

The cab-rank rule is often described as more honored in the breach than in observance.[31] However, it forms an important part of the self-understanding of the legal profession in England and in other legal systems influenced by the English common law, such as Canada, Australia, and New Zealand.[32] It also features frequently in the American debate over criticism of lawyers for representing unpopular clients, if only as an ideal rather than an enforceable rule of professional conduct. However, when invoked in response to public criticism of lawyers, the cab-rank rule stands in need of a moral justification.[33] Otherwise it may appear to the public as if lawyers are trying to hide behind a force field that deflects all criticism without giving an account of why they are entitled to a free pass from the scrutiny that anyone else would be subject to for similar conduct.

The classic statement of the cab-rank rule and its rationale is from Thomas Erskine, who defended the radical writer Thomas Paine against charges of seditious libel:

> I will forever, at all hazards, assert the dignity, independence, and integrity of the English Bar; without which, impartial justice, the most valuable part of the English constitution, can have no existence. From the moment that any advocate can be permitted to say, that he will or will not stand between the Crown and the subject arraigned in the Court where he daily sits to practice, from that moment the liberties of England are at an end.[34]

Erskine's speech is not entirely clear on why the liberties of England will end if an advocate has a choice not to represent any particular client. However, a modern version of the defense of the cab-rank rule, by an eminent British jurist, explains why this might be so: "[I]f counsel could pick and choose, his reputation might suffer if he chose to act for [an unpopular] client, and the client might have great difficulty in obtaining proper legal assistance."[35]

This defense has crossed the Atlantic and is now common in the responses of American lawyers who face criticism for the clients they represent. The late legal ethics scholar Deborah Rhode worried that holding lawyers morally accountability for representing nasty clients could erode legal safeguards against state power, particularly for members of vilified groups:

if... advocates were held morally accountable for their clients' conduct, less legal representation would be available for those most vulnerable to popular prejudice and governmental repression. Our history provides ample illustrations of the social and economic penalties directed at attorneys with unpopular clients. It was difficult enough to find lawyers for accused communists in the McCarthy era and for political activists in the early southern civil rights campaign. Those difficulties would have been far greater without the principle that legal representation is not an endorsement of client conduct.[36]

Similarly, journalist Matthew Yglesias, writing about Ronald Sullivan's representation of Harvey Weinstein, implies that public criticism would be unwarranted if a lawyer were actually bound by the cab-rank rule:

> Sullivan isn't a public defender who's simply taking the clients assigned to him. He's not even a full-time criminal defense lawyer who just takes whichever clients happen to come through his door. He's a busy guy who has classes to teach, a dorm to administer, and various other demands on his time. While it's obviously true that all criminal defendants have a right to an attorney, it's equally obvious that criminal defendants don't have a particular right to Ronald Sullivan's services.
>
> It would be genuinely outrageous to condemn a public defender for catching some heinous clients in the course of pursuing an honorable vocation. But as Sullivan is obviously picking and choosing his clients – and, in Weinstein's case, getting well paid for his time – it doesn't seem unreasonable to draw some inferences based on his choices.[37]

The last sentence is important: If a lawyer has a choice, one may permissibly infer from the clients the lawyer chooses to represent. But infer to what conclusion? Yglesias suggests that at Harvard, where Sullivan was serving as a residential advisor to undergraduates, these students "had some reason reasons to wonder where Sullivan stands." The insinuation here is that students could infer from Sullivan's choice of client that he would not have sufficient appreciation for the social goal of holding powerful men accountable for sexual assault and sexual harassment and would possibly have some sympathy for the backlash against the #MeToo movement.

This is a powerful argument—so powerful, in fact, that it often goes unquestioned by lawyers. There are several weaknesses in it that need to be explored, however. One is empirical. Is it really the case that unpopular clients may go unrepresented if lawyers are subject to criticism? Having something like the cab-rank rule, or not, is only one factor among many in whether unpopular clients can obtain representation.[38] Harvey Weinstein, who at the time of his trial was about as unpopular as anyone could be, had no difficulty in attracting an A-team of talented criminal defense lawyers. A recent survey of English barristers found that the "worse" the client, the greater the attraction for lawyers who want to work on high profile cases. Several survey respondents said that if Anders Breivik, who killed 77 people in Norway, most of them children at summer camp, had been on trial in the United Kingdom, "barristers would have queued around the block to represent him."[39] Perhaps the American equivalent of Anders Breivik, accused of committing the most heinous crime imaginable, was mentioned previously: Dylann Roof, who in 2015 murdered nine African-Americans at a Bible study at a historic church in Charleston, South Carolina, was represented by a team of highly experienced lawyers, including David Bruck, who had previously represented Dzhokhar Tsarnaev, one of the men charged in connection with the Boston Marathon bombing; and Susan Smith, who drowned her two children in a lake and sought to blame the crime on a Black carjacker.[40] Roof, Tsarnaev, and Smith, along with Harvey Weinstein, would surely be on most Americans' list of "worst of the worst," yet all of them were represented by outstanding defense counsel. While this is admittedly not a scientific approach to gathering data, in all of my conversations with lawyers and reading public commentary on lawyers' choices of clients, there does not appear to be a great deal of criticism of criminal defense lawyers, even those like Bruck who represent people accused of doing terrible things. The public seems to get the principle that everyone deserves competent counsel and that a decent society owes fair and dignified treatment to people accused of crimes (as much as that principle is honored in the breach).

Moreover, many lawyers, particularly those who specialize in criminal defense, enjoy working for controversial clients. It is challenging, energizing, and connects with some of their core values such as resisting the exercise of power, both formal state power and informal social sanctions. One of the hypothetical answers Ronald Sullivan could give to The Question is that representing Harvey Weinstein would be a source of real professional and personal satisfaction. And despite some loud critical voices, many nonlawyers who live in democratic rule-of-law societies appreciate the contribution lawyers make to protecting the freedoms of all citizens. The occasional exceptions in which clients have a difficult time finding counsel tend to involve small, isolated, and homogeneous communities, such as the island of Guam, where a plaintiff challenging the territory's restrictions on abortion reported that, in a "relatively small and predominantly Catholic community . . . this case was deemed extremely undesirable."[41]

It is certainly true that the chronic underfunding of counsel for indigent defendants is a real social problem in the United States. Public defenders often labor under such excessive caseloads that it is a constant struggle to provide minimally adequate representation to their clients.[42] But this is a different problem from the one considered here, where social sanctions like intense criticism and ostracism result in the denial of effective representation to unpopular people. Historically, it has happened only infrequently that a class of clients has been socially anathema to such an extent that they had difficulty securing counsel *for that reason*.

The representation of Black clients in the Jim Crow South is one such instance. The so-called Scottsboro Boys, nine Black teenagers accused of raping two white women on a train in Alabama in 1931, were sentenced to death after a hasty proceeding at which they were unrepresented by counsel.[43] The trial judge made a pretense of appointing the entire local bar to represent the defendants,[44] but no lawyer in town wanted anything to do with the case. An out-of-state lawyer, who admitted he was unprepared and unfamiliar with Alabama law, offered to help in any way he could, and this was enough to satisfy the trial judge. The U.S. Supreme Court reversed the defendants' convictions on the ground that the state of Alabama had violated the constitutional requirement due process of law, holding that a fair hearing would be impossible without the assistance of a lawyer.[45] The Supreme Court's recognition of the constitutional significance of legal representation in criminal cases did not extend to civil legal proceedings, however, and throughout the 1950s and 1960s, almost no white southern lawyers would consider representing civil rights protesters, reasonably fearing for their livelihoods or even their safety; some lawyers who advocated against segregation found themselves socially ostracized and harassed by the local bar authorities.[46] Many lawyers incorrectly interpreted the Principle of Nonaccountability as requiring them to keep their beliefs about racial justice separate from their decision to represent clients asserting civil rights claims. As legal historian Jerold Auerbach wrote of white lawyers during the civil rights movement: "Everything in a lawyer's training argued for the separation of client from cause."[47] Claiming to be politically neutral in the representation of powerful corporations while refusing to represent individuals with unorthodox views is a familiar lawyerly stance.[48] But let's not pretend it is a value-neutral decision.

Similar harassment by government officials and social pressure affected the willingness of lawyers to represent unpopular clients during a period whose name has become a synonym for political repression—the McCarthy era. Beginning in 1947 with the Truman Doctrine and Attorney General Tom Clark's list of subversive organizations, and continuing through the investigative activities of the House Un-American Activities Committee (HUAC), the government and private actors such as the entertainment industry set about purging, blacklisting, and prosecuting members of the Communist Party.[49] Wisconsin Senator Joseph McCarthy came to prominence by asserting that he had a list of Communists within the U.S. State Department, prompting the Senate to join the investigative efforts, looking for Communists in such unlikely places as the White House and the U.S. Army.

The government response to the perceived threat was breathtakingly comprehensive, with informants, surveillance and wiretaps, FBI dossiers, grand juries, congressional hearings, and the acquiescence of courts and the organized bar. Anti-Communist hysteria had a chilling effect on other civil rights, such as the rights of speech and association, and severely impacted left-leaning institutions such as the labor movement and universities.[50] Would-be lawyers were forced to answer questions about their affiliations with allegedly subversive organizations and to swear loyalty oaths; the Supreme Court was at best equivocal in protecting the First Amendment rights of bar applicants.[51] The National Lawyers Guild, an association of lawyers formed in the 1930s to promote progressive causes like labor unions, minority rights, and public funding for legal services, was attacked by President Eisenhower's Attorney General as being controlled by "card-carrying Communists and prominent fellow travelers."[52] The range of socially acceptable political views narrowed considerably, with people on the left in particular making strenuous efforts to avoid being seen as disloyal or as "dupes" for Communists.[53] Red-baiting then fused in the South with opposition to the civil rights movement in the wake of the Supreme Court's *Brown v. Board of Education* decision in an unholy reactionary alliance.[54]

For all of this, the effect on the right to counsel and the representation of unpopular clients was equivocal. Most of the defendants in the first Smith Act trials of Communist Party leaders in 1948–49 were represented by a team of volunteer lawyers.[55] The Hollywood Ten, summoned to appear before HUAC, were represented by Ben Margolis, Robert Kenny, and Bartley Crum, three lawyers somewhere on the political spectrum between progressive and radical.[56] After the hearings the lawyers went on to careers with law firms that varied in their political commitments, from apolitical to left leaning. Like John Adams after the Boston Massacre trials, none of them experienced adverse professional consequences as a result of having represented the alleged Communists. On the other hand, a convincing case can be made that official and unofficial intimidation campaigns scared off many lawyers from representing clients accused of membership in the Community Party.[57] The lawyers who represented the defendants in the so-called Foley Square Trial, for violating a federal statute prohibiting advocating the violent overthrow of the government,[58] were held in criminal contempt by the trial judge for disrupting the proceedings, imprisoned, and subsequently disbarred.[59] The contempt charges and disbarments were upheld on appeal by the Second Circuit and the Supreme Court.[60] Numerous defendants in political prosecutions found it impossible or extremely difficulty to retain counsel and an American Bar Association committee found in 1953 that lawyers were subjected to "severe personal vilification and abuse" if they represented suspected Communists.[61]

It is difficult to quantify refusals to represent clients; the individual decisions by lawyers tend not to leave a paper trail. Legal historian Jerold Auerbach sums up the difficulty of evaluating the available evidence:

> It is impossible to calculate with precision the impact of a few conspicuous prosecutions or proceedings on the entire profession, or on those whose caution or fear may have prompted silent acquiescence and consequent anonymity. It cannot be determined how many prospective attorneys for unpopular defendants were deterred by the threat of professional discipline or the risk of economic adversity.[62]

Someone like me who is not a professional historian can always be accused of cherry-picking anecdotes to support a preferred conclusion.[63] There is no doubt that the McCarthy era was characterized by pervasive paranoia and use of political and social power to punish perceived disloyalty. For the most part the organized bar was keen to jump onto the anti-Communist bandwagon. The American Bar Association (ABA), a national voluntary organization of mostly elite lawyers, certainly did not cover itself in glory during the second Red Scare. In 1950, the ABA adopted a resolution supporting President Truman's executive order requiring executive branch employees to swear an oath of loyalty to the United States; the ABA sought to extend the requirement to all lawyers to swear an anti-Communist oath.[64] The ABA did subsequently create a Special Committee on Individual Rights as Affected by National Security, which affirmed the right of defendants to the assistance of counsel and committed the ABA to defending lawyers attacked in public for their defense of unpopular clients. However, that committee was counterbalanced by a separate Special Committee on Communist Tactics, which proposed that lawyers who refused to give testimony about alleged subversive activities should be disbarred.[65]

The Jim Crow and McCarthy periods differ in an important way from the situation facing lawyers for unpopular clients today. Social pressures and the use of government power were aligned behind the goals of racial segregation and anti-Communism. A Black civil rights plaintiff or an alleged member of the Communist Party would have been perceived as threatening the social order as it was understood by a substantial majority of the relevant society at the time. Extraordinary courage would have been required for a lawyer to represent a client so far outside the social and political mainstream. Even the great judge Learned Hand saw the Communist Party of the United States (completely counterfactually) as "a highly articulated, well contrived, far spread organization, numbering thousands of adherents, rigidly and ruthlessly disciplined, [and] infused with a passionate Utopian faith that is to redeem mankind."[66]

I understand the attraction of the Principle of Nonaccountability in these circumstances. Lawyers who believe in it want to think that creating distance in the public's mind between lawyers and the clients they represent will make it less likely that pariah clients will go unrepresented. In the face of a solid wall of public condemnation, however, a few hortatory editorials in the *Wall Street Journal* seem hardly sufficient to screw the courage of lawyers to the sticking point. Picking up on what actually motivated lawyers to represent vilified clients during the civil rights movement and in opposition to McCarthy-ite forces, a better strategy would be appeal to lawyers who are politically motivated and temperamentally inclined to resist government or private power, take up the cause of outsiders, and make waves. An ironic effect of continued reliance on the Principle of Nonaccountability is the disconnection between some of the most challenging, satisfying client representations and the types of lawyers who would be best suited to take them on.

It still may be the case that unwarranted criticism functions as a kind of tax on representation, possibly deterring some lawyers who otherwise would have been willing to take on the client.[67] As lawyers sometimes say with respect to the First Amendment's guarantee of freedom of expression, one can worry about a "chilling effect" on a protected right if retaliation is permitted against someone exercising that right. This is the serious concern that was raised (among a lot of political posturing) when the behemoth law firm Kirkland & Ellis announced that it would no longer represent firearms manufacturers in constitutional litigation.[68] Following the horrific massacre at Robb Elementary School in Uvalde, Texas, some of Kirkland's large institutional clients expressed discomfort at the firm's decision to lend its talents, particularly those of former U.S. Solicitor General Paul Clement, to the efforts to beat back restrictions on the sale and possession of guns. As a result, Clement left the firm, presumably taking his clients with him. Kirkland, for its part, had very little to say publicly, but reportedly it was facing pressure from other clients to distance itself from conservative cause litigation, like Second Amendment cases.[69] Clement, in his *Wall Street Journal* editorial, accused the firm of "acceding to the demands of the woke," and distinguished a law firm from an "ordinary" business that might understandably be concerned about a significant loss of revenue.[70] He blasted the firm, citing the go-to trope of John Adams, and arguing that unpopular clients are precisely the ones who need a highly skilled lawyer to advocate for their rights:

> [D]efending unpopular clients is what we do. The rare individuals and companies lucky enough to be universally popular (for the time being) have less need for lawyers. And the least popular clients are most in need of representation, from the British soldiers after the Boston Massacre to the defendant in the Boston Marathon bombing.[71]

In theory it is possible that a group like gun manufacturers or firearms enthusiasts might find themselves unable to obtain competent representation owing to the "cancelation" of lawyers who take these cases. Perhaps this theoretical outcome could result from lawyers and law firms forming some kind of power elite, sharing a common, presumably left-wing ideology and refusing to accept conservative clients or causes.[72] Given the pervasive ideological polarization in the United States and many other countries, however, it seems highly unlikely that any economic enterprise—including the legal profession—could survive while excluding a substantial proportion of prospective customers.† I would be willing to bet that there will be plenty of top-notch litigators and law firms willing to bring lawsuits under the Second Amendment on behalf of firearms manufacturers, even after Kirkland got out of that business.[73] One could imagine, however, a society with a dominant political and professional culture that systematically excludes and discriminates against an unpopular minority.[74] In that case, turning away clients based on ideological disagreement could undermine the rule of law in that society.[75] Ultimately this is an empirical issue, but it is ever present, lurking in the background of the debate over public criticism of lawyers.

Apart from the empirical claim, about which I am skeptical for reasons discussed previously, there is another basis for opposing canceling lawyers, which Clement has alluded to in public discussions of his departure from Kirkland.[76] The argument is that ideological disagreement over questions like the responsibility borne by firearms manufacturers for gun violence and mass shootings is likely to be intractable. A society could just allow conflict to fester, but it may also make what I regard as a morally significant choice to establish institutions and procedures that attempt to reach a social judgment that represents a fair resolution of disagreement over facts and values.[77] Lawyers and the legal system play a vital role in managing social conflict. In today's much more polarized political climate, when there is nothing like the anti-Communist or racist consensus that left some clients without counsel in the first half of the 20th century, there appears to be no shortage of lawyers willing to represent controversial clients. In the years following the September 11, 2001, terrorist attacks, some of the most prominent lawyers in private practice lent their assistance to suspected terrorists who were repeatedly characterized by Bush administration officials as "the worst of the worst."[78] Gun manufacturers, former Trump administration officials, fossil fuel companies, and activists on all sides of various culture-war issues have not had any difficulty in retaining high-quality lawyers.[79] If lawyers are going to defend the Principle of Nonaccountability, it will have to be on normative, not empirical grounds.

My take on the Clement case is normative, not empirical. I do not believe obnoxious clients—whether deemed so by the right or the left—will be unable to find good lawyers to represent them. It is also probably the case that Kirkland's decision was primarily motivated by economics, not moral

---

† In fairness, conservative critics do make this claim with respect to the entertainment industry.

qualms about representing firearms manufacturers. The case for feeling some indignation on behalf of Clement (and, as we will see in the next chapter, reactive attitudes like indignation are very much a part of this story) is that the firm gave insufficient weight to the reality of reasonable disagreement over the issues raised in the litigated matters on which Clement had been representing the gun companies. Throughout the remainder of the book, I will be developing a justifying story about the role of lawyers that puts the legal system, and the ideal of the rule of law, at the center of practices that enable liberal societies to hold together despite intense conflicts over rights and justice. The deepest reason to promote the rule of law is that legal institutions and procedures, including the legal profession, supports the treatment of individuals as free and equal, even in the circumstances of deeply felt disagreements.[80] But I am not sure this argument translates particularly well to the representation of corporations. At least it is harder to see something like the Remington Arms Company as having the status of a "self-originating source of valid claims," to use John Rawls's language.[81] There may be a complicated story one could tell about how corporations enable people to realize certain objectives that are central to their well-being, but most shares of stock in publicly traded corporations are held by institutional investors, and therefore the connection between human dignity and the rights of artificial persons like corporations is extremely attenuated.

If forced to take a position on this case,[82] I would defend Clement's representation of the gun companies as something that is permissible for reasons related to the rule of law but reserve judgment about his intentions, motivating reasons, and attitudes. As we will see in the next chapter, attitudes and motivations play a central role in the practice of blaming lawyers for representing obnoxious clients. I would like to know whether Clement and other Second Amendment advocates feel any reluctance or qualms about the clients they represent every time there is another news report of a mass shooting.[83] The cultural significance of owning an AR-15 rifle has been described by a board member of the National Rifle Association as "an F-you to the left."[84] It is possible that Kirkland & Ellis had become uncomfortable with its association with clients whose business was driven in large part by taking one side on an extremely divisive culture-war issue. The rule-of-law story based on the law's capacity to settle social disagreements is only part of the justification that critics are looking for when they seek to hold lawyers accountable. Critics also want to know about the lawyers themselves, and their attitudes and reasons. I understand that Clement may not like being subjected to that sort of scrutiny, either by the public or by his employer, and he certainly has the right to respond only with reference to the general ideal of the rule of law. But the right response to this controversy is not the Principle of Nonaccountability but exactly what happened here, in the form of vigorous public criticism and an equally strong response. We should not expect consensus about such a divisive issue, but insulating lawyers from criticism would be a mistaken response to the controversy.

Chapter summary

This chapter made two related points: first, the representation of criminal defendants accused of doing terrible things is strongly justified by the political ideals of the rule of law, deterring police misconduct, and treating individuals with dignity. However, there is a further question one might ask about a lawyer's justified representation of a client—namely, why are *you* interested in taking this case? This question pertains to the attitudes and motivations of the lawyer, which are appropriately considered by others as part of moral evaluation. The second point is that lawyers worry too much that having to answer this first personal question will result in a lack of dedicated counsel for unpopular clients. The historical episodes generally cited in support of this concern, the Jim Crow and McCarthy eras, show that it is not entirely unfounded. There are few, if any, examples in modern times of unpopular clients lacking effective representation. This is due in part to political polarization but also to the fact that many lawyers quite appropriately enjoy taking on challenging cases.

Notes

1. Jodi Kantor & Megan Twohey, "Harvey Weinstein Paid Off Sexual Harassment Accusers for Decades," *N.Y. Times* (Oct. 5, 2017); Ronan Farrow, "From Aggressive Overtures to Sexual Assault: Harvey Weinstein's Accusers Tell Their Stories," *New Yorker* (Oct. 10, 2017).
2. Jan Ransom, "Harvey Weinstein Is Found Guilty of Sex Crimes in #MeToo Watershed," *N.Y. Times* (Feb. 24, 2020).
3. Maureen O'Connor, "Who Would Defend Harvey Weinstein?," *Vanity Fair* (Jan. 5, 2020). Media accounts report fees charged by Weinstein's lawyers into seven-figure

territory. David Thomas, "Harvey Weinstein Sues Former Lawyer to Recover $1 Million," Reuters (May 5, 2021).
4. See Kate Taylor, "Harvard's First Black Faculty Deans Let Go Amid Uproar Over Harvey Weinstein Defense," *N.Y. Times* (May 11, 2019). For additional media accounts and commentary on which this discussion is based, see Conor Friedersdorf, "The Damage that Harvard Has Done," *Atlantic* (May 19, 2019); Lucy Caldwell, "Harvard Was Right to Fire Ron Sullivan," *New Republic* (May 18, 2019); Matthew Yglesias, "The Raging Controversy Over Harvey Weinstein, Ronald Sullivan, and Harvard, Explained," *Vox* (May 17, 2019); Lara Bazelon, "Harvard Shouldn't Punish Harvey Weinstein's Attorney," *Slate* (May 13, 2019); Jan Ransom & Michael Gold, "'Whose Side Are You On?'": Harvard Dean Representing Weinstein Is Hit With Graffiti and Protests, *N.Y. Times* (March 4, 2019).
5. Danu A. Mudannayake & Remedy Ryan, "Harvard, Remove Dean Sullivan," *Harvard Crimson* (Feb. 13, 2019). Interestingly, similar arguments had been raised in connection with Justice Antonin Scalia teaching a class at Harvard Law School, given Scalia's statements and judicial opinions that were understood as comparing same-sex intimacy with bestiality. See Benjamin Eidelson, "The Etiquette of Equality," 51 *Phil. & Pub. Aff.* 97 (2023).
6. Letter, "Harvard Law Faculty Speak in Support of Resident Dean Representing Weinstein," *Boston Globe* (Mar. 8, 2019).
7. Jeannie Suk Gersen, "Unpopular Speech in a Cold Climate," *New Yorker* (Mar. 14, 2019).
8. Randall Kennedy, "Harvard Betrays a Law Professor – And Itself," *N.Y. Times* (May 15, 2019).
9. See Ronald S. Sullivan, Jr., "Why Harvard Was Wrong to Make Me Step Down," *N.Y. Times* (June 24, 2019).
10. Isaac Chotiner, "A Harvard Law School Professor Defends His Decision to Represent Harvey Weinstein," *New Yorker* (Mar. 17, 2019).
11. Barbara Allen Babcock, "Defending the Guilty," 32 *Clev. St. L. Rev.* 175 (1983–84). See also Abbe Smith & Monroe H. Freedman, eds., *How Can You Represent Those People?* (Palgrave Macmillan 2013), an anthology of writing on The Question, including a "spruced up" version of her classic article by Barbara Babcock. Not only American lawyers, but all criminal defense lawyers in common law systems have to answer The Question. For an excellent account of the answers given by Australian lawyers, see Abbe Smith, "Defending the Unpopular Down-Under," 30 *Melb. U. L. Rev.* 496 (2006). For a similar project, although focused more on the phenomenon of burnout among public defenders, see Charles J. Ogletree, Jr., "Beyond Justification: Seeking Motivations to Sustain Public Defenders," 106 *Harv. L. Rev.* 1239 (1993). Ogletree's paper has an important structural feature in common with the major argument of this book, which is the distinction between justifications for criminal defense work and an understanding of what it means for practitioners. Abbe Smith critically examines Ogletree's influential article and adds the values of respect, professional craft, and a sense of outrage at abuses of power in Abbe Smith, "Too Much Heart and Not Enough

Heat: The Short Life and Fractured Ego of the Empathic, Heroic Public Defender," 37 *U.C. Davis L. Rev.* 1203 (2004).

12. Paul Butler, "How Can You Prosecute Those People?," in Freedman & Smith; Paul Butler, "Can Good People Be Prosecutors," in *Let's Get Free: A Hip Hop Theory of Justice* (New York: The New Press 2009), pp. 101–22; Richard Delgado, "Should Good People be Doctors? A Comment on Paul Butler and Anonymous," 72 *SMU L. Rev. F.* 1 (2019).
13. Alan Blinder, "A Top Defender, Sidelined by the Accused in the Charleston Church Massacre," *N.Y. Times* (Dec. 13, 2016).
14. David Bruck, "Decisions of Death," *New Republic* (Dec. 12, 1983); David Bruck, "Is the Death Penalty Only for Killers of Whites?," *Wash. Post* (Oct. 12, 1986).
15. Jelani Cobb, "Letter from Charleston: Inside the Trial of Dylann Roof," *New Yorker* (Feb. 6, 2017).
16. Smith, "Heart and Heat," pp. 1251–59.
17. Babcock, p. 178. See also Abbe Smith, "Representing Rapists: The Cruelty of Cross Examination and Other Challenges for a Feminist Criminal Defense Lawyer," 53 *Am. Crim. L. Rev.* 255, 293–94 (2016)(noting that rape and child sex cases are unusually interesting and challenging for lawyers, as they tend to go to trial, involve forensic evidence, medical and nonmedical experts, issues of memory and suggestibility in child cases).
18. Speech delivered at Rice University (my undergraduate alma mater—go Owls!) on Sept. 12, 1962, available from the John F. Kennedy Presidential Library at https://www.jfklibrary.org/learn/about-jfk/historic-speeches/address-at-rice-university-on-the-nations-space-effort.
19. Smith, "Heart and Heat," pp. 1259–61.
20. Smith, "Representing Rapists," p. 296.
21. See Christine Cauterucci, "What Kind of Woman Defends Harvey Weinstein?," *Slate* (Feb. 14, 2020); Jan Ransom, "She's Harvey Weinstein's Lawyer, and She Thinks #MeToo Is 'Dangerous,'" *N.Y. Times* (Jan. 14, 2020); Maureen O'Connor, "Who Would Defend Harvey Weinstein?," *Vanity Fair* (Jan. 5, 2020).
22. Smith, "Representing Rapists," p. 308.
23. American lawyers incorrectly state that they have a duty to represent every would-be client who wishes to retain them. As for why lawyers think this, one hypothesis is that some lawyers, "confused by self-interest . . . may simply be arguing that they were driven by professional duty in acquiring a personal fortune representing rich but odious clients." Charles W. Wolfram, *Modern Legal Ethics* (St. Paul, Minn.: West Publishing Co. 1986), § 10.2.2, at 571.
24. My colleagues who do a significant amount of criminal defense work for unpopular clients, but *indigent* unpopular clients, were considerably more critical of Sullivan than lawyers who are not professionally committed to representing poor people.
25. The representation of the defendant in a civil lawsuit related to a sexual assault at an elite boarding school came back to haunt a lawyer who had been nominated to the U.S. Court of Appeals for the First Circuit. Prior to serving as Attorney General of New Hampshire the lawyer, Michael Delaney, had been in private practice and in that

capacity had defended St. Paul's School in 2016 in an action brought by the parents of a minor who alleged she had been assaulted there. Criticism focused on a motion to permit disclosure of the name of the complaining witness, which the plaintiffs saw as an attempt at intimidating her. Although I have not seen a reference to Model Rule 4.4(a) in the coverage of this case, let's suppose for the sake of argument that it is a close call, but that the lawyer's conduct did not rise to the level of "means that have no substantial purpose other than to embarrass, delay, or burden a third person." The motion to permit identification of the victim could nevertheless be seen as an aggressive tactic—one that indicates impaired attitudes (to use the language of the next chapter) toward the victims of sexual assault. The criticism would then not be for the identity of the client (the boarding school) but for what the lawyer did in the course of the representation. For coverage of the case, see James Arkin, "Advocacy Groups Raise Concerns Over 1st Circ. Pick," *Law360* (Mar. 10, 2023); Jeremy Diamond & Lauren Fox, "Biden Judicial Appointment Hangs in the Wind as Senators Mull Action in Past Case," *CNN* (Mar. 3, 2023).

26. One of the most influential scholars in the field of legal ethics, the late Deborah Rhode, excoriated renowned litigator David Boies and his firm for accepting the representation of a private investigator firm called Black Cube; the objective of the representation was to help Black Cube develop information to discredit negative information made public about Harvey Weinstein. Deborah Rhode, "David Boies's Egregious Involvement with Harvey Weinstein," *N.Y. Times* (Nov. 9, 2017). Rhode's op-ed was carefully written to focus most of its critical attention on claims that Boies's conduct violated rules of professional conduct regarding conflicts of interest and the use of deception in the course of investigations. However, the intensity of Rhode's condemnation of Boies appears to be rooted not merely in indignation over rules violations but, more importantly, in a sense of betrayal by a lawyer who publicly claims to be committed to "good" causes and the clients who promote them: "Mr. Boies is a renowned litigator, a champion of same-sex marriage and, according to his own statement, an attorney with a long history of 'protecting the rights of women.' When leaders with such high visibility cut ethical corners, it sends a powerful and corrosive message." A similar sense of betrayal by a political fellow traveler seems to have inflamed the anger of critics of Neal Katyal, discussed in Chapter 6.

27. One of the issues addressed in Chapter 5 on boycotts of law firms is whether informal sanctions, like shaming, ostracism, and boycotts can be criticized in ethical terms for poaching on the turf of formal law, which aspires to standards of fairness and impartiality in application. Waheed Hussain argues that informal social pressures such as boycotts are wrong because they intrude upon decisions that should be committed to democratic processes. "As I see it, a central set of questions about ethical consumerism stems from the fact that some decisions in a liberal democracy should be made through a market process, while others should be made through a democratic legislative process." Waheed Hussain, "Is Ethical Consumerism an Impermissible Form of Vigilantism?", 40 *Phil. & Pub. Aff.* 111, 114 (2012). In his view, it is impermissible for individuals and groups to try to use market pressures to bring about social change and should instead "approach the task as a legislative endeavor that is part of the wider

political process." Never mind that many issues of great social importance, at least in the United States, are decided by courts whose judges are accountable to the wider political process in only a very limited way. The decision to recognize a constitutional right to abortion in 1973, in *Roe v. Wade*, and the subsequent decision to overrule Roe in 2022, in *Dobbs v. Jackson Women's Health Organization*, were both made by majorities on a nine-member court, the members having been nominated by the President and confirmed by the Senate, sometimes with thin majorities (certainly in recent years). Beyond that, a deeper problem with Hussain's critique of boycotts is that it places a great deal of weight on the legitimacy of the political process, which the organizers of boycotts presumably contend is not responsive to their concerns. People who believe that the political process is rigged in favor of, say, conservative political interests may believe the only effective avenue for change is to use collective economic power to target powerful actors who contribute to the non-responsiveness of the political system. Something like the boycott of Chick-fil-A for contributing to anti-LGBTQ groups does not have to be seen as an illegitimate attempt to force people to act in ways that are contrary to their principles lest they go bankrupt; rather, it is a political war fought on another front—one that is more advantageous to the combatants. Compare Scott Altman, "Are Boycotts, Shunning, and Shaming Corrupt," 41 *Oxford J. Legal Stud.* 987 (2021)(discussing the Chick-fil-A and Domino's Pizza boycotts, which were motivated by opposition to the companies' support of conservative social causes). Chapter 5 will take up the subject of boycotts targeted at law firms representing large oil and gas companies for their role in exacerbating climate change.

Ames, above. The American rules of professional conduct for lawyers includes a curious rule stating that "[a] lawyer's representation of a client . . . does not constitute an endorsement of the client's political, economic, social or moral views or activities." ABA Model Rules of Professional Conduct, Rule 1.2(b). This rule states Rose's conclusion, that a lawyer should not be identified with her client's position. That may be right, but again, some argument is required to establish this principle.

28. Quoted in Ames, above.
29. Code of Conduct of the Bar of England and Wales, Rule 601 (2002); Charles W. Wolfram, *Modern Legal Ethics* (St. Paul, Minn.: West Publishing Co. 1986) § 10.2.2, at 572. See also John Flood, "Traditions, Symbols, and the Challenges of Researching the Legal Profession: The Case of the Cab Rank Rule and the Bar's Responses," *Int'l J. of the Legal Prof.* 29:3-32 (2022), pp. 5-6, for the nuance of the rules application only to *self-employed* barristers, which I did not previously notice.
30. Flood, pp. 12–13. As Flood notes, there is further sub-specialization, with known chambers of prosecution and defense-side criminal barristers, for example, who would never receive briefs from solicitors who are aware of the clients they typically represent. Flood, pp. 12, 13, 20–21.
31. Ames, above; see also the works of John Flood, cited above and below.
32. In three Australian states, New Zealand, and South Africa, the cab-rank rule applies to in-court advocates. Abbe Smith, "Defending the Unpopular Down-Under," 30 *Melb. U. L. Rev.* 495, 499–501 (2006) (citing Ysaiah Ross, *Ethics in Law: Lawyers' Responsibility and Accountability in Australia* (Chatswood, N.S.W.: Butterworths, 3d

ed. 2001), pp. 199–216). Canada does not have the cab-rank rule. In England and Wales, barristers are engaged ("instructed" or "briefed") not directly by clients but through solicitors retained by clients. Moreover, solicitors deal with barristers not directly but through the clerks employed by barristers or barristers' chambers. These clerks have well-developed techniques for ensuring that unwelcome engagements ("briefs") are avoided. John A. Flood, *Barristers' Clerks: The Law's Middlemen* (Manchester: Manchester University Press 1983). More recent research by John Flood confirms his earlier finding that the cab rank rule is routinely circumvented by barristers who are looking for better cases, with "better" meaning either more remunerative or higher profile. Flood, above, p. 11. It often appears to go unnoticed that the cab-rank rule, as a principle of law or a professional custom, is not self-justifying in moral terms. See Steven Vaughan, "The Unethical Environmental Lawyer," speech on the occasion of Professor Vaughan's inauguration at the Faculty of Laws, University College London, on October 13, 2022 ("I think [barristers] plead the 'cab rank' rule far too often as a blanket justification for the work they do.").

33. An example of the invocation of the cab-rank rule by an English barrister, combined with a persuasive moral justification for it, came out of the criticism of a constitutional barrister, Dinah Rose, for representing the government of the Cayman Islands in litigation over the Territory's statutory definition of marriage as being between a man and a woman. In a striking parallel with the Weinstein case, Dinah Rose was not only a highly accomplished barrister with a distinguished career as a civil rights advocate but was then serving as the President of Magdalen College, Oxford. The representation led to student complaints that it was incompatible with her role at the university because it would involve her in asserting an anti-LGBTQ position in defense of the position of the government of the Cayman Islands that it was not constitutionally prohibited from adopting the heteronormative statutory definition of marriage. Jonathan Ames, "University of Oxford Students' Fury Over Dinah Rose's Same-Sex Marriage Case," *The Times (London)* (Sept. 9, 2021). Some of the most vigorous criticism of Rose came from Edward Cameron, a retired judge on the South African Constitutional Court, the first openly gay member of that tribunal and a long-time activist for access to HIV/AIDS treatment. He contended that, as President of Magdalen College, Rose's actions "put a stain upon the college," undermined the college's mission of inclusivity, and sent a stigmatizing message to members of the Magdalen and Oxford communities. Edwin Cameron, "Statement by Edwin Cameron, Retired Justice, South African Constitutional Court: The President of Magdalen Prosecutes a Homophobic Case to Deny LGBTIQ Persons in the Cayman Islands Equal Rights" *OxHRH Blog* (Jan. 29 2021), available at https://ohrh.law.ox.ac.uk/statement-by-edwin-cameron-retired-justice-south-african-constitutional-court-the-president-of-magdalen-prosecutes-a-homophobic-case-to-deny-lgbtiq-persons-in-the-cayman-islands-equal-rights/ I am grateful to South African law professor Helen Kruuse for bringing this episode to my attention and for spirited conversation about it.

One of the participants in the debate, a senior counsel in South Africa, quite rightly observed, "Recourse to technical bar rules on the obligation to accept briefs serves only to disguise the real issue." Gilbert Marcus, "Why Dinah Rose QC Had an Obligation to Give up the Cayman Islands Brief: A Response to Lord Hendy QC," *OxHRH Blog* (Mar. 2021), available at https://ohrh.law.ox.ac.uk/why-dinah-rose-qc-had-an-obligation-to-give-up-the-cayman-islands-brief-a-response-to-lord-hendy-qc/. The issue was discussed in moral terms and, in my view, decisively concluded by Rose's statement that she was advocating for a political solution to the social conflict in the Cayman Islands over legalizing same-sex marriage, noting that the case was not about the justice of same-sex marriage but "whether the determination of that question should properly be decided by the courts or by the Cayman parliament." Ames, above. Rose he did not, however, provide the kind of justification the Harvard students appeared to be seeking from Ronald Sullivan, namely why this case appealed to her, given her other personal and professional values and commitments.

As I see it, this highly visible but short-lived public controversy played out exactly as it should. Although many lawyers cited the Principle of Nonaccountability, in the specifically British form of the cab-rank rule, many Oxford students and other members of the public were unpersuaded. Being a skilled advocate, Rose then shifted ground; she accepted the demand for accountability and sought to explain the role of lawyer to others, including others at Oxford University, in terms of the societal benefits of the rule of law. Perhaps not all critics were persuaded, but this strategy was at least respectful of the concerns of critics. The stronger version cab of the Principle of Nonaccountability, as exemplified by the cab-rank rule, has the contrary effect of shutting down critical scrutiny of the legal profession and its characteristic ethical norms. Rather than the uncomfortable air of mystification accompanying the strong Principle of Nonaccountability, better to provide a substantive defense based on the value of the rule of law and the activities of lawyers.

It is interesting to speculate about why the controversy at Magdalen College died down while at Harvard it only intensified. I don't think British universities are less politicized than their American counterparts, nor was there any lack of vigor in pressing the critical and supporting cases on both sides. My hypothesis is that Rose was more forthright in her acceptance of the demand for accountability. This is ironic given the salience of the cab-rank rule in public discourse about the English bar. It is also possible that the volume of criticism from a few students makes it appear that the criticism is more widely shared than it is. One post on a human rights and civil liberties blog said it was reported that Rose had the support of the college's elected student representatives. Conor Gearty, "The Case of Dinah Rose, Magdalen and the Bar" (Feb. 25, 2021), available at https://conorgearty.co.uk/2021/02/the-case-of-dinah-rose-magdalen-and-the-bar/ I have no way of independently verifying the claim that a vocal minority of students was driving much of the controversy, although it rings true for someone who has been around the higher education world for a couple of decades.

34. *The Speeches of the Hon. Thomas Erskine*, vol. 2, pp. 90–91 (James Ridgeway ed. 1813) (quoted in John Leubsdorf, *Man In His Original Dignity: Legal Ethics in France* (London: Routledge 2001), p. 19).
35. *Rondel v. Worsley*, [1969] 1 AC 191. The judgment in this case is of Baron James Reid, one of the best-known British judges of the 20th century.

36. Deborah L. Rhode, *In the Interests of Justice: Reforming the Legal Profession* (Oxford: Oxford University Press 2000), p. 54.
37. Matthew Yglesias, "The Raging Controversy Over Harvey Weinstein, Ronald Sullivan, and Harvard, Explained," *Vox* (May 17, 2019).
38. I owe this point to John Leubsdorf, whose said there is no evidence that unpopular clients in France have any difficulty finding counsel, notwithstanding the absence of a French counterpart to the cab-rank rule. He noted that the head of local bar associations can appoint an advocate where necessary, which may be a functional equivalent of the cab-rank rule. An interesting example of the appointment power of local bar organizations in Continental European systems was described to me by Dutch lawyer and University of Amsterdam law professor Jonathan Soeharno. Following Russia's invasion of Ukraine, a group of 20 law firms in the Netherlands signed the "Stand Firm!" declaration, pledging not to represent any Russian clients that did not denounce the invasion. After a law firm in Amsterdam withdrew from representing a Russian client while litigation was pending, the client asked the dean of the bar association in the district of The Hague to appoint counsel. Responding to the Russian client, however, the dean refused to appoint another lawyer, citing, among other factors, sanctions imposed on Russian entities by the European Union and "the oath taken by lawyers, stating that they should not deal with matters or represent interests that they find unjust." The Russian client complained to the Court of Appeal, acting in a professional disciplinary capacity. The court concluded that the EU sanctions do not apply to the provision of legal services and that the dean should appoint counsel notwithstanding the subscription of many Dutch law firms to the Stand Firm Statement. This brief summary is based on a decision of the Court of Discipline, ECLI:NL:TAHVD:2022:132—Court of Discipline—The Hague, 220199, available in Dutch at https://tuchtrecht.overheid.nl/ECLI_NL_TAHVD_2022_132. (I ran the text through Google translate and Soeharno made edits to the translation.) As Soeharno explained, where the court in 4.16 noted that the lawyers' oath would not apply "in a general sense" it was alluding to a very strict subjective test ("in gemoede niet gelove rechtvaardig") for an irreconcilable conflict between conscience and the duties of a lawyer. This has some parallels with the American legal principles that a lawyer may avoid a judicial appointment to represent a client only where the "the client or the cause is so repugnant to the lawyer as to be likely to impair the client lawyer relationship or the lawyer's ability to represent the client." ABA Model Rules, Rule 6.2(c). This is also a subjective test and it would be a fairly unusual occurrence for it to be satisfied. In this way, the Dutch and American legal standards are quite similar. While I make no claim to any expertise regarding the regulation of lawyers in civil law systems, discussions with Leubsdorf and Soeharno suggest that in practical terms the process of client selection by private lawyers and judicial appointment of counsel is fairly similar to practices in the United States.
39. Flood, p. 12.
40. Jelani Cobb, "Letter from Charleston: Inside the Trial of Dylann Roof," *New Yorker* (Feb. 6, 2017); Alan Blinder, "A Top Defender, Sidelined by the Accused in the Charleston Church Massacre," *N.Y. Times* (Dec. 13, 2016).

41. Guam Society of Obstetricians and Gynecologists v. Ada, 100 F.3d 691, 699 (9th Cir. 1996).
42. See, e.g., Richard A. Oppel, Jr. & Jugal Patel, "One Lawyer, 194 Felony Cases, and No Time," *N.Y. Times* (Jan. 31, 2019); Bryan Furst, *A Fair Fight Achieving Indigent Defense Resource Parity*, Brennan Center for Justice Report (Sept. 9, 2019), available at https://www.brennancenter.org/our-work/research-reports/fair-fight. Public defenders have sometimes asserted, generally unsuccessfully, that underfunding and overwork amounts to an interference with their clients' right to counsel under the Sixth Amendment. See, e.g., *Public Defender, Eleventh Judicial Circuit of Florida v. State*, 115 So.3d 261 (Fla. 2013).
43. Their convictions were overturned in a landmark Supreme Court case, *Powell v. Alabama*, 287 U.S. 45 (1932). For an excellent history of the proceedings, see James Goodman, *Stories of Scottsboro* (New York: Pantheon Books 1994). I am grateful to Ekow Yankah for challenging me with this counterexample to my glib statement that even the most unpopular clients have no difficulty obtaining counsel.
44. *Powell*, 287 U.S. at 53–56.
45. *Powell*, 287 U.S. at 68–69.
46. Charles W. Wolfram, *Modern Legal Ethics* (St. Paul, Minn.: West Publishing), § 10.2, at 576; Daniel H. Pollitt, "Counsel for the Unpopular Cause: The Hazard of Being Undone" (1964) 43 *N.C. L. Rev.* 9. Legal historian Jerold Auerbach observed that the unwillingness of white Southern lawyers to represent advocates of racial equality, along with the lack of Black southern lawyers, "promoted another invasion of carpetbaggers across the Mason-Dixon line: Northern lawyers committed to the objectives of the civil rights movement." Jerold S. Auerbach, *Unequal Justice: Lawyers and Social Change in America* (Oxford: Oxford University Press 1976), pp. 264–65.
47. Jerold S. Auerbach, *Unequal Justice: Lawyers and Social Change in America* (Oxford: Oxford University Press 1976), p. 266. For a spirited critique of the stance of neutrality by many law professors toward what should be clearly understood as egregious breaches of standards of professional conduct by lawyers enabling Trump's "Big Lie" about the 2020 presidential election, see Cynthia Godsoe, Abbe Smith, & Ellen Yaroshefsky, "Can You Be a Legal Ethics Scholar and Have Guts?," 35 *Geo. J. Legal Ethics* 429 (2022). They argue that neutrality is itself a political choice, one which privileges the status quo beneath a veneer of objectivity (p. 455).
48. Auerbach, p. 254 (observing, of John W. Davis, that "his Cold War silence strongly suggests a double standard which permitted him to believe that power was repressive, and Liberty Leagues were necessary, only when New Dealers regulated corporations").
49. See, e.g., Richard M. Fried, *Nightmare in Red: The McCarthy Era in Perspective* (Oxford: Oxford University Press 1991); Victor Navasky, *Naming Names* (New York: Viking 1980); David Caute, *The Great Fear: The Anti-Communist Purge Under Truman and Eisenhower* (New York: Simon & Schuster 1978).
50. Fried, pp. 171–73.
51. In a long series of cases—see *Law Students Civil Rights Research Council, Inc. v. Wadmond*, 401 U.S. 154 (1971); *In re Stolar*, 401 U.S. 23 (1971); *Baird v. State Bar of*

Arizona, 401 U.S. 1 (1971); *In re Anastaplo*, 366 U.S. 82 (1961); *Schware v. Board of Bar Examiners of New Mexico*, 353 U.S. 232 (1957); *Konigsberg v. State Bar of California*, 353 U.S. 252 (1957). The Court did protect applicants from being compelled to disclose membership in subversive organizations but upheld the right of state character and fitness committees to ask whether the applicant belonged to an organization advocating the overthrow of the U.S. government by force. *See Wadmond*, 401 U.S. at 164–66; *Konigsberg*, 366 U.S. at 56; *Anastaplo*, 366 U.S. at 96–97.

52. Jerold S. Auerbach, *Unequal Justice: Lawyers and Social Change in America* (Oxford: Oxford University Press 1976), pp. 198–99, 234–36.
53. Fried, pp. 79–80, 87.
54. Fried, pp. 174–76.
55. Ted Morgan, *Reds: McCarthyism in Twentieth-Century America* (New York: Random House 2003); Arthur J. Sabin, *In Calmer Times: The Supreme Court and Red Monday* (Philadelphia: University of Pennsylvania Press 1999); Michal R. Belknap, *Cold War Political Justice: the Smith Act, the Communist Party, and American Civil Liberties* (Westport, Conn.: Greenwood Press, 1977).
56. See, e.g., Erica Bose, "Three Brave Men: An Examination of Three Attorneys Who Represented the Hollywood Nineteen in the House Un-American Activities Committee Hearings in 1947 and the Consequences They Faced," 6 *UCLA Enter. L. Rev.* 621 (1999).
57. Auerbach, pp. 240–49; Caute, pp. 97–99.
58. Caute, pp. 187–88; Michal R. Belknap, "Foley Square Trial," in Michal R. Belknap, ed., *American Political Trials* (Westport, Conn.: Greenwood Publishing Co. 1994).
59. Caute, pp. 192, 196–97.
60. For contempt, see *U.S. v. Sacher*, 182 F.2d 416 (2d Cir. 1950), *aff'd*, 343 U.S. 1 (1952); for the appeals from disbarment, see *Association of the Bar of the City of New York v. Sacher*, 206 F.2d 358 (2d Cir. 1953), *aff'd*, 347 U.S. 388 (1954). The Supreme Court initially disbarred one of the lawyers but subsequently reversed the disbarment after a rules change that, not coincidentally, occurred as anti-Red hysteria was beginning to abate. See *In re Disbarment of Isserman*, 345 U.S. 286 (1953), *rev'd*, 348 U.S. 1 (1954).
61. Auerbach, pp. 248–49.
62. Auerbach, p. 246.
63. Professional historians disparage "law-office history," written for the purpose of advocacy and playing free and loose with evidentiary standards of the discipline. Alfred H. Kelly, "Clio and the Court: An Illicit Love Affair," 1965 *Sup. Ct. Rev.* 119, 122 n.13. Justice Kagan, dissenting in *Brown v. Davenport*, 596 U.S. ___ (2022), criticized the majority's reliance on "law chambers history" in its effort to recharacterize the scope of the federal habeas corpus remedy. She freely admits that she is no historian either but contrasts the indeterminate materials of history with the standards that lawyers should pay attention to when deciding cases: "Although it is more entertaining to play amateur historian, it is past time to put in some work on the technical issue before us: what standard(s) a habeas court should use to decide whether a state trial court's constitutional error was harmless."

64. Michael Ariens, "The Rise and Fall of Social Trustee Professionalism," *J. Prof. Law.* 49 (2016).
65. Ariens, above; Auerbach, pp. 238–39. The Committee on Individual Rights was eventually taken over by southerners who sought to link the civil rights movement with Communism.
66. *U.S. v. Dennis*, 183 F.2d 201, 212 (2d Cir. 1950). In reality the CPUSA was never anything more than "a flea on the dog's back," with a miniscule number of members widely dispersed geographically throughout the country and lacking the organization and discipline necessary to engage in effective strikes or industrial sabotage, let alone a revolution of the proletariat. Caute, pp. 185–86. In a much-cited opinion on libel law, Judge Hand wrote that being called a "fellow traveler" is just as likely injurious to the plaintiff's reputation as being alleged to be a member of the Communist Party, because "it is not uncommon for [those who think ill of Communists] to feel less concern at avowed propaganda than at what they regard as the insidious spread of the dreaded doctrines by those who only dally and coquette with them, and have not the courage openly to proclaim themselves." *Grant v. Reader's Digest Ass'n*, 151 F.2d 733, 735 (2d Cir. 1945).
67. I am grateful to Tim Dare for raising this possibility.
68. Jess Bravin, "Winning Lawyers in Supreme Court Gun Case Leave Firm," *Wall St. J.* (June 23, 2022); Anna Sanders, "Clement Exits Kirkland After Firm Drops Gun Cases," *Law360* (June 23, 2022); Paul Clement & Erin Murphy, "The Law Firm That Got Tired of Winning," *Wall St. J.* (June 23, 2022). Interestingly, Clement had previously left another law firm, King & Spalding, when it withdrew from the representation of an unpopular client. The firm had taken as a client the Republican majority in the House of Representatives after the Obama administration defined to defend the constitutionality of the Defense of Marriage Act, which defined marriage as being between a man and a woman. The Human Rights Campaign, an LGBTQ advocacy organization, criticized the firm for arguing in favor of discrimination; it contended that the representation "brought a shameful stain" on the reputation of the firm. Press Release, "HRC to Law Firm King & Spalding: Defense of Discriminatory DOMA Law is 'Shameful'" (Apr. 18, 2011), available at https://www.hrc.org/press-releases/hrc-to-law-firm-king-amp-spalding-defense-of-discriminatory-doma-law-is-quo. The organization contacted firm clients and used social media in an attempt to pressure the firm to drop the House as a client. See Editorial, "King & Spalding and HRC Do a Disservice to American Values," *Wash. Post* (Apr. 26, 2011). The campaign worked. The firm withdrew from the representation but Clement left the firm in protest. John Gibeaut, "Withdrawing from Controversial Case Was Awkward for King & Spalding, But That's About All," *ABA Journal* (July 1, 2011).
69. Jess Bravin, "Winning Lawyers in Supreme Court Gun Case Leave Firm," *Wall St. J.* (June 23, 2022). Senate Majority Leader Mitch McConnell subsequently sent a letter to the chief judges of the federal courts of appeal, urging that they inquire of law firms whether their decisions regarding representation of clients are influenced by the political views of firm management or other clients. James Arkin, "GOP Sens. Quiz Circuit Chiefs Over Kirkland Gun Cases Shift," *Law360* (Aug. 18, 2022). Needless to

say, Congress has no power to demand that the federal judiciary exercise its supervisory power over lawyers in any particular way.
70. Clement & Murphy, above. This complaint was later echoed in an editorial by legal commentator David Lat—see "Big Law's Cancel Culture," *Boston Globe* (Jan. 30, 2023).
71. Clement & Murphy, above.
72. An inversion of the claim in C. Wright Mills, *The Power Elite* (Oxford: Oxford University Press 1956), that large corporations, the federal government, and the national security apparatus comprised a unified, conservative center of power.
73. Contrary to the view of legal commentator David Lat, that the so-called BigLaw sector of the legal services industry exhibits ideological uniformity—see David Lat, "Big Law's Cancel Culture," *Boston Globe* (Jan. 30, 2023)—some observers see the sector as differentiated into a few conservative-leaning and progressive-leaning firms, with most firms attempting to remain politically neutral. See, e.g., David Enrich, *Servants of the Damned: Giant Law Firms, Donald Trump and the Corruption of Justice* (New York: HarperCollins 2022) (discussing history of Jones Day's embrace of conservative political causes and the tight revolving-door relationship between partnerships in the firm and positions as high-ranking government lawyers in the Trump administration). The Seattle-based firm Perkins Coie, by contrast, has long been regarded as aligned with Democratic Party politics. See Justin Wise, "Perkins Coie Dials Back Politics, Doubles Down on Corporate Work," *Bloomberg Law* (Nov. 2, 2022). A different measure of political affiliation looks at percentage of contributions by firm lawyers to Democratic or Republican affiliated candidates or organizations. Derek T. Muller, "Ranking the Most Liberal and Conservative Law Firms Among the Top 140, 2021 Edition," *Excess of Democracy* (Nov. 8, 2021), available at https://excessofdemocracy.com/blog/2021/11/ranking-the-most-liberal-and-conservative-law-firms-among-the-top-140-2021-edition. The only real ideological uniformity disclosed by this study is that many firms doing a significant amount of plaintiffs' side class-action representation, such as Grant & Eisenhoffer, Hausfeld, Lieff Cabraser, and Cohen Milstein, are 100% in the Democratic column. Kirkland is on the more conservative end of that spectrum—interestingly, considerably more conservative than Jones Day when ranked by percentage of donations to partisan political groups—but it would be a caricature to call it either a "woke" firm or a hard-right firm based on the measure of political donations.

This book was in the copyediting process at the time of the October 7, 2023, attack by Hamas that killed over 1,200 Israeli citizens. A law student at NYU wrote in a message to a student group that Israel bore full responsibility for the massacre and that a "regime of state-sanctioned violence created the conditions that made resistance necessary." The student's job offer at the law firm of Winston & Strawn was withdrawn soon thereafter, an unusual example of literal cancelation as the result of expressing controversial views. Vimal Patel & Anemona Hartocollis, "N.Y.U. Law Student Sends Anti-Israel Message and Loses a Job Offer," *N.Y. Times* (Oct. 11, 2023). Another law firm, Davis Polk & Wardwell, revoked the job offers of three law students who had signed letters by student organizations blaming Israel for the attack, but the firm later said it was investigating whether the students had authorized their signatures on the letters. Maureen Farrell, "A Prestigious Law Firm Rescinded Job Offers for Columbia and Harvard Students, but It May Reverse Itself," *N.Y. Times* (Oct. 17, 2023). Over 100 law firm subsequently signed a letter to law school deans noting "reports of anti-Semitic harassment, vandalism and assaults on college campuses, including rallies calling for the death of Jews and the elimination of the State of Israel." The signatories pointedly reminded the deans that they employed many graduates of their schools and said they "trust[ed] you will take the same unequivocal stance against such activities as we do . . . ." Sam Skolnik, "Wake Up Call: More than 100 Firms Sign on to Antisemitism Letter," *Bloomberg Law* (Nov. 6, 2023).

74. I realize many readers will react to that sentence by saying "Yes, it's *this* society!" But I also think readers will differ on what they use to fill the open variables of the power elite and the unpopular minority. Left-leaning readers will probably imagine poor people, people of color, and LGBTQ people as the excluded group, with Congress (particularly the rural-dominated Senate), large corporations, and special interest groups like the U.S. Chamber of Commerce, and white evangelical Christians as the dominant group. Some conservative readers, on the other hand, may say "Exactly—it's the secular, progressive, 'woke' elite that runs everything and us rural, patriotic, God-fearing real Americans are struggling to take back our country." The fact that such an acrimonious debate is readily imaginable suggests, to me at least, that the fears of one group dominating the other are largely overblown, even if sincerely felt.

75. This is the concern underlying one of the most influential papers in the early theoretical legal ethics literature. See Stephen L. Pepper, "The Lawyer's Amoral Ethical Role: A Defense, a Problem, and Some Possibilities," 1986 *Am. B. Found. Res. J.* 613. Pepper warns that if lawyers are accountable for the clients they represent, they may turn away unpopular clients and the result would be an "oligarchy of lawyers." In response, David Luban argues that there is no such oligarchy, because by definition an oligarchy requires concerted action. David Luban, "The Lysistratian Prerogative: A Response to Stephen Pepper," 1986 *Am. B. Found. Res. J.* 637, p. 641. Implicit in this response is that there is no *tacit* oligarchy either, because lawyers disagree over the contested value propositions that underlie "canceling" unpopular clients; that is, there is no consensus on who the unpopular clients are—firearms manufacturers or Black Lives Matter protesters.

76. Jess Krochtengel, "Clement Decries BigLaw as 'Too Woke,' Too Money-Hungry," *Law360* (Nov. 13, 2022).

77. In this I am very much influenced by Jeremy Waldron's and David Luban's sympathetic reading of Lon Fuller's invocation of the inner morality of law. See Jeremy Waldron, "The Concept and the Rule of Law," 43 *Ga. L. Rev.* 1 (2008); David Luban, "Natural Law and Professional Ethics: A Reading of Fuller," in *Legal Ethics and Human Dignity* (Cambridge: Cambridge University Press 2007), pp. 99–130.

78. See, e.g., Scott Horton, "The Worst of the Worst?", *Harper's* (Oct. 2, 2009).

79. Some controversial clients may have difficulty attracting counsel because they are self-destructive chaos agents, like Alex Jones, or notorious for stiffing people who work for them, like Donald Trump. For Trump's history, see Max J. Rosenthal, "The

Trump Files: Trump's Long History of Getting Sued by His Own Lawyers," *Mother Jones* (Aug. 18, 2020); Steve Reilly, Hundreds Allege Donald Trump Doesn't Pay His Bills," *USA Today* (June 9, 2016). In one particularly amusing anecdote, a lawyer who had represented Trump during his career as a real estate developer visited him at Trump Tower to demand payment of $2 million he was owed. After making "some apologetic noises," Trump said he would not pay the lawyer's bill, but instead offered him a deed to a horse allegedly worth $5 million. "This isn't the 1800's," the lawyer replied. "You can't pay me with a horse." David Enrich, *Servants of the Damned: Giant Law Firms, Donald Trump and the Corruption of Justice* (New York: HarperCollins 2022), pp. 218–19. Trump reportedly had to shell out a $3 million retainer to secure the services of Christopher Kise, an experienced appellate litigator, in connection with the search of his Mar-A-Lago residence. Maggie Haberman, "Trump Hires Former Florida Solicitor General as Lawyer in Documents Case," *N.Y. Times* (Aug. 30, 2022); Betsy Woodruff Swan, "Trump's Save America Paid $3 Million to Cover Top Lawyer's Legal Work," *Politico* (Sept. 15, 2022).

Trump also, famously, not only refuses to listen to sensible legal advice but does things that actively undermine the legal strategy that any competent lawyer would recommend. Bradley Moss, a prominent criminal defense and national-security lawyer, said of Trump that he is "the worst type of client," because he does not listen to his lawyers. *Quoted in* Carolina Bolado, "Trump Attys In Hot Seat After New Revelations In DOJ Filing," *Law360* (Aug. 31, 2022). *New York Times* journalist Maggie Haberman, who has followed Trump for many years, stated in a television appearance that "it takes a huge effort to get him to do so by his lawyers always. This is an ongoing story we've been watching—frankly not just since he became president, but well before, going back to when he was advised by Roy Cohn many decades ago." Quoted in Mary Papenfuss, "Trump Having Hard Time Finding Lawyers Because They Want To Be Paid: Journalist," *Huffington Post* (Aug. 21, 2022). Trump claimed to have returned the documents in response to a subpoena and to have provided "complete cooperation" to the FBI; one of his lawyers also signed a statement attesting that all responsive documents had been returned after a diligent search. Charlie Savage & Maggie Haberman, "Trump's Lawyers May Become Witnesses or Targets in Documents Investigation," *N.Y. Times* (Aug. 31, 2022). Later, however, after the government released a picture of classified documents spread out on the floor of his mansion, Trump explained that the documents had been neatly stored in cartons and dropped by the FBI. Glenn Thrush & Adam Goldman, "How the Picture of Top Secret Folders at Mar-a-Lago Came About," *N.Y. Times* (Aug. 31, 2022). Not only is this no defense to the charge of possessing sensitive national security information, but the statement potentially throws his lawyers under the bus. Subsequent reporting revealed that Trump proposed returning the documents sought by the FBI in exchange for an agreement by the National Archives to produce documents in its custody that Trump believed would support his claim of FBI wrongdoing in connection with its probe of the 2016 election. Maggie Haberman & Michael S. Schmidt, "How Trump Deflected Demands for Documents, Enmeshing Aides," *N.Y. Times* (Oct. 8, 2022). Needless to say, no sensible lawyer would have approved of this strategy.

For his part, Jones made his lawyers' jobs much more difficult, in defense of defamation lawsuits brought by families of school shooting victims, by doing things like alleging that judges presiding over lawsuits against him are "involved in pedophilia and human trafficking" and posting pictures on his website of the presiding judge with laser beams coming out of her eyes. Elizabeth Williamson, "Alex Jones, Under Questioning, Is Confronted With Evidence of Deception," *N.Y. Times* (Aug. 2, 2022); Cara Salvatore, "Combative Jones Mostly Denies Harm In Newtown Testimony," *Law360* (Sept. 22, 2022). During a trial in Connecticut, for example, Jones said in his Infowars broadcast that the proceeding was a political show trial, aimed at silencing him, and later said the trial was "rigged," "staged," and "synthetic as hell." Cara Salvatore, "Jones Calls Sandy Hook Trial 'Synthetic' in Final Evidence," *Law360* (Oct. 5, 2022). Statements like this run contrary to his trial testimony, for example his admission in a Texas civil lawsuit that he now believes the Sandy Hook shooting was "100% real." Janet Miranda, "InfoWars' Alex Jones Admits Sandy Hook Massacre Was 'Real,'" *Bloomberg Law* (Aug. 3, 2022); Associated Press, "Alex Jones Concedes That the Sandy Hook Attack was '100% Real,'" *NPR* (Aug. 3, 2022), available at https://www.npr.org/2022/08/03/1115414563/alex-jones-sandy-hook-case.

Although plenty of people have moral objections to Jones and Trump, a lawyer's refusal to represent either one of them is not necessarily an instance of ideologically motivated cancelation. Lawyers tend to like high-profile clients and challenging cases, even if the clients are socially vilified. Many officials in the Trump administration, including Stephen Miller, the principal architect of the family-separation policy, and pugnacious international trade advisor Peter Navarro, have managed to retain highly qualified defense counsel. That is true even though some of these officials, including Miller, were intimately involved with some of the most morally troubling conduct of the administration. The comparison between these former government officials, on the one hand, and Donald Trump and Alex Jones on the other, suggests that lawyers do not tend to avoid representing bad *people*, but are keenly interested in not being stuck with a bad *client*. Jean Guerrero, *Hatemonger: Stephen Miller, Donald Trump, and the White Nationalist Agenda* (New York: HarperCollins 2020); Betsy Woodruff Swan, Nicholas Wu, & Kyle Cheney, "All the Former President's Lawyers (That We Know Of)," *Politico* (Sept. 7, 2022).

80. Waldron, above; Luban, above.
81. John Rawls, "Justice as Fairness: Political Not Metaphysical," 14 *Phil. & Pub. Aff.* 223 (1985).
82. Tim Dare's marginal comment in the manuscript: "Great case – can't quite figure out what Brad thinks about it."
83. Written on the day the headline of the *Washington Post* was "Nashville School Shooter Who Killed 6 Was Heavily Armed, Left 'Manifesto'" (story by Kim Mueller, Brittany Shammas, Ben Brasch, and Holly Bailey, March 27, 2023).
84. Todd C. Frankel, Shawn Boburg, Josh Dawsey, Ashley Parker, & Alex Horton, "The Gun That Divides a Nation," *Wash. Post* (Mar. 27, 2023)(quoting Grover Norquist, who is not just an NRA board member but a highly visible anti-tax activist).

4
Philosophical Perspectives: Blame, the Meaning of Actions, and the Ethics of Blame

Blameworthiness vs. wrongness

We now come to the heart of the philosophical argument of the book. Chapter 2 introduced Peter Strawson's famous argument that if we attend to what is really going on in moral life, including the prevalence of moral emotions, we will see that practices of holding others responsible are central to morality. For Strawson, the susceptibility to feeling reactive attitudes like resentment and indignation toward people who fail to manifest concern for others is an essential component of human relationships. One of the practices by which we hold others accountable is blame. Blame is part of the "complicated web of attitudes and feelings which form an essential part of the moral life as we know it."[1] One of the most prominent moral philosophers working today, T.M. Scanlon, has recently provided a powerful theory of blame founded in the nature of human relationships. Although I will not follow Scanlon's approach in all respects, I do think understanding blame roughly in the terms he discusses will help us make progress with the questions that are the concerns of this book, pertaining to the accountability and blameworthiness, within a political community, of professionals whose role requires them to perform certain essential functions.

Understanding Scanlon's approach to blame begins with two traditional positions against which his own views are set.[2] One the one hand, blame could be a kind of accounting or assessment of wrongdoing. Scanlon sees this as the "pointless assignment of moral grades,"[3] having no meaningful connection to the social practices that constitute our relationships with others. We care about blameworthiness for a reason, presumably related to the terms of our social engagements with others. The occasions on which we blame others have much to do with the relationships we have with the objects of blame. Blame is therefore more than a process of toting up rights and wrongs but functions to sustain relationships in a moral community. Alternatively, blame could be employed as a sanction in an attempt to bring about better behavior. Scanlon sees blame less about sanctioning wrongdoing and more about sustaining the expectations, intentions, and attitudes that constitute interpersonal relationships.[4] On Scanlon's account, someone is blameworthy when their action reveals something about that person's attitudes toward others, and those attitudes impair the relationship that others can have with them.[5] Blame consists in a revision of the relationships that others have with the target of blame.[*]

The most distinctive feature of this approach to blame is its separation from permissibility. "[W]rongness and blame can come apart," Scanlon says.[6] The *permissibility* of an action—that is to say, whether it is right or wrong, or whether it may be done, consistent with the requirements of morality—depends on the principles that could be invoked to justify it, and whether those principles could not be reasonably rejected by those who are affected by the action. Blame, by contrast, follows from the *meaning* of the action.[7] Meaning depends on the reasons and attitudes that are revealed by the action and which underlie the action and their significance for others. When someone acts in a way that reveals attitudes inconsistent with the norms governing the relationship we have with that person, blame involves an adjustment of our own attitudes toward them.[8] Blame takes the form of a judgment of blameworthiness along with a modification to the terms of the relationship with the other person, in a way that is appropriate to the impairment of the relationship. This two-step process is important, because it shows there may be an ethics of blame—that is, principles that bear on when and in what way it is appropriate to modify one's attitudes toward someone having been judged blameworthy, on an assessment of the meaning of that person's actions.

Scanlon offers a now much-discussed hypothetical of learning that a friend ("Joe") had been bad-mouthing him at a party. What makes Joe's behavior

---

[*] That is Scanlon's approach to blame. In many of the case studies considered in this book, blaming takes the form not only of revising one's relationship with the target of blame but also of calling out, shaming, seeking to influence others to revise their opinion of the target, and other behaviors that do not fit neatly within Scanlon's model of revising relationships. My aim here is not to defend Scanlon's specific view of blame but to use it as an illustration of how reactive attitudes can be expressed in concrete ways in response to an assessment of the intentions, motivating reasons, or attitudes of another. My way of thinking about blame may be closer to Susan Wolf's than Scanlon's. For a nonspecialist reader, however, this distinction is not important.

blameworthy is not just that his actions were wrong, but that they reveal a certain amount of indifference or even cruelty toward someone he claimed to care about. There are certain expectations that constitute a friendship: You will be there for a friend if they need a hand with some project, listen to them talk about their relationship troubles, feel hopeful when they apply for a new job, stick up for them when others bad-mouth them, and so on. Blame follows from actions that reveal attitudes inconsistent with those expectations. Making fun of someone who thought of Joe as a friend behind their back reveals something about the attitudes Joe has toward that person. The upshot of Joe's blameworthy conduct would be a modification of the relationship between the two former friends, such as no longer sharing confidences with Joe, not spending as much time with him, not having his back when other people criticize him, or possibly ending the relationship altogether.[9] In the case of a minor impairment, the other party's reaction of blame may be nothing more serious than a mild scolding or gentle mocking. Joe, on the other hand, may have irreparably damaged the relationship, or at least made it very difficult to restore the expectations that had previously constituted it. In that case blame may not only serve as a modification to the relationship between the former friends but also has a communicative role, indicating to Joe and others that has displayed attitudes inconsistent with the friendship.[10] This communication may call for an acknowledgment or response, such as an apology or a more demanding act of atonement by Joe, in which case the relationship may be repaired.

Scanlon's analysis considers Joe's *attitudes*, but our judgments may also touch on evaluations of the *character* of people who engage in blameworthy actions (although Scanlon himself is careful to distinguish blame from assessment of the character of others).[11] One way of looking at a blameworthy action (although not Scanlon's own view) is that it is one that displays ill will or some character flaw on the part of the actor.[12] Joe's friend would presumably want to know more about *why* Joe did what he did at the party. Some people really do have "hardened hearts and vicious characters,"[13] and we want to know who those people are. Maya Angelou famously told Oprah Winfrey, "When people show you who they are, believe them."[14] Maybe Joe did reveal his true character at the party. On the other hand, he may have been drunk and saying a lot of outrageous things, and maybe his excessive drinking at the party is in turn related to some personal difficulty he is going through. We sometimes say an action is "out of character" for someone, and maybe this is such a case. Maybe Joe is kind of a loudmouth and a trash-talker, and while that can occasionally be difficult, it is also one of the things that makes Joe fun to be around. The inference from someone's actions to their true character can be complicated, and it is possible that one may misunderstand or misinterpret the meaning of another's actions.[15]

For his part, Scanlon discusses blameworthiness not in terms of character but rather the norms constituting the relationship that is impaired by the action, what it reveals about the attitudes of the actor, and the significance of those attitudes for the relationship.[16] While I mostly agree with this approach, one difficulty with it is that not all relationships are as "thick," as philosophers say, as friendships. Thick relationships are those in which certain standards are baked into the description of the relationship.[17] Being a friend *means* having certain attitudes toward another, such as wanting things to go well for them, and also certain dispositions, such as taking their side when they are criticized, and also taking certain actions, like helping a friend with a tedious job like moving or painting a room.[18] Because friendships are thick relationships, it is relatively easy to spot when someone's attitudes are impaired in ways that are significant for the ongoing success of the relationship. Familial relationships are thick in a similar way. There are clear expectations for what attitudes are appropriate for parents and children, siblings, or even more distant relations (and this may vary to some extent by culture) to have with respect to each other. But something like the "moral relationship," which calls for attitudes of concern for all others insofar as they are rational beings,[19] is a much thinner relationship. Scanlon writes:

> A judgment of blameworthiness is one that anyone can make, however distant he or she may be from the relevant agent and action. But the content of *blame* depends on the significance, for the person doing the blaming, of the agent and of what he has done.[20]

In a thin relationship, where someone can be described only as a fellow member of the moral community simply because they are a rational being, there is likely to be little significance to an action, however blameworthy, for that relationship. Yet we observe others engaging in angry blaming behavior with respect to complete strangers. Perhaps this shows that blame does not necessarily follow only from actions that are significant within a particular relationship. The phenomenon of blaming lawyers as if their actions had significance for everyone in the political community shows that Scanlon may be tying blame too tightly to thick relationships.

In any event, returning to the previous chapter, the outpouring of blame from Harvard students directed at Ronald Sullivan for his representation of Harvey Weinstein fit Scanlon's explanation to a T. The students asserted that Sullivan was blameworthy because his representation of Weinstein showed something about him that indicated an impairment of his relationship with the students for whom he was responsible as a residential advisor. The students were in a position with respect to Sullivan that explained why his attitudes were significant to them. Thus, Sullivan was not only blameworthy but an appropriate target for blaming behavior, such as critical columns in the student newspaper and demands for his removal as house dean, and blame in Scanlon's sense of revising the relationship students had with Sullivan. For example, following the decision to represent Weinstein, students may adjust the terms of their relationship by not coming to Sullivan with issues about gender equality or sexual misconduct.

What do you mean by that?

It is still open to Sullivan and his defenders to grant the distinction between permissibility and blameworthiness but to contend that the students are mistaken in some way in blaming him. Perhaps they lack all the facts needed to make a judgment about Sullivan's blameworthiness. Or perhaps they have erred in inferring from the representation of Weinstein to attitudes that impair Sullivan's role as a mentor and counselor to students. Sullivan's reasons, if known, may indicate that he has attitudes, intentions, and expectations that do not in any way impair the relationship he has with the residents of the house in which he serves as dean, or of any members of the Harvard community. He could have been motivated entirely by concerns that Weinstein was not being treated fairly by the legal system, as was the case for other clients he had represented without controversy. Reasonable people can disagree about judgments of blameworthiness. Many of the episodes that get discussed in the never-ending conversation about "cancel culture" involve contestable inferences from the action to attitudes that impair relationships with others. A prominent political journalist retweets a dumb, sexist joke.[21] Does this reveal something about the journalist's attitudes toward others that impairs the relationships that others can have with him? Does it show that the journalist holds sexist attitudes that would impair his ability to work with women at his newspaper? Would failing to take action indicate that the newspaper does not value women journalists?²² These are questions that invite intense disagreement, as well as views that may depend to some extent on the way one's views are affected by social structures—women, for example, may be less patient with the explanation that the tweet showed merely poor judgment, not sexism.²³

The meaning of many actions, particularly those that provoke strong reactive attitudes, will themselves be subject to debate. The contest will likely take place on very tricky evaluative terrain, where conflicting values, competing perspectives, and factual uncertainty come together. The same action may also be compatible with a range of meanings. Consider an example from the ethics of boycotting: The protests against the popular fast food chain Chick-fil-A due to comments made by the company's president in opposition to same-sex marriage and donations by the company's foundations to groups organizing against the legalization of same-sex marriage.²⁴ It seems obvious that there is a difference between going to Chick-fil-A because its chicken sandwich is delicious and eating there as a kind of counter-protest, with the aim of showing support for conservative causes. An intermediate case might be opting for Chick-fil-A over Popeye's (which offers an arguably even more delicious chicken sandwich) at the height of protests over the opening of a new store, when purchasing decisions are under heightened scrutiny. In that case, a consumer who perhaps had no subjective intention to send a message may nonetheless be subject to blame for appearing to convey approval of the company's political objectives. Is this fair? Perhaps not, but the social attribution of meaning inevitably takes place against a background of uncertainty and conflicting evidence.

Take another example, this time from the public criticism of lawyers. A large law firm called Gibson Dunn & Crutcher has been the target of blame from activists who object to its representation of fossil fuel companies.† Relatedly, some critics have discerned a meaningful pattern in the firm's work—a negative attitude toward the legal rights of Indigenous people. The firm had a high-profile role in defending against claims of environmental contamination by Texaco Petroleum in a remote area of the Amazon rainforest. The area is the home of the Huaorani people as well as an extraordinary diversity of plant and animal species.²⁵ On behalf of Texaco and its corporate successor Chevron, the firm conducted a "best defense is a

---

† The next chapter will consider efforts by some climate activists to persuade law students not to go to work for Gibson Dunn.

strong offense" strategy, seeking to establish that the litigation in Ecuador was tainted by serious fraud committed at the direction of the U.S.-based lawyer for the plaintiffs, Steven Donziger. While some proceedings were still pending related to the Ecuador litigation, Gibson Dunn took on a pro bono (that is, for no fee) representation challenging the constitutionality of a statute called the Indian Child Welfare Act.[26] The statute was adopted in 1978 to halt the separation of Native American children from their families and communities and their forced assimilation into non-Native communities.[27] The firm chose to accept the representation and is doing it for free, so critics of the firm assume this must mean it wanted to assist the conservative project of destabilizing tribal sovereignty.[28]

Connecting the constitutional attack on the Indian Child Welfare Act with the defense of Chevron against claims for environmental damage in Ecuador appears, at least to some activists and progressive law students, to clarify the firm's attitudes, which constitute the meaning or significance of the representation:[29] The firm wants to help its clients in the oil and gas industry, many of whom would benefit from weakening sovereignty over Native lands. This reveals at least an attitude of indifference toward the rights of Indigenous people. Sometimes this criticism is expressed more intemperately, as a claim that the firm is expressing racial hostility or even "advocating cultural genocide."[30] An important aspect of the relational account of morality that I am defending here is that relationships imply not only norms of how we should act with respect to others, but how we should feel about our actions.[31] The firm's critics may be inflamed by what they perceive as an absence of any sense of reluctance or regret about the impact of firm lawyers' advocacy on the interests of marginalized communities.‡ Responding to this criticism, the lead partner representing the plaintiffs in the constitutional litigation contends that the firm is interested only in preserving the unity of the adoptive family and the well-being of the children.[32] He may be right about this, and his explanation might be a sufficient response to critics who want to know something about the attitudes of firm lawyers. Perhaps critics were being unfair and motivated by their own ideological beliefs.[33] On the other hand, there is a risk that the partner's explanation will come off as insincere and self-serving, given the firm's pattern of representing clients with interests that frequently conflict with the interests of Indigenous communities.

---

‡ Chapter 8 will consider the phenomenon of experiencing qualms, reluctance, or regret as a result of one's actions.

In no way am I contending that there is only one meaning that can be ascribed to the decision by lawyers at Gibson Dunn to seek to invalidate the Indian Child Welfare Act in connection with the representation of a client. Just as in the case from Chapter 3 involving the defense of Harvey Weinstein, the lawyers may have had a variety of motivations. The partner who originated the case, and firm management, may have many different attitudes and motivations with respect to the representation. It could be commitment to conservative political causes, a policy-based disagreement with the statute, or simply the desire to work on a high-profile constitutional case before the Supreme Court. Meaning is not simply "read off" the facts of a situation; it is an interpretation of the actions of others, influenced by what others say and what they do. As such, it is contestable. As observers we do not have all of the facts about the intentions and attitudes of the lawyers but impute them based on the facts that are known. The firm may insist that its representation can mean only one thing, such as commitment to the rule of law, while its critics can doubt the sincerity of that position. This is all to the good. Debates about the meaning of a law firm's representation of a particular client are an important part of broader public debates about justice and the legal system. If you are looking for clarity, however, it will not be found in the interpretation of the attitudes of others.[34]

The ethics of blaming

The case for representing Harvey Weinstein clearly relies on the values of fairness and due process. This defense seems so obvious to lawyers that many cannot understand how anyone could criticize Ronald Sullivan. Once again, it is important to note the distinction between permissibility and meaning. Scanlon's analysis of blame directs attention to what actions imply about the actor's attitudes; the question is whether the actor's attitudes regarding interpersonal relationships are impaired in some way.[35] We can ask, in addition, whether those blame based on an assessment of those attitudes is warranted, fitting, or appropriate in light of the attitudes exhibited by the lawyer involved and the significance those attitudes have for our relationships, if any, with the lawyer. Having a debate over whether reactive attitudes are appropriate, well-grounded, or fitting helps make sense of the way in which high-profile legal cases tend to function as morality plays. Just as an actual play, like any work of art, can be interpreted without reference to the intentions or expectations of its creator, there may be significance to a highly publicized representation that is not reducible to the mental state of the lawyer.

Further, picking up on Scanlon's idea that there is an ethics of blaming, we can ask further ethical questions: One is, *ought* we to blame either a lawyer for the representation or others for criticizing or attempting to call down public shame on the lawyer? People get mad about these cases—they write editorials, Facebook comments, and tweets—but should they get mad about them, and on what grounds? Or should they be open to taking down the temperature of the criticism, restraining their tendency toward angry blame and looking for other ways of holding others accountable.[36] Another question is the *manner* in which we express blame. "Moral talk" is undoubtedly important as a way of bringing moral considerations down to a practical level and maintaining relationships of accountability.[37] In Scanlon's terms, it may be part of the way in which we adjust our relationships toward someone we blame—that is, judges to have attitudes that are impaired relative to the standards of that relationship. Blame may be used irresponsibly, however, to threaten or intimidate others or as a means of self-promotion.[38]

The principles belonging to the ethics of blame are what philosophers refer to as second-order reasons. We may have a reason to tolerate or not blame someone for doing something even though we believe it to have been wrong. Similarly, we might believe that even if someone is a wrongdoer, there are reasons not to behave in a self-righteous or judgmental manner.[39] The first-order judgment is that the action was wrong; the second-order judgment is to withhold disapproval or blame. The conclusion that something is not properly my concern or that I should cool it and do some research before firing off an angry tweet about a lawyer's representation of a nasty client, is an example of a second-order principle applicable to blaming practices.

1. How wide is the circle of blame?

In ordinary life we recognize that there may be wrongs that are none of our business.[40] We criticize people for being gossips, busybodies, or sticking their noses where they don't belong. To borrow an idea from the law, we might ask who has "standing" or "jurisdiction," to use two legal metaphors to blame the actor.[41] Scanlon's example of friendship provides a clear case of a person who is appropriately situated to hold another accountable for actions and attitudes that indicate an impairment to a relationship that both parties, apparently, have reason to care about. But most people, at least if they are fortunate, do not have to deal with lawyers on a regular basis. Scanlon's paradigm case of blaming a friend therefore does not cover most cases of blaming lawyers. An interesting question for the ethics of blame is whether the central case can be modified or extended beyond intimate relationships such as family and friendships into community, social, or other relatively more impersonal ones.

Recall the case, discussed in Chapter 2, of Anthony Griffin, the Black civil-rights lawyer who represented a leader of the Ku Klux Klan. Scanlon's ethics of blame considers the attitudes toward a person that one takes to be called for by the significance of that person's action for one's relationship with him or her.[42] One may also have relationships with others such that *failing to blame* a wrongdoer would itself impair one's relationships with the victim of that wrong.[43] A Black resident of Vidor, Texas, may believe that she owes it to other members of the local Black community to modify her attitudes toward Griffin as a way of emphasizing the significance of Griffin's representation of the Klan as a manifestation of Griffin's inappropriate attitude of insufficient loyalty to his own people. Something similar seems to underlie the intensely negative reactions of many Harvard students toward Ronald Sullivan's representation of Harvey Weinstein. Blame was grounded not simply on the wrongfulness of Weinstein's actions but on the attitudes Sullivan appeared to manifest toward victims of sexual harassment more generally, which included many of the students in Sullivan's residential house. Griffin and Sullivan are lawyers who are situated within communities in which it is quite plausible to see members of these communities as having authority or standing to blame them because their actions reveal the lawyer's attitudes toward others that impairs the relations that others can have with the lawyer.[44]

The widest scope of blame would be to regard any member of the moral community as potentially blameworthy for failing to exhibit attitudes of respect for others. Negative reactive attitudes are based on a belief that the actor has breached expectations to which we generally hold others.[45] Regarding one another as members of a moral community *means* treating them as agents who can understand and respond to reasons, govern their behavior accordingly, and give reasons in justification of their actions when they affect the interests of others.[46] That may mean holding them accountable, through blaming practices such as criticism and otherwise adjusting the terms of our relationships with them. The upshot of this view is that one is potentially accountable to any observer.[47] The trouble with this broad a scope of standing or jurisdiction to blame, however, is that if blameworthiness follows from a judgment that someone has acted in a way that reveals them to have attitudes that impair their relationships with others, then it really makes sense to have an reactive attitude toward someone with whom a person is in some kind of preexisting relationship.[48] Reactive attitudes and blame outside the context of a relationship may be indistinguishable from an objective judgment, which lacks the emotional quality that is essential to blame.[49] *Blame* specifically, as distinguished from a judgment that someone is a wrongdoer, typically follows from an impairment of a relationship. In more down-to-earth terms, some things are none of your business.[50]

Anyone with even a passing familiarity with modern social media might observe, in response, that people do not appear inclined to limit their angry reactive attitudes to others with whom they are in a relationship. It seems like everybody is angry, at everyone else, all the time. Stories abound of online mobs harassing, threatening, and sometimes succeeding in ruining the lives of perfect strangers.[51] A notorious case involved a woman who tweeted, before boarding an international flight to visit family in South Africa, "Going to Africa. Hope I don't get AIDS. Just kidding. I'm white!"[52] According to its author, the tweet was meant as a critique of her own privilege and the tendency of Americans to ignore problems in the developing world. The irony was clumsily executed, however, and the joke did not land well. Her tweet was widely shared and after a days-long frenzy of public ridicule and demonization, she was fired from her job. She had difficulty finding another job or dating because of course online shaming remains accessible to anyone who can use Google. There is much that can be said in ethical terms about incidents like this, including the disparity between the seriousness of the offense and the resulting punishment, but the extent to which people experience strongly negative reactive attitudes toward complete strangers is a remarkable feature of this kind of ritualistic social media shaming.

Moral philosopher R. Jay Wallace argues that morality is a matter of relationships of interpersonal accountability.[53] He conceives of moral duties as fundamentally relational, on an analogy with legal duties that arise out of a contract or other promise, or in tort law out of a relationship in which one has a duty to use reasonable care to avoid injuring another.[54] One of the novel aspects of his theory is the claim that the relationship of being fellow human beings, or members of the moral community, is sufficient to ground *moral* duties to others. He does not say much to specify, however, the scope of the circle of blame. He says that violations of standards of interpersonal accountability "provide other parties with reasons for reactive and other forms of blame."[55] He also says that interpersonal accountability "involves a preparedness to blame other people when they fail to live up to the expectations to which we hold them in our interactions with them."[56]

Because Wallace does not intend to limit relationships of accountability to preexisting relationships—between friends, family members, and neighbors, for example—it seems fair to read this language of preparedness to hold others accountable to include all members of the moral community. I do not think Wallace had online shaming frenzies in mind when he wrote about blaming other people for falling short of standards of interpersonal accountability to which we hold them. Yet, it is consistent with his view on the scope of the moral community to believe that it is reasonable for others to experience "reactive sentiments" (here, following Strawson) in response to observing people acting in ways that violates reasonable expectations of respect for others. Of course, one can still believe that someone like the woman who tweeted a clumsy joke about her privilege did not violate standards of interpersonal accountability. On Wallace's understanding of blame, however, any member of the moral community has standing to blame others, to the extent it is reasonable to experience reactive attitudes of resentment, indignation, or anger in response to their conduct. The trouble with this approach is that the norms governing how we act with respect to others, and how we feel about these interpersonal interactions, become less specific as we move from relationships characterized by shared history and mutual expectations, toward more thinly described relationships with others simply as members of the moral community. Anthony Griffin was responding to very specific expectations that other members of the Black community in East Texas had about who he would represent and how he would feel about it. That is not to say that a white lawyer in New York City might not have some reaction to Griffin's decision to represent the Klan. The grounds for that critic's reactive attitudes would be very different, however, from those of someone who attended church with Griffin in their hometown.

In any event, as I suggested above, lawyers in high-profile cases often find themselves performing a role in a public morality play. In contrast with a person with a hundred Twitter followers who tweets something dumb, a lawyer who chooses to represent Harvey Weinstein at the height of the #MeToo movement can reasonably expect to be held to a demand for accountability. In response, lawyers can seek to persuade critics of the value of what they do. To emphasize something I said earlier, saying that lawyers are accountable does not mean they are wrongdoers. The practice of blaming, however, is directed at the meaning of an action. It is the attitudes displayed by the lawyers involved that are important. Does the representation of a client reveal attitudes of respect for others in the wider moral community as well as more specific subcommunities in which the lawyer is embedded? In most cases, the answer is yes. For the most part lawyers readily satisfy the demand for accountability arising from the representation of clients accused of committing serious crimes, for example. The cases that become occasions for public criticism of lawyers are usually different in an important respect. The Weinstein-Sullivan case, for example, involved the competing demands on Sullivan resulting from his role as Harvard house dean. The criticism of nominees at judicial confirmation hearings shows the tension between the judicial virtue of impartiality and the expectation that lawyers can represent unpopular clients. In these cases, if the public cares enough to direct resentment and anger at a lawyer, it is likely that the lawyer's representation of a client has touched on something important enough to the moral community to warrant a public discussion. Whatever may be the case for truly private figures caught up in social media frenzies, lawyers have to accept a certain amount of criticism that comes with the territory.

2. What standards apply to determine blameworthiness and appropriate blaming responses?

Scanlon's idea of an impairment to a relationship is readily understandable where there is a normative ideal that specifies what is necessary to have a relationship of a particular type, how people in such a relationship should behave toward each other, and the attitudes they should have.[57] Go back to Scanlon's hypothetical involving his friend, Joe. Reflecting on the attitudes and expectations that are appropriate to the relationship of friendship informs the reaction of blame. An appropriate reaction, for Scanlon, would be a modification in the relationship in a way that is appropriate given the impairment to the relationship. The appropriate response constituting the act of blaming Joe, by contrast, might be an angry phone call, but also might be a more substantial modification of the terms of the relationship, such as keeping Joe at a distance; not trusting him with confidences; not being there for him in tough times; or, in an extreme case, putting an end to the relationship altogether. A less serious failing, like forgetting a friend's birthday, might provoke a milder reactive attitude like annoyance and a response like giving the forgetful party a hard time for being careless. (Even this simple situation may be complicated by a pattern of forgetfulness that may appear to manifest a lack of appropriate concern for the friend's well-being.)

As suggested above, with the example of Anthony Griffin, many relationships carry with them specific expectations about how we will act toward others and how we will feel about those actions. Being a Black resident of East Texas involves a shared history and common expectations with other members of that community. This is what philosophers would refer to as a "thick" relationship, with quite a bit of texture that establishes clear, shared expectations about what is owed to others in that community—not only in terms of actions, but also attitudes, motivations, and sentiments. Outside the context of relationships with clear ground rules, however, it is more difficult to specify the parties' expectations with respect to each other so that we can determine when there has been an impairment of the relationship. Saying unkind things behind someone's back is a clear violation of the ground rules of a friendship, but it may not be blameworthy where the negative comments relate to someone with whom the actor is not in a relationship characterized by expectations of loyalty. There may be relatively clear standards in relationships with neighbors, co-workers, and other people we deal with on a regular basis.[58] But much of the public criticism of lawyers is not coming from their clients or other professional associates but from people who have nothing whatsoever to do with the controversy at hand. In addition to the intuitive reaction that these representations may be none of the business of many observers, there is the further question of what experience these critics have with the norms that govern the provision of legal services, permitting them to identify deviations from appropriate behavior and attitudes. Scanlon's idea that we stand in relationships with everyone in the moral community is difficult to square with the particularity and "thickness" of relationships that ordinary support the evaluation of whether someone's attitudes are deficient in ways that impair the relationship.

A different standard applicable to blaming can be borrowed from the legal concepts of pleading and burden of proof.[59] In law, an aggrieved party cannot simply make unsupported allegations. Someone with a beef against someone else must make more than an "unadorned accusation" but must set out the facts supporting the claim to relief.[60] Then, after some time for investigation and discovery (that is, learning facts known by the other party), the party asserting the claim make a showing, based on evidence introduced into the record, that there is a genuine issue of material fact.⁶¹ Translated from legalese, that means courts will require an aggrieved party to "put up or shut up" at the risk of losing the entitlement to ask the court for some type of relief.

As applied to blaming, an analogous ethical principle would be that it is not appropriate to go off angrily retweeting complaints, signing petitions, or making demands for someone to be penalized in some way, without doing a bit of factual research to determine whether the objection is well founded. (Unfortunately beyond the scope of this book is the application of the law of defamation to public officials and public figures, which includes heightened fault requirements imposed by the Supreme Court to protect the freedom of the press and the public's right to know about newsworthy events.⁶²) Perhaps Sullivan was not representing Weinstein, but a different person with a similar name, so all the hullabaloo was based on a mistake. Or, if someone's criticism of Ronald Sullivan was that he was representing Harvey Weinstein only for the money and it turned out that he was working *pro bono*, that complaint would be unfounded. More realistically, many instances of public outrage about lawyers and their clients turn on a potentially incomplete, mistaken, or tendentious account of the facts or the motivations of the parties. When the venerable consumer products company Johnson & Johnson sought to cap its liabilities related to allegations that its iconic Johnson's Baby Power product contained asbestos, it received legal assistance in the form of a maneuver that involved creating a separate entity, transferring all talc-related liabilities to that entity, and then filing for bankruptcy protection.⁶³ Many critics perceived this as "trying to deny justice to cancer victims."⁶⁴ In fact, however, the company had provided the separate entity it sought to take into Chapter 11 bankruptcy with guarantees of tens of billions of dollars in funding.⁶⁵ It claimed to be seeking a more orderly process for handling a vast number of products liability claims, one that offered advantages over case-by-case adjudication in state courts, in particular in cases where the scientific evidence linking talc exposure to mesothelioma and ovarian cancer was, at best, murky, and more likely inconsistent with the company's liability.⁶⁶

Like losing a legal claim on a motion to dismiss or for summary judgment, an act of blaming could be "dismissed" by the target as being inadequately considered and thus not worth taking seriously if it did not reflect some effort to acquaint oneself with the facts on point. Overheated criticism may be easily dismissed as clearly not the product of any serious undertaking to reflect on the matter. If one aim of blame is to get the target to take the criticism to heart, the loose or inappropriate deployment of terms like "cultural genocide" is likely to be counterproductive.[67] The amount of effort that is required may vary depending on the seriousness with which one intends the criticism to be taken. Liking a tweet criticizing Johnson & Johnson for trying to use the bankruptcy process to avoid liability to cancer victims is different from invoking one's position or expertise to heighten public condemnation of the company. In the latter case, fairness demands a greater degree of care and consistency. To be clear, this is a point about the ethics of blaming; whether it is practically effective to ignore unfounded criticism is another matter. Oftentimes it is possible to score cheap points in a political controversy by mischaracterizing the facts.[68] An *ethical* blaming stance, by contrast, implies making a reasonable effort to understand the issues and become informed about the facts. Intriguingly, the ethics of blame may subject a blamer, himself or herself, to blame—for example for behaving intemperately or merely trying to stir up trouble without engaging seriously with the issues.[69]

Moving beyond the legal analogy, acts of blaming might be given lesser or no weight if they were inconsistent with one's treatment of relevantly similar cases.[70] If it is outrageous for a conservative political official to criticize big-firm partners for representing suspected terrorists detained at Guantánamo Bay, Cuba, then progressive critics should be similarly outraged when Never Trump conservatives (with whom they are temporarily in a political alliance) go after partners at large law firms who represent the Trump campaign in state election challenges. (Both of these episodes are discussed in Chapter 8.) Cheering on the critics of these firms in one case while deploring the criticism in another may be an indication that the critic's stance on lawyer blameworthiness is more strategic than principled.

3. Toleration

Beyond taking care to learn accurate information, there may be other norms regarding reactive attitudes. One of those norms, which seems to be in short supply in public life these days, might be toleration. Toleration can be understood as a disposition or commitment not to act on negative reactive attitudes toward another, notwithstanding a belief that the other has attitudes that impair their relationships with others. My former colleague Charles Wolfram wrote, in an early article about the public criticism of lawyers, that "ethical shunning" is a feature of ordinary life. While not explicitly relying on

Strawson, he described the effect of reactive attitudes on people's willingness to interact with others: "Ethical instincts of this kind seem to inform many people's attitudes and actions in everyday life. Persons with ongoing immoral projects and with prominent immoral acts in their past frequently find themselves avoided by others with whom they might wish to deal."[71] Most of us can think of people we avoid specifically on ethical grounds, not just because they may be unpleasant to deal with. This is not an effort at imposing social sanctions, like a public shaming campaign, but merely a normal human reaction to the attitudes and character displayed by others.

Wolfram goes on to contend, however, that even "moral reprobates" are bearers of human dignity that deserves to be protected.[72] This is one argument for the ideal of toleration. Within ordinary morality, toleration can reflect appreciation that there are some issues on which reasonable people may reach different judgments. This does not mean anything goes, and there are some beliefs or actions that are beyond the pale. It also makes sense to speak of toleration only where the conduct in question is something of which one disapproves and on moral grounds.[73] I do not have to "tolerate" the Black Lives Matter sign in my neighbor's front yard, but toleration would be required if another neighbor chose to fly a Confederate flag. Toleration means putting up with something that one believes to be morally wrong (or at least morally questionable) and has the desire to suppress or drive out, in furtherance of some other value, such as peace or stability.[74] Becoming indifferent to something that was formerly regarded as wrong—as has occurred in Western societies in recent decades with respect to same-sex intimacy, is not toleration.[75] Refraining from "ethical shunning," in the sense of morally motivated refusals to interact in normal ways with a person believed to be a wrongdoer, is the domain of toleration, as is tempering one's criticism of those perceived to be wrongdoers, or at least not resorting immediately to the most inflammatory characterization of a position one disagrees with. Toleration, as a virtue, requires a certain amount of restraint in one's reactive attitudes.

Toleration may underwrite social or political practices that are aimed at fostering peaceful coexistence and sustaining practices of treating others with some degree of respect, even in the face of strongly held beliefs that others are misguided about ethical matters. The rule of law, as I see it, is a virtue of societies that seek to constrain the exercise of raw power in favor of relatively fair procedures for allocating rights and duties to individuals and organizations. One virtue of the rule of law is that it provides a way of interacting with those with whom we have profound and bitter disagreements in a way that manifests respect for them as free and equal. There will be more to say later about this political ideal of toleration. For now, the question related to the ethics of blame is whether toleration is something we should require of ourselves and others in situations of disagreement. Not because of skepticism about ethics or a belief that right and wrong is relative to individual actors (as in the statement one often hears from undergraduates in ethics courses that "it may be wrong for me, but who's to stay it's wrong for you?"). Rather, the ethical value of toleration may be rooted in an appreciation for a plurality of genuine human goods and ideals and also recognition that being able to regard someone as *both* a wrongdoer and a human being worthy of respect is something we should demand of ourselves. I may believe my neighbors who flew the Confederate flag (this really happened when I was living in Virginia, by the way) is expressing harmful racist attitudes but also believe that they deserve autonomy to do things that others believe, with justification, are morally wrongful.[76]

Toleration is the value that underlies some of our most venerated political practices and legal rights, such as the freedom of expression protected by the First Amendment and the academic freedom of university faculty members.[77] As the subtitle of this book suggests, toleration is in tension with accountability to others, enforced through blaming practices like shunning, shaming, calling out, and canceling. What attitudes should we take toward those with whom we not only disagree, but believe to be expressing harmful attitudes or assisting those with harmful goals? An attitude of toleration may be supported by the desire to live in a community where the temperature of conflict is taken down a few degrees and it is possible to treat others with respect despite our disagreements with them.[78] An individual considering another's outrageous behavior may ask, however, why they should care about a community-regarding virtue like toleration when the other person is doing something that they reasonably believe manifest a lack of respect? An answer might be that a community in which we tacitly agree not to express angry reactive attitudes toward others regarding matters about which people may reasonably disagree is, overall, a much less conflictual and emotionally taxing environment. Toleration requires us to forebear from expressing blame where someone does or says something that is within the range of reasonable beliefs and attitudes that someone might have, even if we ourselves strongly disagree.[79]

Since toleration—at least outside the context of official toleration, such as the right of free exercise of religion protected by the First Amendment—is an informal practice, it is subject to familiar collective-action problems. It would be better overall, at least I think, that as a society we do not escalate disagreements immediately to highly charged conflicts. Toleration is a more attractive and appealing way of mediating differences among groups within our society.[80] However, any given person's role in maintaining a culture of toleration is likely to be marginal unless they are a public figure or other influential person. It may be that it is more *personally* satisfying to exhibit a tolerant attitude toward those with whom one disagrees, but this seems to be a contingent matter; some may enjoy the attitude of righteous indignation that is inconsistent with a tolerant public sphere. For my own part I see toleration as an important aspect of a civil culture that supports a diversity of viewpoints, practices, and traditions and is worth fostering for that reason. The collective-action problem is a tough nut to crack, however, as long as individuals get an emotional charge out of engaging in angry blaming behavior.

As applied to blaming lawyers, toleration can mean refraining from blaming someone like Ronald Sullivan who, by one's own lights, is a wrongdoer for representing Harvey Weinstein. In a deeper and more interesting sense, however, appreciating the value of toleration can suggest a way of understanding Sullivan's decision as not blameworthy at all. Even "moral reprobates" deserve to be treated as bearers of dignity.[81] Because of this dual aspect of representation, a lawyer's choice of clients may prompt reactive attitudes in response to either the reprehensible nature of the client or the admirable feature of upholding the client's dignity. Lawyers would very much like to restrict others' reactive attitudes to the latter, insisting that representation is *only* the effort to vindicate the liberal political values of dignity and autonomy. This restriction is not a feature of lawyers' own ethical commitments, however, but of the ethics of blame. Lawyers are asking their critics to be more tolerant. And because toleration is called for only when one disagrees on moral grounds with what another is doing, situations calling for toleration can be exploited by bad faith actors. The last section on the ethics of blame considers the blame that may be directed at those who seek to manufacture outrage to score cheap political points.

4. Don't feed the trolls

I believe there are profoundly interesting theoretical issues raised by much of the public criticism of lawyers, but it would be remiss not to point out that some public criticism is transparently in bad faith. This is a particular problem in judicial confirmation proceedings in the U.S. Senate. Consider, for example, the hearings on the nomination of Nina Morrison to serve as a federal trial court judge in New York.[82] Morrison was senior litigation counsel for the Innocence Project, a public interest organization dedicated to rectifying wrongful convictions. Presumably looking to score political points by linking the Biden administration's policies to recent increases in crime, two Republican senators called Morrison personally "soft on crime" and therefore unfit to serve as a federal judge. Texas Senator Ted Cruz blamed the exoneration of innocent people for the rising crime rate: "Across this country, Americans are horrified at skyrocketing crime rates, at skyrocketing homicide rates, at skyrocketing burglary rates, at skyrocketing carjacking rates. All of those are the direct result of the policies you've spent your entire lifetime advancing." Missouri Senator Josh Hawley vowed to "oppose you and anyone else the administration sends to us who do not understand the necessity of the rule of law." And Arkansas Senator Tom Cotton asked, referring to the comments of a man to the prison warden before his execution, "Are you proud that you encouraged such defiance in convicted murderers?" All of these criticisms blithely ignore the fact that the Innocent Project works within the law to secure the release of innocent people.

The three senators attacking Morrison, who was eventually confirmed,[83] are card-carrying members of the elite conservative legal establishment.[84] Lawyers sometimes seek to explain away public criticism as the result of ignorance of subtleties like the constitutional value of due process or the importance of human dignity. But the three senators going after Morrison for her work with the Innocence Project are not outsiders to the legal system and its norms. They are perfectly well aware of the long professional tradition of representing unpopular clients and would probably be the first to reference John Adams or Atticus Finch in response to criticism from the left of conservative lawyers. Their criticism should not be taken seriously and probably was not intended to be taken seriously. It is merely trolling—that is, inflammatory comments meant to rile up an opponent without any commitment to the soundness of the underlying arguments or, as right-wing provocateurs describe it, "owning the libs," meaning acting in ways that inflame and infuriate opponents, often baiting them into overreaction, without regard to a substantive policy commitment or consistency with one's other beliefs.[85] In fairness, the same response could be offered to some critics from the left, either of conservative judicial nominees or lawyers in private practice representing clients unpopular with progressives. Criticism of lawyers, and the response to it, is not a red state/blue state phenomenon. One can assess the attitudes and motivating reasons of a lawyer apart from the partisan political orientation of critics. As part of the ethics of blame, however, critics can themselves be blamed for displaying attitudes of unseriousness or indifference to the truth.

The distinguished philosopher Harry Frankfurt, who had published a number of influential papers on free will and responsibility, became famous outside of academic circles when a paper he wrote in the 1980s, entitled "On Bullshit," was republished as a short book.[86] Ideas like the "post-truth" society and political satirist Stephen Colbert's "truthiness" were then in the air,[87] so Frankfurt's book became a cultural touchstone. Frankfurt distinguished lies, which require the speaker's awareness of and intent to deviate from the truth, from bullshit, which is blissfully unconcerned with whether a statement is true.[88] A bullshitter, according to Frankfurt, "offers a description of a certain state of affairs without genuinely submitting to the constraints which the endeavor to provide an accurate representation of reality imposes."[89] The Trump administration adopted bullshit as a communication style very early, when White House Senior Advisor Kellyanne Conway appeared on *Meet the Press* and proclaimed with a straight face that the White House press secretary had presented "alternative facts" when he misstated the size of the crowd at President Trump's inauguration.[90] Traditional responses by the mainstream media, such as fact-checking the claim about crowd size,[91] proved to be surprisingly ineffectual in the face of a communication strategy memorably described by advisor Steve Bannon: "The real opposition is the media. And the way to deal with them is to flood the zone with shit."[92]

No sensible observer of judicial confirmation hearings can deny that some of the attacks on nominees are shining examples of bullshit. The ethics of blame provides a way to criticize bad faith, bullshit criticism of lawyers: There is a baseline ethical requirement that serious criticism of lawyers exhibit respect for epistemic (that is, truth-regarding) norms such as consistency and grounding in factual evidence. For example, Senator Hawley's criticism of Morrison for not understanding the necessity of the rule of law is clearly inconsistent with Morrison's advocacy, using legal institutions and procedures, for the exoneration of innocent people. Morrison clearly understands the necessity of the rule of law, and in fact is seeking to support it by helping correct mistakes which have led to injustices. A lawyer in Morrison's situation, like Judge Ketanji Brown Jackson dealing with similar questions in her Supreme

Court confirmation hearing, has little choice but to answer the questions as if they were asked in good faith. As a matter of the ethics of blame, however, observers of these charades may properly blame elected officials who know better for seeking to arouse indignation and resentment against lawyers whose attitudes toward other members of the moral community are not in any way impaired. In other words, bullshit efforts to direct angry blame toward someone who doesn't deserve it are *themselves* blameworthy. They display the hallmarks of blame—impaired attitudes toward an important relationship, in this case the relationship of trust and confidence that senators should feel that they owe to their constituents, which should motivate them to be more honest in the way they represent their constituents' concerns about judicial nominees.

Like many of the examples considered in this chapter, the ascription of bullshit to the critics of President Biden's judicial nominees is a contestable one. The ethics of blame is like ethics generally; it is something we can disagree (hopefully more or less productively and in good faith) about, rather than a tool to end disagreement. Reframing the public criticism of lawyers as a blaming practice, subject to the ethics of blame, helps explain why lawyers and their critics are so often talking past one another. Lawyers want to invoke the Principle of Nonaccountability but critics aren't having it. Rather than meeting the criticism on its own terrain, which is that of blame, lawyers try to deflect it entirely. A different way to understand the response of lawyers, however, is not knee-jerk reliance on the Principle of Nonaccountability but as an attempt to deescalate social conflict by appealing to the value of toleration.[93] If one sees, as I do, the social good promoted by the legal profession as enabling relatively peaceful and orderly coexistence and cooperation in a community characterized by profound disagreement and conflict, then there are reasons to temper angry reactive attitudes. As the next chapter shows, sometimes frustration with this strategy boils over and critics of the legal profession resort to more organized efforts to hit the profession where it hurts—in its pocketbook and social prestige.

Chapter summary

Blame follows from a judgment that someone has attitudes that impair their relationship with others. The response is to adjust one's own relationship with that person. There are not necessarily clear boundaries on what relationships count when assessing blame. Some philosophers extend the scope of concern to the entire moral community. This general approach to blame, as influentially developed by T.M. Scanlon, provides a framework for understanding what is going on in many episodes of shaming or canceling lawyers. Since blame is a response to a perception of the attitudes of another, it does not necessarily follow from a judgment that the other is a wrongdoer. This is another explanation for the intractability of debates over criticizing lawyers because lawyers frequently believe, and rightly so, that they are justified in representing unpopular clients. These debates are further complicated by the ethics of blame—that is, the standards by which one determines whether an adjustment to a relationship is warranted. Toleration is an aspect of the ethics of blame. In a society characterized by pervasive and intense disagreement, toleration is a way of taking down the temperature of social conflict.

Notes

1. David Shoemaker and Emad Atiq provided very helpful feedback on this chapter. Peter Strawson, "Freedom and Resentment," reprinted in Gary Watson, ed., *Free Will*, 2d. ed. (Oxford: Oxford University Press 2003), p. 91.
2. Angela M. Smith, "Moral Blame and Moral Protest," in D. Justin Coates & Neal A. Tognazzini, eds., *Blame: Its Nature and Norms* (Oxford: Oxford University Press 2013).
3. T.M. Scanlon, "Blame," in *Moral Dimensions: Permissibility, Meaning, Blame* (Cambridge, Mass.: Belknap Press 2008), p. 128.
4. Scanlon, "Blame," p. 128.
5. Scanlon, "Blame," p. 128.
6. Scanlon, "Blame," p. 124. I am in agreement with what Victoria McGeer says about blame not necessarily being dependent upon *moral* wrongdoing. "[T]he wrong in question need not be a moral offense. I may blame you for failing to pay a bill on time, or weakly accepting an invitation I know you have good reason to turn down, or forgetting to take the dog out for its morning walk. Yet as Bernard Williams points out, even in such cases the wrongdoing . . has 'some kind of ethical dimension to it'; that is to say, 'for blame to be appropriate, there must be some generally reprehensible characteristic involved in the explanation: the agent must have been careless, or lazy, or self-serving, or something of the sort." Victoria McGeer, "Civilizing Blame," in D. Justin Coates & Neal A. Tognazzini, eds., *Blame: Its Nature and Norms* (Oxford: Oxford University Press 2013), p. 162. What is striking about Scanlon's account is not just admitting the possibility of blame for non-moral wrongdoing, but also for unlucky but non-culpable harms to others. He gives the example of a driver who, through no fault of his own, runs over and kills a neighbor's child (suppose the child darted out from behind some shrubs, giving the driver no time to stop). Scanlon

says the driver is likely to suffer something "somehow akin to blame," implying that it would be appropriate in those circumstances. Scanlon, "Blame," p. 125.
7. While I do not aim explicitly to defend Scanlon, several commentators on drafts of this work (including Tim Dare and Bill Watson) have similarly expressed doubts about pulling apart considerations of permissibility and meaning. The strongest form of this objection is that the meaning of a permissible action should be one that does not warrant a judgment of blameworthiness. I hope to defend an adequate response in the text, but the short response for now is that considering, and evaluating, permissibility and meaning separately may help account for the messiness of the landscape of professional ethics and provide a theoretical foundation for the observation of moral remainders—that is, judgments that a lawyer ought to feel reluctance or regret when engaging in certain legally and morally permissible representations.
8. Susan Wolf, "Blame, Italian Style," in R. Jay Wallace, Rahul Kumar, & Samuel Freeman, *Reasons and Recognition: Essays on the Philosophy of T.M. Scanlon* (Oxford University Press 2011), p. 332.
9. Scanlon, "Blame," pp. 128–30. Wolf points out that withdrawal seems like a paradigmatic mechanism for expressing Scanlonian blame, but in cases of what she calls "angry blame," a different pattern of reaction would be expected. Rather than putting distance between yourself and a wrongdoer, you might want to get in his face or feel the specific reactive emotions of guilt or remorse. Wolf, "Blame, Italian Style," p. 338.
10. Smith, "Moral Blame and Moral Protest," pp. 39–40.
11. Scanlon, "Blame," pp. 153–54.
12. Nomy Arpaly, *Merit, Meaning, and Human Bondage: An Essay on Free Will* (Princeton: Princeton University Press 2006); Gary Watson, "Two Faces of Responsibility," *Phil. Topics* 24: 227–48 (1996). Susan Wolf cautions against inferring too quickly from a blameworthy action to a judgment that someone's character is deficient; it may be the case simply that the person is imperfectly virtuous. Susan Wolf, "Blame, Italian Style," pp. 337–38. This strikes me as an important point to be considered in connection with the ethics of blame, discussed farther down in the text.
13. Wolf, "Blame, Italian Style," p. 339.
14. Sources for this quote abound on the internet. For one example, see Joan Podrazik, "Oprah's Life Lesson From Maya Angelou: 'When People Show You Who They Are, Believe Them,'" *Huffington Post* (May 14, 2013), available at https://www.huffpost.com/entry/oprah-life-lesson-maya-angelou_n_2869235.
15. Wolf, "Blame, Italian Style," p. 341.
16. Scanlon, "Blame," p. 129.
17. Bernard Williams, *Ethics and the Limits of Philosophy* (Cambridge, Mass.: Harvard University Press 1985).
18. Scanlon, "Blame," pp. 132–33.
19. Scanlon, "Blame," pp. 140–41.
20. Scanlon, "Blame," p. 145.
21. See Dominick Mastrangelo, "Washington Post Suspends Dave Weigel Over Retweet of Sexist Joke," *The Hill* (June 6, 2022). Although the episode preoccupied political

Twitter for about 24 hours, it was mostly reported in right-leaning media outlets like the *New York Post* and Fox News, suggesting that its political valence was equated with progressive cancel culture.
22. Scanlon argues that in some cases A's *failing* to blame B may impair the relationships that A has with victims of B's action. Scanlon, "Blame," pp. 169–70.
23. Way beyond the scope of the discussion in text, but for a sophisticated philosophical and social analysis of positionality and identity politics, see Olúfémi O. Táíwò, *Elite Capture: How the Powerful Took Over Identity Politics (and Everything Else)* (Chicago: Haymarket Books 2022).
24. Linda Radzik, "Boycotts and the Social Enforcement of Justice," *Social Phil. & Policy* 34(1): 102–22 (2017); Ginia Bellafonte, "Chick-fil-A and the Politics of Eating," *N.Y. Times* (Oct. 9, 2015).
25. Judith Kimerling, "Lessons from the Chevron Ecuador Litigation: The Proposed Intervenors' Perspective," 1 *Stan. J. Complex Litig.* 241, 261–62 (2013).
26. Julia Lurie, "Why Are Right-Wing Groups Targeting a Law Aimed at Protecting Native Families?," *Mother Jones* (Nov. 7, 2022); Vivia Chen, "Gibson Dunn Pro Bono Case Draws the Ire of Some Native Americans," *Bloomberg Law* (Nov. 23, 2021); Nick Estes, "Why Is the U.S. Right Suddenly Interested in Native American Adoption Law?," *Guardian* (Aug. 23, 2021). The case is called *Brackeen v. Haaland*, 142 S. Ct. 1205 (2022), and comes to the Supreme Court on a writ of certiorari to the U.S. Court of Appeals for the Fifth Circuit, 994 F.3d 249 (5th Cir. 2021) (en banc). Gibson Dunn has acted as counsel for the plaintiffs challenging the statute from the beginning, including the district court decision in *Brackeen v. Zinke*, 328 F. Supp. 3d 514 (N.D. Tex. 2018).
27. Michele Kriegman, "The Supreme Court May Ensure Native Kids' Ancestry Is Erased—Just Like Mine Was," *Slate* (Nov. 8, 2022).
28. Chen, above; Estes, above.
29. See, e.g., a post from a self-proclaimed independent newspaper at Harvard Law School—Rachel D. Varroward, "Whose 'Bono' Is It, Anyway?," *Harvard Law Record* (Nov. 9, 2022), available at https://hlrecord.org/whose-bono-is-it-anyway/.
30. Joe Patrice, "Most Firms Don't Advocate Cultural Genocide Pro Bono, But This Biglaw Firm Will!," *Above the Law* (Nov. 4, 2022), available at https://abovethelaw.com/2022/11/supreme-court-indian-child-welfare-act-gibson-dunn/.
31. Thanks to Emad Atiq for reminding me of the significance of this aspect of the analysis to the Gibson Dunn controversy.
32. Chen, above (quoting Michael McGill).
33. An example of how ideology may complicate the attribution of motives and attitudes to others surfaced in spectacular fashion when a judge on the U.S. Court of Appeals for the Fifth Circuit, Stuart Kyle Duncan, was invited by the Stanford Law School chapter of the Federalist Society to give a talk at the law school. See Chase Feliciantonio, "Stanford Apologizes to Trump-Appointed Judge Shouted Down by Students at Event," *S.F. Chronicle* (Mar. 10, 2023). According to an article in the Stanford student newspaper, activists contended that "Duncan has been a right-wing advocate for laws

that would harm women, immigrants and LGBTQ+ people. The fliers cite examples of his attempts to deny same-sex couples adoption rights and how he served as lead trial and appellate counsel in a case that stopped transgender people from using the bathroom of their choice at state institutions." Greta Reich, "Law School Activists Protest Judge Kyle Duncan's Visit to Campus," *Stanford Daily* (Mar. 11, 2023). One of the grounds for this assessment was an opinion he wrote denying a request by a prisoner to change her name on a judgment to reflect her gender identity. *U.S. v. Varner*, 948 F.3d 250 (5th Cir. 2020). The opinion was characterized as exhibiting needless cruelty. See, e.g., Ian Millhiser, "Trump Judge Lashes Out at a Transgender Litigant in a Surprisingly Cruel Opinion," *Vox* (Jan. 17, 2020). Activists saw his presence at Stanford as objectionable because Duncan "has not only expressed views but has actively, as a lawyer and as a judge, worked to further a homophobic and transphobic agenda" and the invitation by the Federalist Society has the effect of "emboldening narratives of hate and prejudice." Reich, above. Duncan had previously been characterized as "bughouse on the subject of gay people and trans people and any other person whose sexuality gives Duncan the jittery Jesus vapors." Charles P. Pierce, "A Lifetime Gig Should Never Belong to Someone Like This," *Esquire* (Apr. 24, 2018). The thoughtful and (at least to my mind) appropriately cynical First Amendment lawyer and legal commentator Ken White characterizes everyone involved in this dispute as acting in bad faith or, in the best case, in negligent disregard of bedrock free-speech and academic-freedom principles. Ken White, "Hating Everyone Everywhere All At Once At Stanford," *Substack—The Popehat Report* (Mar. 14, 2023). As the subtitle of White's article rightly observes, we shouldn't expect free speech disputes to have heroes. However, in connection with the ethics of blame, it would be almost a heroic act of impartiality to sort through this controversy unencumbered by one's prior views about transgender rights and the use of pronouns based on gender identity. Judge Duncan's opinion reads to me like he went out of his way to be dismissive of the request, particularly given that there is no law compelling a result either way and so it was entirely within the discretion of the district court to use the petitioner's preferred name and pronouns, or not. But to emphasize, that is how it reads *to me*, with the attitudes and beliefs I bring to the social controversy over these issues. It is important to be clear that I do not believe there is some Olympian perspective of objectivity from which to assess the motives, attitudes, and character of those at whom blame is directed. Rather, motives, attitudes, and character are the thing we are debating *about*, and that debate will have to proceed with the usual complication of the assumptions and biases that participants bring along with them.

34. An additional source of uncertainty is suggested by the findings of modern behavioral psychology that, while observers tend to explain actions with reference to the personality traits, dispositions, or attitudes of actors, they overlook the importance of situational factors that channel behavior—often unconsciously—in predictable ways. See, e.g., Lee Ross & Richard E. Nisbett, *The Person and the Situation: Perspectives of Social Psychology* (New York: McGraw Hill 1991); Lee Ross, "From the Fundamental Attribution Error to the Truly Fundamental Attribution Error and Beyond: My

Research Journey," 13 *Persp. on Psychol. Sci.* 750 (2018). This is referred to as the fundamental attribution error. As shown in a classic experiment, the fact that someone is in a hurry is more likely to affect their decision to help a person in obvious distress than the fact that they are a student studying for the ministry or that they had recently been asked to reflect on the parable of the Good Samaritan. John M. Darley & Daniel Batson, "From Jerusalem to Jericho: A Study of Situational and Dispositional Variables in Helping Behavior," 27 *J. Person. & Soc. Psych.* 100 (1973). Similarly, the likelihood that players will keep their mouth shut or rat out the other player in a Prisoner's Dilemma game is significantly influenced by the framing effect of telling the players that the game is called either the "Wall Street Game" or the "Community Game." The mainstream view within moral psychology understands behavior as a complex product of the interaction between personality traits and situational factors, not as determined exclusively by situational factors. John Doris, Stephen Stich, Jonathan Philips, & Lachlan Walmsley, "Moral Psychology: Empirical Approaches," *Stanford Encyclopedia of Philosophy* (2020). Nevertheless, the subtle influence of seemingly inconsequential details of a situation can lead observers to draw mistaken inferences about the attitudes of the actor.
35. Scanlon, "Blame," pp. 127–29.
36. Derk Pereboom, *Wrongdoing and the Moral Emotions* (Oxford: Oxford University Press 2021).
37. Justin Tosi & Brandon Warmke, *Grandstanding: The Use and Abuse of Moral Talk* (New York: Oxford University Press 2020).
38. Tosi & Warmke, pp. 5–6.
39. Gary Watson, "Standing in Judgment," in Coates & Tognazzi.
40. Macalester Bell, "The Standing to Blame: A Critique," in Coates & Tognazzi, pp. 269–70; Radzik, p. 115.
41. Angela M. Smith, "On Being Responsible and Holding Responsible," *J. Ethics* 11: 465–84 (2007), p. 471; Coates & Tognazzi, p. 19.
42. Scanlon, "Blame," p. 159.
43. Scanlon, "Blame," p. 169.
44. Scanlon, "Blame," p. 128; Radzik, p. 116.
45. R. Jay Wallace, *Responsibility and the Moral Sentiments* (Cambridge, Mass.: Harvard University Press 1994), p. 12.
46. Gary Watson, "Responsibility and the Limits of Evil: Variations on a Strawsonian Theme," in *Agency and Answerability* (Oxford: Clarendon Press 2004), pp. 229–33.
47. The philosopher Aaron James argues that the defining characteristic of an asshole, as distinguished from a mere jerk, is a belief in immunity from the complaints of other people. The moral failing of assholes consists in their resentment at being criticized. Aaron James, *Assholes: A Theory* (New York: Doubleday 2012).
48. Here I am following Susan Wolf in distinguishing what she calls the "angry attitudes," that is, affectively charged reactive attitudes from Scanlonian blame, which she hilariously characterizes as "blame for wusses" or "wimpy blame." Wolf, "Blame, Italian Style," p. 336.

49. Wolf, "Blame, Italian Style," pp. 338–39 (noting that Strawson distinguished reactive attitudes from the "objective attitude").
50. Bill Hodes has an interesting take on the Freedman-Tigar debate, discussed in Chapter 2. He agrees that a choice to represent an odious client (or not) should be capable of a hypothetical public justification. But he does not believe he owes anyone an actual justification, with the exception of himself, relatives, and close friends. He may choose to justify himself to a broad audience, but he does not owe them any account for his decision. W. William Hodes, "Accepting and Rejecting Clients—The Moral Autonomy of the Second-to-the-Last Lawyer in Town," 48 *U. Kan. L. Rev.* 977, 989–90 (2000). As he recounts in this article, Hodes provided some legal assistance in the challenge by the white supremacist Matthew Hale to the efforts by the Illinois Committee on Character and Fitness to deny him admission to the bar. If friends or professional colleagues criticized his representation of Hale (as no doubt some did), that would be their right. However—and this may be seen as part of the ethics of blame—Hodes continues: "I would retain the same right to question the judgment of anyone who could not give me (and the adversary system) the benefit of the doubt and work out for themselves what some of my reasons must be." Hodes, p. 990. Hodes could ground his right to refuse to give an account for himself on the legal duty of confidentiality owed to current and former clients, but he does do so, relying instead on a kind of right of conscience as a moral agent, not a professional obligation.
51. See, e.g., Jon Ronson, *So You've Been Publicly Shamed* (New York: Riverhead Books 2016).
52. British journalist Jon Ronson tells the story in the book cited in the previous note and also in an article: "How One Stupid Tweet Blew Up Justine Sacco's Life," *N.Y. Times* (Feb. 12, 2015).
53. R. Jay Wallace, *The Moral Nexus* (Princeton: Princeton University Press 2019), pp. 67–70.
54. Wallace, *Moral Nexus*, pp. 5–6, 47–54.
55. Wallace, *Moral Nexus*, p. 70.
56. Wallace, *Moral Nexus*, p. 71.
57. Scanlon, "Blame," pp. 133–34.
58. Scanlon, "Blame," p. 134 ("Our relationships with neighbors, co-workers, and the tradespeople we deal with are obviously conditional on the contingent fact that we regularly interact in these ways.").
59. I am grateful to Erin Miller for suggesting this approach.
60. *Bell Atlantic Corp. v. Twombly*, 550 U.S. 544, 555 (2007).
61. *Celotex Corp. v. Catrett*, 477 U.S. 317 (1986).
62. The landmark case *New York Times Co. v. Sullivan*, 376 U.S. 254 (1964), imposed the requirement that a public official show a defamatory false statement of fact was made with knowledge of its falsity or reckless disregard of its truth of falsity. This requirement has been extended to public figures—those who "by reason of the notoriety of their achievements or the vigor and success with which they seek the public's attention" are classified as public figures. *Gertz v. Robert Welch, Inc.*, 418 U.S. 323 (1974). Purely private figures may recover on a showing of mere negligence by the speaker.

I mention this here by way of analogy with private-law protections for the reputation of individuals who are falsely accused of doing something that would tend to expose them to "public hatred or contempt, ridicule, share or disgrace"—a pretty good list of Strawsonian reactive attitudes. See *Susan B. Anthony List v. Dreihaus*, 805 F. Supp. 2d 423 (S.D. Ohio 2011).

63. Rather than handle what it perceived to be a flood of claims by women seeking to connect their ovarian cancer to talc exposure, Johnson & Johnson spun off its talc liabilities into a newly created unit called LTL, which then filed for Chapter 11 bankruptcy protection. Under the supervision of the bankruptcy court, LTL could then propose a plan for the fair handling of all claims filed against the company. See Michael B. Marois, "J&J's Strategy on Cancer Suits Questioned by Appeals Court," *Bloomberg Law* (Sept. 20, 2022). Because the transaction took advantage of a provision in Texas corporate law, it became known as the "Texas Two-Step." See Jonathan Randles, "Jurist Noted for Bankruptcy Expertise Will Weigh J&J Talc Appeal," *Wall St. J.* (Sept. 16, 2022). A federal court of appeals held that the spun-off entity, LTL, was not in financial distress because of funding guarantees that had been provided by J&J; therefore, the bankruptcy filing was not in good faith. See *In re LTL Management, LLC*, 64 F.4th 84 (3rd Cir. 2023).

64. See, e.g., Max Kennerly, "How Giant Corporations Are Using Fake Bankruptcies to Hang Consumers Out to Dry," *Balls and Strikes* (Sept. 7, 2022), available at https://ballsandstrikes.org/legal-culture/texas-two-step-bankruptcy/.

65. The effort expended in creating and funding the LTL subsidiary was all for naught, as the Third Circuit Court of Appeals held that a debor not in financial distress cannot take advantage of the safe harbor offered by Chapter 11 bankruptcy proceedings. *In re LTL Management, LLC*, 64 F.4th 84 (3d Cir. 2023). The court's opinion is a good summary of the facts, including the funding guarantees to the LTL subsidiary that could have reached $65.1 billion.

66. In the 1960s some products containing talc also contained asbestos fibers. Asbestos exposure is linked with a variety of illness, most notably mesothelioma, a cancer that develops from the thin layer of tissue found in the lining of the lungs. There is also some evidence that regular genital use of talc is associated with greater odds of developing ovarian cancer. Daniel W. Cramer et al., "The Association Between Talc Use and Ovarian Cancer: A Retrospective Case-Control Study in Two U.S. States," *Epidemiology* 27: 334–346 (2016).. As in all toxic tort cases, however, even if there is some association between an illness and exposure to a substance capable of causing that illness, the plaintiff must still establish that it is more likely than not that the illness was caused by the exposure and not some other cause, such as a genetic predisposition or exposure to some other substance. See, e.g., *Rider v. Sandoz Pharmaceutical Corp.*, 295 F.3d 1194 (11th Cir. 2002).

67. Patrice, above.

68. For example, a Trump nominee for a district court judgeship in the Western District of Michigan withdrew his nomination after ferocious criticism from some Republican senators. The nominee had defending the city of East Lansing in an action against a Catholic couple who had been excluded as vendors from the city's farmers market

after refusing to host a same-sex marriage on their farm. The lawyer's brief compared Catholic opposition to same-sex marriage to the Ku Klux Klan's opposition to interracial marriage. Marianne Levine & Eliana Johnson, "Trump Judicial Nominee Withdraws Amid GOP Opposition," *Politico* (June 11, 2019); Ariane de Vogue & Ted Barnett, "Trump Judge Nominee Withdraws as Republicans Press White House on Vetting," *CNN* (June 12, 2019).

69. Being what Canadians would call a "shit disturber."
70. Lawyers are actually permitted to take inconsistent positions on behalf of separate clients in unrelated cases. See ABA Model Rules of Prof'l Conduct, Rule 1.7, cmt. [24].
71. Charles W. Wolfram, "A Lawyer's Duty to Represent Clients, Repugnant and Otherwise," in David Luban, ed., *The Good Lawyer*, 214, 228–29 (Totowa, N.J.: Rowman & Allanheld 1983).
72. Wolfram, p. 229.
73. Rainer Forst, *Toleration in Conflict* (Ciaran Cronin, trans.) (Cambridge: Cambridge University Press 2013), p. 18; Barbara Herman, "Pluralism and the Community of Moral Judgment," in David Heyd, ed., *Toleration: An Elusive Virtue* (Princeton: Princeton University Press 1996), p. 61; T.M. Scanlon, "The Difficulty of Tolerance," in *The Difficulty of Tolerance: Essays in Political Philosophy* (Cambridge: Cambridge University Press 2003), pp. 187–201.
74. Bernard Williams, "Toleration: An Impossible Virtue?," in Heyd, p. 19.
75. Williams, pp. 20–21. Williams, with characteristic brilliance and economy of writing, notes in this passage that the lessons learned from the European Wars of Religion in the sixteenth and seventeenth centuries may either be (1) a skeptical lesson, that there is no truth, at least no truth discoverable by human beings, about the validity of one's religious beliefs; or (2) a deeper and more substantive discovery about God's purposes, that is, that God does not mind how people worship as long as they do so in good faith.
76. Williams, p. 25.
77. See, e.g., Barry Sullivan, "Private Practice, Public Profession: Convictions, Commitments, and the Availability of Counsel," 108 *W. Va. L. Rev.* 1 (2005).
78. Benjamin Eidelson, "The Etiquette of Equality," 51 *Phil. & Pub. Aff.* 97 (2023); Scanlon, "Difficulty of Tolerance," pp. 190–92.
79. Eidelson, above.
80. Scanlon, "Difficulty of Tolerance," p. 193.
81. David Luban, "Lawyers as Upholders of Human Dignity (When They Aren't Busy Assaulting It)," in *Legal Ethics and Human Dignity* (Cambridge: Cambridge University Press 2007), p. 65.
82. Jennifer Bendery, "Republicans Blame Crime on an Innocence Project Lawyer Tapped for a Judgeship," *Huffington Post* (Feb. 16, 2022); Radley Balko, "Republicans' Buffoonish, Disingenuous Attacks on an Innocence Project Attorney," *Wash. Post* (Feb. 18, 2020).
83. Nate Raymond, "U.S. Senate Confirms Innocence Project Lawyer Morrison to be Federal Judge," *Reuters* (June 8, 2022).

84. Cruz graduated from Harvard Law School, clerked for Court of Appeals Judge J. Michael Luttig and Supreme Court Chief Justice William Rehnquist, and subsequently worked at powerhouse conservative law firm Cooper & Kirk and served as solicitor general for the State of Texas. Hawley received his law degree from Yale before clerking for Judge Michael McConnell on the Court of Appeals and Chief Justice John Roberts on the Supreme Court. He was a lawyer in private practice and a law professor before being elected Attorney General of Missouri. And Cotton, a Harvard law school graduate, clerked for Judge Jerry Smith on the Court of Appeals before working as an attorney at Gibson Dunn and Cooper & Kirk and then entering the U.S. Army as a second lieutenant.
85. See, e.g., Derek Robertson, "How 'Owning the Libs' Became the GOP's Core Belief," *Politico* (Mar. 21, 2021).
86. Harry G. Frankfurt, "On Bullshit," *Raritan Q. Rev.* 6, no. 2 (1986), reprinted in *The Importance of What We Care About: Philosophical Essays* (Cambridge: Cambridge University Press 1998), p. 117. The paper was reprinted as a stand-alone book by Princeton University Press in 2005. Citations are to the book version.
87. Post-truth was defined as "relating to or denoting circumstances in which objective facts are less influential in shaping public opinion than appeals to emotion and personal belief." Amy B. Wang, "'Post-Truth' Named 2016 Word of the Year by Oxford Dictionaries," *Wash. Post* (Nov. 16, 2016). Truthiness, according to Colbert, means "sort of what you want to be true, as opposed to what the facts support . . . a truth larger than the facts that would comprise it—if you cared about facts, which you don't. . . ." Jacques Steinberg, "2005: In a Word," *N.Y. Times* (Dec. 25, 2005).
88. Frankfurt, p. 30.
89. Frankfurt, p. 32.
90. Rebecca Sunderbrand, "How Kellyanne Conway Ushered in the Era of 'Alternative Facts,'" *Wash. Post* (Jan. 22, 2017).
91. Glen Kessler, "Spicer Earns Four Pinocchios for False Claims on Inauguration Crowd Size," *Wash. Post* (Jan. 22, 2017).
92. Sean Illing, "'Flood the Zone with Shit': How Misinformation Overwhelmed Our Democracy, *Vox* (Feb. 6, 2020).
93. Compare the similar suggestion in Eidelson, above.

5
Case Studies: Boycotts of Law Firms and the Ethics of Informal Social Sanctions

Lawyers have a great deal of power. On behalf of clients they structure transactions, give advice, and bring and defend litigation that affects the rights and duties of others. As the old saying goes, you can't fight City Hall, but it is also difficult to fight a wealthy corporation that can afford to employ skilled and dogged lawyers on its behalf. Not surprisingly, critics of lawyers have often targeted their support for powerful interests. These critics may believe—and with some justification—that the legal system is tilted in favor of the powerful. Individuals may be able to organize and vote for changes to the law, but this can be difficult due to the influence of big-money donors and structural factors such as the drawing of legislative districts.[1] Those who believe they are frozen out of the process for bringing about changes to formal law may resort to informal means of exercising power.[2] Some of these include calling for public shaming or shunning of wrongdoers or organizing boycotts to exert economic pressure on perceived wrongdoers.[3] These informal avenues of seeking change attempt to harness social or economic power instead of the coercive power of the state. Although the responsibility for antisocial activities ultimately rests with the client,[4] critics of the legal profession target lawyers for providing assistance to clients in carrying out antisocial objectives, in part for the pragmatic reason that they may be perceived as an easier target.

Something that can be decried as "cancel culture" can also be understood as an attempt to use informal social pressure to hold powerful actors accountable where formal legal means, such as passing new legislation or bringing lawsuits, are likely to be ineffective. Of course, those in power can also employ boycotts or other informal social pressures. The Nazi Party organized a boycott of Jewish businesses on April 1, 1933, soon after rising to national prominence.[5] A modern example (not intending a comparison with Nazis) would be the attempt by conservatives to organize a boycott of Disney theme parks and entertainment in protest of the company's advocacy for LGBTQ rights.[6] The Disney episode was complicated by the concurrent use of official state power, in the form of an effort led by Florida's Republican governor, Ron DeSantis, to eliminate a special tax-assessment district that the state had created for the company decades ago.[7] It also illustrates how the issue of who actually wields power in a society is contestable, with conservatives claiming to be a beleaguered band fighting a desperate rearguard action against the massed forces of "woke capital."[8] Nevertheless, historical events like the Montgomery bus boycott, discussed later in the chapter, tend to create the impression that the use of informal social and economic levers of power is a tool generally employed by those who comparatively lack access to formal political power.

Many of the cases discussed in the book so far can be seen as examples of the resort to informal social pressures where the system of formal laws and legal institutions seemed indifferent to the justice concerns raised by marginalized individuals or groups. The effort to shame the administration of Harvard University for tolerating the representation by a faculty member of Harvey Weinstein asserted that the law was not doing enough to protect the victims of workplace sexual harassment. The demand by clients of Kirkland & Ellis that the firm cease representing gun manufacturers was arguably an attempt to use economic power to circumvent the deadlock in legislatures and courts over reasonable gun control policies. Criticizing or "canceling" lawyers can therefore be understood as a resort to informal power in the absence of meaningful access to formal power. An intriguing and paradoxical case study illustrating profound skepticism of the legal system involves a young generation of energetic lawyers and law students with progressive political beliefs. These students see the legal system and the elite law firms that employ many of the graduates of the leading law schools in America as beholden to wealth and power at the expense of social and environmental justice. It may be tempting to write this off as youthful idealism, but in fact the students' protests are part of a long history of criticism of lawyers for uncritically serving capitalism.

The next section will introduce this dissident strand of thinking about professional ethics with a famous speech by a U.S. Supreme Court Justice highly critical of lawyers who allow their services to be abused by powerful clients. Then we can consider the student-led attempts to boycott large law firms whose clients they believe are contributing to an irreversible climate disaster.

The "obsequious servants of business"?

At the dedication of a new University of Michigan law school building in 1934, Supreme Court Justice Harlan Fiske Stone used the occasion to rip into graduates of such institutions for losing sight of a traditional vision of professional excellence.[9] The law is not an end in itself, Justice Stone argued, but a response to the problem of "bringing individual conduct into harmony with the demands of society."[10] Professional groups, particularly lawyers, play a vital role as "guardians of the law" in bringing economic power under some measure of control. Unless "the more influential elements in society"—and here he is talking to elite law school graduates—act to promote the common good, the only available means of securing social order is "the policeman's club."[11] Lawyers have lost sight of the ideal of advancement of the public interest, however. Instead they see their professional role solely in terms of advancing the interests of powerful corporate clients without regard to social consequences.[12] The pursuit of the wealth available from the representation of these clients has "made the learned profession of an earlier day the obsequious servant of business."[13] Justice Stone's speech harked back to another prominent public dressing down of the legal profession, a 1905 commencement address at Harvard University by President Theodore Roosevelt in which the Bull Moose criticized the "most influential and most highly remunerated members" of the legal profession for providing assistance to clients to enable them to "evade the laws which are made to regulate in the interest of the public the use of great wealth."[14]

Justice Stone's criticism, though suffused with nostalgia for a golden age of public spiritedness that may never have existed, was in line with a great deal of worry at the time about the unchecked power of capitalism.[15] Specific to the legal profession, however, was Stone's question: Why have you, lawyers, not done something to "remedy the evils of the investment market," return concepts like equity and fiduciary duties to commercial transactions, and improve access to justice for ordinary people?[16] He answered his own rhetorical question: because lawyers are too caught up in protecting the narrow interests of their clients to consider the social good.[17] Elite lawyers serving wealthy clients have ceased to function as "the guardians of public interests committed to [their] care."[18] As a result, they can no longer claim the honorable status of a profession but are reduced to a mere guild, seeking the material rewards of a monopoly on the provision of legal services[19] Stone did not say, but contemporary theorists of professions would emphasize that having a monopoly over representing clients should heightened the burden on lawyers to ensure that all clients, not just powerful corporations, can obtain high-qualify legal services.[20]

There is a continuous line from Justice Stone's invocation of social-trustee professionalism to contemporary critics,[21] who see the problem with lawyers in terms of pursuing only the objectives of clients, without some regard for the public good.[22] There is, however, a very important difference. Justice Stone was a Justice on the United States Supreme Court. Many law students and young lawyers today look around and see no one with comparable official power offering any kind of critique of the excesses of capitalism. They are concerned that their classmates have tendencies to get coopted by the system and become all too willing to accept the status quo. Some law students therefore are urging their classmates to resist the siren song of prestige, high salaries, and fancy offices in the so-called BigLaw sector of the legal services market. A few students have gone even further in an effort to create a social stigma around representing clients who may be hastening a planet-wide ecological catastrophe.

Down with Big Oil

Frustrated with what they believe to be government inaction on the great existential threat of our time, progressive law students have sought to stigmatize law firms that perform a significant amount of legal work on behalf of clients in the fossil fuel industry, such as ExxonMobil, Chevron, BP, and Shell. An early sign of the salience of this issue was the opposition by some environmentalists to the possible nomination of D.C. Circuit Judge Sri Srinivasan to replace Supreme Court Justice Antonin Scalia.[23] While in private practice at O'Melveney & Myers, Srinivasan had represented ExxonMobil, leading some activists to complain that he would "side with Big Oil over the American people." President Obama eventually nominated D.C. Circuit Judge Merrick Garland, not Srinivasan, to succeed Justice Scalia, and Senate Republicans refused to even hold a vote on Garland's nomination.[24] The early battle lines were drawn, however, over progressive opposition to legal representation of clients in the oil and gas industry.

The next skirmish in the battle was a student-led boycott of law firms recruiting at Harvard Law School. It was initially directed at the New York-based law firm of Paul Weiss Rifkin Wharton & Garrison.[25] The students sought to stigmatize the firm for its work in the fossil fuel industry and to persuade their classmates not to consider working at Paul Weiss as a way of pressuring the firm to drop ExxonMobil as a client. The aim was to choke off the supply of recent law graduates opting to use their training to protect fossil fuel companies from accountability for contributing to climate change.[26] That effort had precedent in earlier law student activism around issues such as apartheid, where student boycotts aimed at drying up the pipeline of new associates led the law firm Covington & Burling to drop South African Airways as a client.[27]

The second, better organized wave was led by a student group founded at Yale Law School, called Law Students for Climate Accountability.[28] The group produced a "scorecard" showing how firms in the Vault 100 (an online ranking of prestigious law firms) performed on the group's metric of client representations that either accelerate climate change or promote the development of sustainable energy sources. The grades, from A through F, are awarded based on litigation and transactional representations on behalf of fossil fuel companies that, in the judgment of the group, exacerbate climate change.[29] Although many firms received a failing grade, the group seemed to reserve particular ire for the Los Angeles-based firm Gibson, Dunn & Crutcher. On December 2, 2021, the group called for a boycott of the firm (also announcing a hashtag, #DoneWithDunn), for the following activities:

- Gibson Dunn has represented Dakota Access despite significant environmental impacts and its incursion on sacred Sioux land
- Represents a plaintiff in *Brackeen v. Haaland*, a lawsuit seeking to strike down the Indian Child Welfare Act, a vital law protecting against the removal of American Indian children from their communities
- Have aggressively litigated to ensure that Chevron evades liability for dumping billions of gallons of toxic waste that did irreversible environmental damage and caused widespread cancer and birth defects among Indigenous and campesino communities in Ecuador.
- Chevron has used Gibson Dunn to demonize Steven Donzinger, the attorney representing the Ecuadorian plaintiffs.[30]

In a Frequently Asked Questions (FAQ) document included with the call for the boycott, the group stated, "This is not a radical ask: all we're saying is that Gibson Dunn should have some standard guiding its fossil fuel work other than profit. If Gibson Dunn really has no standard other than profit guiding their work, they start to sound a lot like mercenaries."

One aim of the student-led boycotts is to characterize the actions of some corporations as out of bounds, beyond the pale—so clearly harmful that assisting these clients can only be understood as motivated by willful blindness or greed. A similar strategy appears to be working to some extent with advertising and public relations firms, some of whom are reconsidering their work on behalf of oil and gas companies.[31] The effort is aimed at "turn[ing] fossil fuel companies into social pariahs—a sort of New Tobacco" and thereby altering the social meaning of providing professional services in support of their objectives.[32] Big-firm lawyers enjoy a "social license" to represent clients in the fossil fuel industry; someone today is unlikely to be shunned by polite society for working at a law firm representing ExxonMobil.[33] Activists aim to change this state of affairs. "[I]f they refuse to stop helping to destroy the world, well, they deserve to pay a social price for that—maybe they shouldn't be welcomed at the neighborhood BBQ, or allowed to coach Little League, if they're helping to wreck those kiddos' future or poison the neighborhood."[34] To say someone should pay a "social price" or lose their "social license" can mean regarding them as a social pariah on a par with child molesters or neo-Nazis. Or, somewhat less aggressively, the law students are attempting to do to these law firms what progressive activists tried to do to the restaurant chain Chick-fil-A, based on the company's practice of donating to charities that critics perceived as hostile to LGBTQ people,[35] or on the other side, taking a page from the playbook of right-wing politicians and organizations critical of corporations taking progressive environmental or social positions.[36] The effort is aimed not just at reducing the economic returns from selling chicken sandwiches or crude oil, but at changing the taken-for-granted assumption that what these companies are doing is morally acceptable.

The student protesters attempt to associate themselves with a long tradition of boycotts against powerful antisocial actors. The Montgomery bus boycott continues to serve as the moral touchstone for the use of a concerted withdrawal of cooperation as a protest of injustice and a tactic for social change.[37] After Rosa Parks was arrested on December 1, 1955, for violating the bus segregation ordinance of Montgomery, Alabama, by refusing to yield her seat to a white rider, Black civil rights leaders organized a boycott of city buses. Black bus riders, many of them domestic workers, walked or made use of discounted taxicab or carpool rides offered by supporters and harassed incessantly by police,[38] denying from 30,000 to 40,000 fares per day to City Bus

Lines and threatening bankruptcy of the private company headquartered in Chicago.[39]

The action in Montgomery was met with intense hostility from the white community, including arrests of leaders of the boycott, massive pro-segregation rallies led by White Citizens Councils, the bombing of Rev. Martin Luther King Jr.'s house, and an injunction against the carpools as an unlicensed municipal transportation system.[40] At the national level FBI Director J. Edgar Hoover was telling President Eisenhower that the unrest was the result of Communist influence.[41] The eventual result, however, was total victory, including a Supreme Court decision holding the Montgomery segregation ordinance unconstitutional as well as unprecedented national and international visibility for the cause of racial equality. Unsurprisingly, the Montgomery bus boycott continues to inspire similar efforts to employ what has been called "the weapons of the weak against the strong."[42]

By any reasonable measure of social power, law students at Harvard and Yale do not count as the weak. In fact, at first it may seem anywhere from laughable to obscene to mention a group with this much privilege and social capital in the same discussion as Black citizens of Montgomery, Alabama, in the 1950s. But stop for a second and try to take seriously the students' point: the planet is facing an existential crisis. Increasing global temperatures, extreme weather events like floods, hurricanes, and wildfires, and rising ocean levels threaten to render vast areas uninhabitable, adversely impact agricultural production, harm wildlife and ecosystems, increased health risks to untold numbers of people, and possibly even extinction of humankind.[43] At least in the short term the worst effects of climate change will be experienced by poorer people and countries relatively lacking in political power, so inhabitants of wealthy industrialized nations can fiddle while Earth burns. As a Brookings Institution report dryly notes, "important parts of the political class have been indifferent."[44] Even high-profile natural disasters such as Hurricanes Harvey and Irma and terrifying wildfires in California, or the popularity of the allegorical film *Don't Look Up*, do little to move the needle of public opinion, particularly given how divided the issue has become along partisan lines. In the meantime, companies that produce fossil fuels enjoy record profits and the lawyers who represent them are awash in revenue. Perhaps the only way to get the attention of the leaders of ExxonMobil and similar companies is to start treating them like social outcasts; one technique for doing that, which is available to law students, would be to seek to persuade or shame their classmates into avoiding going to work for Paul Weiss and

Gibson Dunn. Quixotic, perhaps, but the students' activism can be understood as a demand for accountability and an effort to influence the meaning attached to the decision by elite law school graduates to employ their talents in this way.[45] It could be said to be "cancel culture in a good sense."

The title of this book is obviously inspired by the analogy between public criticism of lawyers and the effort by activists on the left and the right to make certain actions, beliefs, positions, or even utterances so socially taboo that people deemed wrongdoers will suffer severe reputational and financial consequences. One of the striking features of the cancel-culture debate is the disagreement over the power relations involved. The activists who attempt to anathemize a person or point of view like to claim that they are in a position of powerlessness, while the targets of public criticism tend to respond that it is they who are powerless in the face of a "woke mob."[46] The capaciousness of the term does not help. If it is "cancel culture" when Delta Air Lines (a powerful private entity) has a valuable tax break targeted by the Georgia legislature (exercising state power) because of the company's objection to a vote-suppression bill (aimed at relatively powerless minority voters), it is hard to see cancelation as having anything to do with abuse of power. Or, at least, there is power of different types on each side of the balance. Conservative political officials tend to see themselves as culturally disempowered, with elite institutions, educated managers and professionals, and the so-called creative class leaning toward liberal or progressive politics. On the other side, the left contends that political power in recent years has belonged mostly to conservatives, and increasingly to the hard-right of social conservatives and the base voters electrified by Donald Trump. Cultural and social power is all the left has remaining.

This dynamic, and the profound mistrust accompanying it, tends to result in titanic clashes, such as the conflict in Florida between the Walt Disney Company and Republican Governor Ron DeSantis. Disney, prodded by its progressive employees, objected to proposed legislation, quickly termed the "Don't Say Gay" bill, which would prohibit elementary school teachers from talking about sexual orientation or gender identity before fourth grade or "in a manner that is not age appropriate or developmentally appropriate for students."[47] This led to a furious reaction from DeSantis, an ostensibly pro-business conservative, who convened a special session of the legislature to end a special land-use district over which Disney had formerly had almost complete control (and which itself was the result of the kind of sweetheart deal between state governments and big businesses that critics on the right and the left decry as an abuse of power). Similar battle lines are being drawn around access to abortion pills, with the governor of California threatening to stop doing business with Walgreens after Walgreens reportedly capitulated to threats from Republican state governors that *their* states would stop doing business with Walgreens if its stores mailed abortion pills into states with abortion bans.[48]

The attempts by law students to muster peer disapproval for the law firms representing fossil fuel companies share with the Disney vs. DeSantis imbroglio a certain murkiness about who is relatively powerful and powerless in the situation. Big corporations may no longer have the same unquestioned economic, political, and cultural power they once did. The retaliation by DeSantis served notice that cozy relationships between big business and government should not be taken for granted. Fossil fuel companies, however, continue to report record profits, driven by the recovery from the pandemic and Russia's invasion of Ukraine.[49] The so-called BigLaw sector of the legal services industry is also prospering, with never-before-seen profits per equity partner and entry-level associate salaries.[50] Yale and Harvard Law Schools continue to enjoy outsized prestige and influence, even within the most elite tier of law schools, the so-called T14.[51]

It is tempting to write off the climate boycott efforts as nothing more than "slacktivism" or, more charitably, overzealous idealism without a solid game plan for mobilizing the cultural and economic power the students enjoy.[52] But I want to take these protests seriously and, as an alternative to being dismissive of the students' concerns, consider instead the possibility of understanding them as a demand for accountability, addressed to lawyers working at elite law firms, representing some of the most powerful and wealthy corporate clients in the world. Mocking cynicism is *a* reaction, but what would a thoughtful, morally based response look like? One possibility is to base a moral defense of the representation by law firms of unpopular clients on a social function of the law and the legal system, which is to provide a "social settlement" in the form of a framework for coexistence and cooperation in a society that is deeply divided over questions of morality and justice. Justice Stone's speech suggested responses along these lines, by contending that the role of the legal system is to bring individual conduct into harmony with society. This approach to handling social conflict through formal legal mechanisms contrasts with the sometimes unruly, decentralized effort to ensure accountability for wrongdoers through informal mechanisms such as shunning, shaming, and boycotts.

Reasonable disagreement and the role of the legal system

One approach to legal ethics in the United States regards the most fundamental obligation of lawyers as advising and representing clients within the law, as well as advocating for their clients' legal rights.[53] The U.S. Supreme Court, in an important decision about the attorney-client privilege, said that the reason to protect privileged communications between lawyers and clients is to foster a relationship of trust and confidence that enables lawyers to counsel clients and bring them into compliance with the law.[54] As a lower federal court recognized, "[m]uch of what lawyers do for a living actually consists of helping their clients comply with the law."[55] In response to Justice Stone, a corporate lawyer at the time might have pointed out that their job was not to remedy the evils of the investment market—that is a job for Congress or regulators—but the appropriately modest undertaking of representing their clients competently within the boundaries set by legislation and regulation. The moral value of the lawyer-client relationship inheres in its fiduciary quality. That is, lawyers serve as loyal agents, acting at the direction of their clients and providing the specialized expertise that allows them access to the rights and privileges afforded by the law to individuals and organizations. Contested questions of value are for clients to decide. As long as it is lawful, a lawyer should lend all her skill and diligence to helping accomplish the objective defined by the client.[56]

This may be an accurate description of the American law governing lawyers, but one can still ask *why* the legal profession deserves the respect of other members of the political community when so many lawyers appear to be lending their time and effort to representing clients with antisocial objectives. The answer, I believe, is that one of the most important functions of formal law and the legal system is to provide a means of settling social conflict. We disagree quite passionately about many matters. We disagree about matters of fact and matters of value. At the same time, however, we are all thrown together in a community and have to work out some way of dealing with one another. Assuming we rule out violence, coercion, or trickery as permissible ways of dealing with those with whom we disagree, a pretty good option seems to be electing representatives, passing laws, and establishing tribunals to resolve disputes, following rules of procedure and evidence. Formal law and the legal system are an alternative to letting people work things out on their own, not only by violence but also by informal methods of social control such as gossip, shunning, shaming, and ostracism. Informal techniques of forcing social change can be unruly and can spin out of control; thus, advanced democratic societies maintain various types of formal processes for establishing rules for action in the name of the community as a whole—*our* laws, for the regulation of ourselves.[57] These laws and decisions made by judges applying them do not finally and for all time settle social conflict, but they do calm the waters by providing at least temporary or provisional resolutions.

If formal laws and the legal system are to work in this way, they must be administered by flesh-and-blood people occupying roles within the system, such as lawyer and judge.[58] In the next chapter we will take up the complicated problem of the relationship between these institutional roles and one's status as a human being and moral agent even when acting within a role. For now the point is that the moral value of what lawyers do can be understood in connection with the maintenance of an official system of lawmaking and law-applying. In a democratic society this system should take account of the positions of the individuals and groups who might be affected by some decision that must be made by the government. Elections, judicial nomination and confirmation proceedings, a vigorous free press to report on the administration of the laws, and the ability of private individuals and entities to hire lawyers to represent them are all means to ensure the responsiveness of official law to the needs of the citizens of a political community.

This argument assumes that much social conflict is among people who hold competing *reasonable* views. This does not mean that morality is a matter of opinion, or relative to some framework or set of background assumption that may diverge from others. It may be the case, as I believe, that it is an objective truth about moral ideals and values that they are diverse and sometimes in conflict, reflecting as they do a variety of genuine human goods and forms of life that can be characterized as worthwhile.[59] Writing in the mid-1990s, former Yale Law School dean Anthony Kronman echoed Justice Stone's call to lawyers not to ignore the common good while representing client pursuing their own interests. But he also admitted that what is in the public interest is something reasonable people can disagree about. He wrote that "the wide range of interests that human beings pursue with such passionate intensity" is diverse and human goods are potentially incommensurable, in that there may be no single overarching governing ideal capable of bringing them all into ordered harmony.[60]

It can be difficult to secure agreement about justice not only because of the wide diversity of human values but also owing to the complexity of factual evidence bearing on the resolution of disputes, disagreement over how competing considerations should be weighed or prioritized, and the ambiguity and vagueness of many normative concepts.⁶¹ The American political philosopher John Rawls called these the "burdens of judgment" and believed that they stand in the way of the interest that members of a political community have in establishing a basis for dealing with one another that are not governed purely by power and coercion.⁶² As Rawls concedes, there can also be *unreasonable* grounds for disagreement, such as the "prejudice and bias, self- and group interest, blindness and willfulness," which are familiar facts of political life.⁶³ Nevertheless, a great deal of social disagreement arises from the conflict between competing beliefs about what is morally permitted or prohibited.

Even where there are points of agreement about some matter of social or economic policy, there can be significant areas of contention. To return to the main case study of this chapter, assume for the moment—probably counterfactually—that there is general agreement that climate change is an urgent problem or even an existential threat. The most promising way to address it is to reduce carbon emissions, and one way to do *that* is to reduce the absolute amount and proportion of energy needs that are met by burning hydrocarbons. Doing so might involve reducing energy consumption, which might require raising fuel economy standards for cars and trucks or efficiency standards for home heating and cooling. Carbon taxes can reduce carbon emissions, but they will inevitably be passed along to consumers, who might inflict political costs on legislators who support carbon taxes. For example, a 2018 study by the Energy Policy Institute at the University of Chicago asked survey respondents who believed climate change was a problem whether they would support a tax on their utility bill to mitigate it; 57% supported a $1 per month tax and only 28% supported a $10 per month tax.⁶⁴

Renewable energy sources such as wind and solar are increasingly competitive in price-per-kilowatt terms but require additional investment by governments in infrastructure, which has yet to materialize on a large scale. Other government-coordinated efforts, which are necessary to make a real difference in carbon emissions, may be similarly politically unpopular. As *New York Times* columnist Paul Krugman notes, voters are extremely resistant to even small, short-run costs to avoid a long-term disaster.⁶⁵ Furthermore, meaningful progress in response to climate change will certainly require international cooperation, but developing counties such as India and China remain heavily dependent on fossil fuels. On the other side of the normative ledger, industrialization in these countries has dramatically reduced poverty and increased living standards for hundreds of millions of people. Recognizing the benefit of energy consumption for developing countries, richer countries could help subsidize decarbonization efforts in developing nations. As India's environment minister argued, referring to past emissions by industrialized countries, "We all have to act. But those who have polluted have to act more."[66] So far, however, wealthy countries have not acted on pledges they have made to take concrete actions to slow climate change.[67] Nuclear power, with almost zero carbon emissions, remains politically unpopular in many countries, particularly following the Fukushima power plant disaster in Japan. In some countries political unrest has been triggered by efforts to mitigate climate change. The "yellow vest" protests that paralyzed France in 2018 were initially motivated by President Emmanuel Macron's green tax on diesel fuel.[68] Farmers in New Zealand protested in 2022 when the government proposed taxes intended to reduce greenhouse gas emissions from farms, pointing to the centrality of farming to the country's economy.[69] Finally, at the risk of invoking one of Donald Trump's hobbyhorses, wind turbines kill many birds, though wind energy proponents point out that more birds are killed by domestic cats.[70]

The point here is not to resolve this technical and policy debate, which in any case is greatly oversimplified. Shelves full of books have been written about climate policy and I am not competent to write another one. Rather, the point is to see the connection between responses to the demand for accountability by student activists and the sort of response that could be given by a thoughtful, morally sensitive lawyer who was genuinely concerned about the problem of climate change but was not persuaded that it would be unethical to work for a law firm representing a fossil fuel company. There are engineering, economic, and geopolitical challenges involved in moving to sustainable energy sources,[71] not to mention substantial political opposition in many countries. For example, electric vehicles are a promising strategy for shifting energy usage in the direction of renewable sources, but they present serious ethical problems due to the extraction of metals needed to produce batteries.[72] In the meantime, burning hydrocarbons will continue to supply much of the world's needs for energy for transportation, manufacturing, electricity generation, and home heating. This means exploring for, producing, and transporting oil and gas, which is located all over the world. It would hardly be fair to see representing clients in this industry as per se wrongful.

Litigation can be a means of influencing climate policy for the better;[73] however, it can also be wasteful, inefficient, or unmerited.

The upshot of all of this is that lawyers may dedicate their time and effort to the representation of clients in the fossil fuel industry not because of the cliché that everyone deserves counsel, but because there is something worthwhile about participating in a process through which genuinely difficult technical and normative issues are resolved. This is a systemic account based on the recognition of value pluralism, reasonable disagreement, empirical uncertainty, and the necessity of making hard trade-offs in political and policymaking processes. Critics of this way of thinking see it as a "hard and bitter pill to swallow" an "unpleasant, repulsive, defeatist, minimal liberalism."[74] But one person's defeatism may be another's realism, anti-utopianism, and reluctance to harness the power of professions to accomplish objectives that have been stymied by more democratically responsive institutions. There is a real risk that telling lawyers to act in the public interest or pursue justice in the course of representing clients will transform professional regulation or theoretical legal ethics into politics by other means. If we are going to fight out contested policy issues, let's do it through representative institutions, not through requiring lawyers to discern what is just or in the public interest and act directly on that. That, at least, is the rule-of-law or social-settlement response to the demand for accountability.

Formal and informal power

I have been making arguments like this for many years; it is the major theme of a book published in 2010 called *Lawyers and Fidelity to Law*.[75] I still agree with it, but one consistent criticism of that position, which has always troubled me, is that it places a tremendous burden on the democratic process and the legal system to deal fairly with all sides of contested political, economic, social, and cultural issues.[76] I believe Justice Stone was right to see the function of the law as bringing individual conduct into harmony with the demands of society. But that only works if competing claims about rights and justice are acknowledged as part of the process of reaching a resolution of societal conflict. To state the obvious, the views of Black citizens were not taken into account when deciding that the demands of society required separate but equal schools. Even in the absence of such legalized subordination, many individuals and groups are at a disadvantage when seeking to use the political process to advance their vision of justice.

One of the premises in the law students' argument for shaming the law firms who represent fossil fuel companies is that the oil and gas industry has exercised extensive control over the legislative and judicial-appointment processes. As a result, it is almost laughable to make the argument from reasonable pluralism and the legal system's function of resolving it fairly. There was nothing fair about the process—the fix was in from the beginning. Therefore, anyone concerned with the problem of climate change ought to approve of the use of whatever informal social levers of power are available, including shaming, shunning, or boycotting the law firms who represent clients in this industry.[77] The same can be said for other contested social and cultural issues draw that criticism of lawyers for representing unpopular clients. The decision by Kirkland & Ellis to terminate its association with gun manufacturers, leading Paul Clement to depart the firm in a huff, may have been motivated by the firm's clients' sense of frustration about the impossibility of moving reasonable gun-control legislation through Congress.[78]

Importantly, informal power, exercised through mechanisms like shaming, shunning, and boycotting is not subject to the constraints on the exercise of formal or official state power. When decisions about social or economic policy are made through the democratic political process, they must satisfy certain procedural requirements. Legislation is the most familiar example.[79] For all of its faults (and goodness knows there are many), the legislative process does have certain democratic virtues. It is relatively open and transparent—draft legislation, committee reports, and floor debates are published and nowadays readily available in electronic form. Legislation may be informed by written or oral testimony from experts in the relevant field or people who will be affected by the bill under consideration. Representatives have staff members who consider letters, emails, or phone calls from constituents. They are certainly sensitive to the impact on their chances of re-election of positions they take on contentious issues. Ideally, legislation is the product of deliberation, debate, openness to criticism, and compromise. Although it is less well understood by the general public, the same is true of administrative rulemaking, which at the federal level is governed by the Administrative Procedures Act and an enormous body of judicial decisions ensuring that agencies take reasoned actions, based on relevant evidence and policy considerations, and do not act arbitrarily and capriciously.[80] Finally, adjudication by courts of disputes is governed by rules of procedure and evidence that ensure that both sides have a fair opportunity to present their case and have it decided on the merits.

The results of legislation, administrative rulemaking, and judicial decision-making—again, understanding that in the real world they are subject to predictable forms of dysfunction—reflect at least some degree of input by interested parties and consideration of alternatives. They are, for this reason, democratically *legitimate*. Informal exercises of power, such as boycotts, shunning, and shaming, on the other hand, can be criticized on mirror-image democratic legitimacy grounds, for failing to exhibit any of the virtues of formal lawmaking when addressing issues of common concern. To the extent one believes that the lives of citizens of a political community should be guided by legitimate rules,[81] the exercise of informal power would appear to be a troubling encroachment on the territory of the democratic political process.

Some instances of shunning or other efforts to penalize lawyers for the clients they represent, such as the objections by Harvard students to Ronald Sullivan serving as a house dean after his representation of Harvey Weinstein (see Chapter 3), are essentially private matters. The relationships between the university, the students, and Sullivan are matters committed to a private institution and its own characteristic norms and values. Organized boycotts, however, are often intended as a way of accomplishing public policy objectives that were unattainable through the formal lawmaking process, perhaps because formal processes have been captured by powerful special interests. The students seeking to persuade their classmates not to work for Paul Weiss or Gibson Dunn are explicitly using the boycott to bring about large-scale policy changes that have been stymied at the legislative level. In that case a deep question for political theory is whether a formal legal system is, or should be, the only means of coordinating action, stabilizing society, or working out resolutions to disagreement and conflict within a political community.[82]

Along these lines, one objection to the student boycotts would be that social changes should be brought about *only* through democratically legitimate processes. A variation on this argument would be this: whatever one might say about the ethical obligations of citizens of a political community, the duties of *lawyers* should be oriented primarily toward the legal system. It is one thing for activists to organize a boycott of, depending on their political stance, a corporation like Chick-fil-A or Disney, based on the support of corporate management for allegedly anti-gay or "woke" causes. It would be very different, and potentially concerning, however, for law students to organize a boycott of a law firm based on the clients it represents. Law students are not yet licensed to practice law, but they are beginning to become steeped in the distinctive values and commitments of the legal system. Among these—at least so I have contended—is the belief that reasonable disagreement about social, economic, and environmental policy is a given in a pluralistic society. The fact that a law firm represents clients who have objectives that are different from one's own is only to be expected. What's more, lawyers may have a duty to support and sustain the legal system in performing its function of stabilizing social conflict and resolving disagreement. Perhaps ordinary citizens care more about substantive policies than the procedures by which they were enacted. Lawyers, however, have professional obligations that are best understood as furthering procedural values respecting orderly social change.[83]

The most cogent critique of the climate boycotts would therefore be that the law student organizers are using the wrong means in pursuit of what, from their perspective, is the right objective. I am not sure, however, that publicizing the negative climate effects of representing fossil fuel companies necessarily *conflicts* with formal legal processes for making environmental policy. Once again we encounter the empirical question, raised previously in Chapter 3, of whether unpopular clients will in fact have difficulty obtaining representation. The student group's 2022 climate scorecard awards a grade of F to 39 law firms and a D to 36 firms. By contrast, there are 2 A's and 8 B's among the top law firms. The scorecard has been issued since 2017, so if the boycotts were really driving law firms to turn away Big Oil clients, the distribution of grades would look very different. Apart from this consequentialist argument, however, one could still contend that there is something improper about law students, or lawyers, criticizing other lawyers for representing clients where there is reasonable disagreement about the morality of those clients' objectives. If the legal system is intended, in part, to resolve social disagreement, then lawyers should keep their disagreements to themselves. To put it differently, critics do not have the right kind of authority to impose social sanctions on lawyers for the perceived wrongdoing of representing controversial clients.[84] It is none of anyone else's business whether a law firm chooses to continue representing fossil fuel companies, no matter how urgent the problem of climate change.

That seems like too strong a position to take. Of course, lawyers who are actively representing a client have strict legal duties of loyalty and confidentiality. These duties would prohibit a lawyer from disclosing confidential information that shows the client in a poor light and would arguably also counsel against bad-mouthing an entire industry for contributing to climate change. Lawyers are also sometimes said to have obligations to promote public confidence in the administration of justice. The Preamble to the American Bar Association's Model Rules of Professional Conduct states:

> [A] lawyer should further the public's understanding of and confidence in the rule of law and the justice system because legal institutions in a constitutional democracy depend on popular participation and support to maintain their authority.[85]

The authority of, and public support for, legal institutions cannot be founded on myth-making, however. If there is a problem with the way the legal system is currently functioning, lawyers are in a better position than non-lawyers to expose these issues to public scrutiny. Justice Stone's jawboning of big-firm lawyers for being the "obsequious servants of business" can be seen as an example of attempting to improve public confidence in the legal system by identifying problems and calling for reform. The law student protesters believe they are in a good position to alert the members of the public to a problem they might not have noticed because they are not accustomed to thinking about who provides legal services to industries engaging in harmful behavior.

Many philosophers who write about boycotts object to them for being potentially coercive.[86] Lawyers often assume that criticism is an attempt to intimidate them into avoiding unpopular clients. The law students involved in the climate boycott efforts freely admit that they are attempting to exert economic leverage on law firms. Under the "Take Action" tab, their website says, "We call on law firm clients who take climate change seriously to hire lawyers with values that match their own. If their existing counsel extensively represents the fossil fuel industry, clients should shift their business elsewhere." Members of the organization have also emphasized the effort to change the social meaning of representing fossil fuel companies, to create a stigma comparable to that attached to cigarette companies in the 1990s or anti-gay businesses more recently.[87] In keeping with one of the major themes of this book, the criticism is aimed at the meaning of the firms' representation, not its permissibility. In any case, however, the aim is to affect the economic or reputational interests of law firms as a means of altering their behavior.

This, I believe, is the heart of the objection by lawyers to these protests as well as one of the strongest critiques of "cancel culture" more broadly. Social sanctions like shaming or boycotting may be intended to result in a change to the actions of another. By definition, they are not subject to the constraints of formal lawmaking and law application. There is no requirement that both sides be able to present evidence and have their arguments fairly considered. There are no constraints on what counts as admissible evidence. There is nothing comparable to the principle that like cases should be treated alike, or that sanctions be proportionate to the wrongdoing. One virtue of formal legal processes is also that those subject to legal sanctions perceive them as legitimate and thus deserving of respect. To the extent that informal social sanctions lack legitimacy, they may cause their targets to become hardened in their position and double down on their behavior. Where some reasonable resolution of disagreement may have been possible, an effort to shame or shun a perceived wrongdoer may instead contribute to the intractability of polarization around the issue. Lawyers understandably respect the value of the rule of law, and informal social pressures are unruly in exactly the opposite way that legal processes are "ruly." The Principle of Nonaccountability can therefore be supported based on the virtues of the rule of law.[88]

On the side of accountability, or even cancel culture, is the stubborn problem of the susceptibility of formal legal systems to capture, or at least excessive influence, by powerful actors. Formal law frequently permits or even constitutes substantive injustice.[89] (Of course, people will disagree over whether an outcome of legal processes is unjust.) If the legal system is dominated by the strong, then boycotts, as the weapon of the weak against the strong, are appealing as an alternative to fruitless struggles to be recognized by the formal legal system for bringing about social change. Procedural dysfunctions in the legal system are one reason that the argument from the law's function of settlement reasonable social disagreement may not persuade critics to respect the Principle of Nonaccountability. But what about *unreasonable* disagreement, or contention by parties that are not acting in good faith?

Value pluralists believe that there is a great diversity of genuine human goods and values. There is no one-size-fits-all answer to the eternal question of what constitutes a life well lived.[90] But there is a limit to what is subject to *reasonable* disagreement. The great political philosopher and historian of ideas Isaiah Berlin used the evocative image of a range of differences in the ideals we respect and guide our lives by, which nonetheless are all "within the human horizon."[91] That implies, negatively, that there are some ends, ideals, and systems of belief that are outside the human horizon. History has demonstrated the destructiveness of certain beliefs. The belief in the inherent inferiority of people of African descent, the "natural" subordination of women to men, and the anti-Semitic canards that have historically been used as a basis for persecuting Jews, are not matters upon which reasonable people can disagree. They are outside the human horizon.[92] Out-and-out racist expression or conduct need not be tolerated, even in a society that is otherwise committed to protecting a wide range of views.[93]

However, despite Berlin's evocative language of being beyond the human horizon, as if human nature was fixed for all time, the line between unpopular ideas and those things that are unthinkable for decent people is something that is constantly in flux. One of the things that makes legal ethics a difficult subject is that lawyers, and the legal system more generally, are involved with the limits of toleration for the expression of intolerant points of view in a liberal society. Another hard-won lesson from history is that giving power to the government to decide what beliefs or values are outside the human horizon is an invitation to the abuse of that power.[94] That means lawyers may represent clients who challenge both formal and informal power. A liberal society that provides space for unorthodox ideas, beliefs, and practices is not always a pretty one, but supporting such a society is an important function of the legal profession. The next chapter will consider what happens when an institutional role, like that of the lawyer, involves people in doing things that appear obnoxious or repugnant by ordinary moral standards. This is the problem of role morality, and it is fundamental to understanding what lawyers do and why they often come in for vehement criticism from others in society.

Chapter summary

One influential strand of thinking about professionalism maintains that lawyers should act as guardians of the public interest. Supreme Court Justice Harlan Fiske Stone criticized lawyers for being nothing more than the "obsequious servants of business" by uncritically representing powerful financial institutions. Today, some law student activists are calling for boycotts of law firms who uncritically serve fossil fuel companies. Boycotts are often used by groups who perceive that they have been excluded from the making and implementation of formal law. On the other hand, reliance on formal law and the legal system can be justified in moral terms as a "social settlement" that is required given the persistence and intensity of disagreements over matters of social policy. In defending their representation of unpopular clients, lawyers tend to rely on the moral values underlying formal law. Informal techniques for exercising power, such as boycotts and public shaming campaigns, can be seen as a protest against perceived unfairness and injustice in the formal legal system and a way of holding lawyers accountable for their acquiescence in these failings.

Notes

1. See, e.g., Alexandra Lahav, *In Praise of Litigation* (Oxford: Oxford University Press 2017); Jane Mayer, *Dark Money: The Hidden History of the Billionaires Behind the Rise of the Radical Right* (New York: Anchor 2016).
2. One of the classics of the literature on the relative unimportance of formal law in social ordering is Robert C. Ellickson, *Order Without Law* (Cambridge, Mass.: Harvard University Press 1994). A famous paper by Lisa Bernstein investigated the norms that lend stability to the diamond industry—again, outside of formal law. Lisa Bernstein, "Opting Out of the Legal System: Extralegal Contractual Relations in the Diamond Industry," 21 *J. Leg. Stud.* 115 (1992). Bernstein's study was influential in the economic analysis of law, but in many ways her findings were old hat to legal sociologists, who had long been aware of the importance of so-called relational contracting. See Stewart Macaulay, "Non-Contractual Relations in Business: A Preliminary Study," 28 *Am. Soc. Rev.* 55 (1963). William Ian Miller has investigated the benefits and pathologies of informal dispute-resolution mechanisms and non-legal means of social control in a series of books, including *Bloodtaking and Peacemaking: Feud, Law, and Society in Saga Iceland* (Chicago: University of Chicago Press 1990) and *Humiliation: And Other Essays on Honor, Social Discomfort, and Violence* (Ithaca, N.Y.: Cornell University Press 1995). "*Nomos* and Narrative," Robert Cover's essay on formal law as one competing normative universe among many, has been enormously influential. Robert M. Cover, "The Supreme Court, 1982 Term - Foreword: *Nomos* and Narrative," 97 *Harv. L. Rev.* 4 (1983).
3. See, e.g., Lawrence B. Glickman, *Buying Power: A History of Consumer Activism in America* (Chicago: University of Chicago Press 2009); Monroe Friedman, *Consumer Boycotts* (New York: Routledge 1999); Brian Berkey, "Ethical Consumerism, Democratic Values, and Justice," *Phil. & Pub. Aff.* 49(3): 237–74 (2021); Scott Altman, "Are Boycotts, Shunning, and Shaming Corrupt?", *Oxford J. Leg. Stud.* 41: 987–1011 (2021); Symposium on the Ethics of Boycotting, *J. Applied Phil.* 36(4): 527–91 (2019); Linda Radzik, "Boycotts and the Social Enforcement of Justice," *Social Phil. & Policy* 34(1): 102–22 (2017); Waheed Hussain, "Is Ethical Consumerism an

Impermissible Form of Vigilantism?", *Phil. & Pub. Aff.* 40(2): 111–47 (2012); Mary Lyn Stoll, "Boycott Basics: Moral Guidelines for Corporate Decision Making," *J. Bus. Ethics* 84: 3–10 (2009); see also Caleb Pickard, "Boycott Ethics," Unpublished Ph.D. dissertation, University of Colorado—Boulder, Department of Philosophy (2019). Particularly thanks are due to Scott Altman for detailed and very helpful engagement with this chapter.

4. Katherine R. Kruse, "Beyond Cardboard Clients in Legal Ethics," 23 *Geo. J. Legal Ethics* 103, 133 (2010).
5. "Anti-Jewish Boycott," *United States Holocaust Memorial Museum*, available at https://www.ushmm.org/learn/timeline-of-events/1933-1938/anti-jewish-boycott; Hussain, pp. 117–18. For a fascinating look at the ethical, theological, and pragmatic arguments surrounding an anti-Nazi boycott, see William Orbach, "Shattering the Shackles of Powerlessness: The Debate Surrounding the Anti-Nazi Boycott of 1933–41," *Modern Judaism*, 2(2): 149–69 (May 1982).
6. See, e.g., Hannah Sampson, "Conservatives Want to Cancel Disney. It's Not the First Time," *Wash. Post* (Apr. 18, 2022); Ryan Faughnder, "Inside the Right's 'Moral War' Against Disney' as Florida Culture Conflict Intensifies," *L.A. Times* (Apr. 25, 2022).
7. Disney subsequently sued DeSantis for seeking to use state power to punish the company for speaking out against official policy (the "Don't Say Gay" legislation), which it is entitled to do by the First Amendment. Aaron Gregg & Lori Rozsa, "Disney Sues Gov. Ron DeSantis, Alleging Political Retaliation," *Wash. Post* (Apr. 26, 2023).
8. See, e.g., Susan Ferrrechio, "Big Conservative Wins, Fighting 'Woke' Disney Propel Rising Star DeSantis to New Heights in GOP," *Wash. Post* (Apr. 27, 2022); Derek Robertson, "Disney Didn't Leave the GOP Behind — Culture Did," *Politico* (Apr. 17, 2022).
9. Harlan F. Stone, "The Public Influence of the Bar," 48 *Harv. L. Rev.* 1 (1934).
10. Stone, p. 4.
11. Stone, p. 4.
12. Stone, p. 13.
13. Stone, p. 7.
14. Theodore Roosevelt, "The Harvard Spirit" (June 28, 1905), in IV *Presidential Addresses and State Papers* 407, 419–20 (1910), *quoted in* Charles M. Yablon, "The Lawyer As Accomplice: Cannabis, Uber, Airbnb, and the Ethics of Advising "Disruptive" Businesses," 104 *Minn. L. Rev.* 309, 325 n.77 (2019).
15. Jerold S. Auerbach, *Unequal Justice: Lawyers and Social Change in America* (Oxford: Oxford University Press 1976), pp. 160–67.
16. Stone, pp. 7–8.
17. Stone, p. 9 ("such departures from the fiduciary principle do not usually occur without the active assistance of some member of our profession, and that their increasing recurrence would have been impossible but for the complaisance of a Bar, too absorbed in the workaday care of private interests to take account of these events of profound import or to sound the warning that the profession looks askance upon these, as things that 'are not done' ").
18. Stone, p. 10.

19. Stone, p. 2.
20. I am grateful to Rebecca Morrow for urging me to consider this point.
21. For excellent histories of the concept of "social trustee" professionalism as concern for the public interest, which probably reached its high-water mark during the Progressive Era, see Michael S. Ariens, *The Lawyer's Conscience: A History of American Lawyer Ethics* (Lawrence: University Press of Kansas 2022); Michael Ariens, "The Rise and Fall of Social Trustee Professionalism," 2016 *J. Prof. Law.* 49 (2016); Rebecca Roiphe, "The Decline of Professionalism," 29 *Geo. J. Legal Ethics* 649 (2016). In Roiphe's telling, this vision collapsed under the pressures of economic rationality (including the emphasis on individual liberty over the interests of society) and mistrust of experts, institutions, and government. The complementary trend in political philosophy was the recognition of value pluralism by scholars including John Rawls and Joseph Raz. Anthony Kronman's much-discussed book, *The Lost Lawyer*, was an effort to revive the idea of social-trustee professionalism in the face of these challenges. Anthony T. Kronman, *The Lost Lawyer* (Cambridge, Mass.: Belknap Press 1993). Experienced "lawyer-statesmen" acquired practical wisdom, consisting of the virtues of sympathy and detachment, and employed it to ensure that client objectives were represented in alignment with the public interest. At least in the elite segment of the market for legal services (which is what Kronman was writing about), however, the balance of power has shifted so decisively in the direction of institutional clients that social-trustee professionalism would be extraordinarily difficult to implement in practice.
22. Kate Kruse wryly notes that many scholars assume that clients are "basically self-interested and uncaring toward others" while assuming that lawyers are "primarily motivated to lead moral lives and pursue the public interest." Katherine R. Kruse, "Beyond Cardboard Clients in Legal Ethics," 23 *Geo. J. Legal Ethics* 103, 118 (2010).
23. Elana Schor, "Greens Wary of Sri Srinivasan's Fossil Fuel Past," *Politico* (Feb. 17, 2016).
24. Adam Liptak & Sheryl Gay Stolberg, "Shadow of Merrick Garland Hangs Over the Next Supreme Court Fight," *N.Y. Times* (Sept. 18, 2020). The next President, Donald Trump, nominated Neil Gorsuch after a change to Senate rules, championed by Senate Majority Leader Mitch McConnell, eliminating the filibuster for Supreme Court nominees; this rule change allowed nominees to be confirmed by a simple majority. McConnell then refused to follow his own stated principle when Trump nominated Amy Coney Barrett to fill Justice Ginsburg's seat upon her death late in Trump's term of office.
25. Patrick Smith, "Law Students Protest Outside Paul Weiss's New York Office Over Firm's Exxon Representation," *Law.com* (Oct. 9, 2020); Ben Geman, "Big Law Firms are Facing New Climate Pressure from Students," *Axios* (Oct. 9, 2020); Chris Villani, "Harvard Students Threaten To Boycott Paul Weiss Over Exxon," *Law360* (Jan. 16 2020).
26. Umair Irfan, "The Surprising Protest of Exxon's Law Firm at Harvard Law," *Vox* (Jan. 16, 2020).
27. David E. Sanger, "Law Firm Drops South Africa Client," *N.Y. Times* (Oct. 4, 1985).
28. Aaron Regunberg, "Big Law is Complicit in the Climate Crisis," *Boston Globe* (Sept. 25, 2021). The group's website, including the most recent scorecard grading large law

firm involvement in climate change, is at https://www.ls4ca.org/. Quotations in text are from the 2021 Scorecard. The group has now grown to include students from numerous other law schools. Its 2022–23 Board has representatives from Alabama, Boston University, Colorado, NYU, Penn, Stanford, UC Davis, and UCLA, as well as Harvard and Yale. In 2023, the group began scoring law schools based on a comparison of the rate at which their graduates become associates at law firms representing clients in the fossil fuel industry. Karen Sloan, "Climate Group Turns Focus to Law School as Energy Industry 'Pipelines,'" *Reuters* (Mar. 9, 2023). The report, entitled "Fueling the Climate Crisis: Measuring T-20 Law School Participation in the Fossil Fuel Lawyer Pipeline," is available at https://www.ls4ca.org/blog.

29. The organization's methodology is detailed on pp. 16–19 of its 2021 Climate Scorecard. It was unchanged for the 2022 Scorecard (see pp. 22–27). Law firms received demerits based on litigation in which the firm's position was judged to exacerbate climate change as well as transactional representation where the size of the negative assessment depended upon the dollar amount of the transaction (not the law firm's fee received) for representations including "additional facility construction, asset acquisition, company acquisition, design-build, portfolio financing, primary financing, privatization, refinancing, and securitization) for fossil fuel companies."

30. https://www.ls4ca.org. The firm's role in the *Brackeen v. Haaland* litigation over the constitutionality of the Indian Child Welfare Act is discussed in Chapter 4.

31. Steve Mufson, "More Than 450 Scientists Call on PR and Ad Firms to Cut Their Ties with Fossil Fuel Clients," *Wash. Post* (Jan. 19, 2022).

32. In a January 25, 2022, panel discussion at a conference entitled "Lawyer Shaming, Lawyer Independence, and Bad Clients" at Hofstra Law School, one of the co-founders of Law Students for Climate Accountability, Camila Bustos, talked about the organization's objectives as "eroding the social license" that Big Oil firms currently enjoy. Climate activist Aaron Regunberg is quite explicit about this in print. See Aaron Regunberg, "The Case for Harassing the Climate Arsonists Among Us," *New Republic* (Aug. 12, 2022).

33. I was unaware of an ambiguity in the expression "social license" until Tim Dare pointed it out. In some instances it can mean permission to engage in activities that are *outside* the practices that have ongoing acceptance and approval by the relevant community. I intend the meaning for which Dare argues, that is, that a social license means that the practice is accepted by the community. See Tim Dare, "Social License and Norm Violation," *Aotearoa New Zealand Social Work* 34(1): 139–42 (2022). Thus, the idea is that activists are seeking to influence the acceptability within the relevant community of representing Big Oil clients.

34. Regunberg, "Case for Harassing."

35. Gaby Del Valle, "Chick-Fil-A's Many Controversies, Explained," *Vox* (Nov. 19, 2019); Ginia Belafante, "Chick-fil-A and the Politics of Eating," *N.Y. Times* (Oct. 9, 2015).

36. See, e.g., Ross Douthat, "The Rise of Woke Capital," *N.Y. Times* (Feb. 28, 2018). Douthat mentions the decision of Delta Air Lines to end group travel discounts for members of the National Rifle Association. A subsequent controversy, discussed in

the main text, involved public opposition by Walt Disney Co. to legislation pending in Florida, popularly known as the "Don't Say Gay" bill, which prohibits classroom instruction on sexual orientation or gender identity for elementary school age children. One important feature of morally motivated protests, highlighted by the Disney controversy, is whether government action is involved. Florida Governor Ron DeSantis successfully urged the state legislature to repeal a self-governing enclave called the Reedy Creek Improvement District, created for Disney in the 1960s to attract the company to Florida. Contrast this with progressive protests against Chick-Fil-A which mostly took the form of "kiss ins" by gay couples and displays of Pride flags, but in some cases also involved state action. See, e.g., Lexi Lonas, "NY Lawmaker Seeks to Keep Chick-fil-A out of State Rest Stops," *The Hill* (July 13, 2021); Kelly Tyko, Chick-fil-A Banned from Opening at San Antonio Airport, Council Members Cite LGBTQ Issues," *USA Today* (Mar. 22, 2019).

37. For the history recounted in the text, see Taylor Branch, *Parting the Waters: America in the King Years 1954–63* (New York: Simon & Schuster 1988), pp. 128–205.
38. Branch, pp. 159–60.
39. Branch, pp. 146, 150.
40. Branch, pp. 164–68, 174, 192–93.
41. Branch, p. 182.
42. See, e.g., Lawrence Glickman, "Boycotts Won't Weaken the NRA's Bottom Line—But That's Not the Point," *Globe & Mail* (Mar. 2, 2018).
43. See, e.g., David Wallace-Wells, *The Uninhabitable Earth: Life After Warming* (New York: Tim Duggan Books 2019). The chapter titles of Section II summarize the danger in pithy but apocalyptic language: Heat death, hunger, drowning, wildfire, disasters no longer natural, freshwater drain, dying oceans, unbreathable air, plagues of warming, economic collapse, climate conflict. See also Justice Kagan's dissent in *West Virginia v. Environmental Protection Agency*, 597 U.S. ___ (2022). Her opinion lists the foreseeable harms linked to rapidly warming temperatures (internal quotation marks and citations omitted):

> The rise in temperatures brings with it increases in heat-related deaths, coastal inundation and erosion, more frequent and intense hurricanes, floods, and other extreme weather events, drought, destruction of ecosystems, and potentially significant disruptions of food production. If the current rate of emissions continues, children born this year could live to see parts of the Eastern seaboard swallowed by the ocean. Rising waters, scorching heat, and other severe weather conditions could force mass migration events, political crises, civil unrest, and even state failure. And by the end of this century, climate change could be the cause of 4.6 million excess yearly deaths.

44. Elaine Kamarck, "The Challenging Politics of Climate Change," *Brookings Institution Report* (Sept. 23, 2019), available at https://www.brookings.edu/research/the-challenging-politics-of-climate-change/
45. Radzik, pp. 112–15 (associating expressive boycotts with Darwall's notion of second-personal demands for accountability in a moral community).
46. See generally Aja Romano, "The Second Wave of Cancel Culture," *Vox* (May 5, 2021).

47. See, e.g., Derek Thompson, "This Is How America's Culture War Death Spirals," *The Atlantic* (May 2, 2022); Andrew Atterbury, "DeSantis Revokes Disney's Special Status After 'Don't Say Gay' Opposition," *Politico* (Apr. 22, 2022); Camille Squires, "Florida's Battle with Disney, Explained," *Quartz* (Apr. 22, 2022).
48. Niha Masih, "California Suspends $54M Walgreens Contract over Abortion Pills Policy," *Wash. Post* (Mar. 9, 2023); Niha Masih, "California to Cut Ties with Walgreens over Abortion Pill Sales, Newsom Says," *Wash. Post* (Mar. 7, 2023).
49. Isabella Simonetti, "Exxon and Chevron Report Record Profits on High Oil and Gas Prices, *N.Y. Times* (July 29. 2022).
50. W. Bradley Wendel, "Rumors of the Death of Big Law Are Greatly Exaggerated," 36 *Georgetown Journal of Legal Ethics* 177 (2023) (reviewing Mitt Regan & Lisa H. Rohrer, *BigLaw: Money and Meaning in the Modern Law Firm* (Chicago: University of Chicago Press 2021)). I dislike the term "BigLaw" intensely but the usage is now well established, as evidenced by this book by two serious scholars of the legal profession.
51. T14 is a term, widely used online and among pre-law advisors, for the 14 law schools that have at some time been in the top 10, as ranked by the magazine *U.S. News and World Report*, which as far as I can tell no longer does anything except rank higher education programs. The traditional T14 are Yale, Harvard, Stanford, Chicago, Columbia, NYU, Penn, Virginia, Berkeley, Michigan, Duke, Cornell, Northwestern, and Georgetown. Texas and UCLA have occasionally made an appearance in the top 14, but since they have never been in the top 10 they are not in the "traditional" T14.
52. Engaging in conspicuous displays of pro-social behavior may have a kind of psychological whitewashing effect, tacitly permitting people who engage in it to behave antisocially in private. See Jennifer Jacquet, *Is Shame Necessary?* (New York: Pantheon Books 2015), pp. 51–53.
53. Stephen L. Pepper, "The Lawyer's Amoral Ethical Role: A Defense, a Problem, and Some Possibilities," 1986 *Am. B. Found. Res. J.* 613.
54. *Upjohn Co. v. United States*, 449 U.S. 383, 389 (1981).
55. *United States v. Chen*, 99 F.3d 1495, 1500 (9th Cir. 1996).
56. I have argued that the most fundamental obligation in the law of lawyering is stated in Section 16(1) of the Restatement of the Law Governing Lawyers: "To the extent consistent with the lawyer's other legal duties . . . a lawyer must, within the scope of the representation . . . proceed in a manner reasonably calculated to advance a client's lawful objectives, as defined by the client after consultation." See W. Bradley Wendel, "Constructing a Legal Field: The Restatement of the Law Governing Lawyers," in Andrew S. Gold & Robert W. Gordon eds., *The American Law Institute—A Centennial History* (Oxford: Oxford University Press 2022).
57. Compare the interesting historical argument reviewed by James Whitman, that the decline in shame sanctions in the West was part of a state effort at crowd control, which in turn was linked with the rise of authoritarian governments. James Q. Whitman, "What Is Wrong with Inflicting Shame Sanctions," 107 *Yale L.J.* 1055 (1998), pp. 1082–85. Whitman also recognizes something that is integral to the analysis of formal and informal power touched upon here: "[I]n the American tradition,

there is a consensus that the government cannot permit itself to be guided in its decisionmaking by fear of riots" (p. 1085).
58. Or executioners, as pointed out by Arthur Applbaum's fictionalized Charles-Henri Sanson, who argues that if courts are going to decree the death penalty for criminals, then there must be a public role of executioner: "It is incoherent to desire the capital punishment be executed and condemn the executioner." Arthur Isak Applbaum, "Professional Detachment: The Executioner of Paris," 109 *Harv. L. Rev.* 458, 479 (1995).
59. Isaiah Berlin, *The Crooked Timber of Humanity* (Henry Hardy, ed., Princeton: Princeton University Press 1990); George Crowder, "Pluralism, Relativism, and Liberalism," in Joshua L. Cherniss & Steven B. Smith eds., *The Cambridge Companion to Isaiah Berlin* (Cambridge: Cambridge University Press 2018), p. 229.
60. Anthony T. Kronman, *The Lost Lawyer* (Cambridge, Mass.: Belknap Press 1995).
61. John Rawls, *Political Liberalism* (New York: Columbia University Press, paperback ed. 1993), pp. lx, 55–58.
62. Rawls, p. lxii.
63. Rawls, p. 58.
64. As reported in an article discussing many other examples of people's unwillingness to make personal sacrifices to combat climate change. Kevin Drum, "We Need a Massive Climate War Effort—Now," *Mother Jones* (Jan./Feb. 2020).
65. Paul Krugman, "Climate Politics Are Worse Than You Think," *N.Y. Times* (July 18, 2022). After hundreds of thousands of people in the United States died in the Covid-19 pandemic, the major political result seems to be efforts to hamstring public health officials from responding energetically to any future threat. Lauren Weber & Joel Achenbach, "Covid Backlash Hobbles Public Health and Future Pandemic Response," *Wash. Post* (Mar. 8, 2023). Given the more remote and abstract threat of climate change, the reaction to a highly salient threat like a highly contagious respiratory virus does not bode well for political responses to rising global temperatures.
66. Quoted in Sha Hua & Phred Dvorak, "China, India Complicate Biden's Climate Ambitions," *Wall St. J.* (Apr. 22, 2021).
67. Brady Dennis, "Pandemic, War, Politics Hamper Global Push for Climate Action," *Wash. Post* (May 2, 2022).
68. Jake Ciganiero, "Who Are France's Yellow Vest Protesters, and What Do They Want?," *NPR* (Dec. 3, 2018).
69. Associated Press, "New Zealand Farmers Hit Streets to Protest Cow-Burp Tax Plan," *Politico* (Oct. 20, 2022).
70. Dr. Clare Asher, "How Many Birds Are Killed by Wind Turbines in the UK?," *BBC Science Focus Magazine* (Feb. 15, 2022). It is not only Trump who thinks about the trade-off between wind power and protecting birds; see, for example, this column by a liberal *Washington Post* writer, Eugene Robinson, "Losing Some Bald Eagles May Be Among the Trade-Offs for Clean Energy," *Wash. Post* (Apr. 18, 2022).
71. Cobalt is a crucial ingredient in the batteries used to store electricity, both for electric cars and larger-scale use. Approximately 70% of the world's supply of cobalt comes from the Democratic Republic of the Congo (DRC), where efforts to ensure

safe and ethical production is hampered by government corruption. In short, the same problems with child labor that affect the production of chocolate are present in the production of electric-car batteries. Michael Davie, "Blood Cobalt," *Australian Broadcasting Corporation* (Feb. 23, 2022), available at https://www.abc.net.au/news/2022-02-24/cobalt-mining-in-the-congo-green-energy/100802588. The majority of mining companies in the DRC are Chinese-owned, raising concerns about the potential for supply-chain disruption in the event of a political or military conflict involving China.

72. Aaron Steckelberg, Hannah Dormido, Ruby Mellen, Steven Rich, & Cate Brown, "The Underbelly of Electric Vehicles: What Goes into Making EVs, Where It Comes From and at What Human Cost," *Wash. Post* (Apr. 27, 2023).

73. Lesley Clark, "Climate Litigation Boosted by IPCC Report," *Scientific American* (Apr. 12, 2022), available at https://www.scientificamerican.com/article/climate-litigation-boosted-by-ipcc-report/

74. Steven Vaughan, "The Unethical Environmental Lawyer," speech on the occasion of Professor Vaughan's inauguration at the Faculty of Laws, University College London, on October 13, 2022. For similar criticism, see William H. Simon, "Authoritarian Legal Ethics: Bradley Wendel and the Positivist Turn," 90 *Tex. L. Rev.* 709 (2012).

75. W. Bradley Wendel, *Lawyers and Fidelity to Law* (Princeton: Princeton University Press 2010).

76. See, e.g., Allan C. Hutchinson, *Fighting Fair: Legal Ethics for an Adversarial Age* (Cambridge: Cambridge University Press 2015), ch. 3; Anthony V. Alfieri, "Fidelity to Community: A Defense of Community Lawyering," 90 *Tex. L. Rev.* 635 (2012); William H. Simon, "Authoritarian Legal Ethics: Bradley Wendel and the Positivist Turn," 90 *Tex. L. Rev.* 709 (2012).

77. Radzik, p. 107 ("[B]oycotters target legal wrongdoers when they believe that law enforcement agencies are unable or unwilling to respond adequately.")

78. For the stranglehold maintained by the National Rifle Association and allied gun-rights groups, see Todd C. Frankel, Shawn Boburg, Josh Dawsey, Ashley Parker, & Alex Horton, "The Gun That Divides a Nation," *Wash. Post* (Mar. 27, 2023). After yet another school shooting, this one in Nashville, the needle is still not moving. See Marianna Sotomayor & Liz Goodwin, "In Congress, Little Urgency to Address Gun Violence with Legislation," *Wash. Post* (Mar. 29, 2023).

79. Jeremy Waldron, *The Dignity of Legislation* (Cambridge: Cambridge University Press 1999).

80. Under Section 706(2)(A) of the Administrative Procedure Act, 5 U.S.C. § 706(2)(A) (2012), as interpreted by the *State Farm* case, *Motor Vehicle Manufacturers Ass'n v. State Farm Mut. Automobile Ins. Co.*, 463 U.S. 29 (1983), reviewing courts subject agency decisions to a standard of review that requires their actions to be more than merely rational. Under the "hard look" doctrine, reviewing courts require agencies to "examine the relevant data and articulate a satisfactory explanation for its action including a rational connection between the facts found and the choice made." *State Farm*, 463 U.S. at 43. Review for rationality is based on the reasons articulated by the agency; conclusory statements will not suffice. *Cherokee Nation Of Oklahoma*

v. Norton, 389 F.3d 1074, 1078 (10th Cir. 2004); *Adams Telcom, Inc. v. FCC*, 38 F.3d 576, 582 (D.C. Cir. 1994); *American Min. Congress v. EPA*, 907 F.2d 1179, 1189 (D.C. Cir. 1990); *ARCO Oil and Gas Co. v. FERC*, 932 F.2d 1501, 1504 (D.C. Cir. 1991). In addition, an agency's decision must not only *be* rational, but it must be *shown to be* rational; the explanation must be one that reasonable people would understand as reflecting the considerations pro and con. *Schurz Communications, Inc. v. FCC*, 982 F.2d 1043, 1049 (7th Cir. 1992). There must also be a rational connection between the facts presented to the agency and the policy choice it made. *Humana of Aurora, Inc. v. Heckler*, 753 F.2d 1579, 1582 (10th Cir. 1985); *Center for Auto Safety v. Federal Highway Admin.*, 956 F.2d 309, 313 (D.C. Cir. 1992).
81. Hussain, p. 120 (citing Joshua Cohen, "Deliberation and Democratic Legitimacy," in *Philosophy, Politics, Democracy* (Cambridge, Mass.: Harvard University Press, 2009)).
82. Katherine R. Kruse, "Fidelity to Law and the Moral Pluralism Premise," 90 *Tex. L. Rev.* 657 (2012), pp. 663–64, 669–70.
83. Waheed Hussain, "Is Ethical Consumerism an Impermissible Form of Vigilantism?", *Phil. & Pub. Aff.* 40(2): 111–147 (2012), pp. 115–16.
84. Radzik, p. 116.
85. ABA Model Rules of Professional Conduct ("Model Rules"), Preamble ¶ 6.
86. Hussain, pp. 121–22; Radzik, pp. 118–19; Altman, pp. 998–99.
87. Regunburg, "BigLaw Is Complicit," above.
88. The rule of law is a much-debated concept in legal philosophy. See, e.g., Tom Bingham, *The Rule of Law* (London: Penguin UK 2010); Joseph Raz, "The Rule of Law and Its Virtue," in *The Authority of Law* 210 (Oxford: Oxford University Press 1979); Martin Krygier, "Four Puzzles About the Rule of Law: Why, What, Where? and Who Cares?," in James E. Fleming, ed., *Nomos L: Getting to the Rule of Law* (New York: NYU Press 2011). Robert S. Summers, "The Principles of the Rule of Law," 74 *Notre Dame L. Rev.* 1691 (1999); Antonin Scalia, "The Rule of Law as a Law of Rules," 56 *U. Chi. L. Rev.* 1175 (1989). The Marxist historian E.P. Thompson once referred to it as an "unqualified human good," E.P. Thompson, *Whigs and Hunters: The Origin of the Black Act* (New York: Pantheon Books 1975), provoking astonishment from ideological fellow travelers who understood the law as only an instrument of brute repression employed against the working class. Daniel H. Cole, "'An Unqualified Human Good': E.P. Thompson and the Rule of Law," 28 *J.L. & Soc'y* 177 (2001) I tend to favor more procedural accounts of the rule of law, indebted Lon L. Fuller, *The Morality of Law* (New Haven, CT: Yale University Press, rev'd ed. 1964), emphasizing its virtue as a way of treating the subjects of political authority with respect, as free and equal reasoning agents, following Jeremy Waldron, "The Concept and the Rule of Law," 43 *Ga. L. Rev.* 1 (2008), and David Luban, "Natural Law as Professional Ethics: A Reading of Fuller," in *Legal Ethics and Human Dignity* (Cambridge: Cambridge University Press 1999), pp. 99–130; see also Robert W. Gordon, "The Role of Lawyers in Producing the Rule of Law," 11 *Theoretical Inq. L.* 441 (2010). For my use of this way of understanding the rule of law, see W. Bradley Wendel, "Truthfulness and the Rule of Law," 35 *Notre Dame J.L. Ethics & Pub. Pol'y* 795 (2021).

89. Taking on board, to some extent, a frequent critique of my position. See, e.g., David Luban, "Misplaced Fidelity," 90 *Tex. L. Rev.* 673 (2012), p. 678: "Ultimately, it seems to me, Wendel puts too much faith in existing legal institutions and too much faith in procedure at the expense of substantive justice. In places, he writes as though the existing legal system is about as good as it can get. There is, I fear, complacency here as well as excess willingness to discount substantive injustice as little more than collateral damage in a basically just system."
90. Isaiah Berlin, "The Pursuit of the Ideal," in *The Crooked Timber of Humanity* (Henry Hardy, ed., 1990).
91. Berlin, p. 12; George Crowder, "Pluralism, Relativism, and Liberalism," in Joshua L. Cherniss & Steven B. Smith eds., *The Cambridge Companion to Isaiah Berlin* (Cambridge: Cambridge University Press 2018), p. 229.
92. The so-called Overton window is a concept from libertarian politics and think tanks that has made its way into public discourse; it is roughly comparable to Berlin's image of the human horizon. See, e.g., Derek Robertson, "How an Obscure Conservative Theory Became the Trump Era's Go-to Nerd Phrase," *Politico* (Feb. 25, 2018). The difference is that the Overton window is an empirical concept, representing the range of opinions that are acceptable to the public, which therefore a politician might advocate for as a matter of policy. Berlin's idea is richly normative, involving engagement with the Aristotelian question of the nature of human beings. Martha Nussbaum's scholarship includes a clear exposition of how this derivation is possible. See Martha C. Nussbaum, "Human Functioning and Social Justice: In Defense of Aristotelian Essentialism," *Pol. Theory* 20(2): 202–42 (1992); Martha C. Nussbaum, "Non-Relative Virtues: An Aristotelian Approach," *Midwest Stud. Phil.* 13: 32–53 (1988).
93. The long-running "Dilbert" comic strip drawn by cartoonist Scott Adams was dropped by most newspapers after Adams, who had long expressed sympathies with alt-right positions and conspiracy theories, posted a video on YouTube in which called Black Americans a hate group and said "the best advice I would give to White people is to get the hell away from Black people." Thomas Floyd & Michael Kavna, "'Dilbert' Dropped by the Post, Other Papers, After Cartoonist's Racist Rant," *Wash. Post* (Feb. 25, 2023). Although Elon Musk tweeted in defense of Adams that it is actually the media that is racist—see Will Oremus, "Musk Defends 'Dilbert' Creator, Says Media Is 'Racist Against Whites,'" *Wash. Post* (Feb. 26, 2023)—the story never really had legs as a "cancel culture" controversy, probably because there is broad agreement that virulent racism is beyond the pale, even in a society in which practically everything else seems to be a matter of disagreement. *Dilbert* was also generally viewed as having long since gone stale, making the decision easier for newspapers. See AP Wire, "Rapid Demise of 'Dilbert' Is No Surprise to Those Watching," *Politico* (Feb. 27, 2023).
94. Canonical First Amendment cases such as *West Virginia State Board of Education v. Barnette*, 319 U.S. 624 (1943), stand for the proposition that government imposition of an orthodoxy of beliefs is one of the core threats to the liberty of thought and conscience. For a more recent example, see *United States v. Stevens*, 559 U.S. 460 (2010), declining to recognize an exception to the First Amendment for depictions of

cruelty to animals. For a defense of free speech *culture* apart from First Amendment *law*, see Jonathan Rauch, *Kindly Inquisitors: The New Attacks on Free Thought* (Chicago: University of Chicago Press, rev'd ed., 2013). Rauch (p. 38) sees managing diversity of belief as a problem for any society and defends classical liberalism, with officially tolerated skepticism and refusal to grant any person or institution an immunity from criticism or the final authority to conclude what is right or wrong in the way of belief (p. 45), as the best solution to this problem.

6
Philosophical Perspective: The Challenge of Role Morality

A theme has been developing throughout much of the discussion up to this point. That theme is the tension between two different types of reasons: (1) those having to do with what we, as ordinary human beings, owe to each other; and (2) those having to do with what duties belong to a distinctive social or occupational role. Interpersonal morality, including reactive attitudes and the attribution of meaning and significance to actions, is part of what might be called personal, ordinary, common, background, or "regular folks" morality—that is, not part of the distinctive normative architecture of a social institution like the legal profession.[1] There is nothing mysterious about roles; they are pervasive in our lives.[2] I am a parent, a spouse, a friend, a teacher, a scholar, a lawyer, and a neighbor, each of which creates distinctive reasons to act in particular ways. Sometimes they can conflict. I have colleagues whose children have been students in their classes. As parents they would ordinarily have permission to favor their children's interests over those of others, but as teachers they have an obligation to be impartial and fair in assigning grades.[3] Reasons connected with roles can also conflict with the reasons that apply in the background, as it were, to everyone as part of ordinary moral life. Think back to the example from Chapter 2 of the lawyers whose client confessed that he had committed a murder for which an innocent person was rotting in prison.[4] The professional rule of confidentiality prohibited the lawyers from disclosing this confession without the client's consent, which he refused to give. What should the lawyers do? These are the cases that call for serious moral reflection.

The ends or objectives of a professional role—such as the highly fiduciary ideal of the lawyer-client relationship just described here—can serve as the foundation for a distinctive scheme of rights and duties.[5] When in response to criticism lawyers talk about values like the dignity of their clients, the importance of the government treating all citizens fairly, or the contribution made by the adversary system to safeguarding individual liberty, these are all appeals to what might be called "role-differentiated" morality. The idea is that lawyers' actions are regulated and justified by ends and values that are specific to their professional role. The role is "differentiated" from ordinary morality in that regular folks do not have the same reason to do things like protect confidential information they learned from someone else, let alone do something that exists only in an institutional context, such as cross-examine a witness for the purpose of discrediting her testimony.[6] The role is not sealed off from ordinary morality, however. A professional role has to be the sort of thing that can be justified to nonprofessionals in terms they can understand. People have to be able to say, "Okay, I see why lawyers are required to keep their clients' secrets, or advocate vigorously for a position even if it seems unjust—that makes sense given the importance of what lawyers do in society."[7] From the standpoint of the background morality of ordinary people, role-differentiated morality must be justifiable.

Once someone has taken on a professional role, the question, "What should I do in this situation?" should be answered from an insider's perspective, so to speak.[8] As an example, consider a study of Australian criminal defense lawyers, which found that the most common reason given for representing people accused of committing terrible crimes was some version of, "That's my job, isn't it?"[9] There are deeper reasons underlying the duty of lawyers to represent unpopular clients, but for most lawyers, most of the time, it is sufficient to observe only that one's job requires it. There is something unsettling about this pattern of justification, however. It appears to displace responsibility for wrongdoing from the individual to an institution, such as a corporation, the state, or a profession. In its most extreme form, the excuse that someone who committed an act of serious moral wrongdoing while acting in role was "just doing their job" has been forever discredited by Adolf Eichmann and other officials in the German government under the Nazi regime, who claimed they were acting as instruments, not responsible moral agents.[10] Most lawyers, of course, are not complicit in anything as horrific as the crimes of the Third Reich. Nevertheless, lawyers must resist the temptation to simply attempt to offload the responsibility for their actions onto another role or institution.

The persistence of the personal

A great deal of public criticism of lawyers is rooted in this tension, which is inescapable for lawyers, who have one foot in the role-differentiated morality of the profession—emphasizing as it does the values of legality, toleration, and accommodating plural and conflicting values—and the other in the background moral standards of ordinary folks and the aspirations citizens have for their political and legal systems. Insisting that people remain morally responsible even when acting within social roles is necessary to avoid the "Eichmann problem." The persistence of moral agency within roles, however, leads to charges that lawyers themselves, *personally*, endorsed their clients' objectives. Lawyers struggle to refute this criticism by citing the ideal of the rule of law and the social-settlement story about the function of law, because the separation of the professional role and an individual's moral agency is so potentially threatening for ethics. Determining what criticism is unfair or offered in bad faith can be difficult given the reasonableness of asking about how one remains a moral agent even when acting in a professional role.

Consider a depressingly familiar ritual in American politics: Senate confirmation hearings for nominees to the federal judiciary. Before making history as the first Black woman to be confirmed to serve as a Justice on the United States Supreme Court, U.S. Court of Appeals Judge Ketanji Brown Jackson was subjected to grilling that was based on, among other things, the clients she represented before becoming a judge. One line of questioning related to her having supported the cause of accused terrorists detained at the U.S. military base in Guantánamo Bay, Cuba.[11] South Carolina Republican Senator Lindsey Graham argued that Judge Jackson was advocating for an outcome that would "destroy our ability to protect our country." In one of the cases then-attorney Jackson had represented the client as a public defender. In response she noted that "[f]ederal public defenders don't get to pick their clients."[12] Graham conceded that lawyers who have no choice in the clients they represent, such as public defenders, should not be assumed to share their clients' views.[13]

Then Graham cited a position Jackson had taken in a friend-of-the-court brief filed on behalf of detainees while she was in private practice.[14] He emphasized that Jackson had a choice in that representation. "What made you join this cause?" he demanded. "Did you feel OK in adopting that cause?" Graham went on:

> You sign on to this brief making this argument, but you're saying it's not your position. Why would you do that if it's not your position? Why would you take the client that has a position like that? This is voluntary, no one is making you do this.[15]

Because Jackson was a lawyer in private practice and could choose her clients, Graham apparently wanted viewers to associate Jackson's choice of representation with "joining the cause" of terrorism. Other Republican senators, and the Republic National Committee, picked up the charge of unpatriotically favoring the Taliban over Americans.[16]

A certain amount of senatorial grandstanding is inevitably going to be part of the process of judicial confirmation hearings.[17] More interesting from the theoretical point of view is the uneasy coexistence between the professional and personal dimensions of ethics. It is one thing to accept that the lawyer's professional role builds in a commitment to values such as due process, the autonomy and dignity of clients, and the rule of law. But what happens to someone's *personal* moral commitments when they take on a professional role? Previous Senate confirmation hearings and the careers of Supreme Court Justices have brought out the tension between the judicial ideal of impartiality and the nominee's own moral commitments, religious affiliation, or prior professional experience. Supreme Court Justice Antonin Scalia, for example, was dogged by questions about how he could be a practicing Roman Catholic and yet write judicial opinions upholding the imposition of the death penalty.[18] Interjecting a personal detail, Justice Jackson noted that while she was working on behalf of Guantánamo detainees in private practice, her brother was deployed with the U.S. military in Iraq.[19] This reference to her family suggests that she was not invoking or relying on the Principle of Nonaccountability to avoid explaining her choices, but rather had made a moral decision, taking into account the situation of people like her brother who were exposed to danger from al-Qaeda attacks and its relevance to the positions she took in the Supreme Court briefs.

At this point many lawyers might object to any invocation of a lawyer's "personal self." Any reference to a lawyer's own moral commitments, the argument goes, wrongly implies that representing a client could be taken as agreement with their client's position or values. The rules of professional conduct for American lawyers make this proposition very clear: "A lawyer's representation of a client . . . does not constitute an endorsement of the client's political, economic, social or moral views or activities."[20] Calling Justice Jackson pro-terrorist would be like confusing mild-mannered actor Bryan Cranston with ruthless crystal meth kingpin Walter White, the character he played in the television series *Breaking Bad*.[21] This seems so obvious to lawyers that they sometimes have difficulty taking seriously the criticism leveled at them based on the clients they represent. In fact, however, the idea that one's personal moral agency is not implicated by the representation of a client, although baldly stated in the rules of professional conduct, requires a theoretical justification that is quite controversial. It is tricky to get the relationship between background morality and role obligations right.

Three mistakes about professional roles

There are certain recurring mistakes that professionals and their critics make regarding the relationship between roles and ordinary morality. The first mistake is to see the role as swallowing up background moral concerns. In its extreme form this is the thoroughly discredited Nuremberg defense of "just following orders," but a more attractive version of the mistake arises from excessive devotion or attachment to what are genuinely valuable objectives. The second mistake is the converse. It is giving too little weight to the responsibilities of one's role, such that one acts directly on background moral reasons instead of carrying the obligations of an institutional role, including a public office. The third mistake is a subtle but important one. It comes from giving oneself over entirely to a social role, which results in "bleaching out" one's personal commitments, relationships, and values.[22] Much of the debate in theoretical legal ethics ultimately comes down to the question of the right way to understand the relationship between the roles and background morality. Thus, it may be helpful to look at the mistakes often made by those who occupy professional roles.

Mistake #1: Too much weight on the duties of the role

A fictional example illustrates the first mistake. Consider the character of U.S. Marine Corps Colonel Nathan Jessup, from Aaron Sorkin's play, *A Few Good Men*, memorably portrayed in the film adaptation by Jack Nicholson.[23] Col. Jessup, a decorated infantry officer, was a witness at a murder trial involving two Marines in the unit he commanded at Guantánamo Bay, Cuba. Private Santiago, the dead Marine, was allegedly weak and went outside the chain of command. There was suspicion that he had been subjected to a "code red"— that is, violent extrajudicial hazing that resulted in his death. Confronted at trial by the defense lawyer's demand to know whether he had ordered the code red, Jessup memorably proclaimed to the lawyer, "You can't handle the truth!" The truth, according to Jessup, was that there are difficult, dangerous, sometimes morally compromising jobs that must be done in order that others in society may enjoy the benefits of peace and security:

> Son, we live in a world that has walls, and those walls have to be guarded by men with guns. Who's gonna do it? You? . . . You have the luxury of not knowing what I know – that Santiago's death, while tragic, probably saved lives; and my existence, while grotesque and incomprehensible to you, saves lives. You don't want the truth because deep down in places you don't talk about at parties, you want me on that wall – you need me on that wall. . . . I have neither the time nor the inclination to explain myself to a man who rises and sleeps under the blanket of the very freedom that I provide and then questions the manner in which I provide it.

Jessup's claim is that the reasons that ordinary decent, conscientious people would regard as important or even decisive are not compatible with his role. Importantly, however, he did not merely assert that his role allowed him to behave in a manner that others might find "grotesque and incomprehensible." Rather, he argued that people who value freedom and security should appreciate that these goods are possible only in a world in which there are institutions like the military, actors like tough and ruthless commanders, and actions like extrajudicial punishments of those who deviate from institutional norms. As for not having the time or inclination to explain himself to someone outside the tight community of the U.S. Marine Corps, that should sound like some of the stronger versions of the Principle of Nonaccountability asserted by lawyers.

Of course, Jessup was eventually goaded by Navy Lieutenant Daniel Kaffee, the defense lawyer played by Tom Cruise, into admitting that he ordered the code red and was taken away, fuming and incredulous, to face charges under the Uniform Code of Military Justice. It turns out that Jessup was wrong about the role. Chain of command is essential to military discipline and effectiveness, but some orders, including the code red on Santiago, are illegal. However, I believe the enduring power of this example comes from the viewer's ability to see where Jessup is coming from. Owing to excellent writing by Aaron Sorkin and an iconic performance by Jack Nicholson, we can appreciate that there is something to the argument that a free society depends to some extent on hard-ass professionals who are willing to do things that people with more delicate sensibilities may find shocking. We may prefer not to think about this reality, but the truth is we need people like that on the wall. Of course, there are responses to this argument; for example, military effectiveness is probably not compromised, and may even be enhanced, by respect for the rights of enlisted Marines. Acknowledging the importance of a role is compatible with seeking to reform or improve it. Nevertheless, the mistake of over-identification with a professional role is often caused by a sincere and justified appreciation for the value of the role.

Mistake #2: Too little appreciation for the significance of the role

An example of the second mistake involves a person occupying a humdrum government office: a county clerk whose official duties involve, among other things, issuing marriage licenses. Kim Davis was the clerk of Rowan County, Kentucky. In 2015, after the Supreme Court recognized the constitutional right of same-sex couples to be married,[24] a gay couple residing in Rowan County sought a marriage license from Davis. She refused, citing her religious beliefs, according to which the issuance of a marriage license to a gay couple would be "a Heaven or Hell decision" for her.[25] Couples who had been denied marriage licenses sued, and Davis was held in contempt of court for defying a federal judge's order and eventually sued for violating the constitutional rights of Kentucky citizens who sought marriage licenses.[26] Davis's critics pointed out that, upon becoming county clerk, she took an oath of office promising to perform the duties of her job.[27] Setting aside Davis's constitutional religious-liberty claim,[28] her refusal to issue marriage licenses raises the conflict between the clear requirement of her job and a moral obligation, which she believed was ultimately rooted in "God's authority."[29] Davis said she intended to serve the citizens of Rowan County but could not violate her conscience. If one of the official duties of her office conflicted with what she took to be a requirement of conscience, then she would refuse to perform the official obligation.

Putting aside one's most deeply held religious convictions is not something to be taken lightly, even if it is required by a public office that is subject to the constitution and laws of the United States and Kentucky. But sometimes it is required.[30] In *Justice Accused*, a landmark book about American judges in the antebellum period who were personally committed to ethical principles opposed to slavery, law professor Robert Cover argues that some anti-slavery judges who upheld the Fugitive Slave Laws did not simply surrender their autonomy and moral agency.[31] These were not Nazi functionaries just following orders. Rather, these judges were committed to respecting the law and legal system even while acknowledging that it is imperfect. Law, by its nature, is anti-utopian, pragmatic, and bound to disappoint anyone who expects it to be a vehicle for the transformation of social life. But it is worthy of respect nonetheless. To fail to respect the law would be to exhibit disloyalty to the political community that has entrusted judges with the job of making decisions that are faithful to the community's law, not the judge's idea of what the law should be.[32]

Evidence for Cover's appreciation of the value of an imperfect legal system comes from the opening of *Justice Accused*, which draws a parallel between the situation of anti-slavery judges and Captain Vere in Herman Melville's novella *Billy Budd*. The character of Vere was likely modeled on Melville's father-in-law, Lemuel Shaw, who as a judge on the Supreme Judicial Court of Massachusetts refused to grant a writ of habeas corpus to free an enslaved person, citing the Fugitive Slave Law.[33] Shaw believed that the act was unjust but in a bitterly divided country was a political compromise that was necessary to avert the greater catastrophe of a civil war, which of course happened in the end anyway. Any reader of *Billy Budd* will have observed that Captain Vere perceived himself to be in an agonizing dilemma. He recognized that Billy was innocent, having struck the malevolent petty officer Claggart in response to Claggart's fictitious allegation of conspiring to mutiny. Vere also believed, however, that his role as a naval officer was not to do what was right all-things-considered but to uphold the strict principles of discipline and order that were particularly necessary during wartime.[34]

Kim Davis may have never read Robert Cover, but she might appreciate his influence on scholars of law and religion. One of Cover's deepest insights practically requires theological language to express. Cover compares the imperfection or fallenness of this world with the promise of a new, transformed world, which can only be accomplished by God's creative and redemptive work. Law, as a human institution, simply is not up to the task of redeeming the world, Cover writes:

> If law reflects a tension between what is and what might be, law can be maintained only as long as the two are close enough to reveal a line of human endeavor that brings them into temporary or partial reconciliation. All utopian or eschatological movements that do not withdraw to

insularity risk the failure of the conversion of vision into reality and, thus, the breaking of the tension. At that point, they may be movements, but they are no longer movements of the law.[35]

The language at the end of this passage—"they are no longer movements of the law"—is of paramount importance to understanding what Cover has to say to professional ethicists. It suggests that the ethics of lawyers and judges should have modest ambitions: not to transform the world but to maintain a semblance of just order and stability, as well as also a means through which people can acknowledge each other as free and equal members of a political community. At the same time, however, letting go of the connection with the ideal—"the breaking of the tension"—potentially leads to helpless acceptance of a squalid reality with no hope of redemption.

As with Col. Jessup, I understand where Kim Davis is coming from. She believed she had a higher calling than being a county clerk, and this higher calling justified departing from her official duties. It can be difficult to maintain a commitment to a profession that, by its nature, deals with imperfection, compromise, and always falling short of what might be. A career in law or as a public official seems particularly suited to those with a pragmatic disposition who are not looking for perfect harmony between their personal values and the requirements of a job. It may be that Davis's best option would have been to resign her office if she saw the role of county clerk as incompatible with her responsibility to follow God's law.[36] That's asking a lot, I know; but the exercise of public authority sometimes demands compromises with one what believes are background moral or religious obligations. Not to be glib about it, but there is truth in Harry Truman's aphorism that if you can't stand the heat, stay out of the kitchen. As Chapter 8 will consider in more depth, the "heat" can be serious indeed, and can sometimes lead to intense feelings of remorse or regret. This may be the cost that comes along with roles having a direct connection to the administration of a necessarily imperfect system.

Mistake #3: Excluding personal identity altogether

Many Americans today may not remember Ramsey Clark, but as a high-ranking government official or a lawyer in private practice, he was an important player in some of the most controversial episodes in the latter decades of the 20th century. As described by law professor Lonnie Brown in a fascinating book, Clark, the son of Supreme Court Justice Tom Clark, seems like a "shadowy yet sophisticated Forrest Gump, surfacing in the backdrop to a jaw-dropping array of significant national and international events."[37] As Deputy Attorney General in the administration of Lyndon B. Johnson he investigated and reported on the August 1965 Watts riots with considerable empathy for the grievances of Black residents of the neighborhood; but then as Johnson's Attorney General he authorized prosecutions of the Boston Five (including the publicly revered Dr. Benjamin Spock), for advocating evasion of the draft during the Vietnam war. In the 1970s Clark defended inmates accused of killing a prison guard at New York's Attica State Correctional Facility, and in the 1990s he represented family members of people killed in the FBI fiasco at the Branch Davidian compound in Waco, Texas, in a civil lawsuit against the United States. His involvement in foreign affairs included taking time off from his partnership at Paul Weiss (a law firm we have met previously, in connection with its representation of ExxonMobil) to travel to Vietnam to gather evidence of American war crimes, defending members of the Palestine Liberation Front in connection with the murder of the disabled American tourist Leon Klinghoffer on the cruise ship *Achille Lauro*, representing the government of Libya in a lawsuit against the United States and Great Britain after a cruise missile attack ordered by President Ronald Reagan, and defending Saddam Hussein against war crimes charges in the Iraqi High Tribunal in 2005 and 2006.

Clark's client list and the causes for which he advocated during his lifetime earned him a laundry list of insults, which Brown recounts: "anti-American, a traitor, a Communist, a fool, a kook, a dupe, a knee-jerk leftist, an anti-Semite, and a war criminal's best friend."[38] Why did Clark represent the clients he did? One answer is that this is simply what lawyers do. Lawyers represent clients regardless of any personal, moral, or political disagreement they may have with them, so Clark's representation of Saddam Hussein should not raise eyebrows any more than another lawyer's representation of Samir's Plumbing Service. The Principle of Nonaccountability is meant to short-circuit any inquiry into the *personal* reasons a lawyer may have for accepting or declining any given client. Being a lawyer should therefore be a sufficient answer to anyone who either criticized Clark or merely wondered what motivated him to take on this rogues' gallery of clients.

The trouble with this explanation is that it imagines that individual professionals are interchangeable. On this approach to professional roles, once one becomes a lawyer, one's distinctive character, commitments, relationships, and values disappear into the role. The only answer one can give to a demand for accountability would rely on the distinctive ends and values of the legal profession; one's own attachments, relationships, and values are "walled off" from the explanation. That feels like a conception of professional ethics roles that risks becoming dehumanizing, turning us into a horde of lawyer-robots. A lawyer may then identify only with this stance of detachment from other values, commitments, relationships, and communities.[39] A different approach to understanding Ramsey Clark, which is one I believe most readers of Brown's book are seeking, would rely on some aspect of Clark's character to explain his history of representing unpopular clients. Brown notes, for example, that Clark had a great deal of sympathy for the plight of largely poor and disenfranchised Black Americans. In his book, *Crime in America*, written after completing his service as Attorney General, Clark wrote that crime was the result of "the dehumanizing effect on the individual of slums, racism, ignorance and violence, of corruption and impotence to fulfill rights" and a variety of other social factors.[40]

That is a good explanation for representing marginalized clients such as inmates of Attica State Prison, but it does not account for Clark's penchant for representing war criminals and brutal dictators such as Slobodan Milosevic and Moammar Qaddafi. Perhaps he had a reflexive suspicion of the power of the American government, having seen its administration up close or, as Brown argues, a reflexive suspicion of all power, including the unofficial power involved in targeting some individual or group as an enemy.[41] But this tendency may have gone too far. Some of Clark's critics came to believe that what may have started out as healthy skepticism and constructive opposition morphed into something more extreme. It began to seem like there was virtually nothing that the U.S. government could do with which Ramsey Clark would not somehow find fault.

The "fungible lawyer-robot" way of understanding professional roles is not only unsatisfying as an explanation of Clark's career, but it creates an implausibly strong wall of separation between one's personal and professional lives. This can be further illustrated by a Massachusetts case that created a minor controversy in the late 1990s.[42] Judith Nathanson was a feminist lawyer who limited her representation to women in matrimonial matters. She was dedicated to the cause of eliminating gender bias in the family-law system and believed that, in order to be effective, she had to represent only women. Along came a man, Joseph Stropnicky, who obtained Nathanson's name from a list of divorce lawyers in the area. When Nathanson told Stropnicky that she did not represent men, he filed a complaint with the state anti-discrimination commission, which shocked lawyers by concluding that "an attorney or law office holding itself out as open to the public may not reject a potential client solely on the basis of gender or some other protected class." The case is now widely regarded as an aberration and a comment to the ABA's anti-discrimination rule states that the rule is not violated by lawyers who limit their practice to "members of underserved populations."[43] (Does that include women in divorce litigation?) To the best of my knowledge, no other government anti-discrimination agency has taken action against a lawyer based on a similar categorical decision to represent only certain clients.

As an opportunity for reflection on professional ethics, however, the case of Judith Nathanson remains compelling. Imagine a feminist who goes to law school with the objective of fighting against sex discrimination and being told she could not limit her practice to women. The objection I want to consider is not related to the best way to understand anti-discrimination norms—that is, if they should be interpreted to require strict gender neutrality. Rather, the issue is what we should think about a professional role that excludes personal commitments and values. On this way of thinking about roles, it would be impossible to account for the widespread acceptance of "cause lawyering."[44] Cause lawyers seek to be the opposite of a taxicab "plying for hire," picking up everyone who hails a ride.[45] Instead, they desire to use their training and efforts to advance particular social causes. Cause lawyers exist on the political right as well as the left.[46] They can be dedicated to causes including environmental protection, racial justice, gender equality, LGBTQ rights, the protection of immigrants and asylum seekers, religious liberty, or freedom of expression.

If one of the foundational normative principles of the lawyer's role is separation from the client's values and commitments, it would be difficult to make sense of something most lawyers perceive to be valuable, which is lawyers dedicating their careers to advancing a particular cause. Insisting on the Principle of Nonaccountability also creates puzzles where there shouldn't be any, such as the case talked about in previous chapters of Anthony Griffin, the Black lawyer who represented the Ku Klux Klan. *Of course* that representation will involve more soul-searching, as well as a different type of explanation, than it would for a white lawyer. Similarly, to foreshadow a case discussed in Chapter 8, someone who identifies as "a woman, a feminist, and a criminal defense lawyer" will have a distinctive burden of justifying representing defendants in rape prosecutions.⁴⁷ Finally, the Principle of Nonaccountability obscures the issue in "two hats" cases, where a lawyer wears a second professional hat, such as being a university administrator. A lawyer like Ronald Sullivan, who represented Harvey Weinstein while also serving in an administrative and student counseling role at Harvard University, cannot coherently wall off only the obligations of the professional role as lawyer, while claiming to respect the duties incumbent upon him as a university administrator.

Roles and professional ethics

The important feature of role morality is that professionals claim to have duties and permissions that differ from those of regular folks not acting in professional roles, but at the same time are not separated so completely from ordinary morality that they are strangers to the moral community. Much of the history of professional ethics, however, has aimed at showing that these two domains of value are entirely separate. This effort has proven futile and, I contend, there is now a consensus that the domains of moral and professional obligations must be connected, even while professional obligations retain a distinctive character.

One of the best-known articles in the field of business ethics created considerable notoriety when it was published in 1968 in the *Harvard Business Review*.⁴⁸ Albert Carr contended, in "Is Business Bluffing Ethical?," that it is naïve to think that the standards of ordinary morality apply to people acting in the social role of business manager. Business, Carr contended, is a game constituted by rules, and as long as a businessperson stays within the rules of the game, they cannot be criticized in moral terms. Building on his poker analogy, Carr differentiates between marking cards, which is cheating (and according to numerous movies would have gotten the cardplayer shot in the Old West) and bluffing, or misrepresenting the value of one's hand, which is a strategy made available by the rules of the game. Of course that distinction exists, but the controversy stirred up by Carr's article resulted from how far he carried his analogy to contend that many practices generally believed to be unethical are actually permitted by the rules of the "business game." Industrial spying, according to Carr, is no different than bluffing in poker: "Espionage in business is not an ethical problem; it's an established technique of business competition."⁴⁹ Unlike the economist Milton Friedman, who allowed that the obligation of corporate managers to maximize shareholder value is constrained by the responsibility to respect "the basic rules of the society, both those embodied in law and those embodied in ethical custom,"[50] Carr conceded nothing to ethics. Or, to be a bit more precise, Carr conceded nothing to ordinary or personal morality. For him, business ethics was its own separate field, in which managers are subject to distinctive duties and permissions but only those norms.

An example of Carr's thesis in action can be found in journalist Michael Lewis's first book, *Liar's Poker*, recounting his brief career as a bond salesman at the Wall Street firm of Salomon Brothers.[51] Lewis, then a rookie in the business, was talked by a more experienced bond trader into selling $3 million worth of AT&T bonds to a small customer who Lewis had wooed over a boozy lunch. The sale resulted in Lewis's name being broadcast over the office loudspeaker, known as the "hoot," as having brokered a great trade for the firm. Only then did Lewis realize that he had helped the trader unload a money-losing position, foisting the bonds off onto a customer whose first mistake had been to trust a Wall Street salesman. Lewis also learned that there was an internal code—the rules of the game, in Albert Carr's terms—that transformed his seemingly unethical act of taking advantage of an unsophisticated customer into something that would earn him stature within Salomon. A salesman could claim he was "jamming" by dumping an underperforming asset into the lap of a customer and become a "minor hero" at the firm. The prior description, in ordinary moral terms, of "screwing the customer," was replaced by the description in professional ethics terms, of "jamming."

To this, of course, the obvious response is that a profession cannot magically transform an unethical action into one that counts as an instance of minor heroism simply by making up rules of an esoteric game.[52] Maybe within Salmon Brothers it is considered a good thing to be a jammer, but from the point of view of the customer, who was eventually fired from his firm after taking a $140,000 loss on the position, it was a betrayal of trust. For the rules of the game to perform a legitimating function, several conditions must be satisfied. First, the players must have given actual consent to play the game, with knowledge of what the rules permit and require.[53] They must have a genuine option not to play the game. Arguably any move within the game that causes harm to a player must be necessary for the ongoing success or stability of the game as a mutually advantageous scheme of cooperation.

"Buyer beware" is one of the first rules of the bond market, and Lewis's counterparty could be seen as a victim of his own naiveté. It may be that the market functions tolerably well, with fraud and manipulation kept to a reasonably low level, by placing responsibility on individual participants to use due diligence before investing millions of dollars in a financial asset. But something like this account is needed. The permission to do what is allowed by the rules of the game is a conclusion that must be earned by an argument taking account of relevant moral considerations.

Lawyers have their own version of Albert Carr's notorious article. In 1951, a distinguished Boston lawyer named Charles Curtis published "The Ethics of Advocacy." In it he cheerfully proclaimed that "one of the functions of a lawyer is to lie for his client."[54] Complete candor is an ideal for "the saints, the secure, and the very courageous." For everyone else, sometimes we get into a pickle and need a lawyer who will "make a better fist of it than we can." Like Carr, Curtis distinguished between "the morals which govern a man acting for himself" and the "special moral code" that applies to acting in a professional capacity, as a representative and an advocate for another.[55] As Curtis saw it, a professional is not properly subject to criticism appealing to the usual moral categories of lies, deceit, trickery, manipulation, and so on. The only question is whether something is permissible move within the rules of the game.

Curtis appealed for support to the French essayist Michel de Montaigne, who insisted on a separation between one's professional calling and the personal character of a person who occupies a role:

> The mayor and Montaigne have always been two people, clearly separated. There's no reason why a lawyer or a banker should not recognize the knavery that is part of his vocation. An honest man is not responsible for the vices or the stupidity of his calling, and need not refuse to practise them.[56]

The "knavery" of lying for clients belongs to the role, which permits or requires that conduct, not to the person who lies while acting in a professional role. To put it differently, in terms of blame (see Chapter 4), it is a mistake to blame a person for doing something that is permitted or required by a professional role.[57] If lying in the course of representing clients is nothing more than an aspect of zealous advocacy and zealous advocacy is a duty of lawyers, then it is improper to blame a person acting in the role of lawyer for lying.

Curtis's article did not sit well with other leaders of the legal profession. The then-head of the Massachusetts bar said that Curtis's views were either "in conflict with those of every decent member of the profession or he has expressed them in a manner that can only be described as inordinately stupid."[58] The renowned legal ethics scholar Henry Drinker said he read Curtis's article with "amazement and indignation" and expressed gratitude that he had not read it as a young person choosing a vocation, because he would have avoided a profession he could never respect.[59] Better than Drinker's high dudgeon, however, would be a response that simply denies the premise of Curtis's article. Lying for one's client is not required by the professional role; in fact, one of the most stringent prohibitions *within* the professional role is on lying in the course of representing clients. The rules of professional conduct for American lawyers require that lawyers refrain from making false statements of fact or law to a tribunal and refuse to offer evidence, including the testimony of witnesses, they know to be false.[60] In addition, despite the usual priority of the duty of confidentiality over all other professional obligations, lawyers must take reasonable remedial measures, including disclosure to the tribunal, if they offer evidence and later come to learn of its falsity.[61] Lawyers are also forbidden to make false statements of material fact to third parties.[62] These rules were the basis for the suspension of former New York City Mayor Rudy Giuliani's license to practice law after he lied on numerous occasions in the course of representing Donald Trump after the 2020 presidential election.[63]

This technical quibble about the permissibility of lying by lawyers leads to an observation with broader significance: some of the conduct that people ascribe to professionals and object to on moral grounds is actually impermissible on the standards of the role. In Albert Carr's terms, they violate the rules of the game. Curtis was wrong about lying by lawyers—not about whether the "knavery" belongs to the profession or to the individual, but whether lawyers may engage in it, consistent with the law and ethical norms governing lawyers.[64] Critics of any profession should consider whether the conduct they criticize is actually permitted by the rules of the game. Some of the conduct that outrages observers of the legal profession is just as outrageous to lawyers. In many cases, lawyers face serious professional, financial, and reputational consequences for wrongful conduct. For example, one of the law firms that assisted Enron in the fraudulent transactions that eventually brought down the company paid over $30 million to settle claims related to its role in the fraud.⁶⁵ Gibson Dunn, one of the target of the law student boycotts described in Chapter 5, was sanctioned by a federal judge for "using delay, misdirection, and frivolous arguments to make litigation unfairly difficult and expensive for their opponents" and engaging in a "sustained, concerted, bad-faith effort to throw obstacle after obstacle in front of the plaintiffs" in a dispute with Facebook over the Cambridge Analytica data breach.⁶⁶ As we will see in Chapter 7, many of the lawyers who promoted Trump's Big Lie that the 2020 presidential election was characterized by widespread voting fraud are under investigation by professional regulators for violations of numerous rules of professional conduct. These include prohibitions on bringing legally and factually unsupported legal claims against state election officials and voting machine manufacturers, knowingly making false statements of fact in court or (more controversially) in public, counseling or assisting clients in conduct the lawyer knows is criminal or fraudulent, and engaging in conduct prejudicial to the administration of justice.⁶⁷ In all of these cases, there are ample grounds, internal to the rules of the game (to use Curtis's metaphor), for regarding these lawyers as wrongdoers.

The moral foundations of the lawyer's professional role, at least as I see it, are the recognition by a political community that some institutional mechanism is needed to channel reasonable disagreement about facts and values into some kind of common ground.⁶⁸ The legal system establishes what is sometimes referred to as a "social settlement" of controversies big and small. These can include momentous issues such as the availability of abortion or the permission of same-sex couples to marry, but they also arise in connection with more particularized, but still morally freighted matters. For example, a brief but intense public controversy broke out in 2020 over the representation of two multinational food companies, Nestlé and Cargill, in litigation arising under the Alien Tort Statute.⁶⁹ The lawsuits were brought by citizens of Mali who claimed they were trafficked to work in Côte d'Ivoire on cocoa plantations that supplied ingredients to American companies.⁷⁰ On the defense side was Neal Katyal, who had formerly served as Acting United States Solicitor General in the Obama administration, and who was widely regarded as a progressive lawyer.⁷¹ One substantive issue in the litigation was what constitutes the *purposeful* employment of slave labor. West African cocoa producers are overwhelmingly organized as small family farms, who sell their products to traders who resell up the chain to large wholesale suppliers.⁷² The plaintiffs alleged that the international companies had purchased cocoa knowing that slave labor may have been involved in its production. One can imagine reasonable uncertainty over the factual evidence of knowledge by the food companies. A different, procedural, issue was whether the Alien Tort Statute applies to activity occurring outside of the United States. The Supreme Court ultimately concluded, by a vote of 8-1, that because the alleged child slavery occurred in Ivory Coast and elsewhere in West Africa, jurisdiction is inappropriate in a U.S. court.[73]

The moral argument for the lawyer's role, based on the "social settlement" provided by the law, assumes that it is a good thing to have a resolution of what would otherwise be never-ending controversies. Of course, any individual person might prefer that their preferred resolution is adopted. Perhaps they would rather it be possible for American courts to hear disputes involving allegations of child slavery in West Africa. This is something about which reasonable people can disagree. But while disagreement can be healthy and productive in a democracy, it is also important to establish a basis upon which individuals and corporations can make plans and establish settled expectations. Before sourcing cocoa from a region of the world where it is difficult to monitor labor conditions, a big food company will understandably want to know whether it might be held legally liable if human rights violations occur somewhere in the chain of distribution of the ingredients it obtains. Perhaps it would be better if these companies were potentially liable; then they might use more care to ensure that their suppliers are not engaging in serious violations of human rights. On the other hand, exposure to liability in American courts for rights violations that may be difficult to detect might deter these companies from dealing with West African farmers at all. As one of the companies noted in response to criticism, it would be better if the companies continued to do business in the region while investing in programs to eliminate human trafficking.[74] Whether that is a good faith position or merely a public-relations ploy to deflect criticism is itself something about which reasonable people may disagree. Without the settlement of social controversy provided by the legal system, a great deal of useful planning, cooperation, transactions, and investments would not take place. The law stabilizes expectations and provides resources for interpersonal engagement where other forms of social ordering run into insurmountable obstacles.

You may disagree with that argument generally or in some of its details. The point is, however, that something like this is needed—a fulsome normative defense, not merely a conclusory invocation of the rules of the game.

Are roles exclusionary or just very weighty?

Order, peace, stability, and social solidarity are good things. Let's stipulate to that, for the sake of discussion. Perhaps you would also be willing to grant that representing a huge multinational food corporation in litigation over its liability to being sued in a U.S. court for conduct that occurs in West Africa can be justified as an instance of resolving disagreement within a framework of laws and procedures that is sensitive to considerations such as impartiality, fairness, and efficiency. Nevertheless, there are values on the other side of the ledger. What about the importance of ending trafficking, child slavery, and other human rights violations? From the point of view of background morality, a decent person should have serious doubts about the permissibility of helping a company that is willing to turn a blind eye to gross injustices in order to save a few pennies per pound on its raw materials. Some ethical decision-making procedure, involving the exercise of judgment and practical wisdom, would appear to be necessary in order to reconcile the considerations counting for and against participating in the legal system by representing clients accused of antisocial conduct.[75]

One possibility is that professional role obligations have a dimension of weight that should be taken into account in deliberation. The examples that began this chapter refer to the weight of professional obligations. The mistake of Kim Davis, the Kentucky county clerk, was giving too little weight to her official responsibilities and seeing them as clearly subordinate to her duties under God's law. On the flip side, Colonel Jessup's mistake was investing so much weight in an admittedly important role that he failed to perceive the humanitarian values that should have led him not to order a violent punishment of Private Santiago. Despite its appeal as a trope, two substantial difficulties arise when referring to the dimension of weightiness in connection with professional roles.

The first is that "weight" is an imprecise metaphor when referring to normative considerations. American law is full of balancing tests that don't make much sense in literal terms. The familiar *International Shoe* test for personal jurisdiction is aimed at determining whether allowing a court to entertain a lawsuit against an out-of-state defendant would "offend traditional notions of fair play and substantial justice."[76] The Supreme Court said this test was not "simply mechanical or quantitative" but considered instead "the quality and nature of the activity in relation to the fair and orderly administration of the laws which it was the purpose of the due process clause to insure."[77]

How one assigns a weight to the quality and nature of the defendant's activities within a state, so that they may be compared with the interest in the fair and orderly administration of the laws, is left obscure in this formulation. In administrative law there is an equally familiar test that determines when and what kind of hearing is required before government benefits may be terminated.[78] Due process is a flexible notion, said the Supreme Court, calling for such protection as the situation demands.[79] To determine what is required by due process, a court must balance the private interest affected by the government action; the risk of an erroneous deprivation of that interest; and the government's interest, including the financial and administrative burden of additional procedures.[80] The interest of an individual in receiving Social Security disability benefits and the burden of providing a hearing before terminating those benefits are different things altogether. There is no unit of measurement common to both sides. The idea of weighing or balancing them against each other can only refer to some kind of rough, intuitive judgment by the decision maker.

An analogous problem arises in ethics, when the duties of a professional role are supposed to be weighed against different considerations. Colonel Jessup's justification—the truth he said the defense lawyer could not handle—was that his role was necessary to protect the freedom and security of all American citizens. Sleeping safe and warm under the blanket of freedom provided by Jessup simply cannot be compared with the so-called rights of enlisted Marines in his chain of command. Jessup was wrong about his justification and he was prosecuted for ordering the code red. His incredulousness that anyone could question the legitimacy of his actions shows, however, that a simple, quantitative comparison is impossible between disparate ideas like national security and individual rights.[81]

The second concern is that many genuine professional obligations would disappear if we truly engaged in case-by-case balancing of good and bad consequences. As legal ethics scholar David Luban rightly observes, the marginal harm to the system that results from violating one's professional duty in a particular case is generally slight: "When common morality clashes with role morality the exceptional cases in which the duty must be overridden simply devour the duty itself; role morality usually loses."[82] Role obligations would unwind easily if they were always weighed against ordinary moral considerations. Kim Davis's refusal to issue a marriage license to David Ermold and David Moore was humiliating to the couple in the moment, but they were eventually able to marry. Someone in Davis's position could understandably perceive the harm to the couple as less weighty than the importance of following God's law.

Luban's response to this concern is to concede that professional roles are associated with genuine duties. These duties apply regardless of whether there would be better consequences to violating them. As Luban acknowledges, however, most duties are not absolute; they may be overridden in appropriate cases.[83] The classic, if somewhat trite, example is that a promise to attend your child's music recital creates a duty, but if on the way to the recital you encounter someone in distress and stop to provide assistance, you have not acted wrongly. The duty to keep the promise is overridden by the compelling need of the person in need of assistance. However, a less compelling reason, such as a last-minute opportunity to grab a beer with a friend after work, would not override the duty. Luban says that professional duties should be treated as presumptions and may be overridden in appropriate cases. Quite a bit will turn on the conditions under which professional duties may be overridden. Is it when there is a threat of a grave injustice or a serious harm to another? If so, how should a lawyer deal with the problem that lies at the foundation of the legal system, which is that people reasonably disagree about issues such as when something is an injustice or a grave injustice.

The intractability of disagreement over both substantive issues regarding justice and what lawyers would think of as procedural issues such as jurisdiction, fairness to all parties in a dispute, and finality (most notably in the form of statutes of limitation, providing that the assertion of claims may be barred by the passage of time), led me to advocate for a very strong form of role obligation. Following the late legal philosopher Joseph Raz, I contended that professional roles ought to have an exclusionary effect on the reasons that would otherwise apply, if the person in question were not occupying the role of lawyer.[84] Law, according to Raz, claims authority. Raz rightly saw the law's claim to legitimate *practical* authority as a real puzzle. For one thing, it runs contrary to the ideal of self-determination or autonomy that is often connected with political liberalism. The frequently quoted closing lines from *Invictus*, "I am the master of my fate / I am the captain of my soul," express something close to Immanuel Kant's insight that we are rational beings capable of, and indeed duty bound to, act pursuant to laws we "legislate" for ourselves, independent of any external influence.[85] Raz's solution to this problem is to understand all authority—practical and theoretical—that one claims over another as justified if the subject of the authority is likely to do better at complying with reasons that apply in any event by trying to follow the directives of the authority. Raz himself was a bit skeptical about the authority of law, so I extended his position in a controversial way. My extension of Raz's approach to authority picks up on the relational conception of morality, discussed in Chapters 2 and 4.[86] This way of understanding morality sees relationships of accountability and authority as foundational.

Recall the example from Chapter 2 of stepping on David's swollen toe. David's reaction of indignation is, in effect, a demand for a justification. If the event was the result of an accident, such as being jostled on a crowded subway train, then the person who stepped on David's toe will have offered an adequate reason for the action. In this simple interaction between two persons, it is easy to imagine the exchange of a demand and a justification. In a large-scale political community, the number of people and issues involved exponentially increases the complexity of the interactions for which a justification is demanded. There are countless swollen toes in a society in which individuals constantly interact, directly and indirectly, in ways that others may object to. The climate boycotts discussed in Chapter 5 can be seen as howls of protest by those whose interests are affected by the continuing production and burning of nonrenewable fuels for energy. In response to the objections of citizens who worry, quite reasonably, about a rapidly accelerating climate catastrophe, what response could fossil fuel companies offer by way of a justification of their actions?

My Raz-inspired response has been that, *through lawyers*, the companies can explain that a great deal of complex factual and normative controversy has been settled, at least for the time being, by the Environmental Protection Agency (EPA), the framework of administrative law within which the EPA operates, Congress, and numerous court decisions, all of which attempt to reconcile the social demand for affordable energy sources and the need to reduce carbon emissions. This is a Raz-inspired response because the participants in this debate do better at what they already had reason to do, which is to offer reasons in response to a demand for justification. Law, the legal system, and the role of lawyer all have authority to the extent they enable members of a political community to do better at the demanding task of living alongside one another and resolving the disputes that inevitably arise in a way that is respectful of the agency and autonomy of others.

Relying on the authorization of the legal system to do something is an alternative to exercising raw power over others. For this reason, lawyers are morally permitted to represent almost any client at all, and once the lawyer-client relationship is established, affirmatively required by the law of agency, contracts, and fiduciary obligation to use their professional skill and care to promote the lawful objectives of their client.[87] Lawyers are technicians, problem-solvers, who provide the valuable service of helping their clients do what the law of their community permits them to do.[88] Lawyers also provide what may be thought of as the technology of toleration.[89] In a highly conflictual, increasingly polarized society, law is the stuff that makes possible some minimal degree of coexistence and cooperation, as well as the means to acknowledge others with respect, as bearers of equal dignity with oneself, even in the context of contentious disputes about values, rights, and justice.[90]

If this is the way the lawyer's role is justified, the reasons to do what the role requires or permits have to be seen not as merely weighty, but conclusive of what lawyers should do in a particular case. As Luban notes, no duties are absolute, and there may be occasions when lawyers believe they are morally compelled to "opt out" of the demands of the role. Think about the Alton Logan case, mentioned in Chapter 2, in which a client confessed to two criminal defense lawyers that he had committed a murder for which another person had been wrongfully convicted.[91] Bad enough that an innocent person was in prison, but imagine that he was under a sentence of death and was about to be executed. Suppose further that the strictest state rule of confidentiality—that of California[92]—applied to the lawyers and they were legally obligated not to disclose their client's confession without his consent. At this point most morally, thoughtful people would say, "so much the worse for the law" and disclose the secret entrusted to them by their client.

There is nothing inherent in the concept of professional roles and their associated duties that requires blind, unthinking obedience. The role of lawyer, however, does preempt most reference back to the moral reasons that are implicated in the legal controversy. Otherwise the very disagreement the law was intended to settle would be reintroduced. Lawyers, acting in their professional capacity, support and sustain a process by which it is possible to transcend uncertainty and controversy to permit at least local, temporary cooperation. This is a good thing, morally speaking, from the point of view of the political community and also from the point of view of individuals who can give reasons, rooted in the law, for their actions to those who demand a justification.

I think the story centered around pluralism, disagreement, and the social settlement provided by the legal system is a pretty appealing one to justify what lawyers do. Sometimes the public accepts this story, but not always. In the Alton Logan case, where the lawyers kept secret their client's confession secret, resulting in an innocent man serving 26 years in prison, the lawyers had a very good explanation, appealing to the duties of their role, for not disclosing the confession. Nevertheless, they were subject to vehement public criticism, including demands that they be disbarred or that *they* should have to serve a 26-year prison sentence.[93] The public is not buying the role story in this case. What should we make of that? Perhaps surprisingly, I see it as a good thing. It is useful for lawyers to be reminded that what we do may be justified but it still sometimes makes people uncomfortable. Why? Because the law only imperfectly embodies our aspirations for justice. Unless the legal profession radically reorients the lawyer's role, so that the fundamental obligation of lawyers is to work toward what they believe would be the just result in the matter,[94] there will be instances in which a justified representation results in an unjust outcome. In those cases, people will unleash all manner of angry blame against lawyers. Rather than try to wish this away by asserting the Principle of Nonaccountability, lawyers should understand this blame as a useful reminder that their role is aimed at a social value—one that sometimes requires actions that are difficult, even agonizing, when viewed from the point of view of ordinary morality.

Chapter summary

The deep, structural feature of professional ethics is the problem of role-differentiated morality. The Principle of Nonaccountability relies on a strict separation between the lawyer's professional role and ordinary morality, but the prevailing scholarly view is that the two cannot be fully insulated from one another. Otherwise there is a risk of the "Eichmann problem" of relying on superior orders instead of one's own capacity for responsible action. The tricky part is getting the relationship right between the distinctive duties and permissions of a role and the background moral considerations that matter to nonprofessionals. There are characteristic ways of getting this wrong, as the Kim Davis, Colonel Jessup, and Ramsey Clark examples show. The case for the lawyer's professional role, based on the function of the legal system in achieving a social settlement of factual and normative controversies, is a strong one. However, the moral dimension of meaning and blameworthiness is not foreclosed by the system-level justification relied upon by lawyers. This creates tension between role-based and ordinary moral evaluation, which is entirely to the good, because it prevents roles and ordinary morality from an extreme separation.

Notes

1. David Luban, "Freedom and Constraint in Legal Ethics: Some Mid-Course Corrections to *Lawyers and Justice*," 49 *Md. L. Rev.* 424 (1990), refers to the conflict between "common morality" and role morality. The discussion in this chapter is considerably indebted to Luban's work, as well as Tim Dare's. For the latter see Tim Dare, *The Counsel of Rogues? A Defence of the Standard Conception of the Lawyer's Role* (London: Ashgate 2009). Dare uses the term "ordinary morality."
2. Tim Dare, "Roles All the Way Down," in Tim Dare & Christine Swanton, eds., *Perspectives on Role Ethics* (New York: Routledge 2020).
3. The example is from Dare, *Counsel of Rogues?*, pp. 31–32.
4. Alton Logan with Berl Falbaum, *Justice Failed: How "Legal Ethics" Kept Me in Prison for 26 Years* (Berkeley: Counterpoint 2016).
5. See Dare, *Counsel of Rogues?*, p. 34, understanding role obligations as those moral requirements whose content is determined by the function of the role and which apply by virtue of one's status as an occupant of the role. I have argued that the duties of lawyers as agents and fiduciaries of their clients—not just in litigation representation, but in transactional and compliance counseling work as well—as central to the permissibility of lawyers' actions on behalf of clients. See, e.g., W. Bradley Wendel, "Understanding the Complex Loyalty of Lawyers: Dual-Commission, Governance Mandate, and Intrinsic-Limit Analyses," in John Oberdiek & Paul B. Miller eds., *II Oxford Studies in Private Law Theory* (Oxford: Oxford University Press 2023); W. Bradley Wendel, "Constructing a Legal Field: The Restatement of the Law Governing Lawyers," in Andrew S. Gold & Robert W. Gordon eds., *The American Law Institute—A Centennial History* (Oxford: Oxford University Press 2023); W. Bradley Wendel, "Should Lawyers Be Loyal to Clients, the Law, or Both?", 65 *Am. J. Juris.* 19 (2020).
6. Political philosopher Arthur Applbaum imagines an entertaining but substantively serious dialogue between a journalist and Charles-Henri Sanson, the executioner of Paris, who served under successive governments during the French Revolution. Applbaum has the fictionalized Sanson claim, "I was not needed to *kill* Robespierre—any number of vengeful citizens were prepared to do that but only I could *execute* him." Arthur Isak Applbaum, "Professional Detachment: The Executioner of Paris," 109 *Harv. L. Rev.* 458 (1995), p. 483. One of the core claims of role-differentiated morality is that different descriptions may be given to the same act of taking the life of another person. Killing and executing are different because the latter act proceeds under government authority, which must answer to the demand that its authority be legitimate. (In Applbaum's dialogue, Sanson defends a minimal conception of legitimacy, contending that a death sentence is legitimate if it is issued by a government that maintains a monopoly over the use of force: "I would execute innocents condemned to death by a judicial process authorized by the existing regime, so long as the practice of execution contributed to the maintenance of the rudiments of social order." Applbaum, p. 483.) Whatever one thinks about the success or failure of Sanson's proffered justification in this case, it is a very clear example of the claim that roles change the relevant descriptions of actions: "The act of execution that

the executioner performs on the scaffold does not exist apart from his professional role –it is constituted by it." Applbaum, p. 484. The distinction between those acts that are personal and those that are institutional—here exemplified by killing vs. execution—may be thought to underwrite an institutional excuse for wrongdoing. The blame for chopping off heads, conducting a humiliating cross-examination of a witness, keeping a client's secret, exploiting legal loopholes, and so on, belongs to the legal system, not the actor who performs a role within it. Postema notes that this argument tends to beg the question straightaway, unless there is some way of specifying which wrongs are personal and which are institutional. Gerald J. Postema, "Moral Responsibility in Professional Ethics," 55 *NYU L. Rev.* 63, 80 (1980). As he rightly observes, some acts cannot exist apart from an institution; describing "hitting a home run" necessarily makes reference to baseball. But some wrongs have both a personal and an institutional character. See also Dare, *Counsel of Rogues?*, pp. 30–33. Bernard Williams refers to it as a familiar point that some acts (e.g., harassing witnesses) cannot be done in a non-professional context but that, for other acts, there are multiple, potentially morally relevant descriptions. Bernard Williams, "Professional Morality and Its Dispositions," in *Making Sense of Humanity and Other Philosophical Papers 1982–1993* (Cambridge: Cambridge University Press 1995), pp. 193–94. He suggests differentiating the acts in terms of the dispositions that are characteristic of professionals and non-professionals that are connected with the performance of various acts.

7. While working on this book I encountered many episodes such as the criticism of the consulting firm McKinsey & Company for its work supporting authoritarian governments around the world. Walt Bogdanich & Michael Forsythe, "How McKinsey Has Helped Raise the Stature of Authoritarian Governments," *N.Y. Times* (Dec. 15, 2018). The pattern of criticism of other professions may be similar in that it juxtaposes what is taken as "business as usual" within the profession with the standards of background morality. The defense by the profession of the permissibility of these actions would be very different, however, from that given by lawyers. Lawyers play a vital role in a system that aims at stabilizing conflict in a liberal democracy. To the extent that is a good thing, it can balance out the negative evaluation grounded in background morality. Other professions will have their own characteristic arguments in response to the burden of proof put on them by critics seeking to hold them accountable. The pattern of the debate will be similar, even though the specific justifications offered will vary depending on the social function of the profession.

8. "For the person who maximally identifies with his role, the response 'because I am a lawyer,' or more generally 'because that's my job,' suffices as a complete answer to the question 'why do that?'" Postema, p. 75.

9. Abbe Smith, "Defending the Unpopular Down-Under," 30 *Melb. U. L. Rev.* 496, 505 (2006)

10. David Luban, "The Legal Ethics of Wrongful Obedience," in *Legal Ethics and Human Dignity* (Cambridge: Cambridge University Press 2007), pp. 250-52; Hannah Arendt, *Eichmann in Jerusalem: A Report on the Banality of Evil* (New York: Viking Press

1963); Alasdair MacIntyre, "Social Structures and Their Threats to Moral Agency," *Philosophy* 74: 311 (1999).

11. Jordan S. Rubin, "Jackson's Guantanamo Work Prompts Republican Criticism," *Bloomberg Law* (Feb. 25, 2022). The article notes criticism from the Republican National Committee: "Despite Jackson's claim that she did not get to choose her clients as a public defender, she continued to advocate for Guantanamo terrorists when she went into private practice," See also Jordain Carney, "GOP Raises Red Flag on Supreme Court Nominee's Guantánamo Work," *The Hill* (March. 14, 2022); Charlie Savage, "As a Public Defender, Supreme Court Nominee Helped Clients Others Avoided," *N.Y. Times* (Feb. 26, 2022).

12. Julianne McShane, "A Woman Created the Public Defender Role. Jackson Could Bring That Experience to the High Court," *Wash. Post* (Mar. 23, 2022).

13. Graham said: "The American people deserve a system where everybody's represented, whether you like them or not. And anybody that takes up that cause, no problem with me. You're just doing your job and I think you make our country stronger." Jessica Gresko & Mark Sherman, "Judge Jackson Grilled on Guantanamo Detainee Representation," *AP News* (Mar. 22, 2022). When a controversy arose over Hillary Clinton's representation of an alleged rapist in Arkansas in 1975, Clinton parried the attack by noting that she had been appointed by the court to represent the client. Amy Chozick, "Clinton Defends Her Handling of a Rape Case in 1975," *N.Y. Times* (July 18, 2014).

14. Kimberly Strawbridge Robinson, "Jackson Hearing Highlights Line Between Lawyer's Duty, Beliefs," *Bloomberg Law* (March 22, 2022). For the details of the representation, while she was in private practice at the law firm Morrison & Foerster, see Lori Robertson, "The Facts on Judge Jackson's Defense Work for Gitmo Detainees," *FactCheck.org* (Mar. 22, 2022), available at https://www.factcheck.org/2022/03/the-facts-on-judge-jacksons-defense-work-for-gitmo-detainees/.

15. Alexander Bolton, "Graham Gets Combative with Jackson: 'What Faith Are You, by the Way?,'" *The Hill* (Mar. 22, 2022).

16. Robertson, above, quoting Tennessee Senator Marsha Blackburn and a tweet from the Republican National Committew. Conservative commentator Andrew McCarthy sought to exploit the distinction raised by Senator Graham between service as a public defender and being a lawyer in private practice in order to criticize Jackson for working for accused terrorists. Of the detainees seeking habeas corpus rights in federal court, McCarthy wrote:

> The Constitution does not entitle habeas corpus petitioners to counsel. Only those charged with crimes are guaranteed legal representation. It is thus a commonplace in the American criminal-justice system that imprisoned convicts who file habeas corpus petitions challenging their detention must represent themselves. They are not entitled to counsel, and if they can't afford lawyers, there is no expectation that the taxpayers will subsidize legal representation.

Andrew C. McCarthy, "Not Everybody Is Entitled to a Lawyer," *National Review* (Mar. 22, 2022). McCarthy attempted to head off the invocation of John Adams's defense of British soldiers involved in the Boston Massacre, which seems to be the flag every participant in this debate is trying to capture:

> The lawyers who volunteered their services to represent America's enemies have for years analogized their work as no different from John Adams's defense of British soldiers after the Boston Massacre in 1770. Durbin invoked this episode today. But the British soldiers were criminal defendants accused of murder in a court of law.

McCarthy's attempt to distinguish the example of Adams did not rely, and could not, on Adams being compelled to represent the defendant, because he was not. He distinction, instead, was that they were criminal defendants, but surely the significance of that fact is that they were faced with the prospect of deprivation of their liberty and possibly even their lives, and were facing the power of the state. Since the Guantánamo detainees also suffered the loss of freedom resulting from the exercise of overwhelming government power, the moral case for representing them is on a par with Adams's justification for his representation.

17. Justin Tosi & Brandon Warmke, *Grandstanding: The Use and Abuse of Moral Talk* (New York: Oxford University Press 2020). During the confirmation hearings for Justice Sonya Sotomayor, then-Senator Jeff Sessions objected to the nominee's statement that she would judge with empathy. Empathy seems like one of those things like apple pie—who can be against it?—but Sessions fulminated, "I will not vote for, and no senator should vote for, anyone who will not render justice impartially. Call it empathy, call it prejudice or call it sympathy, but whatever it is, it's not law. In truth, it's more akin to politics, and politics has no place in the courtroom." Robert Barnes, Amy Goldstein & Paul Kane, "In Senate Confirmation Hearings, Sotomayor Pledges 'Fidelity to Law,'" *Wash. Post* (July 14, 2009).

18. See, e.g., Lisa Miller, "Justice Scalia Speaks for Himself on Death Penalty, not the Catholic Church," *Wash. Post* (Oct. 27, 2011).

19. Charlie Savage, "As a Public Defender, Supreme Court Nominee Helped Clients Others Avoided," *N.Y. Times* (Feb. 26, 2022); Fabiola Cineas, "Why Ketanji Brown Jackson's Time as a Public Defender Matters," *Vox* (Mar. 21, 2022).

20. American Bar Association, Model Rules of Professional Conduct, Rule 1.2(b).

21. There is a subtle way in which lawyers may have less distance from the clients they represent than an actor has from a character. Gerald Postema has argued that the characteristic activities of the lawyer involve a large investment of the lawyer's moral faculties. Gerald J. Postema, "Moral Responsibility in Professional Ethics," 55 *NYU L. Rev.* 63, 78–79 (1980). I would say this is true of some lawyering roles, like representing a client at trial or maybe in a highly contested negotiation, although other lawyering roles are more technocratic. Nevertheless, Postema's point is that lawyers who are morally invested in their client's objectives must preserve their own integrity by "drawing a tight circle around himself and his client, allowing no other considerations to interfere with his zealous and scrupulously loyal pursuit of the client's objectives." The risk of this strategy is that the lawyer will come to identify with this very stance of detachment and must "reconcile himself to a kind of moral prostitution."

22. Russ Pearce has long criticized the Standard Conception of legal ethics for underwriting what he calls a "bleached out" conception of professionalism. See, e.g., Russell G. Pearce, Adam Winer, & Emily Jenab, "A Challenge to Bleached Out Professional Identity: How Jewish Was Justice Louis D.Brandeis?," 33 *Touro L. Rev.* 335 (2017); Russell G. Pearce, "White Lawyering: Rethinking Race, Lawyer Identity, and Rule of Law," 73 *Fordham L. Rev.* 2081 (2005). As he acknowledges, Pearce borrowed that term from Sandy Levinson. See Sanford Levinson, "Identifying the Jewish Lawyer: Reflections on the Construction of Professional Identity," 14 *Cardozo L. Rev.* 1577 (1993).
23. Canadian lawyer Andrew Bernstein used this example in an article discussing scholarship on role morality, from David Luban and myself. Andrew Bernstein, "The Ethics of Advocacy: Can Lawyers Handle the Truth?," *Advocates' Journal* (Winter 2021), p. 29. I thought it was a brilliant illustration and am using it with his permission.
24. *Obergefell v. Hodges*, 576 U.S. 644 (2015).
25. German Lopez, "Kentucky Clerk Kim Davis, Explained," *Vox* (Sept. 25, 2015); Sarah Kaplan & James Higdon, "The Defiant Kim Davis, the Ky. Clerk Who Refuses to Issue Gay Marriage Licenses," *Wash. Post* (Sept. 2, 2015).
26. James Higdon & Sandhya Somashekhar, "Kentucky Clerk Ordered to Jail for Refusing to Issue Gay Marriage License," *Wash. Post* (Sept. 3, 2015). In the ensuing constitutional tort litigation, the Sixth Circuit rejected Davis's qualified immunity defense, see *Ermold v. Davis*, 936 F.3d 429 (6th Cir. 2019) and the Supreme Court declined to review that decision. Robert Barnes, "Supreme Court Will Not Hear Kim Davis Same-Sex Marriage Case," *Wash. Post* (Oct. 5, 2020).
27. Noah Feldman, "What the Oath of Office Means to a Kentucky Clerk," *Bloomberg Opinion* (Sept. 3, 2015).
28. Davis's First Amendment claim is complicated by being a government employee. In the context of constitutional speech rights, government employees have somewhat diminished protections due to the employer's interest in an efficient, disruption-free workplace; nevertheless, they do have some right to speak out on matters of public interest. A line of cases including *Pickering v. Board of Education*, 391 U.S. 563 (1968), and *Connick v. Myers*, 461 U.S. 138 (1983), establish a two-part test for speech protection. The freedom-of-religion cases that many are familiar with are concerned with the applicability of state anti-discrimination statutes, particularly those protecting the rights of LGBTQ customers, to business open to the public and whether a business owner can claim an exemption from these statutes. In *Masterpiece Cakeshop, Ltd. v. Colorado Civil Rights Commission*, 584 U.S. _ (2018), held that a state anti-discrimination agency displayed hostility toward a claim by the owner of a bakery that making a wedding cake to celebrate the marriage of a same-sex couple would violate his religious beliefs. (The finding of hostility was important because a prior Supreme Court case, *Employment Division v. Smith*, 494 U.S. 872 (1990), held that the Free Exercise Clause of the First Amendment did not provide a basis for an exception to neutral laws of general applicability, like the anti-discrimination statute in the Colorado case.) Crucial to the plaintiff's constitutional challenge in *Masterpiece*

Cakeshop was the claim that making a cake was expressive activity, requiring the use of his artistic skills. A more recent case involving a website designer is similarly dependent upon the claim that designing a website is an expressive activity. See *303 Creative v. Elenis*, No. 21-376 (argued Dec. 5, 2022). By contrast, the issuance by a county clerk of a marriage license is a ministerial act, not involving artistry or expression. Neither the *Masterpiece Cakeshop* or the *303 Creative* cases should be read to stand for the proposition that a religious liberty claim would be successful if asserted by a government employee performing an action that does not implicate the expressive freedom of the employee.

29. For the "God's authority" explanation, see the district court's order granting the plaintiffs' motion for summary judgment in *Ermold v. Davis*, 2022 WL 830606 (E.D. Ky., March 18, 2022), at *2.
30. Barry Sullivan tells the story of a Christian professor of religious studies at the University of Missouri who had a conversation with a young physician who had just completed his residency. For reasons not made clear in the article, the professor asked the physician what he would do if he had a Muslim patient who was dying and asked for an imam. The physician responded that this request would be personally offensive to him and that he saw it as his duty to try to convert the patient to Christianity. Barry Sullivan, "Private Practice, Public Profession: Convictions, Commitments, and the Availability of Counsel," 108 *W. Va. L. Rev.* 1, 5–6 (2005). Sullivan isn't nearly as outraged as he should be in response to this story. In my view the physician should look for another line of work entirely, as he misunderstands completely the relationship between his own religious commitments and his role as a physician.
31. Robert M. Cover, *Justice Accused: Antislavery and the Judicial Process* (New Haven: Yale University Press 1984). The enactments known collectively as the Fugitive Slave Laws included a clause in Article IV of the federal Constitution and implementing Congressional legislation from 1973 providing for a summary procedure under which slave owners could apply to a federal or state judge for the return of an alleged fugitive (pp. 162–63); an amendment in 1850 provided for a different procedure and opened up new avenues for legal challenge (pp. 175–77).
32. Cover, pp. 151–54 (describing the Garrison-Phillips view of judicial obligation which, in Cover's assessment, was the mainstream position); see also p. 171 ("Realistically, Story and Lemuel Shaw were as close to confirmed opponents of slavery as existed on the bench.... Both Story and Shaw not only perceived their primary obligation, as judges, to the Constitution, but they also affirmed the general principl.es of impersonal, neutral construction; adherence to recent precedent in spirit as well as holding; and obligation to make a good faith effort to effectuate the instrument's purpose even in the face of their own moral beliefs.").
33. *Sims's Case*, 7 Cushing (Mass.) 285 (1851), discussed in Cover, pp. 176–78. For discussion of the connection between Vere and Shaw, see Cover, p. 60.
34. Some law and literature scholars have questioned the conventional reading of *Billy Budd* that takes for granted that Vere had no choice but to conduct the hasty trial and execution of Billy. See Richard H. Weisberg, *The Failure of the Word: The Protagonist as Lawyer in Modern Fiction* (New Haven: Yale University Press 1984). Richard

Posner defends the traditional reading. See Richard A. Posner, "Comment on Richard Weisberg's Interpretation of 'Billy Budd'", *Cardozo Studies in Law and Literature*, 1(1): 71–81 (Spring 1989). I am grateful to John Leubsdorf for reminding me of this critique.
35. Robert M. Cover, "The Supreme Court, 1982 Term - Foreword: Nomos and Narrative," 97 *Harv. L. Rev.* 4, 39 (1983).
36. Cover, *Justice Accused*, p. 158 (reporting that one school of anti-slavery judges saw resignation as the best solution to the "moral-formal dilemma," while another school advocated an adventurous approach to natural law, in which either positive law should be interpreted in line with the demands of natural justice, through a "forced reading" if necessary or, failing that, as "an act of naked power").
37. Lonnie T. Brown, Jr., *Defending the Public's Enemy: The Life and Legacy of Ramsey Clark* (Stanford: Stanford University Press 2019).
38. Brown, p. 2.
39. Postema, above, p. 77.
40. Brown, p. 229.
41. Brown, p. 198 ("In [Clark's] experience, many governments tend to employ demonization in order to create a public enemy and unify support for their agendas.").
42. Chris Reidy, "Ruling Has Lawyers Cross-Examining Own Motives; Once They Had Wide Latitude in Selecting Clients; Now They Are Wary," *Boston Globe* (Mar. 9, 1997); Steve Berenson, "Politics and Plurality in a Lawyer's Choice of Clients: The Case of *Stropnicky v. Nathanson*," 35 *San Diego L. Rev.* 1 (1998).
43. ABA Model Rules, Rule 8.4(g), cmt. [5].
44. For some of the classic sources in what has become a well-developed scholarly literature on cause lawyering, see, e.g., Scott L. Cummings, *An Equal Place: Lawyers in the Struggle for Los Angeles* (New York: Oxford University Press 2021); Austin Sarat & Stuart A. Scheingold, *Something to Believe In: Politics, Professionalism, and Cause Lawyering* (Stanford: Stanford University Press 2004); Gerald P. Lopez, *Rebellious Lawyering: One Chicano's Vision Of Progressive Law Practice* (Boulder, Color: Westview Press 1992); Daniel Farbman, "Resistance Lawyering," 107 *Calif. L. Rev.* 1877 (2019). Abbe Smith's article about defending rape cases, which will be discussed in Chapter 8, specifically sets out to offer a feminist defense ethic. Abbe Smith, "Representing Rapists: The Cruelty of Cross Examination and Other Challenges for a Feminist Criminal Defense Lawyer," 53 *Am. Crim. L. Rev.* 255, 300 (2016). Similarly, David Wilkins's approach to Anthony Griffin's defense of the KKK, discussed in Chapter 2, is an explicitly race-conscious perspective. David B. Wilkins, "Race, Ethics, and the First Amendment: Should a Black Lawyer Represent the Ku Klux Klan?," 63 *Geo. Wash. L. Rev.* 1030 (1995). Numerous scholars have written about religious lawyering. See, e.g., Thomas L. Shaffer, *On Being a Christian and a Lawyer* (Provo, Utah: Brigham Young University Press 1981); Robert K. Vischer, "Catholic Social Thought and the Ethical Formation of Lawyers: A Call for Community," 1 *J. Cath. Soc. Thought* 417 (2004); Russell G. Pearce, "Foreword: The Religious Lawyering Movement: An Emerging Force in Legal Ethics and Professionalism," 66 *Fordham L. Rev.* 1075 (1998); Russell G. Pearce, "The Jewish Lawyer's Question," 27 *Tex. Tech*

L. Rev. 1259 (1996); Sanford Levinson, "Identifying the Jewish Lawyer: Reflections on the Construction of Professional Identity," 14 *Cardozo L. Rev.* 1577 (1993). The possibility of constructing a feminist, race-conscious, Jewish, Catholic, or similar perspective that draws from the resources of one's own personal identity, history, and community would be precluded by a conception of roles that strictly walls off these perspectives.

45. Jonathan Ames, "University of Oxford Students' Fury Over Dinah Rose's Same-Sex Marriage Case," *Times (London)* (Sept. 9, 2021).
46. Ann Southworth, *Lawyers of the Right: Professionalizing the Conservative Coalition* (Chicago: University of Chicago Press 2008).
47. Smith, "Representing Rapists," p. 257.
48. Albert Z. Carr, "Is Business Bluffing Ethical?", 46 *Harv. Bus. Rev.* 143 (1968). As I was workshopping drafts of this book, one of the most consistent suggestions was to include other professions by way of comparison with the evaluation of lawyers in role-specific and ordinary moral terms. I have used the Carr example in my business ethics course and have always loved Michael Lewis's story (below, in the main text) about "jamming"—it's a great way to set up the deeper theoretical point about descriptions of an action in practice or institutional terms. See Arthur Isak Applbaum, *Ethics for Adversaries: The Morality of Roles in Public and Professional Life* (Princeton: Princeton University Press 1999), pp. 85–90. But I did not attempt anything like a survey of the prevalence and terms of public criticism of other professionals. One anecdote that I regret having to cut from the main text for space reasons concerns the reaction to some of the public-relations professionals departing the Trump Administration for the private sector. The day after the January 6, 2021 riot, the chief content officer for *Forbes* magazine warned businesses that it would take note if a company had hired Sean Spicer, Kellyanne Conway, Sarah Huckabee Sanders, Kayleigh McEnany, or other administration spokespersons who had unashamedly lied to the public.

    > Let it be known to the business world: Hire any of Trump's fellow fabulists above, and Forbes will assume that everything your company or firm talks about is a lie. We're going to scrutinize, double-check, investigate with the same skepticism we'd approach a Trump tweet. Want to ensure the world's biggest business media brand approaches you as a potential funnel of disinformation? Then hire away.

    > Randall Lane, "A Truth Reckoning: Why We're Holding Those Who Lied for Trump Accountable," *Forbes* (Jan. 7, 2021).

    Dr. Jerome Adams, who served as Surgeon General during the Trump administration, has said he was rejected from academic and corporate jobs following his government service based on their judgment that he was "too tainted to employ." He faced some criticism related to positions he took on behalf of the administration during the Covid-19 pandemic, but he believed it was more virulent than it otherwise would have been due to the "Trump effect." Manuel Roig-Franzia, "Former Surgeon General Faces His Wife's Cancer—and the 'Trump Effect,'" *Wash. Post* (Nov. 25, 2022).
49. Carr, p. 146 (quoting a pseudonymous "Midwestern business executive").

50. Milton Friedman, "The Social Responsibility of Business Is to Increase Its Profits," *N.Y. Times Magazine* (Sept. 13, 1970).
51. Michael Lewis, *Liar's Poker: Rising Through the Wreckage on Wall Street* (New York: W.W. Norton 1989).
52. An alternative way of seeing the problem is in terms of psychological dispositions. Bernard Williams has argued that ethical considerations must be embodied in the form of dispositions and these dispositions are "somewhat resistant to modification and are not simply malleable by casuistical argument." Bernard Williams, "Professional Morality and Its Dispositions," in *Making Sense of Humanity and Other Philosophical Papers 1982-1993* (Cambridge: Cambridge University Press 1995), p. 199. Seen this way, the problem is that young bond trader Lewis will become socialized into attitudes consistent with an extreme *caveat emptor* attitude toward dealing with the bank and become desensitized to the moral costs of inducing trust in customers and then dumping an underperforming asset on them.
53. Arthur Isak Applbaum, *Ethics for Adversaries: The Morality of Roles in Public and Professional Life* (Princeton: Princeton University Press 1999), pp. 113-24.
54. Charles P. Curtis, "The Ethics of Advocacy," 4 *Stan. L. Rev.* 3, 8-9 (1951).
55. Curtis, p. 16.
56. Curtis, p. 20 (quoting Michel de Montaigne, "On Husbanding Your Will," in Donald M. Frame, trans., *The Complete Essays of Montaigne* (Stanford: Stanford University Press 1958), 3:10. In an important article that has become foundational in the field of philosophical legal ethics, Gerald Postema refers to the complete separation of personal and professional moral standards as a way of minimizing normative conflicts as "Montaigne's solution." Gerald J. Postema, "Moral Responsibility in Professional Ethics," 55 *NYU L. Rev.* 63 (1980).
57. I am grateful to Tim Dare and Sarah Cravens for pressing me on this point.
58. No author attributed, "Curtis Statement on Court Lying Mums Law Professors," *Harvard Crimson* (Sept. 27, 1952).
59. Henry S. Drinker, "Some Remarks on Mr. Curtis' 'The Ethics of Advocacy,'" 4 *Stan. L. Rev.* 349 (1952).
60. ABA Model Rules of Prof'l Conduct, Rule 3.3(a).
61. Model Rules, Rule 3.3(c) & cmt. [10].
62. Model Rules, Rule 4.1(a).
63. *In re Giuliani*, 197 A.D.3d 1, 146 N.Y.S.3d 266 (1st Dept. 2021).
64. Possibly seeking a similar shock value as Curtis's article, Daniel Markovits contends that the "genetic structure" of the lawyer's role requires lawyers to lie and cheat. Daniel Markovits, *A Modern Legal Ethics* (Princeton: Princeton University Press 2008), p. 26. This argument depends on an idiosyncratic definition of lying as attempting to persuade others of a proposition that one disbelieves, and cheating as promoting a cause which one believes to be undeserving. Markovits, p. 35. Many of Markovits's critics have focused on his non-standard definitions of lying and cheating. See, e.g., David Luban, Book Review, 120 *Ethics* 864 (2010); Monroe H. Freedman & Abbe Smith, "Misunderstanding Lawyers' Ethics," 108 *Mich. L. Rev.* 925, 929-31 (2010); Ted

Schneyer, "The Promise and Problematics of Legal Ethics from the Lawyer's Point of View," 16 *Yale J.L. & Human.* 45, 63 (2004).

65. John C. Roper, "Vinson & Elkins Settles with Enron for $30 Million," *Houston Chronicle* (June 2, 2006); Stephen Taub, "Enron Settles with Vinson & Elkins," *CFO* (June 1, 2006), available at https://www.cfo.com/risk-compliance/2006/06/enron-settles-with-vinson-elkins/ The *CFO* article includes a quote from John J. Ray III, Enron's chairman and president in the bankruptcy process. Ray played the same role in the bankruptcy in 2022 of cryptocurrency exchange FTX. Declan Harty & Sam Sutton, "Federal Prosecutors Charge Bankman-Fried with Massive, Yearslong Fraud," *Politico* (Dec. 13, 2022). No doubt reports can be expected of lawyer failures in connection with the FTX scandal.

66. In *re Facebook, Inc. Consumer Privacy User Profile Litigation*, No. 18-md-02843-VC (N.D. Cal., Feb. 9, 2023).

67. See, e.g., *In re Jeffrey B. Clark*, District of Columbia Court of Appeals Board on Professional Responsibility, Docket No. 2021-D193. See also the grievances filed by the bipartisan 65 Project against prominent lawyers such as Kenneth Chesebro, Ted Cruz, Jenna Ellis, Boris Epshteyn, Kenneth Klukowski, and Cleta Mitchell, described in Sam Skolnik, "Trump Lawyer Targeting Push Opens New Front With Bar Rules," *Bloomberg Law* (Oct. 12, 2022). Two prominent commentators on legal ethics in New York (and nationally) cautioned that disciplining lawyers for false statements made to the public but not in a court proceeding, in the course of what is clearly a political debate, raises challenging First Amendment issues. Bruce A. Green & Rebecca Roiphe, "As the Giuliani Case Goes Forward, Courts Should Think Deeply about the First Amendment," *Wash. Post* (June 25, 2021). Their argument is, essentially, that a non-lawyer serving as a campaign spokesperson could have made the same statements that Giuliani did and they would be protected as core political speech. Consider, for example, Kellyanne Conway's notorious appeal to "alternative facts." Contrast that with making false statements in connection with pending litigation, which is something only lawyers could do.

68. Jeremy Waldron refers to the "felt need among members of a certain group for a common framework or decision or course of action on some matter, even in the face of disagreement about what the framework, decision or action should be" as the circumstances of politics. Jeremy Waldron, *Law and Disagreement* (Oxford: Oxford University Press, 1999) at 102. Scott Shapiro has argued the law has a moral aim insofar as it maintains procedures for establishing permissions, rights, and duties in the name of the political community as a whole that distinguish social from individual judgments about what ought to be done in a particular case. Scott Shapiro, *Legality* (Cambridge, Mass.: Harvard University Press, 2011) at 170–73. For my development of these positions in political philosophy and general jurisprudence into an approach to legal ethics, see W Bradley Wendel, "The Limits of Positivist Legal Ethics: A Brief History, a Critique, and a Return to Foundations" (2017) 30 *Can J L & Jurisprudence* 443.

69. For examples of critical commentary see Alex Pareen, "Neal Katyal and the Depravity of Big Law," *New Republic* (Dec. 8, 2020); Mark Joseph Stern, "Prominent Anti-Trump Attorney Asks the Supreme Court to Let Companies off the Hook for Child Slavery,"

Slate (Dec. 1, 2020); Leo Gertner, "Which Side Are 'Liberal' Lawyers On?", *American Prospect* (Aug. 11, 2020). For examples of pushback on the criticism see Eric H. Holder, Jr. "'Lawyers Know Better': Criticizing Lawyers for Defending Unpopular Clients Is Risky, 'Disturbing,'" *Nat'l L.J.* (Dec. 29, 2020); Tom Goldstein, "Confusing Supreme Court Counsel with Their Clients," *SCOTUSblog* (Dec. 2, 2020), https://www.scotusblog.com/2020/12/confusing-supreme-court-counsel-with-their-clients/. The litigation concluded with an 8-1 decision by the Supreme Court holding that the lower court had improperly applied the Alien Tort Statute extraterritorially.

70. For useful background on the problem of child slavery in West African cocoa production, see Peter Whoriskey and Rachel Siegel, "Cocoa's Child Laborers," *Wash. Post* (Jun. 5, 2019).
71. One commentator referred in his critical commentary to Katyal as "a staunch critic of Donald Trump who frequently represents progressive causes." Stern, above.
72. Vivienne Walt, "Big Chocolate's Child-Labor Problem Is Still Far from Fixed," *Fortune* (Feb. 19, 2020).
73. *Nestle USA, Inc. v. Doe*, 141 S. Ct. 1931 (2021).
74. A Hershey spokesperson, quoted in Oliver Balch, "Mars, Nestlé and Hershey to Face Child Slavery Lawsuit in US," *Guardian* (Feb. 12, 2021).
75. Referring again to Arthur Applbaum's fictionalized dialogue between Mercier and Sanson, Mercier poses the question of the relationship between ordinary or background moral reasons and the reasons given by a professional role: "Why should a person be a 'good' professional if 'good' professionals routinely commit horribly bad acts? One should be *morally* good, a good man, Charles-Henri. If a good professional must be a bad man, then it is immoral to be a good professional. Why on earth should a man ignore moral reasons that run against professional ones?" Applbaum, above, p. 484. Sanson responds by insisting that roles must be evaluated at the wholesale, rather than retail level, so to speak: "I do not deny the possibility of a bad professional role that is not worthy of anyone's commitment. But that is a judgment made about the role itself, not particular actions the role requires."
76. *International Shoe Co. v. Washington*, 326 U.S. 310 (1945). A bunch of recent Supreme Court decisions has fundamentally altered the good old *International Shoe* analysis. See, e.g., *BNSF Railway Co. v. Tyrrell*, 37 S. Ct. 1549 (2017); *Bristol-Myers Squibb Co. v. Superior Court*, 137 S. Ct. 1773 (2017); *Daimler AG v. Bauman*, 571 U.S. 117 (2014); *Goodyear Dunlop Tires Operations, S.A. v. Brown*, 564 U.S. 915 (2011). None of these cases alters the point made in text, however, which is that generations of law students learned the *International Shoe* test as if the kind of balancing it called for is possible.
77. 326 U.S. at 319.
78. *Mathews v. Eldridge*, 424 U.S. 319 (1976).
79. 424 U.S. at 334.
80. 424 U.S. at 335.
81. There are also conflicts *within* ordinary morality, among different types of values that cannot be represented in terms of a common scale on which disparate quantities can be measured or balanced. Thomas Nagel, "The Fragmentation of Value," in *Mortal Questions* (Cambridge: Cambridge University Press 1979), p. 131.

82. Luban, "Freedom and Constraint," pp. 431, 445; see also Dare, above, p. 38.
83. Luban, "Freedom and Constraint," p. 432.
84. W. Bradley Wendel, *Lawyers and Fidelity to Law* (Princeton: Princeton University Press 2010), § 3.1.1, at p. 107. Raz's service conception of authority is developed in many works, including: Joseph Raz, "Authority, Law, and Morality," in *Ethics in the Public Domain* (Oxford: Oxford University Press 1994); Joseph Raz, *Practical Reason and Norms* (Princeton: Princeton University Press, 2d ed., 1990); Joseph Raz, *The Morality of Freedom* (Oxford: Oxford University Press 1986); Joseph Raz, "Authority and Justification," *Philosophy and Public Affairs* 14: 3–29 (1985). For a very clear summary of the philosophical literature, see Thomas Christiano, "Authority," *Stanford Encyclopedia of Philosophy* (2012).
85. Andrews Reath, "Autonomy of the Will as the Foundation of Morality," in *Agency and Autonomy in Kant's Moral Theory* (Oxford: Oxford University Press 2006), pp. 121–72.
86. W. Bradley Wendel, "Should Lawyers Be Loyal to Clients, the Law, or Both?", 65 *Am. J. Juris.* 19 (2020); W. Bradley Wendel, "The Rule of Law and Legal-Process Reasons in Attorney Advising," 99 *B.U.L. Rev.* 107 (2019).
87. Restatement (Third) of the Law Governing Lawyers § 16(1) (2000).
88. See the justly influential paper by Stephen Pepper on the lawyer's role being best understood as providing access to law. Stephen L. Pepper, "The Lawyer's Amoral Ethical Role: A Defense, A Problem, and Some Possibilities," 11 *Am. B. Found. Res. J.* 613 (1986).
89. Rainer Forst, *Toleration in Conflict: Past and Present* (Ciaran Cronin, trans.) (Cambridge: Cambridge University Press (2013), pp. 28–29.
90. Forst, p. 29.
91. Alton Logan with Berl Falbaum, *Justice Failed: How "Legal Ethics" Kept Me in Prison for 26 Years* (Berkeley, Cal.: Counterpoint Press 2018).
92. California has always stood out among U.S. jurisdictions as having the most uncompromising approach to client confidentiality. Lawyers may not disclose confidential information without their client's informed consent unless "disclosure is necessary to prevent a criminal act that the lawyer reasonably believes is likely to result in death of, or substantial bodily harm to, an individual." Cal. R. Prof'l Conduct 1.6(b). In the Alton Logan case, disclosure would be necessary to prevent the death of the wrongfully convicted person but disclosure is not necessary to prevent a criminal act and therefore would not be permitted by the rule.
93. Logan & Falbaum, above.
94. Simon makes this the maxim of what he calls the Contextual View of legal ethics: "Lawyers should take those actions that, considering the relevant circumstances of the particular case, seem likely to promote justice." William H. Simon, *The Practice of Justice* (Cambridge, Mass.: Harvard University Press 1998).

7
Case Studies: McCarthyism or Legitimate Criticism? Canceling Government Lawyers

From the Trump administration back to polite society?

The presidency of Donald Trump was extraordinary in many ways, but for a lawyer one of the most notable features of the Trump years was the administration's incessant defiance of norms of respect for the judiciary and the legal process. These informal guardrails, not legally enforceable, had been a significant source of stability during previous presidencies. Trump's willingness to simply ignore them proved to be a source of power that was difficult for other institutions to check.[1] For example, while many presidents have expressed dissatisfaction with court decisions that did not go the way they had hoped,[2] Trump's numerous and sometimes personal attacks on judges conveyed an attitude of contempt for the authority of courts and thus for the legitimacy of legal restraints on his power.[3] He openly sought to use official power to pursue personal vendettas, such as his long-running feud with Jeffrey Bezos and Amazon.[4] He fired internal agency watchdogs, such as inspector generals at the State, Defense, and Transportation Departments, whose findings he disliked.[5] And he frequently attempted to influence actions of the Justice Department, for instance by criticizing former Attorney General Jeff Sessions's recusal from the investigation of Russian influence in the 2016 presidential election, demanding the firing of Special Counsel Robert Mueller, and pressuring the DOJ to declare the results of the 2020 election invalid owing to widespread fraud.[6]

In the memorable words of Republican political consultant Rick Wilson, everything Trump touches dies.[7] During the Trump years, however, the legal profession and the judiciary did better than most public institutions at withstanding the assault on democratic and rule-of-law norms.[8] Public criticism of lawyers who worked in various capacities within the Trump administration risks overlooking the ways in which many lawyers resisted the pressure to do nothing more than acquiesce in the assertion of presidential power. Particularly in the tumultuous period between the 2020 presidential election and the January 6, 2021, riot at the Capitol building, many lawyers who may have been aligned with many Trump administration policies nevertheless refused to provide legal cover for the interference with a democratic election.[9]

Nevertheless, some critics believed that lawyers who worked in the administration deserved to lose the honorable status that usually attaches to professionals who have held high government offices. To take one example, in the waning months of the Trump administration, the widely read legal commentator Dahlia Lithwick wrote to publicly and preemptively shame elite law firms who she believed would hire former government lawyers, thereby laundering the reputational stain they had acquired while serving the administration.[10] As she saw it, at least some high-level government lawyers shared the moral blame for actions ordered by Trump, including the "zero-tolerance" border policy that resulted in the separation of numerous minor children from their families.[11] Particularly severe criticism was directed at Deputy Attorney General Rod Rosenstein for his involvement in implementing the policy; one columnist in the *New York Times* compared him with Nazi functionary Adolf Eichmann.[12] (It was perhaps unfortunate, then, when one of the published defenses of Trump administration lawyers was that they, like Eichmann, were "just doing their jobs."[13]) Lithwick was undoubtedly disappointed when Rosenstein landed a partnership at the prestigious law firm of King & Spalding after stepping down as Deputy Attorney General.[14]

What, exactly, was Rosenstein accused of doing? The zero-tolerance policy had been adopted by then Attorney General Jeff Sessions in April 2018, around the time that conservative media outlets were hyping reports of a so-called migrant caravan headed toward the U.S.-Mexico border.[15] Trump had reportedly "ranted" and gone on a "tirade" in which he ordered the Department of Justice to prosecute as many migrants as possible.[16] The zero-tolerance policy directed U.S. attorneys in offices along the southwestern border to criminally prosecute adult migrants for illegal entry offenses, rather than allowing the Department of Homeland Security to handle their cases administratively if adults crossed the border in family units, with accompanying children.[17]

The policy was delayed in implementation because a problem had arisen: if the criminal prosecution of adult migrants was not handled very expeditiously, their children would have to be committed to the custody of the Office of Refugee Resettlement within the Department of Health and Human Services.[18] As it transpired, that agency did not have the capacity to care for and keep track of children separated from their families and given the status of "unaccompanied alien children" (who were "unaccompanied" only because their parent or other adult companion had been taken into federal custody).[19] The delay infuriated Trump's senior advisor Stephen Miller, who reportedly regarded the separation of migrant families "not as an unfortunate byproduct but as a tool to deter more immigration."[20] Miller convened a meeting of senior administration officials, including Attorney General Sessions, the Health and Human Services Secretary, the Secretary of State, and Homeland Security Secretary Kirstjen Nielsen. Miller reportedly said anyone who disagreed with the zero-tolerance policy was "a lawbreaker and un-American" and that failure to enforce the policy would mean "the end of our country as we know it."[21] The assembled officials voted to direct federal agencies to enforce the policy, and the next day Secretary Nielsen instructed agencies within Homeland Security to refer apprehended adult migrants for prosecution.[22]

As the Justice Department's Inspector General subsequently reported, several U.S. attorneys from border states had raised concerns about the directive to prosecute adult migrants accompanied by children. In particular they wanted to know what would happen to the children in the custody of Health and Human Services after they were separated from their parents and how they would be reunited with their parents.[23] In several conference calls with the U.S. attorneys, Deputy Attorney General Rosenstein reminded them of how significant the zero-tolerance policy was to the Attorney General and that they should not decline to prosecute an adult migrant solely on the basis of being accompanied by children; discretion not to prosecute should be exercised only on the basis of exceptional circumstances such as illness or inability to communicate in Spanish.[24]

Rosenstein later sought to blame individual U.S. attorneys for not exercising discretion not to prosecute in cases in which children would be separated from their families.[25] That is a classic bit of bureaucratic blame-shifting, but it does seem unreasonable to fault Rosenstein for the policy directive itself. The zero-tolerance policy was adopted by senior political officials, including the Attorney General, at the direction of the President and his senior advisor Stephen Miller. In that sense Rosenstein was "just following orders." But using reasonable efforts to carry out the lawful instructions of clients is the essence of the professional function of lawyers.[26] Rosenstein would have been permitted to try to talk Sessions out of ordering the zero-tolerance policy,[27] but given repeated public statements (and probably others in private) by Sessions, Miller, and Trump, it almost certainly would have been a fool's errand. He could have resigned but might have reasonably believed that Trump and Sessions would simply appoint a yes-man in his place.[28]

The severe criticism of Rosenstein, including the comparison with Eichmann, fits exactly with the model of blame discussed in Chapter 4.[29] Blame involves an assessment of the motivating reasons, intentions, and attitudes of another.[30] Readers of editorials interpreting Rosenstein's actions are meant to reach a judgment that his conduct was blameworthy, in the sense that the actions reveal him to hold attitudes that impair his relationships with others, and also to hold him liable to blame, which has special significance for those with whom he is in a relationship.[31] For someone in the legal profession, that judgment marks a change in the relationship they have with Rosenstein, calling for an adjustment in attitudes toward him. An appropriate adjustment might include a reluctance to hire him as a partner in an elite law firm, with its characteristic commitments to values such as legality and the protection of human rights.* The question is, of course, whether the conclusions reached by critics about Rosenstein's attitudes and motivating reasons are warranted. As we have seen, attitudes must be inferred on the basis of actions and other evidence. The ultimate conclusion for which Lithwick and others are arguing is that professional shunning or ostracism of Rosenstein is an appropriate adjustment in other lawyers' attitudes toward him, given Rosenstein's attitudes, as revealed in his conduct in connection with the zero-tolerance policy.

While this is an interpretive question and others may disagree, in my judgment a careful examination of the Justice Department's Inspector General report does not support the conclusion that Rosenstein in blameworthy, in the sense of failing to manifest attitudes of respect and concern for others.[32] Given the callousness of some within the Trump administration, particularly Stephen Miller but also Jeff Sessions, toward the traumatic experience of separating children from their families, it is understandable that some observers would blame anyone who had anything to do with implementing

---

* Before the Covid-19 pandemic changed the connotation of this term, Scanlon's approach to blame was known as "social distancing," to convey the idea of others revising their attitudes toward and relationships with the target of blame. I am grateful to Emad Atiq for this interesting tidbit.

the zero-tolerance policy. Rosenstein has expressed regret for his role in implementing the family separation policy, without merely pointing fingers at others. In a statement to NBC News, he said:

> Since leaving the department, I have often asked myself what we should have done differently, and no issue has dominated my thinking more than the zero tolerance immigration policy. It was a failed policy that never should have been proposed or implemented. I wish we all had done better.[33]

Former Homeland Security Secretary Kirstjen Nielsen, by contrast, struck a defiant tone regarding her role. She told an interviewer, "I don't regret enforcing the law. . . . It's heartbreaking that any family felt at any time that they had to cross the border illegally because it is a terrible, dangerous journey."[34] (Nielsen was later reported to have agreed with Alex Azar, the secretary of Health and Human Services, to resign in protest if Trump resumed the family separation policy.[35])

Of course, judgments of blameworthiness do not depend entirely on public statements. Talk can be cheap, although it is not easy to accept blame openly, as Rosenstein did. It also matters a great deal what the actor actually did, their reasons for taking the action, what they knew about the consequences of their decisions, and what other options were available to them. One aspect of the ethics of blame is the responsibility of critics to look carefully and honestly at the factual record before concluding that someone has a character that is inconsistent with the obligations arising from relationships with others, in a personal or professional capacity. At least as I read the factual record, Rosenstein did not act with indifference toward the well-being of families in federal custody. He thought that individual U.S. attorneys would exercise discretion not to prosecute adults who had caregiving responsibility for minor children, believing he had communicated clearly enough that expectation. He may also have been operating on the understanding that prosecutions of adults would be concluded in a matter of hours, so that no lengthy separation from children would be required.

To be clear, I also believe the decision to adopt the zero-tolerance policy knowing, or even intending, that it would result in the separation of children from their families, was an egregious moral wrong. Stephen Miller deserves to be shunned by all decent people for masterminding this tragedy. The situation of *lawyers* is complicated, however, by the division of normative labor in the lawyer-client relationship. In most cases, responsibility for deciding whether an action is morally permissible is the client's. The job of the lawyer is to act with reasonable competence and diligence to advance the lawful objectives of the client.[36] The key word here is "lawful," not "moral." The lawyer's job is not to second-guess moral decisions made by the client.

In the case of executive branch lawyers, the division of labor is complicated further by the democratic accountability of the President. Tens of millions of people voted for Donald Trump, and among them some number was motivated at least in part by his hardline anti-immigrant rhetoric. Government lawyers sometimes say they are different from private lawyers because they represent the nation. A line from a speech by Griffin Bell, the Attorney General under President Jimmy Carter, is frequently quoted: "Although our client is the government, in the end we serve a more important constituency: the American people."[37] When a government lawyer is trying to ascertain the will of the American people, however, the Constitution has established a mechanism for determining its content, in the form of elections and presidential appointment of agency heads.[38] For Rosenstein or any other high-ranking lawyer in the Justice Department to go around the instructions of the President and the Attorney General would not only be insubordinate but would constitute a breach of the lawyer's fiduciary duty to follow the lawful instructions of the client—in this case, the American people, whose objectives were determined through the presidential election.[39]

This last point about the will of the people suggests a further objection to the social practice of blaming lawyers. The title of this section and the reference to criticism of Rosenstein make reference to exclusion of certain ex-government officials from "polite society." One of the clear lessons of the Trump years, however, is that there is more than one thing called American society, and one must be careful making assumptions about what "we" think about lawyers or other officials who served in the administration.[40] I and many people I know would have nothing to do with Stephen Miller, but he is regarded as admirable by a substantial number of my fellow citizens. It is too glib to dismiss these varying reactions as the byproduct of propaganda or disinformation. Rather, our society is characterized by disagreements that are so deep and intensely felt that it is hard to see how they could be reconciled within a single coherent worldview. We might be well on our way to a society characterized as a loose affiliation of communities with profoundly irreconcilable expectations about what we owe to each other (and to whom, as shown by Miller's contempt for immigrants from Latin America).

One small hope that I hold out is that the law, the judiciary, and the legal profession serve as a repository of enough shared values to underwrite a sense of social solidarity, even if it is fairly thin. These values include fairness, due process, respect for factual truth, hearing both sides, impartiality in adjudication, and the ability to tolerate difference. If lawyers are working to sustain these shared social practices, then the ethics of blame suggest that we should withhold blame based on political disagreement, because disagreement is what makes the law important in the first place. Simply representing a client one regards as reprehensible or taking a position with which one disagrees should not, by itself, be regarded as blameworthy, absent some other evidence suggesting that the lawyer's attitudes are inconsistent with what is owed to others.

Blame and the Big Lie

The importance to legal ethics of respecting the law and legal system helps explain another round of criticism of Trump's lawyers. Following the 2020 presidential election, some activists sought to embarrass law firms they believed were representing the Trump campaign in challenges to state election procedures. The Lincoln Project, a group made up of Republican political strategists alarmed at the direction Trump had taken the party (and the country) in, pointedly attacked the law firms of Jones Day and Porter Wright for supporting "Donald Trump's unwarranted and dangerous attacks on our democracy."[41] In a series of tweets, the Lincoln Project suggested not only that employees of these firms resign in protest, but that other clients of the firms, including Walmart, General Motors, and Amazon, might consider whether they wished to continue to be represented by law firms involved in the election challenges.[42]

The Lincoln Project was incorrect about the identity of Jones Day's client; the firm was representing the Pennsylvania Republican Party, not Trump himself.[43] However, the lawsuit attracted unwelcome attention for the firm given the importance of Pennsylvania to the presidential election. The controversy grew out of litigation related to mail-in ballots in the context of the Covid-19 pandemic. Despite a statute requiring mail ballots to be received by 8:00 p.m. on Election Day, the Pennsylvania Supreme Court had permitted counting of ballots postmarked by Election Day and received within three days.[44] Jones Day stepped in to file a petition for review ("certiorari," in legal lingo) in the United States Supreme Court of the Pennsylvania court's decision.[45] This was well in advance of the election itself and the increasingly unhinged claims made by Trump that the election had been stolen. The Supreme Court eventually denied review and the number of late-received mail-in ballots would not have made a difference to the result in any case.[46] But the firm drew considerable public criticism nonetheless, possibly owing to former Trump administration lawyers having rejoined the firm and working on election litigation.[47] In addition, and perhaps taking a cue from the climate boycotts described in Chapter 5, students at the University of Michigan Law School urged their classmates not to interview with or work for law firms that had worked for the Trump campaign, including Jones Day.[48]

Following the same playbook, after the *New York Times* reported that Foley & Lardner partner Cleta Mitchell had been on the phone call in which Trump urged Georgia Secretary of State Brad Raffensperger to "find more votes" and change his state's results,[49] the Lincoln Project publicly identified Major League Baseball as a client of the firm.[50] Mitchell resigned a few days later, citing "a massive pressure campaign in the last several days mounted by leftist groups via social media and other means against me, my law firm and clients of the law firm."[51] Mitchell went on to become one of the leading lawyers pushing the false narrative of a stolen election. (The *Washington Post* referred to her as one of the "leading voices in the election-denier movement."[52]) A bipartisan watchdog group filed a complaint with the regulatory authorities in Mitchell's jurisdiction of admission, the District of Columbia, contending that Mitchell counseled or assisted Trump in conduct she knew to be a crime, by participating in the phone call with Raffensperger and threatening him and other Georgia state officials with criminal charges if they did not get with the program.[53]

The conduct of lawyers related to election challenges and the January 6 insurrection is an example of how the line between who a lawyer represents and what the lawyer does in the course of the representation can be blurry.[54] There is an important difference between counseling or assisting a client's crime, which goes to the heart of the role of attorneys as officers of the court, and representing a controversial client through legally permissible means. It can be all too easy at times, however, to muddy those waters by claiming that criticism or even a bar grievance proceeding is motivated solely by political disagreement. It is therefore an understandable priority for lawyer regulators and legal profession scholars to defend neutral, nonpolitical norms of conduct in connection with the representation of clients. As a result, however, many of these proceedings have a technocratic air to them, preoccupied with showing that a lawyer knew that such-and-such factual assertion was false when it was made, or that a lawsuit was factually and legally meritless. Observers may understandably believe that professional regulators are losing the forest for the trees. The real problem is not that a lawyer like Cleta Mitchell crossed a specific legal line but that she was part of a concerted effort to overturn a democratic election.

Following the election there were legitimate challenges raised under the election laws of various states. Jones Day and Porter Wright represented Republican organizations in these lawsuits that were adequately supported by factual evidence and legal arguments and also quickly resolved by courts against the challengers. A fair-minded, nonpartisan observer of the legal profession should have no complaint whatsoever with the firms providing this type of legal assistance. Indeed, candidates from both parties regularly file challenges under the Constitution and federal and state election statutes, as did Georgia Democratic gubernatorial candidate Stacey Abrams in 2018.[55] In the words of the Wisconsin Supreme Court case considering some of the Trump campaign's arguments, there are "technical issues that arise in the administration of every election."[56] Election lawyers representing Democratic and Republican challengers routinely pursue these types of claims. As it turned out, the 24-hour news cycle moved on, the controversy provoked by the Lincoln Project tweets abated, and Jones Day and Porter Wright weathered the very brief storm.[57] As much as I enjoyed some of the Lincoln Project's hard-hitting tweets aimed at Trump himself, I believe it was a mistake to target these law firms for blame.

Cleta Mitchell, however, was part of a categorically different effort to oppose the election results, having much more in common with the outlandish allegations, unsupported by any credible evidence, made by lawyers like Rudy Giuliani, Lin Wood, and Sidney Powell.[58] The lawsuits filed by those lawyers resulted in the imposition of sanctions on the lawyers by federal district courts judges for the lawyers' failure to comply with procedural rules requiring that filed pleadings be based on an adequate factual record with a sufficient legal basis. Legal scholars called for these lawyers to be referred to state authorities for investigation and possible professional discipline.[59] There were legitimate—which is to say, without the bounds of ethical lawyering—challenges that could have been raised to the 2020 election but there were also tactics that went beyond the bounds of permissibility for lawyers, for example, by relying on known false statements of fact or, in Mitchell's case, knowingly assisting a client in conduct known to be criminal or fraudulent.[60] Criticism of Trump administration lawyers could therefore vary depending on whether the lawyers acted with sufficient legal and factual grounds or engaged in dishonest or manipulative lawyering.

Another lawyer whose conduct warrants both legal and moral condemnation is a conservative constitutional law professor, John Eastman, who advised the Trump campaign on political and legal strategy following the 2020 presidential election.[61] Despite a public statement by Attorney General William Barr that there was no fraud in the election, and a communication directly to President Trump from the Deputy Attorney General that "after dozens of investigations, hundreds of interviews, the Department of Justice had concluded that the major allegations of election fraud are not supported by the evidence developed,"[62] Trump continued to press allegations of fraud and to look for lawyers who would support his fantastical claim to be the actual winner of the election. Eastman stepped up, writing a memo in which he proposed a plan by which Vice President Mike Pence would refuse to count the electoral votes from seven states, resulting in an Electoral College victory for Trump.

Eastman met with Trump, Pence, and the vice president's counsel and chief of staff on January 4 and 5; in these meetings, Pence and his advisors pressed Eastman into conceding that his plan would violate the Electoral Count Act and likely be rejected by a unanimous Supreme Court.[63] Nevertheless, Eastman continued to advocate for his plan, both in meetings with Pence and Trump and in a speech to Trump supporters outside the White House on January 6. In that speech Eastman said:

> And all we are demanding of Vice President Pence is this afternoon at 1:00 he let the legislators of the state look into this so we get to the bottom of it, and the American people know whether we have control of the direction of our government, or not. We no longer live in a self-governing republic if we can't get the answer to this question.[64]

A couple of hours later, an armed mob stormed the Capitol building, overwhelmed law enforcement officers, and sought to prevent the certification of election results by Congress. Pence's lawyer Greg Jacob emailed Eastman to say, "thanks to your bullshit, we are now under siege."[65]

There is a big difference between adverse personal or professional consequences, such as being denied lucrative private sector employment, based on disagreement with conservative political principles versus supporting the violent overthrow of a democratically elected government. There is also an important difference between the types of challenges pursued by firms like Jones Day and Porter Wright and the fanciful arguments of John Eastman. Eastman himself all but conceded that there was no legal basis for the vice president to refuse to certify the election results. His own memo referred to his position as "BOLD, Certainly," but justified by his belief that the election had been "Stolen by a strategic Democrat plan to systematically flout existing election laws."[66] He stated in an email exchange with another lawyer for the Trump campaign, Kenneth Chesebro, that his legal advice was "not based on the legal merits but an assessment of the justices' spines, and I understand that there is a heated fight underway" within the Supreme Court.[67] Chesebro replied that the odds of the Supreme Court becoming involved would be better if the justices feared that "there will be wild chaos on Jan. 6" unless they intervened. That is, of course, exactly what happened.

A federal district court, ruling on Eastman's assertion of attorney-client privilege, concluded that Eastman's arguments were not a good faith interpretation of the Constitution and federal statutes, but an obviously illegal attempt to disrupt the joint session of Congress on January 6, 2021.[68] Eastman's memo was comprehensively refuted by politically conservative lawyers, including Greg Jacob, the vice president's counsel; and J. Michael Luttig, a prominent former federal judge for whom Eastman had clerked. Following the January 6 insurrection attempt, White House lawyer Eric Herschmann told Eastman that he was "out of his mind," said the only words he wanted to hear from Eastman were "orderly transition," and recommended that Eastman find a good criminal defense lawyer because he was going to need one.[69] At times even Eastman agreed that his plan was contrary to historical practice and the Electoral Count Act.[70] All of this pushback, including from ideologically allied lawyers, shows that Eastman's position was not good faith legal advice but "a coup in search of a legal theory."[71] That is the critical distinction between Eastman's representation of the Trump campaign and the work by law firms like Jones Day, who have never been credibly alleged to have offered advice that was not sufficiently well-grounded in law and fact.

The professional and informal sanctions directed at lawyers like John Eastman reflect not ordinary partisan disagreement but something much deeper, relating to the rule of law and the norms necessary to sustain a constitutional democracy. Eastman's efforts to supply a purportedly legal justification for the vice president to reject legitimate slates of electors is not best understood as a Republican position, with which Democrats disagree on ideological grounds, but an assault on a process intended to handle political disagreement in an orderly way. This criticism depends, however, on there being a tenable distinction between a creative, but with adequate legal support *and therefore legitimate* argument for the result sought by Eastman and an interpretation that lacks a sufficient foundation in law and fact.

This distinction is particularly important for critics trying to generalize from the experience with lawyers representing Trump after the election challenges and the January 6 insurrection. If this episode is not understood correctly, the wrong lessons might be learned from it. For example, a board member of the law student group organizing boycotts of law firms representing fossil fuel companies referred to the nearly unanimous condemnation by lawyers of Rudy Giuliani as evidence that criticizing lawyers in moral terms can be an effective strategy to accomplish social change:

> Big law firms themselves know their work is never value-neutral. Consider the vitriolic condemnation many of these same voices (rightly) directed toward Rudy Giuliani for representing Donald Trump's attempts to overturn the results of the 2020 presidential election. As Trump's suits were being filed, legions of corporate attorneys called for Giuliani to be disbarred, showing recognition that lawyers do, in fact, have a degree of responsibility for the clients they choose to represent. But as repugnant as Giuliani's behavior was, it's not clear why helping a would-be fascist attack our democracy is morally or ethically worse than helping corporate polluters condemn countless children like mine, born in the smoke and flames of the Anthropocene, to a future of climate catastrophe.
>
> The Giuliani cases also illustrate how game-changing it can be when lawyers hold themselves to a moral standard. Facing immense backlash for representing Trump's campaign, elite law firms overwhelmingly refused to aid Giuliani's efforts to overturn the election, and that made an enormous difference.[72]

Vitriolic as the condemnation of Giuliani may have been, however, any calls for him to be *disbarred* (as opposed to being criticized or shunned by prospective employers) must have been based on his violation of applicable rules of professional conduct. There is all the world of difference between "helping a would-be fascist attack our democracy" and knowingly making false statements of fact, or filing meritless, abusive litigation in furtherance of an attack on our democracy. One could do both, and perhaps Giuliani should be both subject to professional discipline and criticized for playing a role in an attempted interference with the lawful transition of presidential power.[73] However, the interim suspension of Giuliani's law license was based on specific findings of false public statements, though for the most part not made in connection with court proceedings, that violated Rules 4.1, and 8.4(c) of the New York Rules of Professional Conduct.[74]

It is possible that "legions of corporate attorneys" really were judging Giuliani by a moral standard, reacting with horror to his willingness to deceive the public about the discovery of fabricated mail-in ballots in Pennsylvania, dead people (including famous boxer Joe Frazier) voting in Philadelphia, machines manufactured by Dominion Voting Systems manipulating the ballot count, and tens of thousands of underage voters casting ballots in Georgia.[75] Trump was reported to have said that no "sane lawyers" would represent him in election challenges because they had been "pressured."[76] Plenty of sane lawyers, at Jones Day and other prestigious law firms, represented Trump in non-crazy election challenges, avoiding making false statements of fact or filing frivolous lawsuits. The best interpretation of the fate of the outlandish characters who represented Trump, including Giuliani, Sidney Powell, and Lin Wood, is as a cautionary tale about playing fast and loose with the rules in the belief that one is representing a just cause. And, as the next section will discuss, much of the handwringing about lawyers avoiding the representation of Trump can be explained on nonmoral grounds.

Whose side are you on? The "Department of Jihad"

During the Obama administration, conservative groups saw an opening to attack the administration's national security policies. A group called "Keep America Safe," founded by conservative columnist William Kristol, former Vice President Dick Cheney's daughter Elizabeth Cheney, and the sister of an American Airlines pilot killed in the September 11, 2001, attacks, produced a series of videos criticizing the administration's "radical" policies that weakened the nation.[77] The attacks became more specific and concentrated on Attorney General Eric Holder and the Department of Justice, which the group referred to as the "Department of Jihad."[78] As Cheney's group eagerly pointed out, many lawyers hired by the Justice Department had represented, while in private practice, detainees who had been captured by U.S. or allied forces in Afghanistan or elsewhere, believed to have had some connection to the September 11th attacks, and indefinitely held on the U.S. military base in Guantánamo Bay, Cuba. The Murdoch-owned *New York Post* editorialized: "It's just insane that a lawyer who defended Osama bin Laden's driver and bodyguard—and who sought constitutional rights for terrorists—could be one of the Obama administration's top legal officials."[79] In response to the furor in the right-wing press and among congressional Republicans Holder would name only two Justice Department lawyers who had represented detainees, prompting Cheney's group to insinuate that he or the unnamed lawyers must be on the side of terrorists: "Holder will only name two. Why the secrecy behind the other seven? Whose values do they share? . . . Americans have a right to know the identity of the Al Qaeda Seven."[80]

The attacks by Cheney's group can be seen as a continuation of the criticisms that had been leveled by conservatives at the time against the lawyers representing detainees in their challenges to the legality of the post-9/11 structure of military commissions and indefinite detentions.[81] Charles "Cully" Stimson, deputy assistant secretary of defense for detainee affairs in the Bush administration, sought to shame the corporate clients of major law firms who were providing representation to detainees. In a radio interview he named the firms and suggested that their clients should think twice about whose side they are on: "I think, quite honestly, when corporate CEOs see that those firms are representing the very terrorists who hit their bottom line back in 2001, those CEOs are going to make those law firms choose between representing terrorists or representing reputable firms."[82] He also noted that the firms were not representing their clients pro bono (that is, without pay), but were "receiving moneys from who knows where," leaving readers to draw their own conclusions about the source of the funds.

Stimson's suggestion that some law firms were on the side of terrorists was met with swift and public condemnation by lawyers, including conservatives such as former Solicitor General Charles Fried. In an op-ed in the *Wall Street Journal*, Fried turned the table on the perennial criticism of large law firms coming from the political left, implying that if criticism for representing these clients was fair, the left could hardly complain now if lawyers had to answer for representing detainees.[83] (Fried's point could be made against today in response to the criticism by progressives of law firms, discussed in Chapter 5.) The firms on Stimson's hit list, Fried noted, "represent large employers defending discrimination and disability suits, major corporations accused of price fixing, securities fraud and pollution." Stimson might have been misled, Fried suggested, by progressive attacks on firms for representing these clients:

> All that can be said in explanation, if not mitigation, of Mr. Stimson's egregious statements is that he may have been led on by the extravagant rhetoric of ideologues at the other end of the spectrum, who regularly inveigh against law firms which make their living by defending corporate interests accused of abusing employees, consumers and the environment. It was a regular event on law school campuses to see such ideologues picketing campus recruiters from these law firms, and to hear speeches by professors and even law school deans deploring the fact that graduates regularly took up employment in them.

There is no moral argument that can be made from the left or the right, Fried contended, that could penetrate the Principle of Nonaccountability. If liberals want to represent accused terrorists, that is their right: "It is the pride of a nation built on the rule of law that it affords to every man a zealous advocate to defend his rights in court, and of a liberal profession in such a nation that not only is the representation of the dishonorable honorable (and any lawyer is free to represent any person he chooses)." But the same must go for the decision by lawyers at these firms to represent Big Tobacco, Big Pharma, or Big Oil.

The approach defended in this book, which emphasizes accountability to the moral community, is very different from Fried's. Rather than objecting to the request, or demand, that one provide a justification for representing Guantánamo detainees, a lawyer should welcome the opportunity. Why take cases on behalf of accused terrorists? Because the process by which the government can label someone an enemy combatant and thereby deprive an alleged terrorist of the constitutional rights available to anyone accused of criminal acts is anathema to the values of our country. Because the system of military tribunals gives even more power to an already mighty federal government whenever national security considerations are invoked (or at least if we're going to vest such power in military tribunals, Congress should have some say in the matter). Because reasonable, humane citizens of a constitutional democracy believe that dehumanizing and torturing anyone, no matter what they are accused of doing, is unacceptable. Because it is vital that the judicial branch have the final say in the administration of core constitutional protections, such as the right to seek a writ of *habeas corpus*.

In the later iteration of the conservative criticism of defense lawyers, Cheney's group overplayed its hand, and its McCarthy-esque language questioning the loyalty and patriotism of government officials and demanding that the Attorney General name names called forth a backlash from otherwise politically allied lawyers.[84] Twenty lawyers and national security experts, many with experience at senior levels in the Bush administration, and notably including former Independent Counsel Kenneth Starr, signed a statement defending "[t]he American tradition of zealous representation of unpopular clients." The statement did more than repeat yet again that John Adams had represented British soldiers accused of taking part in the Boston Massacre. It sought to ground the response to the attacks on the lawyers' loyalty by demonstrating the connection between representing detainees and the value of the rule of law. The novel legal questions presented by the so-called War on Terror require full development of the factual record and competing legal positions. Adjudication and policymaking decisions on contested issues, in judicial, legislative, and executive forums, depend for their reliability and legitimacy on adversarial presentation of the views of both sides. Speaking directly to the question "whose side are you on?," the drafter of the statement contended that effective advocacy on both sides is necessary for lasting, effective, institutionalized responses to difficult questions of counterterrorism policy.[85]

Bringing this controversy to its current form, conservative political pundit Andrew McCarthy accused Democrats of trying to have it both ways, defending Judge Ketanji Brown Jackson's nomination to serve as a U.S. Supreme Court Justice against charges that she harbored sympathies for accused terrorists because she had filed an amicus brief in support of habeas corpus rights for Guantánamo Bay detainees, while going after lawyers who represented the Trump campaign in election-law matters:

> Progressive Democrats have taken the position that former president Trump and those who worked with him to challenge the results of the 2020 election are not entitled to legal representation. They have put enormous pressure on lawyers and firms to drop these people as clients. There is now an ongoing project to have lawyers disciplined and disbarred if they played any role in enabling Trump to file legal challenges to the election. One needn't be persuaded by these legal challenges—I think most of them were

frivolous—in order to acknowledge that Trump had the right to file them and to retain counsel for that purpose.[86]

He exaggerates by claiming there is a project to have lawyers disciplined if they played *any* role in challenging election results and that it is solely a Democratic effort. If he meant to refer to the 65 Project,[87] which seeks to "hold[] accountable the lawyers who bring fraudulent lawsuits seeking to overturn legitimate election results or who otherwise violate their professional responsibilities to undermine our democracy," that organization is intentionally bipartisan and also concerned with lawyers who commit violations of professional conduct rules such as lying under oath, aiding and abetting crimes or fraud by clients, or filing frivolous lawsuits. One can look long and hard at the grievances filed by the 65 Project for any against a lawyer who pursued factually and legally adequately grounded litigation. Nevertheless, there is a rhetorical or political payoff to blurring the distinction between seeking professional discipline on the basis of violating applicable rules of professional conduct and doing anything that supported a challenge by the Trump campaign or its allies (such as the Pennsylvania Republican Party, represented by Jones Day) to any aspect of the administration of the presidential election.

To be clear about my own position, I would not support an effort to impose professional discipline or even to direct intense social criticism at lawyers who pursued potentially meritorious election litigation in good faith on behalf of the Trump campaign or allied groups. The shaming, shunning, ostracism, and exclusion from polite society that constitutes an appropriate blaming response to the conduct of Trump administration lawyers should be reserved for those like John Eastman, who exhibited the attitude of contempt for the rule of law and the constitutionally prescribed democratic process of certifying elections. This is intended as a neutral, apolitical standpoint on which criticism may be grounded. The risk is that if this standpoint is not, in fact, neutral and apolitical, it may be "weaponized" and used as just another political tool among others to be used against one's opponents. Predictably, Eastman and his supporters have sought to characterize the complaint filed by the State Bar of California, seeking his disbarment for his role in the January 6, 2020, insurrection, as nothing more than a naked attempt to use the disciplinary process as politics by other means. I believe it is possible to distinguish good faith interpretation of the law, even if somewhat creative or aggressive, from what Eastman is accused of, which is urging his client to act based on a completely unsupported legal position. Making this point stick, however, requires some appreciation of how the law itself establishes limits on what lawyers may advocate on behalf of their clients or advise their clients that they are lawfully permitted to do. The next case study refers to an earlier episode where the advice given by lawyers was challenged as manipulative or abusive and not a candid, independent account of what the law actually permits or requires.

Fidelity to law vs. abusive legal advice

In one of the earlier episodes of criticizing lawyers for representing Guantánamo detainees, conservative lawyer Ted Olson joined the widespread pushback against Liz Cheney and William Kristol's "al Qaeda Seven" smear. His defense of the lawyers' conduct added an interesting critique of the outrage now being expressed on behalf of the lawyers who had formerly represented detainees. Where were these supporters of the representation of unpopular clients, Olson asked, when lawyers within the Bush administration had provided legal advice that proved to be highly unpopular when public disclosed, concerning the treatment of these very same detainees?

> I of course think it's entirely appropriate for members of the legal profession to have provided legal services to detainees. . . . It is a part of the responsibility of lawyers and in the finest tradition of the profession to represent unpopular persons who are caught up in the criminal justice system or even in the military justice system. I think that people who do so, do so honorably," said Olson, whose arguments before the Supreme Court helped win the presidency for George W. Bush in 2000.
>
> But I also think that some of the people being highly critical now of the criticism of the lawyers in the Justice Department, have been completely silent when it came to attacks—vicious attacks—on lawyers in the Department of Justice and the Defense Department who were providing legal assistance and advice to the United States of America during the last administration in connection with the attacks on the United States by terrorists.[88]

On its face, this looks like nothing more than a plea for consistency, or more sharply, a critique of the other side playing politics with their attacks on lawyers. Fairness demands that if it is "honorable" for lawyers to represent detainees, then it is equally honorable to have provided legal assistance to the Bush administration in the wake of the 9/11 attacks. To the extent conservative critics of the Obama administration were making *just the same point* as liberal critics of the Bush administration, then it would be an intellectual and moral failure to have failed to stand up publicly for the lawyers who were doing nothing other than providing competent, if sometimes controversial, legal representation.[89]

But that is not the argument many critics leveled against lawyers in the Bush administration. Their argument was not that it was a bad thing for a conscientious and decent person to work in the Bush Justice Department, but that some of these lawyers were wrongdoers as judged by professional ethical standards. In particular, critics claimed that the lawyers provided legal advice that certain methods of interrogation were lawful, when in fact they constituted torture prohibited under international and domestic law.[90] The "enhanced interrogation techniques" authorized by high-ranking government lawyers, including waterboarding, stress positions, sleep deprivation, and slamming detainees headfirst into walls,[91] were gross human rights abuses, and any purported legal opinion authorizing their use was not worth the paper it was written on. To borrow a term from the philosophy of law, there are content-independent criteria that can be used to determine whether a lawyer's advice is sufficiently well supported to be deemed lawful, as distinguished from a contrived employment of legal-sounding terms that is in fact an end run around the law.[92]

Fully vindicating this claim would require actually digging into the legal arguments offered by the lawyers, the sources of domestic and international law they relied upon (including cases, statutes, state practice, and other sources that are customarily relied upon by lawyers and judges as authoritative sources of law[93]), and also the norms and traditions of legal interpretation. This last point can be difficult to convey to non-lawyers. Legal education has the goal, among other things, of teaching students to "think like a lawyer" or developing professional judgment. Part of what that means is acquiring a feel for difference between, on the one hand, arguments that are well supported and likely to be acceptable within a community of professional interpreters of law and, on the other hand, those arguments that may superficially appear to be grounded in authoritative sources of law, but in reality are unpersuasive because they do not exhibit the right inferential relationship among facts, law, and interpretive techniques. Importantly, this analysis should not come down to simply whether other lawyers agree (in part because there will probably be a number of lawyers who *disagree*) with the interpretive judgment. There should be something beyond counting noses in the professional community that determines whether a legal interpretation is a genuine effort to get the law right and not a results-driven exercise of raw power by a lawyer or a court.

It takes considerable training and experience to tell the difference between a position taken in bad faith, albeit one with a veneer of legal argument covering it, and one that is sufficiently supported by the factual record and the law. "No formula or algorithm exists for sorting out the plausible-but-wrong arguments from the silly . . . Legal plausibility is a matter for case-by-case judgment by the interpretive community . . ."[94] However, legal judgment should not be a black box within a theory of ethical lawyering, treated as some mystery that is beyond the understanding of non-lawyers. (One of the tacit arguments for the Principle of Nonaccountability is that non-lawyers just don't understand what lawyers do, so their reactions to a lawyer's representation of a client can safely be ignored.) The criticism leveled by many lawyers and legal scholars of the Bush administration lawyers was that they distorted or manipulated the law in giving advice that the "enhanced interrogation techniques" did not violate applicable domestic and international legal prohibitions on torture. To fully understand this critique, there is really no substitute for reading and engaging with the legal arguments on both sides.[95] Maybe you will be persuaded that John Yoo, Jay Bybee, and other lawyers who provided this advice went too far in bending or distorting the law to serve their client's stated objectives. Or maybe you will think that they stayed on the right side of the line between a legitimate interpretation of law and one that would earn a failing grade on an international criminal law exam.

A similar analysis may be undertaken of Rod Rosenstein's involvement in the family separation policy during the Trump administration. It may be the case that he worked diligently within the law and norms regarding prosecutorial discretion to resist implementing the Stephen Miller-designed policy in a way that actually resulted in children being separated from their families. It is possible, however, that he could have done more within the law, short of reigning in protest. That is an issue requiring specialized legal knowledge and familiarity with the factual record to fully address. The same is true with respect to the assessment of the constitutional arguments advanced by John Eastman intended to embolden Vice President Pence to refuse to certify the results of the 2020 presidential election.

In any case, the important point is that there is a difference between criticism of the way lawyers did their job and criticism that amounts to political or ideological disagreement with the client's objectives. One could coherently see the Cheney/Kristol attacks on lawyers for detainees as a smear campaign while faulting the lawyers in the Bush Justice Department who authorized the interrogation program. Doing so, however, requires engaging in good faith with the legal arguments for and against the authorization of enhanced interrogation techniques, and for this there is no substitute for legal experience and judgment.

Of course, one could also rightly argue that torture is a great evil, full stop.[96] It does not matter whether it is legally permitted or not; no morally reflective person should participate in designing or authorizing a program of interrogation that inflicts excruciating physical pain and demonic psychological harm on human beings. The same can be said of a policy—lawful or not—that separates the minor children from their families, no matter how they enter the United States. That is certainly true, but it is also the case that there is something wrong, in specifically professional ethical terms, with lawyers claiming to give legal advice which distorts or misrepresents the applicable law. The distinctive kind of wrongdoing connected with abusive legal advice is connected with the value of legality or the rule of law. If there are good moral reasons to care about the distinction between raw power and legally authorized actions, as I believe there are, then lawyers may also be criticized in these terms.[97]

Finally, there is a possibility that has received relatively little attention from legal scholars or moral philosophers. Suppose for the sake of discussion that the law does permit something that would be regarded by ordinary, decent human beings as wrong. Full-on torture is prohibited by both law and morality, but imagine there are some interrogation techniques that do not constitute torture under international or domestic law, but which a reasonable person would ordinarily feel qualms about using. (This is not an appeal to some fanciful "ticking bomb" story,[98] but the possibility of doing something less than torture that would nevertheless make an ordinary person queasy.) If that person is in the role of a lawyer advising a state intelligence service about the permissibility of conducting the interrogation using the aggressive techniques, the lawyer may feel a profound sense of guilt, reluctance, or regret when advising that, in the lawyer's judgment, the interrogation is legally permitted. And yet, faithful performance of the lawyer's professional duties requires giving this advice. The next chapter considers the origin and effect of qualms and regrets—whether they are simply irrational and can be ignored, or whether they play an important role in a fully worked-out system of professional ethics. It should be no surprise that I favor the second answer, but working out exactly how these "moral remainders" function in ethics will take us back for a bit more moral theory.

Chapter summary

Government lawyers who face public criticism may wish to write it off as nothing more than politics by other means. Some of what lawyers did in the course of representing the Trump campaign or working within the administration is unobjectionable. Other conduct is either outright unlawful or a serious violation of standards of professional ethics. The same observation can be made about criticism from the political right of lawyers who defended accused terrorists and subsequently joined the Obama administration. Distinguishing partisanship from a well-grounded ethical objection to a lawyer's actions necessarily requires an understanding of the relevant law and facts. Taking this too far, however, leads to the Principle of Nonaccountability, which I reject. The meaning of an action, referring to attitudes and motivations of lawyers, still bear on whether the lawyer is blameworthy. As before, reasonable people can disagree about whether any given lawyer—for example, Rod Rosenstein—is blameworthy even if they acted lawfully. It can be hard to disentangle partisan politics from moral evaluation, but it is possible, at least in principle.

Notes

1. David Montgomery, "The Abnormal Presidency," *Wash. Post* (Nov. 10, 2020). The article quotes Harvard Law School Professor Jack Goldsmith's observation that "shamelessness in a president is really empowering." For reform proposals aimed at limiting this power, see Bob Bauer & Jack Goldsmith, *After Trump: Reconstructing the Presidency* (Washington, D.C.: Lawfare Press 2020).
2. For a useful catalog of historical examples, including Theodore Roosevelt's excellent comment that he could "carve out of a banana a judge with more backbone than that," see Daniel I. Weiner & Alicia Bannon, "How to Criticize a Judge," *U.S. News & World Report* (Mar. 6, 2017), also available from the Brennan Center for Justice at https://www.brennancenter.org/our-work/analysis-opinion/how-criticize-judge. Efforts to

call out, shame, or (to use a basketball term) "work the refs" with judges are often motivated by frustration with the appointment and confirmation process. For a more recent example, an opinion piece in the *Washington Post* cited as a problem the fact that "America's judiciary is dominated by conservatives issuing an endless stream of rulings that help corporations, the rich and the bigoted while hurting working-class people, women and minorities in particular." The response: Shame, or "[a] sustained campaign of condemnation." Perry Bacon, Jr., "There Is Only One Way to Rein in Republican Judges: Shaming Them," *Wash. Post* (Feb. 19, 2023).

To which there are two responses—one political and one theoretical. The political response is Barack Obama's frequently quoted line that elections have consequences. Chuck McCutcheon & David Mark, "'Elections Have Consequences': Does Obama Regret Saying That Now?," *Christian Science Monitor* (Nov. 21, 2014). In our constitutional scheme the president has the right to appoint justices of the Supreme Court, with the advice and consent of the Senate. The election of Donald Trump as President, and the previous election of a Senate majority that empowered Mitch McConnell to block the confirmation of Merrick Garland to the Supreme Court, enabled the current majority.

The theoretical response relies on the ethics of blame, as developed in Chapter 5. For example, in criticizing a Fifth Circuit decision affirming a district court order invalidating President Biden's student loan forgiveness program, Bacon writes that "the president should have immediately brought some people struggling with college debt to the White House for a news conference where both he and the college debtors would blast those judges by name." Maybe. But it is not clear that the judges deserve blame (or shame) for having attitudes inconsistent with the ethical obligation of impartiality. The issue in the student loan cases is whether the Department of Education had to follow the notice and comment procedures of the Administrative Procedure Act (APA) or whether it was exempt from the notice-and-comment requirement under a statute allowing the Secretary of Education to promulgate relief measures for people who suffered direct economic harm as a result of a national emergency. *Brown v. U.S. Dept. of Educ.*, 640 F. Supp. 3d 644 (N.D. Tex. 2022), cert. granted before judgment on appeal, 143 S. Ct. 541 (2022). I'm no expert on administrative law, but this seems to me like an issue upon which reasonable lawyers can disagree.

On the approach I defend to the ethics of blame, one should be hesitant to ascribe nefarious motives, such as being in the tank for Trump or merely wanting to help out rich corporations, where there are valid non-nefarious reasons supporting an action. Combining the political and ethical arguments, the Fifth Circuit today is strikingly conservative and that is the result of repeated presidential and senatorial elections going for Republicans in those states. If reasonable lawyers disagree on issues such as the appropriateness of nationwide injunctions, the interaction between the APA and a separate statute, or generally how broadly one reads remedial statutes like the HEROES Act at issue in this case, then one should expect differences along ideological lines among judgers. These differences are not necessarily reducible to "support Trump" or "support Biden" but may reflect commitments to methods of statutory interpretation or positions on executive vs. legislative power that may tend to fall out on

party lines. I don't know if Bacon is a lawyer, and I really don't mean to pick on him, since many supporters of the Biden administration have criticized this decision, but I do think that someone with a prominent national platform should be aware of the legal issues in play in a case like this and whether they are arguable or so clearly one-sided that the judge is likely to be playing politics.
3. Will Baude, "The Deadly Serious Accusation of Being a 'So-Called Judge,'" *Wash. Post* (Feb. 4, 2017). Trump's most notorious attack on a judge came when he was a candidate and referred to the Indiana-born (that is, American) judge presiding over a class-action lawsuit against Trump University as inherently biased against him because of his signature campaign promise to "build a wall" on the U.S.-Mexican border and Trump's belief that the judge is "a Mexican." Jia Tolentio, "Trump and the Truth: The 'Mexican' Judge," *New Yorker* (Sept. 20, 2016). Trump's reference to a district court judge who had enjoined the administration's ban on migrants from Mexico seeking asylum in the United States as an "Obama judge" promoted an unusual comment from Supreme Court Chief Justice John Roberts, who said: "We do not have Obama judges or Trump judges, Bush judges or Clinton judges. What we have is an extraordinary group of dedicated judges doing their level best to do equal right to those appearing before them." Undaunted, Trump merely continued tweeting criticism of the district judge and the Ninth Circuit. See Robert Barnes, "Rebuking Trump's Criticism of 'Obama Judge,' Chief Justice Roberts Defends Judiciary as 'Independent,'" *Wash. Post* (Nov. 21, 2018).
4. Damian Paletta & Josh Dawsey, "Trump Personally Pushed Postmaster General to Double Rates on Amazon, Other Firms," *Wash. Post* (May 18, 2018). Amazon had alleged that it lost a $10 billion contract to provide cloud-computing services to the Defense Department due to Trump's hatred of the company. Alina Selyukh, "Pentagon Scraps $10 Billion Contract With Microsoft, Bitterly Contested By Amazon," *NPR* (July 6, 2021).
5. Aaron Blake, "Trump's Slow-Motion Friday Night Massacre of Inspectors General," *Wash. Post* (May 18, 2020).
6. Katie Benner, "Trump Pressed Justice Dept. to Declare Election Results Corrupt, Notes Show," *N.Y. Times* (July 30, 2021); Michael S. Schmidt & Maggie Haberman, "Trump Ordered Mueller Fired, but Backed Off When White House Counsel Threatened to Quit," *N.Y. Times* (Jan. 25, 2018); Peter Baker, Michael S. Schmidt, & Maggie Haberman, "Citing Recusal, Trump Says He Wouldn't Have Hired Sessions," *N.Y. Times* (July 19, 2017).
7. Rick Wilson, *Everything Trump Touches Dies: A Republican Strategist Gets Real about the Worst President Ever* (New York: Simon & Schuster 2018).
8. W. Bradley Wendel, "Pluralism, Polarization, and the Common Good: The Possibility of *Modus Vivendi* Legal Ethics," 131 *Yale L.J. Forum* 89 (Oct. 24, 2021).
9. As discussed later, several high-ranking government lawyers, including White House Counsel Pat Cipollone, Vice President Pence's counsel Greg Jacob, Acting Attorney General Jeffrey Rosen, White House lawyer Eric Herschmann, and conservative legal icon and outside legal advisor J. Michael Luttig all refused to lend assistance to Trump's various schemes to overturn the results of the election. Several pushed back forcefully on proponents of stolen-election claims, such as John Eastman.

10. Dahlia Lithwick, "What Will Happen to the Lawyers Who Aided and Abetted Donald Trump?," *Slate* (Nov. 1, 2020). For a reporter's take on the controversy, see Dan Packel, "Will Service in the Trump Administration Be a Scarlet Letter in Big Law?," *Am. Law.* (Jan. 11, 2021).
11. Department of Justice, Office of the Inspector General, *Review of the Department of Justice's Planning and Implementation of Its Zero Tolerance Policy and Its Coordination with the Departments of Homeland Security and Health and Human Services* (originally released Jan. 14, 2021, and revised Apr. 13, 2022). See also Caitlin Dickerson, "We Need to Take Away Children: The Secret History of the U.S. Government's Family-Separation Policy," *Atlantic* (Aug. 7, 2022).
12. Jennifer Senior, "Rod Rosenstein Was Just Doing His Job," *N.Y. Times* (Oct. 20, 2020).
13. Stephen L. Carter, "Trump's Lawyers Are Just Doing Their Jobs," *Bloomberg Opinion* (Nov. 13, 2020).
14. Kerry Kennedy & Erika Andiola, "The Architects of Trump's Family Separation Policy Have Landed on Their Feet," *Slate* (Aug. 11, 2021).
15. DOJ Inspector General Report, pp. 9, 20.
16. Bess Levin, "Report: The Trump Administration Let Sex Offenders Off Because It Was Too Busy Separating Migrant Babies from Their Parents," *Vanity Fair* (Oct. 7, 2020).
17. DOJ Inspector General Report, pp. 9-15. The Department of Homeland Security (DHS) is the federal agency that includes the offices of U.S. Customs and Border Protection (CPB) and Immigration and Customs Enforcement (ICE), which are responsible for enforcing entry requirements into the United States.
18. DOJ Inspector General Report, p. 6.
19. Julia Ainsley & Jacob Soboroff, "Trump Cabinet Officials Voted in 2018 White House Meeting to Separate Migrant Children, Say Officials," *NBC News* (Aug. 20, 2020); DOJ Inspector General Report, pp. 12-13, 49-51. The Inspector General Report states that several DOJ officials told investigators that Sessions knew the zero-tolerance policy would result in family separations and in fact intended that result. DOJ Inspector General Report, pp. 2, 24-26. Sessions stated in a public speech on May 7, 2018, that if a family cross the border with a child "that child will be separated from you." DOJ Inspector General Report, p. 37. He is reported also have said, on a conference call with U.S. attorneys, that "[w]e need to take away children." Michael D. Shear, Katie Benner & Michael S. Schmidt, "'We Need to Take Away Children,' No Matter How Young, Justice Dept. Officials Said," *N.Y. Times* (Oct. 6, 2020). In an interview given nearly three years after the end of his presidency, Trump stated that his administration's decision to separate families at the border was intended as a deterrent: "When you hear that you're going to be separated from your family, you don't come," he said. Brett Samuels, "Trump Defends Family Separation Policy in New Interview," *The Hill* (Nov. 9, 2023).
20. Ainsley & Soboroff, above.
21. Ainsley & Soboroff, above; Suzanne Gamboa, "'White Supremacy' Was Behind Child Separations—and Trump Officials Went Along, Critics Say, *NBC News* (Aug. 22, 2020).
22. The May 3, 2018, meeting described in the NBC News reporting is referred to in the DOJ Inspector General Report at pp. 31-33, and resulted in a directive from Homeland Security Secretary Nielsen to refer all apprehended adults for prosecution.

23. DOJ Inspector General Report, p. 39.
24. DOJ Inspector General Report, pp. 41–42.
25. DOJ Inspector General Report, p. 56.
26. The Reporter for the ALI's Third Restatement of Agency has written that the most fundamental obligation of all agents is to follow the lawful instruction of their principal, interpreted reasonably in light of the principal's wishes as the agent understands them. Deborah DeMott, "The Fiduciary Character of Agency and the Interpretation of Instructions," in Andrew S. Gold & Paul B. Miller eds., *Philosophical Foundations of Fiduciary Law* (Oxford: Oxford University Press 2014), p. 321. The Restatement of the Law Governing Lawyers states what I regard as one of the core duties for lawyers: "[A] lawyer must . . . proceed in a manner reasonably calculated to advance a client's lawful objectives, as defined by the client after consultation." Restatement (Third) of the Law Governing Lawyers § 16(1) (Am. L. Inst. 2000). I have defended Rosenstein's conduct along these lines. See W. Bradley Wendel, "Pluralism, Polarization, and the Common Good: The Possibility of Modus Vivendi Legal Ethics," *Yale L.J. Forum* (Oct. 24, 2021). Milan Markovic criticizes this narrow conception of the lawyer's role when applied to prosecutors, who he sees as having a special obligation to do justice, particularly in the context of making discretionary charging decisions. Milan Markovic, "The Legal Ethics of Family Separation," 57 *U. Rich. L. Rev.* 487 (2023). I disagree with that on the substance of the duties of prosecutors, but here I want to focus on the meaning or significance of Rosenstein's actions, assuming for the sake of argument they were permissible. It could very well be that he deserves shame, shunning, or ostracism *even though* one could give an argument along the lines that considerations of democratic accountability justify deferring to chain of command (the Attorney General's directives) and the instructions of high-ranking officials in the White House.
27. ABA Model Rules of Prof'l Conduct, Rule 2.1.
28. Former Office of Legal Counsel Attorney Erica Newland said that she believed "a critical mass of responsible attorneys staying in government might provide a last line of defense against the administration's worst instincts. Erica Newland, "I'm Haunted by What I Did as a Lawyer in the Trump Justice Department," *N.Y. Times* (Dec. 20, 2020). But she now thinks that a mass resignation by lawyers committed to democracy and the rule of law would have left the administration with only the kinds of "second-rate lawyers who lack the skills to maintain the president's charade"—goofballs like Sidney Powell and Rudy Giuliani. See also Grace Panetta, "William Barr and Jared Kushner Both Referred to the Trump Campaign's Legal Efforts to Overturn the Election as a 'Clown Show,' Book Says," *Business Insider* (July 20, 2021). David Luban notes that Hannah Arendt regarded this reasoning as at best self-deception and self-flattery, and at worst complicity under the guise of resistance. David Luban, "Complicity and Lesser Evils: A Tale of Two Lawyers," 34 *Geo. J. Legal Ethics* 613, 621 (2021). One of the principles he distills from Arendt's writing on the behavior of Germans during the Nazi regime is this: "Don't justify participation by saying the next person would be worse." Luban, p. 623. Rosenstein's replacement, Jeffrey Rosen, actually behaved quite honorably following the election when, as Acting Attorney General following William Barr's resignation, he resisted Trump's demands to appoint a special counsel

to investigate Dominion Voting Systems and send a letter to Georgia election officials suggesting that the Justice Department was investigating voter fraud in that state. The threat by numerous senior DOJ officials to resign *en masse* if Trump forced out Rosen led Trump to back down from his plan of replacing Rosen with the pliable Jeffrey Clark, who had been working with Trump to cast doubt on the election results. Katie Benner, "Trump and Justice Dept. Lawyer Said to Have Plotted to Oust Acting Attorney General," *N.Y. Times* (Jan. 22, 2021). Trump's national security officials, including the Secretary of Defense and the Chairman of the Joint Chiefs of Staff, faced a similar dilemma. See Susan B. Glasser & Peter Baker, "Inside the War Between Trump and His Generals," *New Yorker* (Aug. 8, 2022).

29. T.M. Scanlon, "Blame," in *Moral Dimensions: Permissibility, Meaning, Blame* (Cambridge, Mass.: Belknap Press 2008), pp. 128–31. As I noted in Chapter 4, Scanlon's account of blame is the most prominent n the literature, so it makes sense to talk about blame with reference to Scanlon. However, my own way of thinking about blame probably inclines a bit more toward Susan Wolf's approach. See Susan Wolf, "Blame, Italian Style," in R. Jay Wallace, Rahul Kumar, & Samuel Freeman, *Reasons and Recognition: Essays on the Philosophy of T.M. Scanlon* (Oxford: Oxford University Press 2011), p. 332.

30. Scanlon, "Blame," p. 153.

31. Scanlon, "Blame," pp. 145 ("the content of *blame* depends on the significance, for the person doing the blaming, of the agent and of what he has done"), p. 212 ("a conclusion that someone is blameworthy is a conclusion about that person's attitudes").

32. Scanlon, "Blame," p. 140 ("morality requires that we hold certain attitudes toward one another simply in virtue of the fact that we stand in the relation of 'fellow rational beings'").

33. Julia Ainsley & Jacob Soboroff, "Justice Officials Respond to Report on Family Separation by Blaming Trump, Expressing Regret, *NBC News* (Jan. 14, 2021). Other government lawyers have apologized publicly for their role in implementing Trump administration policies, including a lawyer formerly in the DOJ's Office of Legal Counsel. Erica Newland, "I'm Haunted by What I Did as a Lawyer in the Trump Justice Department," *N.Y. Times* (Dec. 20, 2020). She subsequently expanded on this editorial in a law review article, stating that in hindsight her decision to remain in office helped to maintain an image of stability and respectability in the administration. Erica Newland, "A Practitioner's Perspective on Complicity and Lesser Evils," 34 *Geo. J. Legal Ethics* 681 (2021).

34. Nicole Narea, "Kirstjen Nielsen was Asked to Answer for Family Separations in Her First Interview Since Leaving Office," *Vox* (Oct. 23, 2019); Amanda Holpuch, "'I Don't Regret Enforcing the Law': Nielsen Defends Family Separation at Summit," *The Guardian* (Oct. 22, 2019).

35. Peter Baker, "Cosmetics Billionaire Convinced Trump That the U.S. Should Buy Greenland," *N.Y. Times* (Sept. 14, 2022).

36. Restatement (Third) of the Law Governing Lawyers § 16(1) (Am. L. Inst. 2000)

37. Griffin B. Bell, "The Attorney General: The Federal Government's Chief Lawyer and Chief Litigator, or One Among Many?," 46 *Fordham L. Rev.* 1049, 1069 (1978).

38. Geoffrey P. Miller, "Government Lawyers' Ethics in a System of Checks and Balances," 54 *U. Chi. L. Rev.* 1293 (1987).
39. I have defended this position for many years in debates about the ethical duties of government lawyers. See W. Bradley Wendel, "Pluralism, Polarization, and the Common Good: The Possibility of *Modus Vivendi* Legal Ethics," 131 *Yale L.J. Forum* 89 (Oct. 24, 2021); W. Bradley Wendel, "Government Lawyers in the Trump Administration," 69 *Hastings L.J.* 275 (2017); W. Bradley Wendel, "Sally Yates, Ronald Dworkin, and the Best View of the Law," 115 *Mich. L. Rev. First Impressions* 78 (2016); W. Bradley Wendel, "Government Lawyers, Democracy, and the Rule of Law," 77 *Fordham L. Rev.* 1333 (2009).
40. A different issue is that the norms of polite society might be so tilted in the direction of conflict-avoidance that even the worst wrongdoer will not be shunned. Not intending to compare Stephen Miller (who I regard as loathsome) with Antonin Scalia, one of the remarkable anecdotes in NPR legal journalist Nina Totenberg's book about her friendship with Supreme Court Justice Ruth Bader Ginsburg occurred at a dinner party hosted by Totenberg and her husband, a surgeon who had treated numerous victims of gun violence. Scalia had just written the majority opinion in *D.C. v. Heller*, a case recognizing a broad right under the Second Amendment to gun ownership, not tethered to the "well regulated militia" language in the Amendment. Totenberg and her husband set the table with plastic squirt guns at each place, which reportedly was regarded as hilarious by the guests. See G.S. Hans, "Book Review: 'Dinners With Ruth' and Without Any Semblance of Journalistic Standards, By Nina Totenberg," *Balls & Strikes* (Sept. 21, 2022), available at https://ballsandstrikes.org/legal-culture/dinners-with-ruth-review/. To emphasize, I believe Scalia was wrong as a matter of constitutional interpretation and the *Heller* has had terrible social consequences, but I am not comparing his character with Miller's. To the extent shunning and shaming occurs in rarified social settings, however, the anecdote about the dinner party with Antonin Scalia suggests that well-connected lawyers and judges have little to fear from social sanctions.
41. Jeff John Roberts, "Backlash Against Jones Day, the Law Firm Aiding Trump's Election Challenge, Begins to Escalate," *Fortune* (Nov. 12, 2020); Xiumei Dong, "Lincoln Project Lobs Attacks Against Jones Day, Porter Wright," Law360 (Nov. 10, 2020), https://www.law360.com/articles/1327686/lincoln-project-lobs-attacks-against-jones-day-porter-wright.
42. This would be an example of a secondary boycott. Linda Radzik, "Boycotts and the Social Enforcement of Justice," *Social Phil. & Policy* 34(1): 102–22 (2017), p. 106–107.
43. See Jones Day's Nov. 10, 2020, press release, available on *Business Wire*. When I appeared at a book talk event at Cardozo Law School with *New York Times* reporter David Enrich, I received a letter from Kevyn Orr, Jones Day's Partner in Charge of all U.S. offices. The letter was highly critical of Enrich's reporting and asked that I clarify that the Lincoln Project shaming efforts were "promoted by admittedly false media reports about the nature of Jones Day's involvement in pre-election litigation." As frustrating as this may be for the firm, I am actually less interested in who the firm actually represented than in the public reaction to the report that the firm had represented the Trump campaign. The intense public criticism and—as was reported

in the sources cited above—pushback from other firm clients is evidence for the public's rejection of the Principle of Nonaccountability.
44. *Pennsylvania Democratic Party v. Boockvar*, 238 A.3d 345 (Pa. 2020).
45. Petition for Writ of Certiorari to the Supreme Court of Pennsylvania in *Republican Party of Pennsylvania v. Boockvar*, No. 20-542, 2020 WL 6273543.
46. *Republican Party of Pennsylvania v. Degraffenreid*, 141 S. Ct. 732 (2021) (denying cert.). Justice Thomas's dissent from the denial of certiorari has details about the course of the litigation, including the Court's order to segregate the late ballots.
47. David Enrich, *Servants of the Damned: Giant Law Firms, Donald Trump and the Corruption of Justice* (New York: HarperCollins 2022), pp. 285, 294–95.
48. See https://peoplesparity.org/trumpfirmspledge/, cited in Roy Strom, "Big Law's Nightmare: Ethics Issues Scare Away New Recruits," *Bloomberg Law* (Sept. 15, 2022).
49. Michael S. Schmidt & Kenneth P. Vogel, "Trump Lawyer on Call Is a Conservative Firebrand Aiding His Push to Overturn Election," *N.Y. Times* (Jan. 4, 2021); Michael Kranish, "Cleta Mitchell, Who Advised Trump on Saturday Phone Call, Resigns from Law Firm," *Wash. Post* (Jan. 5, 2020); Amy Gardner, "'I Just Want to Find 11,780 Votes': In Extraordinary Call, Trump Pressures Georgia Secretary of State to Recalculate the Vote in His Favor," *Wash. Post* (Jan. 3, 2021; see also *Eastman v. Thompson*, 594 F. Supp. 3d 1156 (C.D. Cal. 2022).
50. Aebra Coe, "Foley & Lardner Faces Ire over Partner's Role on Trump Call," *Law360* (Jan. 4, 2021).
51. Michael S. Schmidt & Maggie Haberman, "Lawyer on Trump Election Call Quits Firm After Uproar," *N.Y. Times* (Jan. 5, 2020).
52. Rosalind Helderman, Patrick Marley, & Tom Hamburger, "Trump Called a Protest. No One Showed. Why GOP Efforts to Cry Foul Fizzled This Time," *Wash. Post* (Nov. 9, 2022).
53. The 65 Project, *Ethics Complaint Against Trump Attorney Cleta Mitchell* (Mar. 7, 2022), available at https://the65project.com/ethics-complaint-against-trump-attorney-cleta-mitchell/ See also Roy Strom, "Trump Lawyer Cleta Mitchell Targeted in Group's Ethics Complaint," *Bloomberg Law* (Mar. 7, 2022).
54. The conservative but now consistently anti-Trump columnist Jennifer Rubin wrote: "All criminal litigants deserve a vigorous defense, but lawyers have no obligation to represent those who raise meritless claims. They cannot conspire with clients to undermine the Constitution. Just as the Justice Department must prosecute the insurrectionists who stormed the Capitol, so, too, must lawyers, who are officers of the court, be held accountable for their role carrying out Trump's schemes. This is the essence of the rule of law." Jennifer Rubin, "Trump's Enablers Must Face Consequences, Too," *Wash. Post* (Mar. 1, 2023). If the only role the lawyers played in carrying out Trump's schemes was raising meritless claims or engaging in a criminal conspiracy, then in the terms introduced in Chapter 7, the blame is on them *qua* lawyers, for failing with reference to the standards of their role. This would not be an instance of directing angry blame, in moral terms, at the lawyers for doing something they were permitted to do, albeit on behalf of a highly divisive client.
55. Matthew Brown, "Federal Judge Upholds Georgia Election Law in Challenge Brought by Abrams," *Wash. Post* (Oct. 1, 2022).

56. *Trump v. Biden*, 951 N.W.2d 568 (Wis. 2021).
57. Steven Lubet, "Should Those Who Served the Trump Administration Reluctantly Now Feel Remorse?", *The Dispatch* (Dec. 28, 2020), available at https://perma.cc/TQS7-XZGV. Lubet is a severe critic of the Trump administration yet he specifically exempts Jones Day and Porter Wright from criticism since they refused to represent Trump in the unfounded election challenges.
58. These lawsuits were dismissed by federal district courts, often accompanied by lengthy opinions detailing the evidentiary and legal shortcomings of the pleadings filed by the challengers. See, e.g., *O'Rourke v. Dominion Voting Systems*, 552 F. Supp. 3d 1168 (D. Colo. 2021); *Bowyer v. Ducey*, 506 F. Supp. 3d 699 (D. Ariz. 2020); *King v. Whitmer*, 505 F. Supp. 3d 720 (E.D. Mich. 2020). Although they incorrectly lump some of the lawsuits filed by Jones Day in with the frivolous election challenges, two legal journalists recognized early on that there is an important difference between legally and factually unsupported claims and "disputes between two candidates with meritorious claims." Dahlia Lithwick & Mark Joseph Stern, "Of Course We Should Scorn Trump's Sleazy Election Lawyers," *Slate* (Nov. 16, 2020). For Mitchell's continuing involvement with groups denying the basic facts on the ground—that is, that there was no evidence of improper conduct by election officials or significant voter fraud in the 2020 presidential election—see Alexandra Berzon, "Lawyer Who Plotted to Overturn Trump Loss Recruits Election Deniers to Watch Over the Vote," *N.Y. Times* (May 30, 2022).
59. Scott Cummings, Nora Freeman Engstrom, David Luban, & Deborah L. Rhode, "It's Time to Consider Sanctions for Trump's Legal Team," *Slate* (Nov. 23, 2020). A group called the 65 Project referred numerous lawyers to their admitting states' disciplinary authorities for conduct relating to the 2020 election. Roy Strom, "Trump Lawyer Cleta Mitchell Targeted in Group's Ethics Complaint," *Bloomberg* (Mar. 7, 2022).
60. Roy Strom, "Trump Lawyer Cleta Mitchell Leaves Firm After Georgia Call," *Bloomberg* (Jan. 5, 2021). After the publication of the final report of the Select Committee to Investigate the January 6th Attack on the United States Capitol, the former top ethics lawyer in the Trump White House (I know, the jokes write themselves) took a leave of absence from the Milwaukee law firm Michael Best & Friedrich. The lawyer, Stefan Passantino, allegedly advised Cassidy Hutchinson, an aide to White House Chief of Staff Mark Meadows, to testify falsely to the January 6 Committee. Justin Wise, "Trump Lawyer Takes Leave from Firm After Jan. 6 Panel Allegation," *Bloomberg Law* (Dec. 21, 2022); Dave Simpson, "White House Aide Says Atty Told Her to Mislead Jan. 6 Panel," *Law360* (Dec. 22, 2022). See also the disciplinary complaint filed on Feb. 15, 2023, with the State Bar of Georgia, by the 65 Project, regarding Passantino's representation of Hutchinson at the January 6 Committee hearings. If these allegations are true, they represent a serious violation of the rules of professional conduct for lawyers, quite apart from any moral condemnation the lawyer might deserve for seeking to obstruct the investigation into an effort to overthrow a democratically elected government.
61. This discussion is based on the district court's order on claims of attorney-client privilege and attorney work product asserted by Eastman in response to a subpoena by

the committee of the House of Representatives investigating the January 6, 2021, riot at the U.S. Capitol. *Eastman v. Thompson*, 594 F. Supp. 3d 1156 (C.D. Cal. 2022). For an analysis of Eastman's theory that is more sympathetic than most, see David McGowan, "Lawyers and the Theory of the 'Big Lie'", manuscript available from SSRN, https://ssrn.com/abstract=4231550.

62. *Eastman*, 594 F. Supp. 3d at 1169 (alterations in original removed). Barr has tried to rehabilitate his public image, stating in his book that he tried to tell Trump that his claims about massive election fraud were bogus. Numerous reviewers of the book have responded that most of Barr's book consists of a full-throated culture-war defense of Trump's policies and attacks on critics of the administration. See, e.g., Lloyd Green, "One Damn Thing After Another Review: Bill Barr's Self-Serving Screed," *The Guardian* (Mar. 12, 2022); Dana Milbank, "Have You Heard About How Bill Barr Saved Democracy? Let Bill Barr Tell You," *Wash. Post* (Mar. 4, 2022); Martin Pengelly, "William Barr's Trump Book: Self-Serving Narratives and Tricky Truths Ignored, *The Guardian* (Mar. 3, 2022); Devin Bartlitt, William Barr's Memoir Blasts Trump and Giuliani—and Ignores His Own Partisan Excesses, *Wash. Post* (Mar. 1, 2022); Jennifer Szalai, "William P. Barr's Memoir Is Part Lawyerly Defense, Part Culture-War Diatribe," *N.Y. Times* (Feb. 27, 2022). The different reactions to Barr and other former Trump administration lawyers illustrates the complexity and contestability of judgments of blameworthiness.

63. *Eastman*, 594 F. Supp. 3d at 1170–71 (quoting deposition of Greg Jacob, counsel to the vice president).

64. *Eastman*, 594 F. Supp. 3d at 1171 (quoting John Eastman, Speech to the "Save America March" and Rally, C-SPAN (Jan. 6, 2021)).

65. *Eastman*, 594 F. Supp. 3d at 1173.

66. *Eastman*, 594 F. Supp. 3d at 1170.

67. Luke Broadwater & Maggie Haberman, "Trump Lawyer Cited 'Heated Fight' Among Justices over Election Suits," *N.Y. Times* (June 15, 2022).

68. *Eastman*, 594 F. Supp. 3d at 1195.

69. Kyle Cheney "Select Committee Points to Evidence Trump Lawyer's Election-Related Efforts Resumed After Jan. 6," *Politico* (June 14, 2022).

70. *Eastman*, 594 F. Supp. 3d at 1194.

71. *Eastman*, 594 F. Supp. 3d at 1198.

72. Aaron Regunberg, "Big Law Is Complicit in the Climate Crisis," *Boston Globe* (Sept. 25, 2021).

73. Giuliani was found by a committee of the District of Columbia Bar to have violated the prohibition in the D.C. Rules of Professional Conduct on bringing frivolous lawsuits. In closing argument, D.C. Bar Counsel Hamilton "Phil" Fox argued that this was not a garden variety frivolous lawsuit but one that also violated Giuliani's oath to support the constitution and an attempt to undermine the legitimacy of the election. Kyle Cheney & Josh Gerstein, "D.C. Bar Panel Finds Giuliani Violated Attorney Rules in Bid to Overturn 2020 Election," *Politico* (Dec. 15, 2022).

74. *In re Giuliani*, 197 A.D.3d 1, 146 N.Y.S.3d 266 (2021).

75. As detailed in the disciplinary action cited above.

76. In their book *Peril* (New York; Simon & Schuster 2021), Bob Woodward and Robert Costa report that Trump said, of Giuliani: "He's crazy. He says crazy shit. I get it. But none of the sane lawyers can represent me because they've been pressured. The actual lawyers have been told they cannot represent my campaign."
77. Mark Memmott, "Liz Cheney Launches "Keep America Safe"; Video Skewers Obama," *NPR* (Oct. 13, 2009); Dahlia Lithwick, "More Than Words," *Slate* (Mar. 5, 2010); Chris McGreal, "Liz Cheney Accused of McCarthyism over Campaign Against Lawyers," *Guardian* (Mar. 11, 2010). Cheney later was elected to the House of Representatives and was part of the House Republican leadership until voting to impeach Donald Trump during his second impeachment trial arising out of the January 6, 2021, insurrection. Cheney subsequently became, along with Adam Kinzinger, one of only two Republican members of the House committee investigating the Capitol riots, a decision for which they were censured by the Republican National Committee for taking part in the "persecution of ordinary citizens engaged in legitimate political discourse." Burgess Everett, Marianne Levine, & Olivia Beavers, "Senate GOP Backlash Smacks RNC After Cheney-Kinzinger Censure," *Politico* (Feb. 7, 2022). Cheney subsequently lost the Republican primary in Wyoming, thus losing her seat in the House, in an indication of how strong Trump's grip on the party remained 18 months after the January 6 insurrection. See, e.g., Shane Goldmacher, "Here's What Liz Cheney's Lopsided Loss Says about the State of the G.O.P.," *N.Y. Times* (Aug. 17, 2022). One of Cheney's staunchest supporters among anti-Trump Republicans has been Bill Kristol, who was part of the campaign to stigmatize Obama administration lawyers who had represented detainees. I do not quite know what to make of the contrast between their current opposition to Trump and their previous attacks on lawyers for representing accused terrorists. Whether the common factor is their neoconservative foreign policy hawkishness or other grounds for disliking Trump is an interesting question. Nicholas Lemann, "The Larger Lesson of Liz Cheney's Ouster," *New Yorker* (May 16, 2021).
78. Ashby Jones, "Did 'Department of Jihad' Language Go Too Far?," *Wall St. J.* (Mar. 5, 2010).
79. Editorial, "Come Clean, Mr. Holder," *N.Y. Post* (Jan. 27, 2010).
80. Ben Smith, "Cheney Group Questions Loyalty of Justice Lawyers," *Politico* (Mar. 3, 2010).
81. David Luban, "Lawfare and Legal Ethics in Guantánamo," 60 *Stan. L. Rev.* 1981 (2008).
82. Editorial, "Unveiled Threats: A Bush Appointee's Crude Gambit on Detainees' Legal Rights," *Wash. Post* (Jan. 12, 2007); Neil A. Lewis, "Official Attacks Top Law Firms Over Detainees," *N.Y. Times* (Jan. 13, 2007).
83. Charles Fried, "Mr. Stimson and the American Way," *Wall St. J.* (Jan. 16, 2007).
84. John Schwartz, "Attacks on Detainee Lawyers Split Conservatives," *N.Y. Times* (Mar. 9, 2010); Ben Smith, "Republicans Scold Liz Cheney," *Politico* (Mar. 8, 2010). The statement is included at the end of the March 8 *Politico* article and can also be found at the website of the Brookings Institute, the institutional home of its primary drafter. See Statement on Justice Department Attorney Representation of Guantánamo Detainees

(March 8, 2010), available at https://www.brookings.edu/opinions/statement-on-justice-department-attorney-representation-of-guantanamo-detainees/.
85. Benjamin Wittes, "Presumed Innocent? Representing Guantánamo Detainees," Brookings Institute (Mar. 24, 2010), available at https://www.brookings.edu/opinions/presumed-innocent-representing-guantanamo-detainees/.
86. Andrew C. McCarthy, "Not Everybody Is Entitled to a Lawyer," *National Review* (Mar. 22, 2022).
87. https://the65project.com/about/.
88. Quoted in Ben Smith, "Republicans Scold Liz Cheney," *Politico* (Mar. 8, 2010) (noting that, at her district court confirmation hearing, Republican Senator Charles Grassley cited her representation of detainees as reason for "some concern about how you will handle terrorism cases that may come before you").
89. A point made more polemically in Marc A. Thiessen, "The 'al-Qaeda Seven' and Selective McCarthyism," *Wash. Post* (Mar. 8, 2010).
90. The literature on the post-9/11 response by the Bush administration, including the national security and legal institutions of American government, is vast. Well-reported accounts and thoughtful analysis on which I have relied in previous work include Harold H Bruff, *Bad Advice: Bush's Lawyers in the War on Terror* (Lawrence: University Press of Kansas 2009); Jane Mayer, *The Dark Side: The Inside Story of How the War on Terror Turned into a War on American Ideals* (New York: Doubleday 2008); Philippe Sands, *The Torture Team: Rumsfeld's Memo and the Betrayal of American Values* (New York: Palgrave Macmillan 2008); Eric Lichtblau, *Bush's Law: The Remaking of American Justice* (New York: Pantheon Books 2008); Jack L Goldsmith, *The Terror Presidency: Law and Judgment Inside the Bush Administration* (New York: WW Norton 2007); David Luban, "The Torture Lawyers of Washington," in *Legal Ethics and Human Dignity* (Cambridge: Cambridge University Press 2007).
91. These techniques were described in a confidential report by the International Committee of the Red Cross. For citations to the report and other sources, see W. Bradley Wendel, "The Torture Memos and the Demands of Legality," 12 *Legal Ethics* 107 (2009).
92. H.L.A. Hart, *Essays on Bentham* (Oxford: Oxford University Press 1982), pp. 254–55. "A reason is content-independent if the validity of the reason is independent of the validity of its content." Scott Shapiro, "On Hart's Way Out," in Jules Coleman, ed., *Hart's Postscript: Essays on the Postscript to* The Concept of Law (Oxford: Oxford University Press 2001), p. 175.
93. Hart famously posited a "rule of recognition" followed by judges that identifies the primary rules of obligation of a legal system. H.L.A. Hart, *The Concept of Law* (Oxford: Clarendon Press, 2d ed. 1994), pp. 94–95.
94. Luban, "Torture Lawyers," p. 193. Two of the three questions considered in David Luban's chapter on the advice given by Bush administration lawyers in connection with interrogation policy are addressed to this issue: "(2) Given a contentious legal issue, how much leeway does the candid advisor have to slant the law in the client's direction? (3) What is the difference between illicitly slanted advice and advice that is merely wrong?" Luban, "Torture Lawyers," p. 163. The remainder of the chapter

then vindicates the position that the torture memos represent contributed, "spun," or manipulated legal advice, because that is what the clients wanted. Crucially, it does that in legal terms, by careful examination of international law (including the Geneva Conventions and the Convention Against Torture), U.S. law on the recognition of treaties, and domestic criminal law prohibiting torture.

95. Goldsmith, above; Luban, "Torture Lawyers"; Jeremy Waldron, "Torture and Positive Law: Jurisprudence for the White House," 105 *Colum. L. Rev.* 1681 (2005).
96. David Luban, *Torture, Power, and Law* (Cambridge: Cambridge University Press 2014); Henry Shue, "Torture," 7 *Phil. & Pub. Aff.* 124 (1978).
97. W. Bradley Wendel, "Executive Branch Lawyers in a Time of Terror: The 2008 F.W. Wickwire Memorial Lecture" (2008) 31 *Dalhousie L.J.* 247.
98. As the philosopher Henry Shue has pointed out, ticking bomb stories trade on completely fanciful factual assumptions: "The proposed victim of our torture is not someone we suspect of planting the device: he *is* the perpetrator. He is not some pitiful psychotic making one last play for attention: he *did* plant the device. The wiring is not backwards, the mechanism is not jammed: the device *will* destroy the city if not deactivated...." Shue, p. 142.

8
Philosophical Perspective: Regret and Moral Costs

Excruciating cases

One of the major themes in this book has been the separation between the permissibility of representing nasty clients—as well as the things lawyers do in the course of representing them—and the meaning of those actions, in light of the motivating reasons, intentions, and attitudes of lawyers. This separation may account for a sense of reluctance, regret, and the moral remainders that go along with carrying out an obligation of one's professional role. A powerful illustration of the moral remainders that may arise in the practice of law comes from a feminist criminal defense lawyer and law professor, Abbe Smith, who wrote a remarkably candid and personal essay about "how it actually feels to confront and cross-examine alleged victims of sexual assault, knowing (or strongly believing) that they are telling the truth, and how to come to terms with those feelings."[1] Throughout this discussion it is important to remember that Smith is strongly committed to the role obligations of criminal defense lawyers. She believes that vigorous representation is justified, even for people accused of committing terrible crimes, even if the lawyer believes that they are in fact guilty, and even if it means doing things like cross-examining a witness the lawyer believes to be truthful with the objective of undermining her credibility.[2] Uncompromising criminal defense is justified by the problem of mass incarceration; the poverty and racism that underlies so many social injustices; the disparity in power between individuals and the state, preventing officials from rushing to judgment and wrongfully convicting a suspect; the importance of upholding constitutional protections including the right to counsel and the presumption of innocence; and the recognition that ideals of human dignity and due process of law are hollow promises without skilled, experienced, committed counsel who are willing to represent even the proverbial worst of the worst.[3]

That is not the end of the matter, however. There is still what may be seen as the personal dimension or the question of the meaning of a lawyer's actions. Smith describes one case in which her client admitted to her that he had raped an 11-year-old girl.[4] The defense theory was that the child's mother's boyfriend, not the defendant, had committed the crime—a theory which had some support in the police report, in which the girl had said she thought it was her mother's boyfriend climbing into bed. As Smith acknowledges, effective defense lawyering often involves exploiting "the challenges, vagaries, and uncertainty of memory itself."[5] After a cross-examination that was intended to gain the trust of the child and get her to admit facts that would set up a closing argument that she had falsely identified the defendant, there came a break in the proceedings. The child sought out Smith in the hallway of the courthouse and wanted to talk to her. Smith of course understood that it would be wrong to allow the child to think of her as a friend but could not help feeling a human connection with a vulnerable person who had been terribly wronged. She writes:

> I liked her, too, and would have been happy to talk about camp, softball, whatever she wanted to talk about. . . . I wanted to tell her I was sorry, so sorry – about what had happened to her, what my client had done, and what I was doing now. I wanted to tell her she was going to be okay, that she would get through this and have a good life, that she was strong and resilient. I would have done all this if only I was not the *lawyer on the other side*. . . . Defense lawyers do not get to apologize – no matter how much we may want to. To do so would be narcissistic and vain.[6]

This passage captures a central feature of working as a lawyer that receives surprisingly little notice or discussion. As a defense lawyer, Smith understood her job as providing skilled, effective defense to her client, which in this case required cross-examining the complaining witness to lay the foundation for a defense of mistaken identity. This is legally permissible for criminal defense lawyers, even where the client has admitted to his lawyer that he committed the crime.[7] Cross-examining the state's witness in a criminal prosecution, with the aim of making her recollection seem shaky and unreliable, is a permissible feature of loyal, "zealous" defense representation, intended to ensure that the government proves its case beyond a reasonable doubt. Not only is effective cross-examination required by legal duties to the client and under the Bill of Rights, but there are good moral reasons to support a criminal defense lawyering role that calls for such tactics and to *be* such a lawyer: the desire to sustain the rule of law and the civil rights of the accused; the importance of affirming human dignity; sympathy for poor or marginalized people; the importance of standing by someone in need, particularly one who is facing the awesome power of the state arrayed against him; a more general anti-authoritarian mindset and desire to resist the maldistribution of power and resources in society, including along racial lines; and the intrinsic satisfaction of doing extremely challenging work.[8]

But that is not the end of the analysis; there is the further question, from the first-person point of view, of how she should feel about what she did or evaluate it retrospectively. Too often the debate in professional ethics does not go beyond permissibility. As a result, it sometimes seems that permissibility is conclusive of other aspects of morality, such as whether it is appropriate to feel sentiments of regret or reluctance as a result of what one has done. Ask yourself this question: Do you think a lawyer who had a meeting in the hallway like Smith described would, or should, simply be able to go home and sleep well at night, secure in the knowledge that she did the right thing? Most of us, I think, would expect her to feel some disquiet or even guilt afterward. For her part, Smith writes that she remains haunted by the encounter: "I still think about that little girl. I wonder what became of her. I hope she got past what happened to her. I hope she has no memory of me."[9] That response strikes me as empathetic, humane, and decent, even in the context of a system that Smith herself concedes can be profoundly dehumanizing.[10] It is extremely important, however, to hold on to a paradoxical idea while thinking about this case: Smith is not agreeing with critics of criminal defense tactics that she violated any legal or moral standards by conducting the cross-examination. She is saying instead that she did the right thing, both as a lawyer and as a human being occupying a professional role, but yet it is appropriate that she experience, and possibly expressly publicly somehow, a sense of guilt, sorrow, or regret.

Another example comes from a famous episode from the history of American legal ethics, known as the Lake Pleasant bodies case.[11] That case illustrates how the distinction between permissibility and meaning can explain a lingering sense of regret or reluctance. Two criminal defense lawyers were retained to represent a client accused of murdering a hiker at a campground in Upstate New York. Following a map drawn by the client, the lawyers went out into the woods and viewed the bodies of two other hikers who had been missing. Their disappearance had not been connected with the first hiker's murder and the defendant was not yet a suspect in their killing. Upon learning that the lawyers were representing the defendant in connection with the first hiker's murder, the anguished father of one of the missing hikers asked one of the defense lawyers if he had any information about his daughter. In compliance with the rule of professional conduct regarding confidentiality, the lawyer said nothing about having seen the body of the missing woman. The police did not discover the other two bodies until several months later.

An intense public controversy broke out after the client was ultimately convicted of the murder of the hikers and it was revealed that the lawyers had known the location of the bodies. Much of the scholarly discussion of the Lake Pleasant case is therefore about the permissibility of maintaining client confidences.[12] In retrospect, the case was a pivotal moment in the establishment of what is by now a professional consensus that lawyers are not just permitted but required to keep secrets in these circumstances.[13] The reason is that a lawyer need to be able to reassure a client that any information revealed to the lawyer will not come back to haunt the client. As the U.S. Supreme Court has said, in connection with the attorney-client privilege, the relationship of trust and confidence between lawyers and clients is necessary so that clients can make "full and frank" disclosures to their lawyers.[14] In turn, lawyers can learn what they need to know in order to represent their clients effectively. In the Lake Pleasant case, the lawyers were developing a defense of insanity for their client and needed to know the circumstances of all of the crimes he had committed. They needed to learn as much as possible from their client, who of course would clam up if he believed his lawyers would ever disclose information revealed to them in confidence. As one of the defense lawyers later stated in a television interview, the constitution provides "even a bastard like" the defendant with the right to "a proper defense, having adequate representation, [and] being able to trust his lawyer as to what he says."[15]

As I see it, the most important aspect of the Lake Pleasant case is not the constitutional right to counsel and the importance of protecting client confidences. Rather, it is the inevitable tension between those professional obligations and the regret or reluctance that accompanies them, which is rooted in the basic humanity of the people who occupy professional roles. The defense lawyers knew they were causing pain to the families of the missing hikers by refusing to disclose what they knew. As one of the lawyers vividly observed, "Your mind [is] screaming one way 'Relieve these parents!' ... Shouldn't you report it? One sense of morality wants you to relieve the grief." The lawyer saw the conflict between the duties of a lawyer and the fact that "I have a dead girl, the fact that her body's there" and his knowledge of "the breaking hearts of her parents." (The daughter of one of the lawyers was in the same high school class as the sister of one of the missing hikers, so the lawyer had a particularly personal connection with the case.[16]) Later in the interview the lawyer admitted, "I caused [the parents] pain ... What do you say? Nothing I could say would justify it in their minds. You couldn't justify it to me."[17] The words chosen by the lawyer are revealing. He does not doubt that his action in defense of the client were justified, only that nothing he could say would justify it to the grieving parents. The public criticism directed at the defense lawyers, which forced them to leave town for a time to protect their safety,[18] confirms that the defendant's constitutional rights and the duty of confidentiality owed to the client are not the only considerations that factor into the assessment of the significance of the lawyers' representation.

How moral remainders arise (and what to do with them)

Much of the public debate over criticism of lawyers for the clients they represent takes the form of a stark, bipolar choice between only two alternatives: Either it is permissible or not to represent a particular client and to take certain actions in the course of representing that client. Lawyers tend to cite well-worn principles—almost clichés—such as "everyone deserves counsel," the importance of competent counsel to the functioning of the adversarial system of justice, the long professional tradition of representing vilified clients, and the mistake of identifying lawyers with their clients.[19] The Principle of Nonaccountability is supposed to follow from this type of justification. Not only that, but a further aspect of nonaccountability is that a lawyer should be able, literally and metaphorically, to sleep well and night and not be troubled by any qualms related to the identity of the client or the justice of the client's objectives. If the representation or something done in furtherance of the client's objectives is impermissible, that's one thing,[20] but it cannot be the case *both* that the lawyer's actions are permissible and that the lawyer should feel any sense of reluctance or regret about having done something permissible. In either case, however, the conclusion of a moral argument is that the lawyer's actions are permissible or impermissible, full stop, and there is nothing more to be said about any feeling of reluctance or guilt that is appropriate in the circumstances. Moral obligations are believed to override any other reasons a lawyer may have, such as concern for the experience of the complaining witness or the grieving parents.[21] These other reasons are superseded or "canceled" (not in the sense of cancel culture) by the moral requirements of the lawyer's role.

I want to introduce a possibility that has received less attention from lawyers, legal scholars, and moral philosophers, but which helps explain why so many of the cases we have considered in this book are hard. This alternative maintains that there are good reasons to support the professional role of advocate or advisor to clients, even those clients who are unpopular, and even if they are deservedly unpopular because they have antisocial objectives. There are also good reasons to resist disappearing into a professional role, either the discredited defense of "just following orders" or "Montaigne's solution" of displacing all accountability onto the role itself and assuming none of it personally (Chapter 6). Maintaining professional roles while avoiding the erosion of moral agency threatened by roles requires a sensitivity to the moral costs of actions within roles and appropriate responses to the recognition of these costs.

The British philosopher Bernard Williams referred to the lingering moral costs that arise from the concerns, interests, and needs of others that would otherwise count as a reason not to do something as "moral remainders."[22] One of Williams's many insights about ethical dilemmas is that one of the available options may have "deliberative priority,"[23] meaning it is the thing that, upon careful reflection, has the best support from all the considerations that bear on what one should do. Even if one option has deliberative priority, however, the interests or concerns of others that lost out, so to speak, in the deliberation may still be experienced by the actor as reasons to feel regret or reluctance. In the Lake Pleasant bodies case, for example, almost all lawyers would agree that keeping the client's confidences and not revealing the location of the bodies is the option to be done; it has deliberative priority. But a decent human perspective on representing the client is more than a matter of "getting the moral math right."[24] It is also a matter of responding in the right way to the anguish of the parents and the terror in the community. The qualms or reluctance experienced by a lawyer in a case like that one does not mean it is impermissible to represent that client and keep the location of the hidden bodies secret. I believe it would also be inappropriate, however, to find that representation easy, straightforward, and uncomplicated. A morally sensitive person in the role of lawyer in that case should feel troubled and uneasy.

I have always understood the role of lawyers and the legal profession, and therefore its characteristic ethical stance, as having much to do with human imperfection and social conflict. The implication for lawyers is that there will be gaps between what they would like the world to look like—perhaps for very good reasons—and those things that are a necessary feature of an occupation that has as its subject tempering or channeling the human tendencies to behave self-interestedly, harm or exploit others, or at least not pay sufficient attention to what we owe to each other. Williams's response is that professional training and socialization—to which I would add thinking ethically in connection with acting as a professional—should adopt "a general structure or tone that makes it clear that the imperfections of the world in which the professionals operate include the fact that they cannot entirely reconcile what they need to do with what they would like only to have to do."[25]

This may mean, however, accepting a certain amount of public criticism. It may seem unfair to lawyers, who are steeped in a professional morality that accepts conflict and imperfection as foundational. Ordinary folks are not as familiar with or comfortable in this world and may therefore regard lawyers as somewhat peculiar, even distasteful.[26] The answer is not to try to bring professional morality closer to the background morality of the wider community, because the community's moral concerns already include an appreciation for the value of toleration and the role that lawyers play in sustaining the rule of law as an alternative to the exercise of raw power and domination. To act as a lawyer means to do things that people who have not gone through the same professional training and socialization may have a hard time doing. Even lawyers have a hard time with some of these cases, as in the example from Abbe Smith that opened this chapter. The implication, however, is not that we should try to eliminate these moral remainders but to recognize and respond to them in an appropriate way.

The idea of moral remainders is related to a long tradition in political theory that distinguishes the virtues of rulers from those of ordinary people. Niccolò Machiavelli famously counseled Italian princes that they must "learn how not to be good,"[27] and the 19th-century German social theorist Max Weber instructed politicians that "in numerous instances the attainment of 'good' ends is bound to the fact that one must be willing to pay the price of using morally dubious means" and that "anyone who fails to see this is . . . a political infant."[28] Refusal to get one's hands dirty may mean being able to accomplish the ends of a political or institutional role.[29] The challenge for philosophers working in this hard-headed realist tradition is to acknowledge the separation between public and private morality while avoiding the tendency to collapse into cynicism or a nihilistic detachment from ordinary standards of right and wrong.[30]

What is frequently misunderstood is that Machiavelli, Weber, and their modern followers are not counseling politicians to embrace evil, but to understand the paradoxical ideal that doing good in a messy world full of conflicts and unscrupulous people sometimes requires the use of means that would otherwise be abhorrent to morally sensitive individuals.[31] One implication is that we want politicians and professionals to have qualms about the tragedy that is necessarily part of their public calling. Internalization of moral costs is important, because only an actor who is hesitant to incur the personal moral costs of engaging in wrongdoing to further the community's interests, when it is truly necessary to do so, will have any hope of avoiding wrongdoing when it is not necessary, or of not rationalizing self-interested conduct as the inevitable moral costs of exercising public power.[32] In one of his inimitable turns of phrase, Bernard Williams wrote that "a habit of reluctance is an essential obstacle against the happy acceptance of the intolerable."[33] Moral remainders may be a useful safeguard against self-deception.[34] And, to pick up on one of the central themes of this book, a sense of trepidation or reluctance may be imposed on the politician by public criticism. Public criticism enforces accountability, in part through the mechanism of regret or reluctance.

As an example of the role played by a "habit of reluctance" in life-and-death political decision-making, consider an interview with President Barack Obama, near the end of his second term. Asked about criticism from the left about his administration's use of drone strikes in Pakistan and other countries, President Obama said he actually welcomed it. Taking this moral criticism seriously ensured that the decision to launch a lethal strike would not be made too readily:

> I'm glad the left pushes me on this. I've said to my staff and I've said to my joint chiefs, I've said in the Situation Room: I don't ever want to get to the point where we're that comfortable with killing.... [T]he critique of drones has been important, because it has ensured that you don't have this institutional comfort and inertia with what looks like a pretty antiseptic way of disposing of enemies.... I think America will continue to have work to

do in finding this balance between not elevating every terrorist attack into a full-blown war but not either leaving ourselves exposed to attacks or, alternatively, pretending as if we can just take shots wherever we want, whenever we want, and not be answerable to anybody.[35]

Importantly, Obama's argument is not that critics are wrong, and that drone strikes should continue, but that the critics are *right*, and strikes should continue. Simultaneously maintaining these seemingly inconsistent beliefs provides a check against complacency and comfort with "antiseptic" killing, while also recognizing that drone strikes may be the best means to accomplish the nation's national-security objectives.

The view being defended here (which you might disagree with) is, we don't want a president whose moral stance would not permit him to authorize targeted assassinations of terrorist leaders where necessary to protect American lives. But we also don't want a president who would do so without reluctance or scruples. We don't want just anyone to order these strikes; we want this person to do it, precisely because he approaches the task with a morally motivated sense of reluctance.[36] Importantly, this position is not "Montaigne's solution" of sloughing off moral responsibility for wrongdoing onto an institution. Acceptance of some moral guilt for the wrongdoing involved in a public role is necessary to ensure the right kind of connection between the duties of the role and ensuring that one remains a decent person even when acting within the role. The person who can do the right thing, even when it is hard to do so, is someone we should honor. However, we cannot recognize this possibility if doing the right thing is always a matter of simply reasoning in the right way. In other words, it should be possible to recognize the lawyers in the stories that opened this chapter as honorable people, but not those for whom doing the right thing was straightforward or easy.[37]

This deeply paradoxical position should not be understood as a claim that *anything* is permissible as long as it is accompanied by a sense of reluctance or regret.[38] For example, one of the legal advisors in the Justice Department during the Bush administration, who advised the government on the permissibility of using "enhanced interrogation techniques" to learn information that could be used to thwart terrorist plots, once stated that the President has the authority to order an interrogator to crush the testicles of the child of a suspected terrorist.[39] In the face of a threat to national security, it is conceivable that a civilian law enforcement officer or a military or CIA interrogator may have to do things that ordinary people would find horrifying. The interrogator may feel tremendous regret, shame, or guilt for having done those things. Nevertheless, there must be some line beyond which even someone in an institutional role requiring some measure of ruthlessness must be prepared to say, "No way—I'm not doing *that*." The location of that line will vary by circumstances, including the objectives of the role and the importance of the values it implicates. But it is an important feature of the Machiavelli/Weber "dirty hands" tradition that it does not permit everything so long as it is done with a sense of reluctance or regret. Rod Rosenstein's expression of regret for his role in the Trump administration's family-separation policy, referred to in the last chapter,[40] does not retrospectively excuse his actions, if in fact they were wrongful. It might, however, serve as a warning for future high-level government lawyers not to become involved in similar projects or to act more energetically to limit their harmful effects.

That being said, much is permitted by the distinctive morality of the legal profession that ought to be the occasion for moral remainders. This is because the legal system is imperfect and permits injustice, but to pursue justice directly and disregard the obligations of one's professional role would be contrary to the value of the rule of law. I do not mean that every act of conscientious objection or civil disobedience will destabilize political institutions. The point instead is that to the extent there is value in maintaining institutions and professions dedicated to the resolution of social conflict, there is *disvalue* in acting on one's own views—however well grounded—about justice. Recall that in Chapter 6 there was a discussion about law professor Robert Cover's study of cases in which judges, despite their own ethical commitments to anti-slavery principles, rendered decisions under the Fugitive Slave Laws that had the effect of returning enslaved persons to their bondage.[41] Cover saw this as a question of "whether the moral values served by antislavery outweighed interests and values served by fidelity to the formal system when such values seemed to block direct application of the moral or natural law proposition."[42]

Importantly, Cover does not see judges who upheld the application of the Fugitive Slave Laws as "just following orders," the defense notoriously asserted by Nazi functionary Adolf Eichmann. Instead, these judges believed there was good reason to respect the legitimacy and authority of formal law, even though they experienced cognitive dissonance as a result of the clash of the requirements of law with the demands of morality.[43] Cover suggests that a judge would have, and *should have*, experienced regret and reluctance either way, based on either a decision upholding the Fugitive Slave Laws or an act of civil disobedience that went against the application of the law. Cover does not contend that either the obligations of role—which, let's assume, require entering a judgment returning an enslaved person to his owner—or the obligations of conscience must stand in an exclusionary relationship. One set of obligations may have deliberative priority, and Cover appears to concede that it is the professional role that determines what an anti-slavery judge ought to do when deciding a case under the Fugitive Slave Law. Nevertheless, the deliberative priority given to the obligations of the judicial role do not fully settle all of the normative questions one may ask. Again, it is not a stark, binary choice between (1) following the obligations of the judicial role and then going home and sleeping easy, or (2) following the obligations of conscience and entering an order that runs contrary to law and then going home and sleeping easy. A decent public morality may counsel judges that, in either case, they should act only with qualms, hesitation, reluctance, or regret.

Why not seek to bring morality closer to the ideal, rather than live with qualms and regret? The answer is related to Cover's deeper point, which I referred to as quasi-theological: the kind of perfection to which we aspire, and which serves as an ideal toward which the law reaches, is impossible to obtain in a non-transformed world.[44] A secular version of Cover's insight would deny that there is a rational solution available to the problems arising out of the conflicts of goods and ideals in human societies. As the political philosopher Isaiah Berlin has argued, it involves giving up this vision of harmony within reason:

> All true solutions to all genuine problems must be compatible: more than this, they must fit into a single whole: for this is what is meant by calling them all rational and the universe harmonious . . . If the universe is governed by reason, then there will be no need for coercion; a correctly planned life for all will coincide with full freedom – the freedom of rational self-direction – for all.[45]

Moral costs arise from letting go of the aspiration to bring an unruly community within the governance of reason. That does not mean surrendering to brute passions and power, however, but seeking order and stability while attempting to remain respectful of the views of those with whom we disagree. We can think about how things could be better while recognizing that, at least as far as we are currently capable, there is no way to get there without infringing on others' reasonable conceptions of the good life. Mediating between the ideal and the actual is a pretty good description of what lawyers do, and it is therefore not surprising that the role is accompanied by inevitable moral costs.

This leads to the remaining question: What is to be done with, or about, the recognition of imperfection and loss? The example of President Obama and drone strikes suggests that awareness of moral costs helps insulate against the tendency to ignore or undervalue the interests of those other than a client or another object of a professional's loyalty and dedication. Lawyers love to quote a speech by an English barrister defending his aggressive advocacy on behalf of the estranged wife of King George IV, in defense of what was in effect a charge of adultery. The barrister, Lord Henry Brougham, claimed that in the course of carrying out the duty of zealous representation, an advocate "must not regard the alarm, the torments, the destruction which he may bring others."[46] An attitude of indifference to the suffering of others, however, may in the long run desensitize lawyers to subtle signals that something has crossed the line from a regrettable necessity—like a cross-examination designed to make a witness appear uncertain or unreliable—to an instance of prohibited conduct.[47] Many disciplinary actions and judicial sanctions orders against lawyers appear to have begun with aggressive conduct that is close to the line between permissible and unlawful. Training oneself to ignore "the alarm, the torments, the destruction" brought to others may facilitate a gradual slide into illegality.[48]

Slowing down a rush to wrongdoing is not the only role played by the recognition of moral costs, however. It may also motivate something in the way of apology or atonement. Williams notes that in these cases of inevitable moral wrongdoing, "the moral disagreeableness of these acts is not merely canceled, and this comes out above all in the consideration that the victims can justly complain that they have been wronged."[49] The idea that those who experience moral costs can "justly complain that they have been wronged" is connected with the scope of accountability for lawyers and the possibility that they may be subject to reasonably grounded criticism even in cases in which their actions are legally and morally permissible. The problem of moral costs cannot be solved exclusively by calling upon lawyers to suffer inwardly for having made difficult and painful choices among professional and ordinary moral alternatives. There also must be some acknowledgment—some social expression—of regret or reluctance.[50] The political tradition of civil disobedience, as found for example in Martin Luther King, Jr.'s *Letter from Birmingham Jail*,[51] emphasizes that in violating unjust laws one must also accept punishment, which acknowledges the legitimacy of the laws and legal order maintained by one's fellow citizens.[52] King's approach to resistance to legal injustice, inspired by his study of Mahatma Gandhi's resistance to British rule in India, highlights his fundamental belief that both the oppressor and the oppressed are members of the same political community in which justice must be fully realized.[53] As such, civil disobedience cannot appeal only to individual conscience but to the community's shared conception of justice, as embodied in its laws. Its open nature and the willingness of those who engage in civil disobedience to accept punishment manifest respect for other members of the community.

At the risk of descending from the sublime (great political thinkers like Machiavelli and King) to the ridiculous (mean tweets), I will suggest that taking public criticism seriously is a way of acknowledging the moral costs of representing antisocial clients and thereby accepting accountability to the political community for the practice of a professional role. The lawyers in the Lake Pleasant bodies case not only anticipated serious, morally motivated criticism for keeping the location of the bodies secret, but they accepted its legitimacy. One of the lawyers, Frank Armani, said if he had been in the position of the grieving parents, nothing would have justified to him the refusal to alleviate the parents' suffering. He followed the obligations of the professional role, including preserving his client's confidences, but never sought to deflect or undermine the criticism directed at him by the parents and other members of the public. Abbe Smith, the lawyer whose account of representing defendants in rape cases opened the chapter, contends *both* that what she does as a defense lawyer is justified and that criticism for doing so is justified. She says, with remarkable honesty, "Victims of serious crime get to hate us. It is the least we can do for them."[54] Members of the community may also be entitled to hate lawyers, and one of the things lawyers can do in recognition of the moral costs of representing unpopular clients is to accept the legitimacy of much of the criticism directed our way.

It may sound silly to emphasize public criticism of lawyers, particularly since much of it can be vitriolic or not particularly well thought out. But I really do see a vigorous debate about the morality of representing antisocial clients as an important part of the connective tissue that links professions and the broader community they serve. Bernard Williams, who wrote with acute sensitivity about the moral psychology of professionals, saw it as vitally important that respect for the professions "take[] the form of appropriate sentiments . . . expressed in certain practices." The alternative, Williams believed, was to "fall back on mystification."55 The theme of accountability as sustained through reactive attitudes and the characteristic practices in which they are manifested has been central to the analysis of public criticism of lawyers. This chapter has attempted to show that some criticism is inescapable, largely because in an imperfect world, populated by disputatious people, there will always be a gap between the ideal and the actual, between the world as we would like it to be and those things that are necessary to get by in the world as it is. Lawyers are the professionals who help their clients navigate this world, and in some cases that will require doing things, having intentions and attitudes, or being a type of person that "in virtue of some more general ethical dispositions we regard poorly."56

One of the important questions left unanswered by this way of looking at the ethics of lawyers is what types of people will be attracted to a profession that requires them to endure public criticism—some of it not particularly intelligent—and accept that there are occasions on which living with regret, discomfort, qualms, and reluctance comes with the territory. There is some risk that the people who remain in the legal profession will be those who are insensitive or easily inured to moral costs.57 Are only serious jerks going to want to become lawyers? That concern may be overblown, however, given that most lawyers, most of the time, do not face anything like the wrenching dilemma of the lawyers in the Lake Pleasant bodies case. Even criminal defense lawyers do not encounter the truly agonizing cases all that frequently. Smith contrasts the difficult cross-examinations of rape victims to cases in which her role requires her to "cross a police officer, jailhouse snitch, rival gang member, phony expert, or officious neighbor with a penchant for exaggeration,"58 implying that cases in the latter category do not unsettle her much. In any case, the answer to the problem of attracting jerks to the practice of law should not be to wish away moral costs or adamantly refuse to acknowledge them, through the invocation of the Principle of Nonaccountability. On the contrary, accepting accountability may create room for morally sensitive people to practice as lawyers and mitigate some of the moral costs of representation.

Consider again the case of Rod Rosenstein. He stated in an interview with NBC news that he feels regret over the "zero tolerance" policy advocated by Attorney General Jeff Sessions and political advisor Stephen Miller. Rosenstein said:

> Since leaving the department, I have often asked myself what we should have done differently, and no issue has dominated my thinking more than the zero tolerance immigration policy. It was a failed policy that never should have been proposed or implemented. I wish we all had done better.[59]

Critics say the apology is woefully inadequate in light of the deliberate cruelty that was always part of the family-separation policy, and that it was at best naïve for Rosenstein to simply trust that the Department of Homeland Security was diligently attempting to comply with its legal obligations and that the Department of Health and Human Services would be able to keep track of the children entrusted to its care and ensure their prompt reunification with their families, particularly given the generalized dysfunction within the administration.[60] One reading of Rosenstein's apology in light of detailed reporting by journalists and the Department of Justice Inspector General is that his contrition resulted from finally being confronted with the actual facts of the program as it was being implemented, including children being taken away on the pretext of being given a bath and then not returned to their parents, parents being told their children would be put up for adoption and they would never see them again, Border Patrol agents taunting parents by shouting "Happy Mother's Day" as their children were taken away, or a father who hanged himself after his three-year-old son was forcibly pulled from his arms.[61]

The best case for Rosenstein is that he didn't know *that* was going on. He was the Deputy Attorney General, tasked with managing the Justice Department's implementation of the policy at a central level, in conjunction with other federal agencies and their own senior officials, such as Department of Homeland Security Secretary Kirstjen Nielsen and Health and Human Services Secretary Alex Azar. From his position in Washington it had appeared that "logistical problems" were the root cause of the crisis,[62] and that separation of children was caused by interagency coordination problems rather than being the explicit objective of the policy.[63] There are psychological and institutional reasons that high-level officials sometimes have blind spots when it comes to ethical decision-making.[64] Unlike many low-level staffers, Rosenstein had never seen the pictures of the faces of separated children, bearing looks of fear or devastation. (This does not *excuse* the wrongdoing but explains it in a way that is consistent with a conclusion that Rosenstein is not a monster.) Other officials similarly blamed logistics or "messaging." The reporting, intense public scrutiny, and eventual abandonment of the policy forced high-level officials, including lawyers like Rosenstein, to understand the family-separation policy specifically as a *moral* disaster. The most important reason to recognize regret, reluctance, and uneasiness as important aspects of professional ethics may be to keep the minds of lawyers open to the possibility that a seemingly routine action may actually be leading to a moral disaster.

Writing about Max Weber's defense of politics as a vocation, the American political philosopher Michael Walzer confesses that he has a certain amount of admiration for Weber's description of the "mature, superbly trained, relentless, objective, responsible, and disciplined political leader"[65] who also is conscious of the moral costs that may be incurred as part of carrying out a public role. He is skeptical, however, of Weber's "suffering servant" stance adopted by Rosenstein:

> Here is a man who lies, intrigues, sends other men to their death – and suffers. He does what he must do with a heavy heart. None of us can know, he tells us, how much it costs him to do his duty. Indeed, we cannot, for he himself fixes the price he pays. And that is the trouble with this view of political crime. We suspect the suffering servant of either masochism or hypocrisy or both, and while we are often wrong, we are not always wrong.[66]

Notice that I did not refer to Rosenstein's stance as a pose or a pretense. He may be entirely sincere in his regret and acceptance of blame for his role in the family-separation disaster. We want people who occupy important public roles to have an inner life that includes sentiments of guilt and regret. But two conditions must be satisfied for these sentiments to be admitted as a satisfactory element of professional ethics.

First, there must be some appropriate response beyond the private, subjective feelings of remorse or shame: "The self-awareness of the tragic hero is obviously of great value. . . . But sometimes the hero's suffering needs to be socially expressed (for like punishment, it confirms and reinforces our sense that certain acts are wrong)."[67] The social expression of regret can help safeguard against the psychological tendency to engage in antisocial behavior in private as long as it is accompanied with public displays of prosocial attitudes.[68] There is a risk that some of these social practices may serve as "whitewashing" or a cheap price to buy forgiveness for one's transgressions.[69] It is difficult to say anything in general about what qualifies as a serious acceptance of a moral remainder and not a performative practice unaccompanied by any real sense of regret (because by definition the social practice is visible while the sentiments are internal), but the idea of insincere apologies is familiar enough to provide some normative guidance. The publicity of serious expressions of acceptance of residual guilt also reinforces the relationship of accountability between professionals and others in the political community, which has been a major theme of this book. Second, there must be some line between acts that may be committed with a sense of reluctance and those that any decent person, including one occupying a public role, would simply refuse to perform.[70] The dirty hands tradition recognizes that some acts are absolutely off limits for a public official, even while others may be performed only with considerable reluctance and accompanied by practices that manifest a fitting sense of regret or remorse.

Like so many issues in ethics, these are matters on which reasonable people may disagree. Many readers will believe that, on the dimension of permissibility, Rosenstein could—and should—have done more to put a stop to the family-separation policy and, failing that, should have resigned rather than carried out the instructions of Attorney General Sessions. I see this as a case in which resignation was an option, as it almost always is, but where Rosenstein also could have chosen to remain in the position while doing as much as his position and influence would allow to mitigate the most severe impacts of the policy. Legal ethics scholars tend to appreciate the nobility of criminal defense representation, and therefore are willing to grant the permissibility of the cross-examination described by Abbe Smith or the lawyers' decision to keep the client's confidences in the Lake Pleasant bodies case. Serving in an advisory capacity within a government agency is an important role as well, however, and may justify a lawyer in conduct that imposes moral costs even while being justified. If that is right, then this chapter has suggested a way to think about public criticism of Rosenstein and his publicly expressed contrition as an appropriate response to the moral remainders that arise in the gap between the world as it is and the world as we wish it were.

By way of closing, I should say that it is important not to exaggerate the pervasiveness of moral remainders in the practice of law. There are some categories of legal practice in which sentiments of regret or reluctance are highly unlikely to be part of the normative landscape. My wife once met a lawyer whose job was negotiating contracts for the purchase of trucks by the U.S. Postal Service. That lawyer probably never had any trouble sleeping at night. Even criminal defense lawyers mostly handle fairly routine cases in which nothing as dramatic as cross-examining a truthful complaining witness in a rape case or refusing to tell grieving parents the location of their child's body occurs.⁷¹ Much of what lawyers do is uncomplicatedly permissible, in moral as well as legal terms. There are also instances in which conduct is clearly *impermissible*, such as the filing of bogus lawsuits challenging the results of the 2020 presidential election, discussed in Chapter 7. Moral remainders are uncommon, but that does not mean the phenomenon is unimportant. It tells us something important about the relationship between professional roles and the moral community in which professions are located. The rare, dramatic moments described in this chapter are an important subject for reflection even if most lawyers never have to encounter them.

Chapter summary

In some particularly difficult representations, lawyers may experience discomfort, qualms, or regret. I contend they *should* feel those things as an appropriate way of recognizing the moral costs of what is otherwise a justified representation. Abbe Smith's story and the Lake Pleasant bodies case are both instances in which decent, humane lawyers believed they did the right thing but nevertheless acknowledged the moral remainder. The difficult follow-on question is what effect moral remainders should have. Slowing down a rush to wrongdoing and potentially motivating some form of apology or reparation are possibilities, but in some cases lawyers may have no choice but to acknowledge where public criticism is coming from.

Notes

1. Abbe Smith, "Representing Rapists: The Cruelty of Cross Examination and Other Challenges for a Feminist Criminal Defense Lawyer," 53 *Am. Crim. L. Rev.* 255 (2016).
2. Abbe Smith, "Defending the Unpopular Down-Under," 30 *Melb. U. L. Rev.* 496 (2006); Abbe Smith, "Too Much Heart and Not Enough Heat: The Short Life and Fractured Ego of the Empathic, Heroic Public Defender," 37 *U.C. Davis L. Rev.* 1203 (2004); Abbe Smith, "Defending Defending: The Case for Unmitigated Zeal on Behalf of People Who Do Terrible Things," 28 *Hofstra L. Rev.* 925 (2000). Smith also takes the strong position that "[e]xploiting prejudice is part of advocacy." Smith, "Representing Rapists," p. 284; see also Smith, "Defending Defending," pp. 949–55 (discussing the appeal to homophobia by defense counsel for Justin Volpe, the New York City police officer accused of brutally raping Abner Louima); Abbe Smith, "Burdening the Least of

Us: 'Race-Conscious' Ethics in Criminal Defense," 77 *Tex. L. Rev.* 1585 (1999). In her article on representing rapists she admits that "[i]t goes without saying that sexism is inextricably connected to the defense of a charge of acquaintance/date rape" because the defense generally asserts that the sexual activity was consensual. Thus, it is entirely predictable and, in Smith's view, justifiable, that defense lawyers would appeal to "sexist canards" such as what the woman was wearing, whether the woman invited the man into her house, whether there had been previous flirting or consensual sexual activity, the use of alcohol or drugs, and so on. Smith, "Representing Rapists," p. 284. In this she is strongly opposed to progressive critics of criminal defense, particularly Anthony Alfieri. See, e.g., Anthony V. Alfieri, "Race Trials," 76 *Tex. L. Rev.* 1293 (1998); Anthony V. Alfieri, "Defending Racial Violence," 95 *Colum. L. Rev.* 1301 (1995).

3. Smith, "Representing Rapists," pp. 257–61 (noting sheer number of prisoners, the excessive length of sentences, and racial disparities among those behind bars, and "hysteria-driven, hyper-punitive response" to sex crimes), pp. 289–90 (imagining standard criminal-defense lawyer reasoning for zealous representation: "Okay, says the lawyer, my client may have committed the crime. But has the Government played fair? Have they exercised restraint in charging, been scrupulously truthful in their pleadings and representations to the court, and comported with their obligation to disclose favorable evidence? The Government's constitutional and ethical obligations are the same, whether or not my client is guilty. Have they met them?"); Smith, "Defending Defending," p. 952 ("[C]riminal punishment is regarded as the answer to almost all of our social problems. We cannot seem to build prisons fast enough, and we are on the road to the virtual banishment of young African American men from society."); Smith, "Heart and Heat," pp. 1209–10. See also David Luban, "Are Criminal Defenders Different?," 91 *Mich. L. Rev.* 1729 (1993); Stephen B. Bright, "Counsel for the Poor: The Death Sentence Not for the Worst Crime but for the Worst Lawyer," 103 *Yale L.J.* 1835 (1994). One of Smith's strongest objections to progressive critics of criminal defense is that, of all the people or institutions who can be blamed for systemic injustice, why blame the beleaguered, outgunned advocates who are actually doing something tangible to stick up for the interests of poor people? "Of all the political and institutional actors upon whom Alfieri might focus, why us? We did not create the laws calling for greater punishment for poor, black lawbreakers, which have led to the virtual banishment of young African-American men from society. We are not behind the record pace of incarceration, prison construction, or capital punishment, all of which have had a disproportionate impact on racial minorities and the poor. We do not have the power to decide whom to prosecute or what charge to bring, nor do we have the power to determine guilt or innocence, or to formulate a sentence, all of which contribute to the institutional and social status of racial minorities in this country." Smith, "Burdening the Least of Us," pp. 1587–89.
4. Smith, "Representing Rapists," pp. 276–77.
5. Smith, "Representing Rapists," pp. 279–80. Smith cites in several places journalist Janet Malcolm's excellent nonfiction exploration of the age-old question "what is truth?"—see Janet Malcolm, *The Crime of Sheila McGough* (New York: Knopf 1999).
6. Smith, "Representing Rapists," p. 277.

7. Lawyers representing clients in civil litigation are required by the rules of professional conduct and the rules of civil procedure to refrain from taking positions that the lawyer does not reasonably believe have an adequate grounding in both the law and the evidentiary record—that is, the facts that are known to the lawyer or might reasonably be learned through investigation and discovery. ABA Model Rules of Professional Conduct, Rule 3.1; Fed. R. Civ. P. 11. Some of the lawyers representing the Trump campaign after the 2020 presidential election have been sanctioned by courts for asserting claims that were not well-founded in this way. See, e.g., *King v. Whitmer*, 556 F. Supp. 3d 680 (E.D. Mich. 2021); *O'Rourke v. Dominion Voting Systems*, 552 F. Supp. 3d 1168 (D. Colo. 2021). The discussion in Chapter 7 of the bogus theory asserted by John Eastman that Vice President had the discretion to reject state electors is another example of the legal limitations on making frivolous arguments.

It can be quite surprising to learn that none of these rules apply to criminal defense representation. In a landmark case, *In re Winship*, 397 U.S. 358 (1970), the U.S. Supreme Court held that the Due Process Clauses of the Fifth and Fourteenth Amendments, applicable to the federal and state government respectively, prohibit conviction for a crime unless the prosecution proves each element of the offense beyond a reasonable doubt. The flip side of the prosecution's burden of proof is a legal presumption that the defendant is innocent until proven guilty. In practical terms this means the defendant and the defendant's lawyers do not need to introduce any evidence of innocence. It is enough to show that the prosecution's evidence fails to establish guilt beyond a reasonable doubt. ABA Model Rule 3.1, cited previously as standing for the prohibition on bringing claims or contentions without adequate legal and factual support, expressly excludes criminal defense representation: "A lawyer for a defendant in a criminal proceeding... may nevertheless defend the proceeding as to require that every element of the case be established" by the prosecution.

In theory, a criminal defense lawyer can "put the state to its proof" and simply argue to the jury that the prosecution has not sustained its burden of proving guilt beyond a reasonable doubt. Experienced criminal defense lawyers know, however, that jurors are persuaded by *stories*, not dry recitations of facts or deficiencies in the state's proof. In a well-known article, a criminal defense lawyer argued (persuasively, I believe) that giving effect to the presumption of innocence requires that criminal defense lawyers be permitted to put on an affirmative case that they know to be factually unsupported. John B. Mitchell, "Reasonable Doubts Are Where You Find Them: A Response to Professor Subin's Position on the Criminal Lawyer's 'Different Mission,'" 1 *Geo. J. Legal Ethics* 339 (1987). That is not the same thing as introducing evidence the lawyer knows to be false, which is prohibited by Rule 3.3(a) of the Model Rules. See also *Nix v. Whiteside*, 475 U.S. 157 (1986). But there is no prohibition on constructing a story based on bits of factual evidence that are true—such as the girl in Abbe Smith's story who remembered her mother's boyfriend getting into bed with her—and arguing that the evidentiary material developed by both sides, through direct and cross-examination of witnesses as well as documentary and physical evidence, supports a story that is inconsistent with the defendant's guilt. This position is recognized in Rule 3.1 of the Model Rules.

There is a well-known ethics opinion from the Michigan State Bar Association illustrating the permissibility of constructing a story inconsistent with the defendant's guilt out of true bits of evidence, even if the defense lawyer knows the implication of the narrative to be false. Michigan Ethics Op. CI–1164 (1987). I use an embellished version of the hypothetical when teaching this topic. In my version, a man is charged with assault, based on the victim's report that he was hit over the head with a blunt object and robbed at midnight near an automated teller machine. The accused retains an attorney and admits to the attorney that he committed the robbery and truthfully states that the crime occurred at 2:00 a.m. The victim apparently was mixed up about the time since, after all, the defendant hit him over the head and stole his watch. As luck would have it, the defendant was playing poker at midnight with a priest, a rabbi, and the mayor of the town, all of whom have a sterling reputation in the community for honesty and integrity. The attorney's investigator talked to all three poker buddies and they all remembered clearly that they were playing cards at midnight with the defendant. The attorney believes that if she introduces the testimony of the three friends, the jury will believe them and conclude that the prosecution has not proved its case beyond a reasonable doubt. There is no question that, as a matter of the law governing lawyers, the defense attorney is permitted to put the three friends on the stand, elicit the testimony that they were playing poker with the defendant and midnight, and then without explicitly stating the fact (which the attorney knows to be false) that the defendant did not commit the robbery, make a closing argument along these lines: "The victim testified that he remembers the robbery happening at midnight. You have heard the uncontradicted testimony of three pillars of the community—the priest, the rabbi, and the mayor—all of whom said they were playing poker with the defendant and midnight. So I ask you, ladies and gentlemen of the jury, has the prosecution proven its case beyond a reasonable doubt?" John Mitchell has a similar example, involving a shoplifting charge, in his "Reasonable Doubts" article, which is a must-read for anyone interested in the ethics of truth-telling in criminal defense practice.

8. See a number of published articles by Smith, as well as a couple of well-known papers by Barbara Babcock and Charles Ogletree: Abbe Smith, "Defending the Unpopular Down-Under," 30 *Melb. U. L. Rev.* 495 (2006); Abbe Smith, "Too Much Heart and Not Enough Heat: The Short Life and Fractured Ego of the Empathic, Heroic Public Defender," 37 *U.C. Davis L. Rev.* 1203 (2004); Abbe Smith, "Defending Defending: The Case for Unmitigated Zeal on Behalf of People Who Do Terrible Things," 28 *Hofstra L. Rev.* 925 (2000); Charles J. Ogletree, Jr., "Beyond Justifications: Seeking Motivations to Sustain Public Defenders," 106 *Harv. L. Rev.* 1239 (1993); Barbara Allen Babcock, "Defending the Guilty," 32 *Clev. St. L. Rev.* 175 (1983–84).
9. Smith, "Representing Rapists," p. 277.
10. Smith quotes extensively from several memoirs, including that of Alice Sebold, who experienced the trial of her rapist as undermining, making her appear inadequate, uncertain, foolish, and even "a bit insane," and conveying the overall message that the system approved of the crime. Smith, "Representing Rapists," pp. 287–88 (quoting Alice Sebold, *Lucky* (New York: Scribner 1999)).

11. Discussed in David Luban, *Lawyers and Justice* (Princeton: Princeton University Press 1988), pp. 53–55, 185–86; David Luban, "Freedom and Constraint in Legal Ethics: Some Mid-Course Corrections to *Lawyers and Justice*," 49 Md. L. Rev. 424 (1990), pp. 425–32; Alan Donagan, "Justifying Legal Practice in the Adversary System," in David Luban, ed., *The Good Lawyer* (Totowa, N.J.: Roman & Allanheld 1983), pp. 139–45; Monroe H. Freedman, *Lawyers' Ethics in an Adversary System* (Indianapolis: Bobbs-Merrill 1975), pp. 1–8; Leslie C. Griffin, "The Lawyer's Dirty Hands," 8 Geo. J. Legal Ethics 219, 222–25 (1995). One of the lawyers involved, Frank Armani, participated in a panel at the ABA's National Conference on Professional Responsibility, with law professors Lisa Lerman, Monroe Freedman, and Tom Morgan. Lisa G. Lerman et al., "The Buried Bodies Case: Alive and Well After Thirty Years," 2007 *Prof. Law.* 19 (2007). I was present at that session and remember Armani's demeanor as humble yet confident that he had done the right thing, and also that the assembled lawyers and law professors treated him as a genuine professional hero.

12. One of the principles that is now clearer than it was at the time is that a lawyer who knows of the location of physical evidence that could incriminate the lawyer's client if it is discovered by law enforcement (that includes the body of a murder victim) has no obligation to reveal the location of the evidence but may not move or conceal the item or do anything to alter its evidentiary significance. The attorney-client privilege protects the lawyer's knowledge of the location of the item if disclosing the location would be tantamount to revealing the content of a privileged communication (e.g., "the murder weapon is in the basement of my house under some cider blocks – go take a look"). If the lawyer takes possession of the item, however all bets are off—the lawyer is now potentially subject to criminal liability as an accessory after the fact to the crime. See *U.S. v. Russell*, 639 F. Supp. 2d 226 (D. Conn. 2007). Nor may the lawyer counsel the client to get rid of incriminating evidence. ABA Model Rules of Professional Conduct, Rule 1.2(d). This is an intricate and fascinating little sub-area of the law governing lawyers, best approached through a handful of leading cases and a couple of very good law review articles. See *Wemark v. State*, 602 N.W.2d 810 (Iowa 1999) (murder weapon); *Commonwealth v. Stenhach*, 514 A.2d 114 (Pa. Super. Ct. 1986) (murder weapon); *Hitch v. Pima County Superior Court*, 708 P.2d 72 (Ariz. 1985) (victim's watch); *People v. Meredith*, 29 Cal.3d 682, 175 Cal. Rptr. 612, 631 P.2d 46 (1981) (wallet belonging to the victim); *Morrell v. State*, 575 P.2d 1200 (Alaska 1978) (handwritten map and kidnapping plan); *In re Ryder*, 263 F. Supp. 360 (E.D. Va. 1967) (bag of money stolen in bank robbery); *State v. Olwell*, 64 Wash. 2d 828, 394 P.2d 681 (1964) (murder weapon); Gregory C. Sisk, "The Legal Ethics of Real Evidence: Of Child Porn on the Choirmaster's Computer and Bloody Knives Under the Stairs," 89 Wash. L. Rev. 819 (2014); Stephen Gillers, "Guns, Fruits, Drugs, and Documents: A Criminal Defense Lawyer's Responsibility for Real Evidence," 63 Stan. L. Rev. 813 (2011). In Canada the trial of Paul Bernardo and his ex-wife Karla Homolka for a series of horrific rapes and murders spun off a satellite proceeding against one of Bernardo's lawyers, Ken Murray, who had taken possession of videotapes of some of the crimes, which would have revealed that Homolka was a willing accomplice and not herself a victim of Bernardo. The lawyer was acquitted on the ground that the law

in Canada at the time was unclear as to whether the lawyer had a disclosure obligation or whether the tapes were protected by the attorney-client privilege. See, e.g., "Court Finds Bernardo Lawyer Not Guilty," CBC News (Jun. 14, 2000), available at https://www.cbc.ca/news/canada/court-finds-bernardo-lawyer-not-guilty-1.252668.

13. Lerman, pp. 20–22.
14. *Upjohn Co. v. United States*, 449 U.S. 383, 389 (1981).
15. Quoted in David Luban, "Freedom and Constraint in Legal Ethics: Some Mid-course Corrections to Lawyers and Justice," 49 *Md. L. Rev.* 424, 425 (1990).
16. Lerman, p. 27.
17. Heidi Li Feldman, "Codes and Virtues; Can Lawyers Be Good Deliberators?", 69 *S. Cal. L. Rev.* 885, 900 (1996). The lawyers who kept the secret of their client, Andrew Wilson, who had confessed to the murder of a McDonald's security guard for which an innocent person, Alton Logan, was incarcerated, similarly believed they did the right thing by not revealing their client's confidences, but also regretted very much the impact of that decision on Logan. In a series of interviews, Berl Falbaum, who co-authored a book with Logan about his experience, asked the lawyers questions about what we would refer to here as moral remainders: How did they live with the burden of knowing an innocent man was in prison? How did they raise families, take vacations, and engage in even the most mundane tasks when in possession of information that could free an innocent man from prison? One of the lawyers, Jamie Kunz, said he was "anguished" about the situation and found the decision "wrenching," but never doubted it was the right thing to do. Alton Logan with Berl Falbaum, *Justice Failed: How "Legal Ethics" Kept Me in Prison for 26 Years* (Berkeley, Cal.: Counterpoint Press 2018), pp. xiii–xiv.
18. Lerman, p. 31, including the memorable detail, related by Armani in his presentation to the ABA Professional Responsibility conference, that in addition to vandalism and obscene phone calls, Armani once found a dead fish wrapped in a newspaper on the front seat of his car. He explained: "For those of you out there that are Italian, you know that a fish wrapped in a newspaper is a sign of death, you know."
19. Classic examples of the genre include Paul Clement & Erin Murphy, "The Law Firm That Got Tired of Winning," *Wall St. J.* (June 23, 2022); Eric H. Holder, Jr., "'Lawyers Should Know Better': Criticizing Lawyers for Defending Unpopular Clients is Risky, 'Disturbing,'" *Nat'l L.J.* (Dec. 29, 2020); Michael Paradis & Wells Dixon, "In Defense of Unpopular Clients—and Liberty," *Wall St. J.* (Nov. 18, 2020); Randall Kennedy, "Harvard Betrays a Law Professor—and Itself," *N.Y. Times* (May 15, 2019); Charles Fried, "Mr. Stimson and the American Way," *Wall St. J.* (Jan. 16, 2007).
20. Notable examples on this side of the debate include Andrew C. McCarthy, "Not Everybody Is Entitled to a Lawyer," *National Review* (Mar. 22, 2022); Alex Pareen, "Neal Katyal and the Depravity of BigLaw," *New Republic* (Dec. 8, 2020); Dahlia Lithwick & Mark Joseph Stern, "Of Course We Should Scorn Trump's Sleazy Election Lawyers," *Slate* (Nov. 16, 2020); Deborah L. Rhode, "David Boies's Egregious Involvement with Harvey Weinstein," *N.Y. Times* (Nov. 9, 2017).
21. C.A.J. Coady, "Dirty Hands," *Stanford Encyclopedia of Philosophy* (2018).

22. Bernard Williams, "Ethical Consistency," in *Problems of the Self: Philosophical Papers 1956–1972* (Cambridge: Cambridge University Press 1973), pp. 166–86. The discussion in the text will also refer to two additional papers by Williams: "Politics and Moral Character," in *Moral Luck: Philosophical Papers 1973–1980* (Cambridge: Cambridge University Press 1981); and "Professional Morality and Its Dispositions," in *Making Sense of Humanity and Other Philosophical Papers 1982–1993* (Cambridge: Cambridge University Press 1995). For discussion in the context of theoretical legal ethics see Iris van Domselaar, "Law's Regret: On Moral Remainders, (In)commensurability and a Virtue-Ethical Approach to Legal Decision-Making," *Jurisprudence* (Jan. 18, 2022), open access availability at https://doi.org/10.1080/20403313.2021.2014709.
23. Williams, "Ethical Consistency," pp. 184–86. See also Williams, "Politics and Moral Character," p. 60: "It will often be true of these cases that so long as the agent takes seriously the moral frames of reference or reasons which support each of the courses of action, it will be clear what he should do."
24. Postema, p. 69.
25. Williams, "Professional Morality," p. 198.
26. Williams, "Professional Morality," p. 200 (observing that some of what seems like disapproval of lawyers "is the product of our needing things done that cannot be done, or cannot be well done in present circumstances, without the help of activities which in virtue of some more general ethical dispositions we regard poorly").
27. Niccolò Machiavelli, *The Prince* (Luigi Ricci, trans., E.R.P. Vincent ed., Oxford: Oxford University Press 1935), p. 84.
28. Max Weber, "Politics as a Vocation," in Hans H. Gerth & C. Wright Mills, eds., *From Max Weber: Essays in Sociology* (New York: Oxford University Press 1946), pp. 77–128, at 121, 123.
29. "To refuse on moral grounds ever to do anything [morally disagreeable] is more than likely to mean that one cannot seriously pursue even the moral ends of politics." Williams, "Politics and Moral Character," p. 60.
30. Thomas Nagel, "Ruthlessness in Public Life," in Stuart Hampshire, ed., *Public and Private Morality* (Cambridge: Cambridge University Press 1978); Michael Walzer, "Political Action: The Problem of Dirty Hands," *Phil. & Pub. Aff.* 2: 160–80 (1973); Williams, "Professional Morality and Its Dispositions," above; Williams, "Politics and Moral Character," above.
31. Giovanni Giorgini, "The Drama of Politics and Its Inherent Evil," in Thomas Nys & Stephen De Wijze, eds., *The Routledge Handbook of the Philosophy of Evil* (London: Routledge 2019), pp. 55–69. David Luban writes, referring to two lawyers who served in the German government during the Third Reich: "[T]here is something unsatisfying, dissonant, about judging these biographies solely in consequentialist terms of how many expected lives they saved. Intuitively: character matters, motives matter, moral vision matters, self-honesty and self-deception matter, the day to day texture of life matters, complicity matters." David Luban, "Complicity and Lesser Evils: A Tale of Two Lawyers," 34 *Geo. J. Legal Ethics* 613, 657 (2021). Phenomena like regret and remainders are an important part of a full moral analysis that must take into account these considerations of character, motive, moral vision, and so on.

32. Williams, "Politics and Moral Character," pp. 62–63.
33. Williams, "Politics and Moral Character," p. 63.
34. David Luban warns about the potential for self-deception that flows from a lawyer's belief that he must be hard-nosed and realistic to accomplish even a small amount of good among a bunch of hard-liners who are determined to push the boundaries of the law into immoral conduct. His example is Jack Goldsmith, who as head of the Office of Legal Counsel was widely credited with reining in the worst excesses of the interrogation policies established by political officials including Vice President Dick Cheney and his aide David Addington. David Luban, "The Torture Lawyers of Washington," in *Legal Ethics and Human Dignity* (Cambridge: Cambridge University Press 2007), p. 190. Luban does not make the argument that a sensitivity to moral remainders might have prevented reading Goldsmith from writing a memo that purported to authorize unlawful conduct, but it is a fair of his critique of Goldsmith's conduct.
35. Jonathan Chait, "Five Days That Shaped a Presidency," *New York Magazine* (Oct. 2, 2016).
36. A famous passage from Walzer's "Dirty Hands" article explains the connection between sentiments of regret or reluctance and the acceptability of wrongdoing from the standpoint of the community served by the politician:

> Because he has scruples of this sort, we know him to be a good man. But we view the campaign in a certain light, estimate its importance in a certain way, and hope that he will overcome his scruples and make the deal. It is important to stress that we don't want just anyone to make the deal; we want him to make it, precisely because he has scruples about it. We know he is doing right when he makes the deal because he knows he is doing wrong. I don't mean merely that he will feel badly or even very badly after he makes the deal. If he is the good man I am imagining him to be, he will feel guilty, that is, he will believe himself to be guilty. That is what it means to have dirty hands.

Walzer, p. 166.
37. Walzer, p. 168.
38. "The point of this is not at all that it is edifying to have politicians who, while as ruthless in action as others, are unhappy about it." Williams, "Politics and Moral Character," p. 62. In conversation David Luban has cautioned against an appeal to moral remainders that amounts to what he calls "Jewish grandmother guilt," that is, do wrong and feel bad about it. Compare Augustine's melancholy soldier, cited in Walzer, p. 167. One lawyer who had worked in the Trump administration wrote a column in the *New York Times* after leaving government service confessing that she was "haunted" by the realization that her service in the Office of Legal Counsel (an elite division within the Justice Department that advises the Executive Branch on the legality of proposed actions) had the effect of insulating harmful policies, such as Trump's Muslim ban, from effective court review. Erica Newland, "I'm Haunted by What I Did as a Lawyer in the Trump Justice Department," *N.Y. Times* (Dec. 20, 2020). This may be a case in which after-the-fact regret is a distant second-best to the realization at the time that the action was legally and morally impermissible. Admittedly, there is a follow-on question concerning the options a lawyer has in that situation,

including resignation, public disclosure ("whistleblowing") or various strategies of internal resistance, like bureaucratic foot-dragging. See, e.g., Adam Shinar, "Dissenting from Within: Why and How Public Officials Resist the Law," 40 *Fla. St. U. L. Rev.* 601 (2013). I am not contending that Newland was wrong to stay on the job, but I am also not contending that a retrospective *New York Times* editorial expressing contrition is necessarily a sufficient acknowledgement of her regret. In fairness, the lawyer's plan was probably not "do wrong and feel bad about it later." She probably felt isolated and unsupported in her job and unsure about how to proceed.

39. See, for example, Conor Friedersdorf, "The U.S. Constitution Is Worthless When John Yoo Interprets It," *The Atlantic* (Jan. 11, 2012); Sidney Blumenthal, "Meek, Mild and Menacing," *Salon* (Jan. 12, 2006). For a review of five books about the Bush administration's response to the 9/11 attacks and the ongoing threat of terrorism, including one by John Yoo, the lawyer quoted as saying the President has the power to order the crushing of children's testicles, and an overview of the moral issues for lawyers, see W. Bradley Wendel, "The Torture Memos and the Demands of Legality," 12 *Legal Ethics* 107 (2009).
40. Julia Ainsley & Jacob Soboroff, "Justice Officials Respond to Report on Family Separation by Blaming Trump, Expressing Regret, *NBC News* (Jan. 14, 2021).
41. Robert M. Cover, *Justice Accused: Antislavery and the Judicial Process* (New Haven: Yale University Press 1984).
42. Cover, p. 197. The value of formal law was related to its grounding in the presumptive consent of the political community to the Constitution (p. 151); because the Constitution embodied a compromise and because natural law did not speak with one voice (p. 152), it would be "tyranny" for a judge to breach the fiduciary duty to interpret the law impartially—a subversion of "the values that are supposedly served by participatory government" (p. 153). The important thing to see here is that the values of neutral, impartial adjudication and fidelity to law are not simply rote rule-following but respect for the responsibility of self-determining citizens of a political community. Cover argues (pp. 199–200) that these judges erred by over-valuing the formal stakes, retreating to mechanical formalism, or shifting responsibility to the institution ("Montaigne's solution," in Chapter 6). But he takes the problem of conflict between role obligation and the demands of conscience very seriously.
43. Cover, pp. 226–27.
44. Robert M. Cover, "The Supreme Court, 1982 Term—Foreword: Nomos and Narrative," 97 *Harv. L. Rev.* 4, 39 (1983). I call this a quasi-theological stance because it resonates with my own Lutheran perspective on the distinction between the kingdom of God and anything that humans can bring about by their own actions. See, e.g., Martin E. Marty, *Lutheran Questions, Lutheran Answers* (Minneapolis: Augsburg Books 2007). A secular version of this position, applied specifically to the public's irritability with lawyers, was beautifully articulated by Robert Post:

> Lawyers . . . bestride the following cultural contradiction: we both want and in some respects have a universal, common culture, and we simultaneously want that culture to be malleable and responsive to the particular and often incompatible interests of individual groups and citizens. We expect lawyers to fulfill

both desires, and so they are a constant irritating reminder that we are neither a peaceable kingdom of harmony and order, nor a land of undiluted individual autonomy, but somewhere disorientingly in between. Lawyers, in the very exercise of their profession, are the necessary bearers of that bleak winter's tale, and we hate them for it.

Robert C. Post, "On the Popular Image of the Lawyer: Reflections in a Dark Glass," 75 *Cal. L. Rev.* 379, 386 (1987). Compare Machiavelli's provocative claim that a public official cannot simultaneously satisfy the duty to rule responsibly and pursue his own personal salvation. Giorgini, p. 55. Recently Liz Anker has argued that critical theory has been preoccupied with the logic of paradox, finding it potentially redemptive as against the claims of authority asserted by legal systems. Elizabeth S. Anker, *On Paradox: The Claims of Theory* (Durham: Duke University Press 2022). Following Cover and Post, I do not see the tension between the ideal and the actual as potentially liberating for lawyers or the subjects of law, but instead as an occasion for regret and the recognition of inevitable loss.

45. Isaiah Berlin, "Two Concepts of Liberty," in *Four Essays on Liberty* (Oxford: Oxford University Press 1969). See also Thomas Nagel, "The Fragmentation of Value," in *Mortal Questions* (Cambridge: Cambridge University Press 1979). Closer to our topic of law and the legal profession, the great legal philosopher H.L.A. Hart argued for the conceptual separation of law and morality on many grounds, among them that to hold that "what is utterly immoral cannot be law or lawful ... will encourage the romantic optimism that all the values we cherish ultimately will fit into a single system, that no one of them has to be sacrificed or compromised to accommodate another." H.L.A. Hart, "Positivism and the Separation of Law and Morals," 71 *Harv. L. Rev.* 593, 620 (1958).

46. Quoted in Monroe H. Freedman, "Henry Lord Brougham, Written by Himself," 19 *Geo. J. Legal Ethics* 1213, 1215 (2006); Tim Dare, *The Counsel of Rogues? A Defence of the Standard Conception of the Lawyer's Role* (London: Ashgate 2009), p. 6.

47. Williams, "Professional Morality and Its Dispositions," p. 199.

48. One theme in recent work in moral psychology and the psychology of judgment and decision-making is the prevalence of unconscious effects that contribute in subtle ways to wrongdoing by people who would have described themselves as having a good moral character. See, e.g., Max H. Bazerman & Ann E. Tenbrunsel, *Blind Spots: Why We Fail to Do What's Right and What to Do About It* (Princeton: Princeton University Press 2011); Jonathan Haidt, *The Righteous Mind: Why Good People Are Divided by Politics and Religion* (New York: Vintage 2011); John M. Doris, *Lack of Character: Personality and Moral Behavior* (Cambridge: Cambridge University Press 2002); Jennifer K. Robbenolt & Jean R. Sternlight, "Behavioral Legal Ethics," 45 *Ariz. St. L.J.* 1107 (2013); John M. Darley, "The Cognitive and Social Psychology of Contagious Organizational Corruption," 70 *Brooklyn L. Rev.* 1177 (2005).

49. Williams, "Politics and Moral Character," p. 60.

50. Walzer, in criticizing Max Weber's view of the politician as a tragic hero, insists that the problem of dirty hands cannot be solved solely "within the confines of the individual conscience": "We want the politician to have an inner life at least something

like that which Weber describes. But sometimes the hero's suffering needs to be socially expressed (for like punishment, it confirms and reinforces our sense that certain acts are wrong)." Walzer, p. 177.
51. Martin Luther King, Jr., "Letter from Birmingham Jail" (Apr. 16, 1963), in Hugo Adam Bedau, ed., *Civil Disobedience in Focus* (London: Routledge 1991), pp. 68–84.
52. See Rawls's definition of civil disobedience as "a public, nonviolent, conscientious yet political act contrary to law usually done with the aim of bringing about a change in the law or policies of the government." John Rawls, *A Theory of Justice* (Cambridge, Mass.: Harvard University Press 1971), p. 363.
53. Robert K. Vischer, *Martin Luther King Jr. and the Morality of Legal Practice* (Cambridge: Cambridge University Press 2013), pp. 210–13.
54. Smith, p. 277.
55. Williams, "Professional Morality and Its Dispositions," p. 198.
56. Williams, "Professional Morality and Its Dispositions," p. 200.
57. "This leads to a third possibility, that we should have professionals who lack to some degree the general dispositions. This is unlikely to go to the length of the professionals' having a different morality . . . but they could be seen by some others as up to a point rather horrible people. They can be consistently seen like this even by people who also think that there is a good justification of their profession and that the justification does require some of them to be like that." Williams, "Professional Morality and Its Dispositions," p. 196.
58. Smith, "Representing Rapists," p. 256.
59. Quoted in Charles P. Pierce, "Rod Rosenstein Feels Very Bad about Family Separation Now So It's All Good," *Esquire* (Jan. 14, 2021).
60. Pierce, above; Liz Dye, "Rod Rosenstein Is Real Sorry about All Those Kids Separated from Their Parents. Oopsies!," *Above the Law* (Jan. 15, 2021). For more nuanced criticism based on careful, detailed reporting, see Caitlin Dickerson, "We Need to Take Away Children: The Secret History of the U.S. Government's Family-Separation Policy," *Atlantic* (Aug. 7, 2022).
61. All details documented in chapter 6 of Dickerson's article.
62. Dickerson, ch. 7.
63. Dickerson reports that officials at Immigration and Customs Enforcement were concerned that if the parents were prosecuted too quickly their children would still be waiting at Border Patrol Stations, not yet transferred to the custody of HHS. The head of enforcement and removal operations, Matt Albence, *saw this as a bad thing* and sought procedural changes that made it more likely that parents would be separate from their children for much longer.
64. Max H. Bazerman & Ann E. Tenbrunsel, *Blind Spots: Why We Fail to Do What's Right and What to Do About It* (Princeton: Princeton University Press 2011); Robert Jackall, *Moral Mazes: The World of Corporate Managers* (Oxford: Oxford University Press 1988); Irving Janis, *Groupthink* (Boston: Wadsworth, 2d ed. 1982); Linda K. Treviño et al., "Behavioral Ethics in Organizations: A Review," 32 *J. Mgmt.* 951 (2006); Ann E. Tenbrunsel & David M. Messick, "Ethical Fading: The Role of Self-Deception in Unethical Behavior," 17 *Soc. Just. Res.* 223 (2004).

65. Walzer, p. 177.
66. Walzer, p. 177.
67. Walzer, p. 178. Sydney Stanley, a student in my theoretical legal ethics class at UVA, pointed out a passage whose significance I had not previously appreciated: "[The politician] lies, manipulates, and kills, and we must make sure he pays the price. We won't be able to do that, however, without getting our own hands dirty, and then we must find some way of paying the price ourselves." Walzer, p. 180. Her point was that any sort of social practice of punishing lawyers or holding them to account to community norms, for actions that are permitted by the professional role, are themselves tainted by criticizing the occupant of a public role for doing things that the community expects to be done by occupants of the role. Thus, the public doesn't get to keep its hands clean when criticizing lawyers for dirty-handed actions.
68. Jennifer Jacquet, *Is Shame Necessary?* (New York: Pantheon Books 2015), pp. 51–53.
69. A student in my legal ethics seminar at Cornell said she always makes a donation to LGBTQ advocacy organizations after eating at Chick-fil-A. To her credit, she seemed very sheepish about this practice.
70. Walzer quotes with approval Weber's qualification that a political actor, "aware of a responsibility for the consequences of his conduct . . . reaches a point where he says: 'Here I stand; I can do no other'" (p. 177, n.21). He criticizes Weber for not doing more to articulate a line between dirty-handed but permissible actions and those that ought to prompt the Martin Luther-esque stance. I suspect that this fuzziness, which is not found only in Weber, is a significant factor in the doubts many philosophers have about the dirty-hands tradition.
71. I am grateful to John Doris for this point.

9
Some Concluding Thoughts

I used to teach a course in business ethics at the graduate school of management at my university. MBA students and business school faculty would sometimes ask if there was a "tool" my co-teacher and I could provide for ethical decision-making, meaning some stripped-down technique, system, or algorithm. While I appreciate the interest in rigor and attention to process, and I do think summary lists of ethical considerations can be useful in some cases, I would generally nod sadly and respond that there are no tools that can replace thoughtful engagement in ethics. At best a checklist or flowchart can identify people and their interests that may be affected by a proposed action, so that they are not overlooked in deliberation.[1] But there is no substitute for judgment, or "practical wisdom," to use the term popularized by Aristotle.[2] If you have made it this far, you probably have gathered that I believe interesting cases are almost always hard, which means that reasonable people can reach differing conclusions, based on a wide range of considerations that defy simplification or resolution into some unifying method or concept. That's fine, but it's not particularly helpful as a guide to thinking more carefully about the public criticism of lawyers. I would like to leave readers with *something*, even if not a "tool," which will be useful the next time a controversy is whipped up in response to the representation of an obnoxious client. Here is my list of things to keep in mind, which I hope the book has established:

1. *System-level justifications are not always decisive on their own.* I believe the professional role of lawyers is justified, in moral terms, by the story woven through the book about conflict and disagreement, the social settlement provided by the law, and the ideal of the rule of law understood as a way of manifesting respect when acting in ways that affect the interests of others. Lawyers believe the Principle of Nonaccountability follows from that, or some similar system-level justification. To put the idea differently, once a professional role is justified wholesale, so to speak, there can be no criticism at the retail level for actions taken by professionals within the role.[3] Nor can there be an inquiry into what intentions, attitudes, and motivating reasons

any particular professional has. The only question is whether the profession itself, and the duties specified by the professional role, can be given a justification in terms that others within the political community can accept.[4]

As human beings, however, we care about more than whether an action is justified. We also care about the intentions and attitudes of others and perhaps also their character.[5] Some profound, foundational scholarship in moral philosophy considers the importance of intention to evaluating actions.[6] Much of the frustration experienced by lawyers in the seemingly never-ending debate over representing unpopular clients seems to stem from critics not accepting defenses based on the rule of law and the social function of the legal system in resolving conflicts over rights and justice. Lawyers have a right, even a duty, to represent unpopular clients for those reasons—don't you see? I think people do see that, but they want to know more about the motivating reasons and attitudes of the lawyers themselves. In some cases, critics make unfair assumptions about these intentions, and the unfairness can appear to be compounded by duties of confidentiality and loyalty that prohibit lawyers from talking about their representations in ways that might compromise their clients' interests. No one ever said being a lawyer was an easy job. But the irritation felt by lawyers in having to deal with what sometimes seems like criticism offered in ignorance in even bad faith should not obscure the genuine importance of the motivating reasons and attitudes of the individual human beings who occupy institutional roles. Reactive attitudes are fundamental to morality, and the angry blame that is sometimes directed at lawyers is a reminder that the legal profession does not exist above or apart from the rest of society.

2. *The rule of law is a valuable ideal, but it isn't the whole story.* The systemic or institutional justification that lawyers give for representing obnoxious clients is a powerful one. The recognition of social conflict and polarization motivates a resort of formal processes of legislation, rulemaking, and adjudication to settle what would otherwise be intractable disagreements. Properly structured and administered, formal processes of making and applying laws also manifest respect for the dignity and agency of those whose interests are affected by the actions of others.[7] Something along these lines strikes me as the strongest justification for representing unpopular clients. But this justification necessarily rests quite a bit of weight on the fairness and inclusiveness of the official public processes used to establish the legal rights and duties of citizens. Many of the lawyer shaming or "canceling" episodes discussed in

this book arise out of the representation of clients in matters involving issues where it appears that the official process of establishing and interpreting formal law has been captured by powerful interests. The utter domination by the National Rifle Association and allied groups of the debate over gun control may be one of the reasons that clients of Kirkland & Ellis sought to use their economic clout to persuade the law firm to stop representing firearms manufacturers in constitutional litigation, in an episode described at the end of Chapter 3.[8] The student-led boycotts of law firms representing fossil fuel companies, which was the principal case study in Chapter 5, seem to be similarly motivated by exasperation with political gridlock over the climate crisis, attributable to the influence of Big Oil on the political process.

Some lawyers find the resort to extralegal methods like shaming, shunning, or boycotting to be a threat to the rule of law. Any decent legal system, however, must tolerate informal channels of protest and dissent. One of the most important policies underlying the First Amendment's near-absolute protection for political speech is to enable those with less political power to criticize government officials and other powerful individuals and corporations, even in vitriolic terms. It is no fun to endure dissenting speech and protests, but it comes with the territory for those who hold political power or public influence.

3. *Remaining a moral agent while acting in a professional role is tricky business.* One of the central moral lessons learned out of the horrors of the 20th century is that obedience to authority or following the orders of one's superior is no excuse for involvement in wrongdoing.[9] Yet, when pressed on a case that appears to raise moral questions, like pleading the statute of limitations on behalf of a client who genuinely owes the debt to avoid the obligation to repay,[10] the immediate response of most lawyers and law students is that the rules of the game allow for it. The case can be described in two different ways: One is a description in ordinary moral terms, as helping someone (the client) commit an unjust act of weaseling out of the obligation to repay what one owes. The second is an institutional description that refers to legal duties to repay as well as various procedural rules such as jurisdiction and the rule that stale claims are time-barred.[11] Lawyers tend to only "see" the second description, but it has to be the case that something like the first description persists and provides a standpoint from which to evaluate the lawyer's actions.[12] It remains possible to describe the client's action as "cheating" or "going back on an obligation" and the lawyer's actions as assisting in this

wrongdoing.* I know, I know—lawyers consider it perfectly routine and unproblematic to rely on procedural defenses like the statute of limitations. I do too, but it is important not to let go of the perspective of regular folks who have not been trained and socialized as lawyers. Otherwise there is a real risk that the legal profession will been seen as a cartel or a "caste,"[13] not anything deserving of deference or respect.

I suspect the most controversial part of this book will be the effort to preserve the ordinary moral point of view when evaluating the choices lawyers make in the clients they represent. The first two Philosophical Perspective chapters introduced the ideas of reactive attitudes and blame that look to the motivating reasons, intentions, and attitudes underlying actions. These are part of the furniture of ordinary morality. The interesting question is how professional roles fit in with these practices of holding others accountable. Many lawyers with whom I have talked about this problem are simply incredulous that they owe any explanation beyond the general, institutional social settlement or rule-of-law story. Why is a full commitment to the values served by the legal system—assuming those values are good ones— not a sufficient explanation in any instance where a lawyer is criticized for representing an obnoxious client? There are several answers to that question that have been explored in this book. One is that displacing moral responsibility onto institutions is something to be regarded with intense suspicion. The institution had better be worthy of the trust placed in it by those who act in institutional roles. Another, related, response is that the law only imperfectly accomplishes its objective of *fairly* settling the range of social controversy it addresses. The agonizing quality of many of the cases we have considered, from the northern anti-slavery judges deciding cases under the Fugitive Slave Laws, to Alton Logan's wrongful imprisonment, to deciding whether to continue representing gun manufacturers in Second Amendment litigation, arises from the gap between the ideal of justice and the way it is realized through a flawed legal system. Lawyers understandably see themselves as pursuing the ideal, but people outside the legal profession perceive the shortcomings of formal legal processes.

---

* Recall from Chapter 6 the story told by Michael Lewis about his time as a bond salesman at Salomon Brothers, when he learned that the ordinary moral description of "dumping crappy financial assets on an unsuspecting customer" could be described in professional terms as "jamming" and could make a rookie salesman a hero for the day.

That's what this book was really all about: What is the right way to think about the relationship between being a human being, capable of being moved by concerns about justice, truth, and fairness, and acting in a professional role that filters all of those concerns through a process that embodies them only incompletely?[†] I know lawyers get tired of dealing with what they may perceive to be uninformed or bad faith criticism. Blaming big-firm lawyers who represent fossil fuel companies, for example, may appear to be politics by other means, not a serious question about the responsibility of professionals who, in the view of these activists, are blithely cashing large paychecks while furthering activities that are leading to a global catastrophe. Similarly, Rod Rosenstein may seem like merely a convenient punching bag for critics of the Trump administration's immigration policies. But the inquiries into the motivating reasons and attitudes of these lawyers is an important feature of the necessary relationship of accountability between the legal profession and the wider society. In some cases, the attitudes a lawyer *ought* to feel in context of a morally troubling representation is something in the neighborhood of regret, sorrow, or reluctance. This is not an everyday phenomenon, but the idea of moral remainders helps explain some of the most wrenching episodes discussed here, such as the dilemma of the lawyers in the Lake Pleasant bodies case.

There is no tool, but the ideas of moral agency, accountability, reactive attitudes, motivating reasons, and blame help sort through the over public criticism of lawyers. Unfortunately for the lawyers involved in these cases, there are no easy answers. The institution-level story about resolution of social disagreement and the rule of law may be persuasive, but it still leaves open many of the hardest questions about how to remain a decent person while acting in a professional role on behalf of unpopular clients. In many cases the lawyers involved will have a good answer—an account for themselves they can offer to those with whom they are in a relationship that is important to maintain, like that between civil rights lawyer Anthony Griffin and Black residents of East Texas (Chapter 3) or between the lawyers in Upstate New York and their neighbors who were horrified about the missing hikers (Chapter 8). That doesn't mean lawyers need to react to every social media campaign directed against them. Much of that is noise that can safely be ignored. In the serious cases, however, even those who are not closely connected to the lawyers involved will want to know something about how

---

[†] The analogy with Plato's cave is irresistible here.

this lawyer justifies the representation. One function of these cases is to serve as public morality plays, providing resources for an ongoing conversation about the relationship between the legal profession and the society it is intended to serve.

Notes

1. This is how checklists are employed in aviation. They don't tell you how to fly the plane but help prevent accidents caused by inattention or task saturation, leading to oversights such as failing to set takeoff flaps or lower the gear for landing. Many centers for business ethics or practical ethics publish decision-making frameworks or guidelines. See, e.g., "A Framework for Ethical Decision Making," Santa Clara University—Markkula Center for Applied Ethics, available at https://www.scu.edu/ethics/ethics-resources/a-framework-for-ethical-decision-making/; "Ethical Decision Making for Investment Professionals," CFA Institute, available at https://www.cfainstitute.org/en/ethics-standards/ethics/ethical-decision-making. For an example in a specific normative domain—respectful use of language—that is explicitly labeled a "tool," see UC Santa Cruz, "Tool: Recognizing Microaggressions and the Messages They Might Send," https://perma.cc/D74C-VNLB.
2. Yes, "popularized by Aristotle" was meant to be a joke. The centrality of *phronesis*—Aristotelian practical wisdom—was central to a book that made a big splash right around the time I was in law school, Anthony T. Kronman, *The Lost Lawyer* (Cambridge, Mass.: Harvard University Press 1993). Kronman's argument was intricate, but some of the most important strands are the recognition of moral pluralism, which is something I very much agree with (see Chapter 6); a pronounced nostalgia for 19th-century-style social trustee professionalism, which is something I strongly disagree with; the belief that lawyers, through training and experience, acquire practical wisdom, which he further defines as the complementary virtues of sympathy and detachment, which enables them to counsel and represent their clients in a way that harmonizes the private ends of clients with the public interest; and a moderately pessimistic assessment of the modern conditions of the practice of law and its suitability for developing practical wisdom in lawyers.
3. As discussed in the notes to Chapter 1, this is the position of Sanson, the executioner of Paris, in Applbaum's fictionalized dialogue with a critic. Arthur Isak Applbaum, "Professional Detachment: The Executioner of Paris," 109 *Harv. L. Rev.* 458, 484–85 (1995). The critic, Mercier's, response is, among other things: "What sort of man chooses such a gruesome trade?" (p. 477).
4. See Applbaum, p. 476, where Mercier demands from Sanson a justification for his role "on grounds that we can share" and Sanson goes on to provide a pretty good account of the moral reasons for having a legal system, the criminal law, the death penalty, and hence the role of executioner.

5. Mercier again, this time the real Mercier, as quoted by Applbaum from an essay written after the Terror, about the real Sanson: "I should love to love to know what goes on in that head of his, and whether he considers his appalling duties simply as a profession . . . How does he sleep after receiving the last words and the last glances of all those severed heads?" Applbaum, p. 460 (quoting Louis-Sébastien Mercier, *Le Nouveau Paris* (1795)).

6. G.E.M. Anscombe, *Intention* (Cambridge, Mass: Harvard University Press 2000) (first published in 1957); G.E.M. Anscombe, "Modern Moral Philosophy," *Philosophy*, Vol. 33, No. 124 (Jan. 1958), pp. 1–19; Philippa Foot, "The Problem of Abortion and the Doctrine of the Double Effect," in *Virtues and Vices* (Berkeley: University of California Press 1978). Anscombe's philosophical work on intention was partly motivated by her objection to Oxford awarding an honorary degree to Harry Truman, who as U.S. President had ordered atomic bomb attacks on the Japanese cities of Hiroshima and Nagasaki, with the knowledge that the bombings would result in the deaths of hundreds of thousands of civilians. G.E.M. Anscombe, "Mr Truman's Degree," in *Ethics, Religion and Politics: Collected Philosophical Papers, Volume III* (Oxford: Basil Blackwell 1981), pp. 62–71. This connection is noted in an engaging popular introduction to the trolley problem and the doctrine of double effect, David Edmonds, *Would You Kill the Fat Man?* (Princeton: Princeton University Press 2014).

7. See Jeremy Waldron, "The Concept and the Rule of Law," 43 *Ga. L. Rev.* 1 (2008); David Luban, "Natural Law and Professional Ethics: A Reading of Fuller," in *Legal Ethics and Human Dignity* (Cambridge: Cambridge University Press 2007), pp. 99–130.

8. For a deeply reported story on the gun-control debate in the United States over several decades, into the era of seemingly routine school shootings, see Todd C. Frankel, Shawn Boburg, Josh Dawsey, Ashley Parker, & Alex Horton, "The Gun That Divides a Nation," *Wash. Post* (Mar. 27, 2023). For reporting on the departure of former U.S. Solicitor General Paul Clement as a result of the firm's decision, see Jess Bravin, "Winning Lawyers in Supreme Court Gun Case Leave Firm," *Wall St. J.* (June 23, 2022); Anna Sanders, "Clement Exits Kirkland After Firm Drops Gun Cases," *Law360* (June 23, 2022). Clement and one of the partners who departed the firm with him published their response in a *Wall Street Journal* editorial. Paul Clement & Erin Murphy, "The Law Firm That Got Tired of Winning," *Wall St. J.* (June 23, 2022).

9. David Luban, "The Ethics of Wrongful Obedience," in *Legal Ethics and Human Dignity* (Cambridge: Cambridge University Press 2007), pp. 237–66.

10. The case, *Zabella v. Pakel*, 252 F.2d 452 (7th Cir. 1957), is discussed in many classic contributions to theoretical legal ethics scholarship, including Charles Fried, "The Lawyer as Friend: The Moral Foundations of the Lawyer-Client Relation," 85 *Yale L.J.* 1060 (1976); and Gerald J. Postema, "Moral Responsibility in Professional Ethics," 55 *NYU L. Rev.* 63 (1980). I can think of few supposedly troubling cases that trouble lawyers less than *Zabella*. Most of them don't even see the issue, and I don't think this is a pose. It is so taken for granted that a lawyer may interpose a valid defense on behalf of a client—even one who deserves to lose—that lawyers have a hard time seeing what the problem could be in ethical terms.

11. See Tim Dare, *The Counsel of Rogues? A Defence of the Standard Conception of the Lawyer's Role* (London: Ashgate 2009).
12. Arthur Isak Applbaum, *Ethics for Adversaries: The Morality of Roles in Public and Professional Life* (Princeton: Princeton University Press 1999), pp. 85–90.
13. "Professional Morality and Its Dispositions," in *Making Sense of Humanity and Other Philosophical Papers 1982-1993* (Cambridge: Cambridge University Press 1995), pp. 192–93 ("A complete separation from the public is most naturally associated with a caste rather than simply with a profession.").

Acknowledgments

I presented portions of this book, or earlier versions of some of the ideas that made their way into the book, at academic conferences, seminars, and faculty workshops at Cornell Law School, the interdepartmental Moral Psychology Working Group at Cornell University, the University of Georgia School of Law, Hofstra Law School, the University of Southern California School of Law, the Sturm College of Law and the Department of Philosophy at the University of Denver, the University of Tennessee School of Law, Wake Forest School of Law, Washington and Lee University (where Greg Cooper kindly used the book as a text in his legal ethics seminar), and the Ninth International Legal Ethics Conference (ILEC) at UCLA (at which I selfishly put together a panel on my own book manuscript). Thanks to the organizers of these events for their support and for participants for their many helpful questions and comments.

For more sustained conversation, feedback, suggestions, and criticism along the way, sometimes in the form of extensive written comments (for which extra thanks, and probably a round of beers, is due), I am especially grateful to Scott Altman, Emad Atiq, Ben Barton, Sara Bronin, Lonnie Brown, George Cohen, Greg Cooper, Sarah Cravens, Scott Cummings, Tim Dare, Josh Davis, John Doris, Bob Gordon, Gautam Hans, Felipe Jiménez, Sheri Johnson, Greg Keating, Kate Kruse, Helen Kruuse, Alexi Lahav, David Lat, John Leubsdorf, David Luban, Diogo Magalhaes, Erin Miller, Greg Mitchell, Rachel Moran, Rebecca Morrow, Ellen Murphy, Richard Painter, Russ Pearce, Liz Peck, Derk Pereboom, Andy Perlman, Dana Radcliffe, Aziz Rana, Alex Reinert, Dana Remus, Becky Roiphe, Amy Salyzyn, Paula Schaefer, Sarah Schendel, Tony Sebok, Dave Shoemaker, Abbe Smith, Jonathan Soeharno, Steven Vaughan, Eli Wald, Bill Watson, Ken White, David Wilkins, Ekow Yankah, and Ben Zipursky. The students in my philosophical legal ethics seminar at Cornell and in a short course at the University of Virginia in the spring 2023 semester were an outstanding sounding board for many of the ideas in this book and, in some cases, helped spark insights that made their way into the final version.

Friends and family members of varying levels of interest in and connection to the legal profession, who served as invaluable beta readers, and for whom I am most grateful, are Chris Ford, Tracy Kuczenski, Kim Michaels, Angie Purdy, and Ben Wendel.

I gratefully acknowledge the research funding provided by the Judge Albert Conway Memorial Fund for Legal Research, established by the William C. and Joyce C. O'Neil Charitable Trust. Thanks are also due to Cornell Law School Dean Jens Ohlin for research support and a sabbatical leave to work on the first draft of the book.

A Zoom panel at the 2022 Association of American Law Schools annual meeting on writing a book kicked off this project in a very helpful way. I don't recall all of the participants in the panel, but literary agent Lucy Cleland made several smart suggestions that informed my writing from the start, including (1) take the reader along on a journey—start with a question and bring the reader along as you solve the puzzle; (2) claim and own a space of expertise—why are *you* writing this book instead of someone else?—but also think of the book as a conversation with readers; and (3) it helps to be surprising or counterintuitive. I hope the book is responsive to those suggestions. The debate about criticizing lawyers for the client they represent has a real *Groundhog Day* feel for someone who has been a lawyer and academic legal ethicist for a long time, but I think I know why. The reason is that both sides are onto something. What makes a whole book necessary, as opposed to a law review article (or as Sam Bankman-Fried would insist, a three-paragraph blog post), is that each side is onto a piece of something slippery, subtle, and calling for theoretical as well as practical expertise. At least that's my answer to the question of why I am writing the book instead of someone else, given how many lawyers, legal journalists and commentators, and other interested observers have weighed in on these questions over the years. I also think there are surprising and counterintuitive things in the book—it certainly seemed to make many lawyers mad when I was workshopping drafts! In the course of working on the project I came to understand Lucy's suggestion that all authors are, in a sense, mystery authors as a framing device to see the case studies as the mysteries to be solved. Working in that way convinced me that the theoretical apparatus in the book is actually necessary to solve the mystery. Too many puzzles remain in these cases if we don't attend to the underlying philosophical problems. We'll see if readers agree.

Much appreciation, as always, goes to Anne Lamott for writing *Bird by Bird*, without which I would not be able to get a single word on the page. The songs of James McMurtry, Margo Price, and Ray Wylie Hubbard kept me sane during the writing process.

This book is dedicated to my wife, Liz Peck, with inexpressible gratitude for her constant love and support, even during the ups and downs of a major writing project. Thanks for listening to all of this and believing in me.

Index

For the benefit of digital users, indexed terms that span two pages (e.g., 52–53) may, on occasion, appear on only one of those pages.

#MeToo movement, 66, 72, 112–13
65 Project, 215

A Few Good Men, 167–69
accountability, viii–ix, 3, 5–6, 10–11, 12, 13, 40–41, 45, 51, 70, 110–12, 118, 244–46, 248–49
Adams, John, vii–viii, 7–9, 80–81, 83, 200, 214
Alien Tort Statute litigation, 179–81
alternative facts (Kellyanne Conway), 121
American Bar Association (ABA), 14–15, 81–82
Appiah, Kwame Anthony, x–xi
attitudes of the actor, ix, 17–18, 19–20, 39, 49–50, 72–73, 85–86, 101–4, 105–6, 107–9, 110, 112–14, 202, 233, 262–63, 266
attitudes, reactive. *See* reactive attitudes
Auerbach, Jerold, 79–80, 81

Babcock, Barbara, 69–70, 71
Berlin, Isaiah, 150–51, 243
Bernardo case (Canada), 236
Billy Budd, 170
blame, viii–ix, 85–86, 101–5, 185–86, 202, 263, 266–67
  ethics of, 46–47, 55, 108–22, 203, 205
  standing, 109–11
Boies, David, 74
Boston Massacre, 8–9
Boycotts, 147–48, 149, 150
  conservative boycott of Disney, 132–33
  conservative boycott of Walgreens, 139–40
  law student boycotts of law firms, 135–37, 184, 210, 263–64
  Montgomery bus boycott, 132–33, 137–38

Nazi boycott of Jewish businesses, 132–33
Breveik, Anders, 77–78
Brougham, Lord Henry, 11, 244
Brown, Lonnie, 171–73
Bruck, David, 70, 77–78
bullshit, 121–22
burdens of judgment (Rawls), 142–43

cab-rank rule, 75–77, 174
cancel culture, ix–x, 43–45, 74–75, 132–33, 139, 150
Carr, Albert, 175–76, 178–79
cause lawyering, 174–75
character, 103–4
charivari, 43
Cheney, Elizabeth, 211–12, 214, 216
Chick-fil-A, 106, 137, 147–48
Chontiner, Issac, 68–69
civil disobedience, 5, 242–43, 244–45
Clark, Ramsey, 171–74
Clement, Paul, 83–86, 146
climate change, x–xii, 138–39, 143–45, 263–64
confidentiality, duty of, 6–7, 48–49, 53, 148–49, 163–64, 185, 235–36, 263
confirmation hearings, 165–66
Cotton, Tom, 119–20
Cover, Robert, 169–71, 242–43
Covington & Burling, 135–36
Cravath Swaine & Moore, 1–4, 17–21, 47–48, 51, 54–55
criminal defense, 21
cross-examination, 234–35, 244, 246
Cruz, Ted, 119–20
Curtis, Charles, 177–78

Davis, Kim (Kentucky county clerk), 169, 170, 171, 181, 182–83
deliberative priority, 238–39, 242–43

Demjanjuk, John, 10–12
dirty hands, 239–40, 241–42, 248–49
disagreement, reasonable, x, 142, 144–45, 147–48, 150–51, 179–80, 183–84, 204
disagreement, unreasonable, 150–51
Disney vs. Ron DeSantis controversy, 132–33, 139–40, 147–48
due process, 44–45, 68–69, 150, 181–82
Duncan, Stuart Kyle, 107

Eastman, John, 208–10, 215–16
Eichmann, Adolf, 164, 200, 202, 242–43
Erskine, Thomas, 76
ethics rules, 14–15
ExxonMobil, 137, 138–39

family separation policy, 200–1, 218, 219, 241–42, 247
fiduciary duties, lawyers, x, 163–64, 184–85, 203–4
Finch, Atticus, 13
First Amendment, 67, 80, 83, 118–19, 264
Frankfurt, Harry, 121
Freedman, Monroe, 10–11, 54–55
Fried, Charles, 212–13
Fugitive Slave Laws, 169–70, 242–43, 265
fungibility of lawyers, 173–74

General Motors, 11
Gibson Dunn & Crutcher, 178–79
    defense of Chevron in Ecuador, 106–7, 136
    Indian Child Welfare Act litigation, 106–8, 136
    representation of fossil fuel companies, 136–37
Giuliani, Rudy, 178, 207–8, 210–11
Graham, Lindsey, 165–66
Griffin, Anthony, 52–54, 110, 112, 114, 174–75, 266–67
Guantánamo Bay detainees, 166, 211–14

Harvard University, 66–67
Hawley, Josh, 119–20
Herschmann, Eric, 209
Ho, James, ix
Holder, Eric, 211–12

House Un-American Activities Committee, 80–81
Hume, David, 39–40, 50

intention, 263

Jackson, Ketanji Brown, 121–22, 165–66, 214
Jacob, Greg, 208, 209
January 6, 2020, insurrection, 215–16
Jessup, Col. Nathan (fictional character), 167–69, 181, 182
Johnson & Johnson talc bankruptcy, 115
Jones Day, 205–6, 207, 209, 211
Jones, Alex, 84
judicial confirmation hearings, 119–22

Katyal, Neal, 179–80
"kill all the lawyers" (Shakespeare), vii
King, Jr., Martin Luther, 244–45
Kirkland & Ellis, 83–86, 133, 146, 263–64
Kristol, William, 211–12, 216
Kronman, Anthony, 142, 262
Ku Klux Klan, 52–53, 174–75

Lake Pleasant Bodies case, 235–37, 238–39, 245, 246, 249, 266
legislation, 146–47
legitimacy, 147–48, 150, 183–84
Lewis, Michael, 176–77
liberalism, 5–6, 145, 151, 183–84
Lincoln Project, 205–6, 207
Lithwick, Dahlia, 200
Logan, Alton, 48–49, 185–86, 237, 265
Luban, David, 182–83

Machiavelli, Niccolò, 239–40, 245
Mayer Brown, 9–10
McCarthy, Joseph, 80, 214
meaning of actions, ix, 17–19, 39, 72–73, 85–86, 102, 106, 108, 149, 233–34
Michell, Cleta, 206–8
Mill, J.S., 43
Miller, Stephen, 200–4, 246
mob rule, x, 2–3, 75
Model Rules of Professional Conduct, 14–17, 149

Montaigne's solution, 41, 177, 238, 241
moral agency, 41
moral community, 55, 73, 110–11, 112
moral costs, 49–50
morality, definition, 38
moral remainder, 219–20, 233, 238–39, 240, 242, 248–50, 266
Morrison, Nina, 119–22

Nathanson, Judith, 173–74
Nestlé, 179–81
Nielsen, Kirstjen, 200–1, 203, 247–48
Nonaccountability, principle of, 4, 12–13, 17, 20–21, 70, 75, 79–80, 82, 122, 150, 172, 174–75, 185–86, 237–38, 246, 262–63
Nuremberg defense, 167

Obama, Barack, 240–41, 244
Olson, Ted, 216
ostracism, 43, 74–75, 141–42, 202, 215–16
Overton window, 151

Paul Weiss Rifkin Wharton & Garrison, 135–36, 138–39, 171–72
permissibility of actions, ix, 19–20, 72–73, 102, 235, 237–38
Pluralism, moral, 117–18, 142, 145, 150–51
Porter Wright, 205, 207
power, 139, 146–47, 151
practical wisdom, 262

qualms, xi–xii, 13–14, 17, 85–86, 219–20, 237–39, 240

Rawls, John, 142–43
Raz, Joseph, 183–84
reactive attitudes, 40–42, 49–50, 69–70, 110–11, 116–18, 184, 202, 245–46, 263, 266–67
redescription of acts and events, 176–77, 264–65
regret, viii–ix, xi–xii, 48, 107, 167–68, 202–3, 219–20, 233, 235, 236–37, 238–39, 241–43, 248–49
relational morality, 54, 73, 101–4, 107, 202

reluctance, viii–ix, xi–xii, 7, 19, 48, 85–86, 107, 219–20, 233, 235, 236–37, 238–39, 241, 242–43
repugnant clients, vii, 15–16
responsibility, 42
Rhode, Deborah, 76–77
role-differentiated morality, 4–5
Roof, Dylann, 70, 77–78
Rose, Dinah, 76
Rosenstein, Rod, 200–3, 241–42, 246–49, 266
rule of law, 45, 75, 84–85, 117–18, 150, 239, 263–64
rules of the game, 175–77, 178–79, 180, 264–65

Sanson, Charles-Henri (Executioner of Paris), 12, 13, 46, 164
Scalia, Antonin, 166
Scanlon, T.M., 38, 101–4, 109–10, 202
Scottsboro Boys, ix, 79–80
sentiments, 5–6, 39–41, 45–46, 112, 235, 245–46, 248
settlement of social conflict, 141–42, 147–48, 150, 179–80, 184, 185–86, 262–64
shame, 43, 133, 138–39, 141–42, 150
shunning, 43, 44–45, 116–17, 141–42, 147, 202, 210–11
Smith, Abbe, 71–72, 233–35, 239, 245, 249
social media, 43, 111
social trustee professionalism, 135
solidarity, 205
Standard Conception of legal ethics, 4
"Stand Firm!" declaration (Netherlands), 78
Stanford Law School, 107
stigma, 2–3, 135, 149
Stimson, Charles "Cully", 212–13
Stone, Harlan Fiske, 134–35, 145–46, 149
Strawson, Peter, 40–42, 101, 112
Sullivan, Ronald, 66–69, 72–74, 77, 105–6, 110, 115, 119
Swiss bank case, 1–4, 17–18, 21, 47, 49–50, 51

The Good Place, viii–ix
Tigar, Michael, 10–13, 54–55
To Kill a Mockingbird, 13

toleration, ix–x, 5–6, 116–19, 184–85, 239
torture memos controversy, 217–18, 219, 241–42
Trump, Donald, 84, 178–79, 199–200, 211
truthiness (Stephen Colbert), 121

Wallace, R. Jay, 111–12
Walzer, Michael, 248–49
Weber, Max, 239–40, 248
Weinstein, Harvey, 66–67, 74–75, 77, 110, 112–13
Wilkins, David, 52, 54–55
Williams, Bernard, 238–39, 240, 245–46
Woke, defined, ix
Wolf, Susan, 101–2
Wolfram, Charles, 116–17

Yale Law School, ix–x
Yglesias, Matthew, 77

zealous advocacy, 11, 214, 234–35